Captain "Hell Roaring" Mike Healy

NEW PERSPECTIVES ON MARITIME HISTORY AND NAUTICAL ARCHAEOLOGY

UNIVERSITY PRESS OF FLORIDA

Florida A&M University, Tallahassee
Florida Atlantic University, Boca Raton
Florida Gulf Coast University, Ft. Myers
Florida International University, Miami
Florida State University, Tallahassee
New College of Florida, Sarasota
University of Central Florida, Orlando
University of Florida, Gainesville
University of North Florida, Jacksonville
University of South Florida, Tampa
University of West Florida, Pensacola

Michael A. Healy, 1880. Photograph courtesy of Archives, College of the Holy Cross.

CAPTAIN "HELL ROARING" MIKE HEALY

From American Slave to Arctic Hero

Dennis L. Noble and Truman R. Strobridge

FOREWORD BY GENE ALLEN SMITH AND JAMES C. BRADFORD

UNIVERSITY PRESS OF FLORIDA

Gainesville / Tallahassee / Tampa / Boca Raton

Pensacola / Orlando / Miami / Jacksonville / Ft. Myers / Sarasota

22 21 20 19 18 17   6 5 4 3 2 1

First cloth printing, 2009
First paperback printing, 2017

Portions of this work appeared with permission in:
Truman R. Strobridge and Dennis L. Noble, *Alaska and the U.S. Revenue Cutter Service,
1867–1915*. Annapolis, Md.: Naval Institute Press, 1999.
Portions of chapter 10 are condensed from *Naval History* with permission; Copyright 2001
U.S. Naval Institute/www.usni.org.

Library of Congress Cataloging-in-Publication Data
Noble, Dennis L.
Captain "Hell Roaring" Mike Healy : from American slave to Arctic hero / Dennis L. Noble
and Truman R. Strobridge ; foreword by Gene Allen Smith and James Bradford.
p. cm. — (New perspectives on maritime history and nautical archaeology)
Includes bibliographical references and index.
ISBN 978-0-8130-3368-6 (cloth: alk. paper)
ISBN 978-0-8130-5485-8 (pbk.)
1. Healy, Michael A., 1839–1904. 2. United States. Revenue-Cutter Service—Officers—
Biography. 3. Ship captains—Alaska—Biography. 4. African American sailors—Alaska—
Biography. 5. Alaska—Gold discoveries. 6. Alaska—History—19th century. 7. African
Americans—Biography. 8. Slaves—Georgia—Biography. 9. Passing (Identity)—United
States—Case studies. I. Strobridge, Truman R. II. Title.
HJ6647.H43N63 2009
363.28′6—dc22 [B]   2009008372

The University Press of Florida is the scholarly publishing agency for the State University
System of Florida, comprising Florida A&M University, Florida Atlantic University, Florida
Gulf Coast University, Florida International University, Florida State University, New Col-
lege of Florida, University of Central Florida, University of Florida, University of North
Florida, University of South Florida, and University of West Florida.

University Press of Florida
15 Northwest 15th Street
Gainesville, FL 32611-2079
http://upress.ufl.edu

For Loren Alice Noble

—Dennis L. Noble

To my wife, Mary Witeck Strobridge
(27 August 1932–14 April 2002),
and her wonderful family, neighbors,
and friends in Oconto and Green Bay, Wisconsin,
who helped shape her into the fabulous person she was.

—Truman R. Strobridge

It is hard when looking at the pasts of other people to understand the fine points of their lives. It is difficult to know the exact shadings of dates which were never written down and to know the intricacies of events which we have not lived through ourselves but only viewed from the distances of time and space.

—Alistar MacLeod

CONTENTS

Series Foreword xi

Preface xv

Acknowledgments xvii

Introduction 1

1. The Georgia Plantation 16

2. Down to the Sea 29

3. Love and the Sailor 45

4. Eastern Interlude 66

5. Healy's Polar Passion 84

6. Cannons, Expeditions, Shipwrecks, and Reindeer 120

7. The Captain and the Immortal *Bear* 137

8. "Monster Healy" 150

9. The Czar of the North 172

10. "I Steer By No Man's Compass But My Own" 201

11. "A Desperate and Dangerous Man" 226

Epilogue 253

Appendix 1. Important Dates in the Life of Capt. Michael A. Healy 267

Appendix 2. The Family of Michael Augustine Healy 271

Appendix 3. Charges Brought Against Capt. Michael A. Healy
in 1896 Trial 275

Notes 277

Selected Bibliography 305

Index 317

About the Authors 327

Series Foreword

Water is unquestionably the most important natural feature on earth. By volume the world's oceans compose 99 percent of the planet's living space; in fact, the surface of the Pacific Ocean alone is larger than that of the total land bodies. Water is as vital to life as air. Indeed, to test whether the moon or other planets can sustain life, NASA looks for signs of water. The story of human development is inextricably linked to the oceans, seas, lakes, and rivers that dominate the earth's surface. The University Press of Florida's series "New Perspectives on Maritime History and Nautical Archaeology" is devoted to exploring the significance of the earth's water while providing lively and important books that cover the spectrum of maritime history and nautical archaeology broadly defined. The series includes works that focus on the role of canals, rivers, lakes, and oceans in history; on the economic, military, and political use of those waters; and upon the people, communities, and industries that support maritime endeavors. Limited by neither geography nor time, volumes in the series contribute to the overall understanding of maritime history and can be read with profit by both general readers and specialists.

Dennis L. Noble and Truman R. Strobridge's biography of Mike Healy represents the mosaic that is truly American. Born in September 1839 to an Irish Catholic father and a Georgia slave, by law Mike and his siblings were half black. The father took the precaution of sending his six fair-skinned children—including Mike—out of the South to the College of Holy Cross in Worcester, Massachusetts, for a Catholic education. This emphasis on education and religion ultimately gave the fair-skinned children an opportunity to escape the stigma of race and to blend quietly into white society. Young Mike matriculated at Holy Cross in 1850, but he lacked the temperament for academic success and left the college shortly after entering. Then sent to a Catholic seminary in Douai, France, the fifteen-year-old Mike again fled, this time going to sea. Entering the merchant marine as a boy, or the lowest rank on a merchant ship,

Mike threw himself into his chosen profession, and learned his job from the bottom up—"coming up through the hawse pipe"—to become an officer. At age twenty-six, already with ten years of experience at sea, he joined the U.S. Revenue Cutter Service.

Mike Healy spent most of his career stationed along the Pacific Coast, making seasonal cruises (April to November) to the Arctic; he ultimately spent twenty-two years, eight months on the Pacific Station, and of that time he served nine years and six months in Alaskan waters. No other officer of his era had as much service in those turbulent seas. In essence, he became recognized as the service's Arctic expert as well as the sole representative of the federal government on Alaska's isolated maritime frontier. In that role he enforced federal laws, provided search and rescue for sailors, and treated the native peoples of Siberia and Alaska with respect; his concern about the ultimate fate of the Eskimo resulted in the introduction of reindeer to Alaska.

Renowned as an unquestioned Ice Master, Healy also gained a reputation for being a hard-drinking, strict disciplinarian. His junior officers generally bore the brunt of his hard-driving attitude while the sailors believed him to be just and concerned for their well-being. In 1890 junior officers charged Healy with inhumane treatment toward merchant seamen and with drunkenness. He was exonerated, but six years later in San Francisco he again faced a series of charges, including one for drunkenness, from junior officers. Convicted in this instance, the service dropped Healy to the bottom of the list of captains and placed him on the awaiting orders list for four years. Healy finally regained a command post in 1900 and ultimately was restored to his previous position on the captain's list (number 7), but his final years did little to win for him a place in the annals of the service or in the popular imagination. In July 1900 he attempted suicide and subsequently spent time in the Washington State Institution for the Insane; in October 1903 the service reprimanded him for conduct unbecoming an officer, including the use of indecent language in the presence of his officers and crew. Within a year of this last reprimand, Mike Healy died of a heart attack.

Although this biography focuses on the dramatic life and exploits of Mike Healy, it also offers a number of interesting insights. It reveals the Cutter Service's exploits in Arctic waters and how officers such as Healy established an American federal presence. It embraces the topic of race and how the light-skinned, blue-eyed Healy passed himself off not as a white Irish Catholic nor as a black man but rather as a sailor who ultimately rose to a level of distinction within the U.S. Revenue Cutter Service. The authors also confront the questions of Catholicism and alcohol during the late nineteenth century, and how Healy's life challenged the growing social and religious trends of the era. In effect, Healy represented the old-time archetypal sailor, but also one who chose voluntarily to be thrown into the officer's world of refinement and expectation. And while he could exhibit the polite manners of society, ultimately he could not live up to societal expectations, especially those of the refined officer corps. Healy demanded strict obedience of his junior officers, swore profusely, and drank to excess. And these traits did not represent the qualities that Victorian Americans demanded from their heroes.

This biography of "Hell Roaring Mike" Healy reveals the extent to which race and religion influenced seafaring institutions during the late nineteenth century. Healy, technically born a slave, downplayed and disguised his race and embraced his Irish Catholic lineage to advance as a U.S. Customs Revenue officer. Yet despite his race or his religion Healy represented one of the last of a vanishing breed—the archetypical nineteenth-century sailor whose courage and expertise helped to define the Alaskan maritime frontier.

Gene Allen Smith
James C. Bradford

PREFACE

The complexity of Michael Augustine Healy's life means those who wish to tell his story must sail into treacherous waters. The greatest danger comes from the lack of diaries, papers, and other observations recorded by the man and his contemporaries. In Healy's time, most sailors did not write. Furthermore, in the Far North, where Healy operated for much of his career, there were few people to record their impressions of the man. The next greatest danger lies in the "discovery" of Healy's racial heritage in 1971, an event that would eventually wrap the man in myth. The myth of who Healy was then became entrenched in many undocumented articles and passages in books. Trying to unearth the man beneath the layers of legend yields an endless array of questions. Answer one, and five more appear. To offer some answers to the many questions concerning Healy's life, we have decided to pose only the few that fit logically into the narrative we pursue and discuss many of the others in the notes. This approach allows the story to unfold without the constant interruption of stopping and starting to explore the details of these many questions.

For many years, around May Captain Healy departed his home port of San Francisco for the Far North and did not return until October or November. Those who follow the sea know that not every day upon the ocean is exciting. Between the memorable events lie long stretches of monotonous routine. To detail every moment in Captain Healy's time at sea would soon bog down the narrative. Therefore, we have selected the most important details that illuminate the life of this amazing seaman. In other words, between these pages the reader will not find a day-by-day account of Captain Healy's life.

The lack of documentation paired with an abundance of myth has caused us to make certain presumptions about what transpired in Captain Healy's life. Some of these ideas are based upon our own experiences at sea, others upon circumstantial evidence and what took place on other ships during Healy's time. The narrative clearly states what cannot be documented, and the bases for the presumptions we make are available within the notes. In most cases, the notes also offer the reader opinions that depart from our own. The epilogue departs from the other chapters by discussing only the greatest questions that remain about Captain Healy.

The narrative also provides an explanation of the federal seagoing service within which Captain Healy served, the U.S. Revenue Cutter Service. The organization operated under many names. We, however, have chosen to consistently use "U.S. Revenue Cutter Service" to avoid confusing our readers by continually changing the title. In normal correspondence, the service shortened the names of many of its cutters. The *Thomas Corwin*, for example, became the *Corwin*. We record the full name of a cutter the first time it appears and use the more common shortened version thereafter.

The spelling of place-names in the Bering Sea and Arctic regions has changed over the years. We will use the names most common during Healy's time, with the modern spelling provided in brackets after the name's first appearance; thus, Holy Cross Bay [Zaliv Kresta], Siberia.

It is now customary to identify the native people of Northern Alaska as Inupiat. Again, following the conventions of Captain Healy's time, we will use the word "Eskimo" to describe the natives of Northern Alaska.

The authors first became interested in trying to answer some of the questions concerning the life of Capt. Michael A. Healy over thirty years ago. Over the years, as we gathered material and discussed the man, we thought that Healy's story needed a place in the history of the United States. If this biography makes Americans recognize one of their great, unsung maritime heroes, then our long journey is successfully completed.

Acknowledgments

No one can undertake to write a book without the help of others. We received assistance from many people who devoted a great deal of their valuable time to helping us on our voyage to find the man behind the myth of Capt. Michael A. Healy.

We wish to thank The Foundation for Coast Guard History for providing a grant that helped with some of the expenses we incurred while researching this book.

Prof. James M. O'Toole, of Boston College, the first scholar to document the history of the Healy family to the year 1920, became a beacon for our work. His work on the family of Michael Morris and Eliza Clark Healy proved invaluable. Anyone wishing to learn about Michael A. Healy must first read Professor O'Toole's excellent book. He also gave us a great deal of his time, encouragement, and knowledge.

Two members of the current generation of the Healy family, Tom Riley and Clay Young, took time out of their busy schedules to help us. Both responded graciously to questions that many families would not care to have a stranger asking.

We received a great deal of help from three people: Candace Clifford combined her knowledge of technology and of U.S. Coast Guard records in the National Archives to provide us with digitized copies of needed records; Edward W. Phillips, of New England Ancestry Revealed, went above and beyond the call of duty to dig out the genealogy of Mary Jane Healy and to look into the Boston Custom House records; and Len Barnett, of London, who specializes in British maritime history, spent a good deal of time and effort attempting to locate Michael A. Healy's records in the British Merchant Marine.

At the National Archives and Records Administration in Washington, D.C., through their knowledge of the records, Richard W. Peuser, Head of Old Military and Maritime Records Section, and Kim Y. McKeithan, Archives Specialist, Old Navy and Maritime Records, found the elusive *Jumna*. Charles Johnson quickly and helpfully provided needed documents.

Loren A. Noble accompanied Dennis L. Noble as he searched through material in libraries and archives. She read the manuscript and offered insightful comments. Loren also put up with absences and tantrums when the writing proved difficult.

Peggy Norris, yet again, used her keen eye to search out inconsistencies and provided excellent comments on the manuscript. William R. Wells II, who has studied the service for many years, offered very helpful material and comments pertaining to U.S. Revenue Cutter Service officers. Ernest and Sue Wells offered much help in tracking Mary Jane Healy. Michelle and Sean Condon provided a great place to stay and helped in finding an easy path through the maze of Los Angeles to the Huntington Library. Harry and Pam Norweb offered a peaceful harbor during hectic research in Massachusetts.

Mr. James W. Moore and Dr. Harold T. Pinkett of the National Archives and Records Administration and Mr. Bernard C. Nalty of U.S. Air Force History proved extremely helpful in sharing their knowledge of, and insight into, the history and experiences of African Americans, especially those who served in the U.S. military. Chief Warrant Officer Joseph Greco, Jr., U.S. Coast Guard, first introduced Truman R. Strobridge to Capt. Michael A. Healy and Fr. Albert S. Foley, S.J., in 1970, and proved to be a treasure-trove on Captain Healy, the U.S. Coast Guard, and its predecessors. Dr. Mark D. Mandeles, president of the J. De Bloch Group, a defense consulting firm, provided valuable technical and other support. Other individuals that provided technical and other support were Heather M. Bell of Woodbridge, Virginia, Larry and Linda Hurzon of Alexandria, Virginia, Cheryl L. Weston of Atlanta, Georgia, and Elizabeth White of Reston, Virginia.

Master Chief Petty Officer of the U.S. Coast Guard (MCPO-CG) Vincent W. Patton III (Retired) supported this project from the beginning. As the first African American to hold the most senior enlisted position in the service, his views greatly benefited us. We could not have asked for a more enthusiastic person, no less one who never tired of answering a request or question.

At U.S. Coast Guard Headquarters, Dr. Robert M. Browning, Jr., Historian of the U.S. Coast Guard, and his staff of Scott Price and Christopher Havern quickly and efficiently responded to our questions and requests. They made the work easier.

The U.S. Coast Guard Headquarters public affairs staff and the following people of the U.S. Coast Guard Commander, Pacific Area—Historian Dr.

David Rosen, Lieut. Comdr. Glynn Smith, and Chief Petty Officer (CPO) Veronica Bandrowsky—helped guide a request for time on board the icebreaker *Michael A. Healy.*

Capt. Daniel Oliver, and the officers and crew of the U.S. Coast Guard icebreaker *Michael A. Healy,* provided a great deal of help. Their work aided our understanding of modern-day icebreaking in the area wherein Capt. Michael A. Healy operated.

Lieut. Jamie Frederick, and the crew of U.S. Coast Guard Station Cape Disappointment, Washington, allowed Dennis L. Noble a quiet place to work on the final draft of the manuscript and a forum to test ideas about Captain Healy. Master Chief Boatswains Mate (BMCM) Charles "Skip" Bowen, Janet Bowen, and the crew at Station Marathon, Florida, also provided a place to stop, discuss the manuscript, and take some needed time out. Skip now moves into his new duties as the Master Chief Petty Officer of the U.S. Coast Guard. The service is in good hands.

Lieut. Comdr. John Luce deserves special mention. A lawyer of the U.S. Coast Guard, John, on his own time, reviewed the trial records of Captain Healy. His comments were invaluable. CWO4 Ronald G. Long, Commanding Officer of the Port Clarence Loran Station, offered to search for the landing spot of the first reindeer at Port Clarence. Comdr. Michael F. White, Jr., proved a good listener and offered helpful suggestions.

While working on his own book concerning the Overland Relief Expedition, John Taliaferro exchanged ideas with us, made suggestions for books we might read, and offered encouragement. He is also a great icebreaker sailor and shipmate; it would be a pleasure to ship out with him again.

Rosemary Carlton, Curator of Collections of the Sheldon Jackson Museum, Sitka, Alaska, offered a great deal of assistance while working at the museum and cheerfully provided answers to many follow-up questions. She is the type of helpful person a researcher wishes to meet.

At the Huntington Library in San Marino, California, one of the most beautiful and helpful institutions at which to conduct research, Mora Shulman proved of great help. Rev. Peter Hogan, S.S.J., of the Archives of the Josephite Brothers, Baltimore, Maryland, provided helpful, cheerful assistance. Sister Therese Pelletier, S.C.I.M., came in from her retirement to help find material in the Archives of the Diocese of Portland, Maine. At the College of the Holy Cross, Mark W. Savolis, Head of Archives and Special Collections, Lois Hamill, Assistant Head, and Jo-Anne Carr, Archival Assistant, made research enjoyable. Robert Johnson-Lally, Archivist/Records Manager, Archdiocese of

Boston, quickly provided needed information. David Pearson, of the Columbia River Maritime Museum, provided helpful information. The staffs of the Manuscript and Music Divisions, Library of Congress, and the Archives of Georgetown University, Washington, D.C., supplied needed material quickly and efficiently. At Santa Clara University, California, Carol Lamoreaux, Registrar, and Sheila Conway, Assistant Archivist, quickly provided information on Frederick A. Healy. Ray Hudson helped us identify some people who lived in Unalaska in the nineteenth century. Frederick Sherman, Research Director of the Genealogical Society of California, provided material on Frederick A. Healy. Norleen Gooden, of the Georgia Archives, provided cheerful and helpful assistance. Nicole Bouche, of the Special Collections at the University of Washington Library, proved of great help. Robin Smith helped in the early editing of this project.

The staffs of the following institutions were helpful: the California Historical Society; the Historical Society of Sausalito, California; and the Alaska State Museum. The library staffs of the New Bedford Whaling Museum, Massachusetts, the Peary-MacMillan Arctic Museum at Bowdoin College, Brunswick, Maine, and especially Laura Pereira of the Mystic Seaport, Connecticut, provided needed material.

We obtained many books and articles through the interlibrary loan service of the North Olympic Library System (NOLS), Port Angeles, Washington, whose staff cheerfully provided this service. We thank Margaret Richie and Mary Elizabeth Barr of NOLS for their help.

At the University Press of Florida, the following people were instrumental in bringing this book into publication: Gene Allen Smith, one of the coeditors of the series, quickly recognized the value of the work, while Meredith Morris-Babb, director of the Press, strongly supported the book. Project Editor Susan Albury guided the work, while answering many questions. Penelope Cray carefully copyedited the manuscript.

The writing of this book was an experience akin to traveling by dog sled from Icy Cape, Alaska, to Point Barrow, Alaska, in January. We could not have finished without the help of all those mentioned above and of many others who go unmentioned who, we hope, will excuse the oversight. Where the book has merit, it is because we listened to all of the people who helped us. Where the book falters, it is because we ignored their advice.

INTRODUCTION

On Saturday, January 18, 1896, reporters waiting inside the Appraisers Building in San Francisco witnessed an unusual sight. Preventing curious onlookers from entering room 83, an officer of the U.S. Revenue Cutter Service stood "in full dress uniform, with a scabbard containing an ugly-looking cutlass hanging by his side."[1] Soon a trial would begin of a high-ranking officer. Reporters watched from a distance as three senior captains of the U.S. Revenue Cutter Service entered the room. Shortly afterwards, officers from all the cutters in port at San Francisco and "several Japanese sailors off the [cutter] *Bear* . . . in their pretty blue and white uniforms" arrived.[2] At one o'clock in the afternoon, the senior captain of the trial board brought the room to order, and the proceedings against Capt. Michael Augustine Healy began.

The New York *Sun* described Captain Healy as "the ideal commander of the old school, bluff, prompt, fearless, just." The *Sun* also pointed out that Healy ranked as "a good deal more distinguished [a] person in the waters of the far Northwest than any president of the United States."[3] Healy, as the most senior government official in the Far North, reported the San Francisco *Call*, found himself "frequently called upon to exercise his judgment in matters of national and international importance that gained for him a worldwide reputation."[4] All of this meant little, however, given that the fifty-six-year-old officer faced charges that threatened to ruin a career spanning over forty years at sea. "Looking a trifle nervous and anxious," Healy sat at a long table in the front of the room.[5] The coming trial would be worthy of the fiction of Herman Wouk, whose best-selling novel of World War II featured a naval trial.

Healy pleaded not guilty to six charges dealing with conduct unbecoming an officer and a gentleman, including the charge that, on specified occasions, he had been drunk while on duty in command of the cutter *Bear*, thereby placing the ship in danger. The most serious charge centered on the endangering of Healy's cutter. Even in the twenty-first century, such a charge would result in, at least, immediate loss of command, if not dismissal from the service. Very early in the trial, Bradley Henley, Healy's civilian attorney, characterized this trial as a "melancholy case, as melancholy as any recorded in the naval or military records of our country."[6] Henley confessed his fear that the results of the proceedings might erase the name of Captain Healy forever from history.

A strange thing developed early in the trial. In the nineteenth century, most officers on merchant and naval ships stood together. Very few officers gave much thought to the sailors they commanded. In Healy's trial, however, the junior officers of the *Bear* testified against their captain. The grizzled warrant officers and the enlisted sailors, on the other hand, rose to Healy's defense. At one point during the proceedings, the enlisted men of the *Bear* risked the serious charge of mutiny, when trying to put forth their views. Throughout the trial, no junior officer came to Healy's defense, while the enlisted men invariably said nothing bad about him. For example, the following exchange took place when the prosecutor tried to examine an incident in which some of the junior officers accused Healy of mistreating his Japanese steward:

> "Did Captain Healy strike, kick, or ill-treat you, early in the morning of the 7th of June last?"
> "I have no remembrance of that . . ."
> "Did Captain Healy use any profane language to you?"
> "I have no remembrance of it."
> "Did not Captain Healy say to you, 'You damned son-of-a-bitch, get up!' or words to that effect?"
> "He did not say that."
> Attorney Henley then asked the steward, "Did Captain Healy treat you kindly always?"
> "Captain Healy was very kind to me. And besides, he asked Mr. Hamilton to teach English to me. For that reason, I think the Captain was very kind to me."[7]

For over a month, the trial continued. When asked, officers repeatedly said that they had observed Captain Healy drunk at various times on board the *Bear* and while ashore. The enlisted men, on the other hand, said that they always had seen their captain sober.

At one point during the trial, Captain Healy testified:

> I play no favorites. I go [to Alaska] to do my duty and do right as far as I can, and I expect every officer to do the same. I seldom speak to an officer roughly, unless it is the third time I have to speak. I want to say,

though, that when I am in charge of a vessel, I think I always command. I think that I am there to command, and I do command, and I take all the responsibility and all the risks, and the hardships that my officers would call upon me to take. I do not steer by any man's compass but my own. I do not phrase my words with an "if you please." I say "set the mainsail" or whatever the order may be.

The prosecutor asked Healy, "Do you always treat your officers justly?"

"Yes," replied Healy.

"Then why are there so many complaints of unjust treatment?"

"I cannot account for it at all, I think that I have been too good to them."

On March 5, 1896, the trial found Capt. Michael A. Healy guilty. The sentence needed the approval of the secretary of the treasury. Not until June 8, 1896, did the Secretary announce the final sentence: Captain Healy was to be put ashore for four years, dropped to the bottom of the captain's list, and, if convicted of drunkenness in the future, summarily dismissed from the service.

With the announcement of the secretary of the treasury's ruling, the junior officers of the *Bear* celebrated their victory of removing an older officer from the service. They, however, did not really know Healy. On the other hand, Healy and his wife, Mary Jane, may have felt their lives could not plunge any lower. They, too, did not understand the tragedy of Michael A. Healy's life.

For years, amateur historians with an interest in maritime history presumed a simple explanation for Captain Healy's fall from grace. Most of these historians suggested John Barleycorn felled the captain. Healy, like many sailors before and after him, drank, sometimes to excess. As the years passed, he could not control his alcoholism. This suggestion contains an element of truth. Like most simplistic explanations of human circumstance, however, the reason Healy sat before a trial in San Francisco is more complicated. His life echoes the Greek myth of Sisyphus, doomed forever to push a large boulder uphill. Just as he nears the top of the hill, the boulder rolls back down again, and Sisyphus must repeat the cycle. Like Sisyphus, Healy struggles for fame. Just as he begins to receive great recognition, he plunges into despair. Healy then repeats the cycle.

The key to understanding why Michael sat before a group of officers in the Appraisers Building in San Francisco lies within the family he was born into. His Irish-born father, Michael Morris Healy, migrated to Georgia and became a successful plantation owner in Jones County. Sometime around 1829, Michael Morris Healy took as his wife Eliza Clark.[8]

In the antebellum South, white society judged a person's place in the community by their liquid assets: amount of slaves owned and amount of land owned. Michael Morris Healy earned enough ready cash to lend money to nearby neighbors. Of five hundred slaveholders in the county, he ranked eighteenth in terms of number of slaves owned. Michael Morris Healy placed thirty-third in improved acreage out of 412 property owners in Jones County. Michael Morris Healy's position meant his nine children could move easily among the upper levels of white society in nearby Macon.[9] True, the nagging problem of the family's Irish *and* Catholic heritage had to be endured. At this time in American history, many in mainstream society looked down upon the Irish and the Catholics.

Despite the twin obstacles of ancestry and religion, Michael Morris Healy's position offered his children the chance to live life in a way denied to many. Most sons of wealthy whites in the early South traveled to the North for college or university. The six sons of Michael Morris Healy and Eliza Clark attended the College of the Holy Cross, in Worcester, Massachusetts, near Boston. At this time, the institution functioned as a secondary school and a college. Unlike many others in the South, Michael Morris Healy and Eliza Clark also sent their three daughters to the North.

Eliza Clark died suddenly on May 19, 1850, followed by Michael Morris Healy on August 27, 1850. Their wealth allowed their children the opportunity to pursue any course in life they chose. Six of their progeny entered the Catholic Church. The eldest son, James A. Healy, became the Bishop of Portland, Maine. Hugh C. Healy, the second son, after graduating Holy Cross, started a career in business in New York City, but died young in a tragic accident. Patrick F. Healy, the third son, became the second president of Georgetown University. The fourth son, Alexander S. Healy, was a rising star in the church, but died young. Martha A. Healy, the fifth child, entered the Catholic Church, but left to marry before taking her final vows as a nun. Daughters Eliza D. Healy and Amanda J. Healy also entered the church. Amanda J. Healy died young. Noted for her teaching, Eliza D. Healy, known as Sister Mary Magdalen, became a Mother Superior in charge of a number of convents and schools, including an academy at St. Albans, Vermont. The youngest child of Michael Morris Healy and Eliza Clark, Eugene Healy, drifted away from the family.[10]

James, Patrick, and Alexander Healy were prolific diarists. James A. Healy's early entries reveal detailed descriptions of life at Holy Cross but, strangely, no comments about their home in Georgia. Throughout their lives, the famous brothers avoided any mention of their mother and father. Although James and Patrick Healy traveled widely throughout the United States and Europe, no record has been found of them ever returning to Georgia.

Born on September 22, 1839, Michael Augustine Healy arrived at Holy Cross in 1850 at the age of eleven. His older brothers expected great things of their younger brother. After all, James A. Healy was the first valedictorian to graduate from Holy Cross. Hugh, Patrick, and Alexander Healy also thrived on scholarly and religious pursuits. Michael A. Healy, on the other hand, proved totally different from his older brothers and was extremely difficult to discipline. He rebelled against the atmosphere at Holy Cross and began running away, although not for very long, or very far. Patrick F. Healy recorded in his diary that his younger brother was "a source of great anxiety" for both himself and James, and that "his conduct hitherto gives no reason to hope for a change."[11] James A. Healy, now the patriarch of the family, decided to send the rebellious boy to the English College, a seminary at Douai, France. He related to a priest that he did not intend "to make a priest of him, but to give him a chance to redeem his lost time and character." "His conduct," James added, "has not corresponded to my hopes."[12] If James A. Healy thought that moving Michael A. Healy to France would settle the young man down, he badly misjudged his brother's adventurous spirit. Michael A. Healy ran away to sea before turning sixteen. He never returned from the sea.

Some historians interested in the sea knew that Michael A. Healy entered the sailing merchant marine as a "boy," the lowest rank on a merchant ship. Historians also know that he made the difficult transition from ordinary sailor to officer, known to old salts as "coming up through the hawse pipe." Most seamen during the Age of Sail who shipped in deepwater ships could expect little except terrible living conditions, harsh treatment, and an early death. Death came in a multitude of forms. Many succumbed to disease and others the sea took. The life toughened the men who survived. In both sea lore and historical fact, the sailors who decided to try to come up through the ranks had to be able to cower, physically or mentally, anyone in the lower ranks. Healy reached the position of second mate, the third highest officer on a merchant sailing ship. By the age of twenty-six, he chose to enter the U.S. Revenue Cutter Service as a third lieutenant, the lowest officer rank in the service. (The U.S. Revenue Cutter Service and U.S. Life-Saving Service merged in 1915 to form the U.S. Coast Guard. All of these federal maritime organizations operated under the Treasury Department.)

Some who know part of the story of Michael A. Healy point out that they did not need a degree in psychology to understand that Healy's life experiences to the year 1865 produced an individual who craved fame so he could win the recognition of his older illustrious brothers. Maritime historians recognized that his experiences in the sailing merchant marine would produce an officer who expected no one to question his orders. Again, some early researchers were right about parts of Healy's life, but they still had not completely grasped the man.

Just before signing on board the U.S. Revenue Cutter Service, Healy married Mary Jane Roach, the daughter of a Boston Irish immigrant. His thirty-nine-year marriage to Mary Jane emerged as another of the important aspects of Healy's life that early amateur maritime historians overlooked. Mary Jane Healy endured long separations from her husband. Every year from 1880 to 1895, Healy departed for the Arctic in April and returned in November. In times of Healy's despair, Mary Jane Healy supported her husband when other women might have left.

Michael A. Healy rose steadily through the officer ranks of the service. Very early in his career, he showed the trait of expecting those who served under him to act quickly and without question on any order he gave.

In 1880, Healy gained his first dose of fame. Serving in the cutter *Corwin* out of San Francisco, he helped in the search for the ill-fated *Jeannette* Expedition. The United States had launched this naval expedition specifically to seek a sea and land route to the North Pole. When news of the exploring ship *Jeannette* failed to reach San Francisco, the U.S. Revenue Cutter Service began a long search for it above the Arctic Circle. The American public had a voracious appetite for any news from the mysterious Far North. Although the crew of the *Corwin* failed to locate the *Jeannette*, the San Francisco newspapers treated Healy and his shipmates much like Americans did the first astronauts that returned from the moon.

Like the Sirens' call in the *Odyssey*, San Francisco's infamous Barbary Coast seductively beckoned the returning sailors to its bars and brothels. Healy made a good accounting of himself, carousing with hard-drinking sailors, the type of people he had spent the last twenty-six years of his life among. From this traditional shore-time sailor custom came the nickname "Hell Roaring Mike," which no one, of course, ever dared call him to his face. Reporters searching sailor hangouts eagerly sought out any crewman of the *Corwin* who was willing to tell a good story. There they found the forty-one-year-old Healy, well loosened by grog, more than willing to tell them stories of his adventures in the Far

North. Jack London was only four at the time. Had he been older, he would have been furiously scribbling in his notebook stories full of Healy's adventures. Many sailors can tell sea stories, but only a few become truly skilled in the art of storytelling. Healy ranked among these select experts. Reporters recognized and cherished a good source. Over the coming years, they kept returning to him for colorful stories.

Healy's fame increased astronomically. Historians point out that Captain Healy became the sole representative of the federal government on Alaska's maritime frontier. He enforced federal laws and provided a search and rescue service for sailors in the Arctic. In 1885, for example, Healy and his crew rescued fifty-four whalers, whose ships ran afoul of the Arctic ice. In one case, while trying to rescue the whaler *Mabel*, Captain Healy gave orders to take the *Corwin* into the treacherous breaking waves, or breakers, near the beach. Even in the twenty-first century, mariners enter these surf zones at their own peril. In extreme conditions, "pressures in excess of one ton per square foot have been measured in breaking waves, while wind waves rarely exceed 10–12 pounds per square foot." Healy, however, had the seamanship to judge that, with his skill, and luck, he might be able to help the *Mabel*'s crew. As it turned out, the *Mabel*'s anchor cable snapped before its crew could secure a towline from the *Corwin*. The whaler went to pieces on the beach, but no one fell victim to the sea. Healy took the castaways aboard his cutter.[13]

One of Captain Healy's greatest reputations after his abilities as a seaman centered on his concern for the native people of the Far North. He once told his officers to "never break your word to a native."[14] As a result, the people of Siberia's and Alaska's coastlines welcomed the tough sea captain.

In a downtown San Francisco hotel in December 1889, there gathered a large number of important owners and captains of the Pacific whaling industry. The dignitaries presented Captain Healy with awards for his service to the whaling fleet. This should have been the starting point for even greater fame for the Arctic hero. Instead, one month after receiving great accolades, angry crowds marched through the streets of San Francisco carrying banners proclaiming him "Monster Healy." Healy stood accused of committing "inhuman" acts while putting down, in a drunken state, an alleged mutiny on board a whaling ship in the Bering Sea. The new West Coast Seaman's Union and the California chapter of the Woman's Christian Temperance Union formed a strange coalition to press the charges against Healy. Despite being exonerated of all charges, such a blemish on an officer's record could easily spell the end of a career. Healy's fame, however, increased.

Once vindicated, Captain Healy again departed for the Far North. Recognizing his need for help in his battle with alcohol, he asked Mary Jane Healy to accompany him and help him defeat his cravings. Although his wife feared the time in the ice pack, she sailed with Healy because, as she confided to her diary: "My husband needs me."[15] Early in this patrol, Healy lost four crewmen in an exploring accident. No other U.S. military service suffered more casualties during the exploration of Alaska. Healy must have reached his nadir. But, the myth of Sisyphus held.

The next patrol, in 1891, marks the beginning of one of the most unusual aspects of Healy's fame and the one most mentioned in histories of Alaska. Captain Healy had long been concerned with the fate of the Eskimos. For the previous ten years, reports surfaced from Alaskan visitors that the natives in the Far North faced starvation because of interference with their traditional way of life. During the 1891 patrol, the missionary Dr. Sheldon Jackson, who was visiting missionary schools along the northwestern coast of Alaska, sailed in the cutter *Bear*. During the long Alaskan evenings, the tough sea captain and the missionary talked about the fate of the Eskimo. Healy pointed out that the Chukchi of Siberia had proven to be excellent herders of reindeer. Like the Lapps of Norway, their animals provided everything they needed to survive in a hostile environment. Although reindeer were not native to Alaska, Healy had earlier learned from a naturalist that the vegetation in Alaska could support reindeer. If the animals could survive being transported to Alaska and the natives could be trained to herd them, starvation in the Far North could be prevented.

Doctor Jackson quickly recognized the value of the project. Two problems needed solving. The first centered on where to find the money to purchase and transport the animals. Jackson wanted the federal government to provide the funds. The other obstacle to overcome involved the superstitions and questions raised by the Chukchi about selling their reindeer. Healy and Jackson hammered out a plan of action. Captain Healy would use his influence among the Chukchi and, with the approval of headquarters in Washington, D.C., transport the reindeer to Alaska. Jackson would use his abilities to raise funds and win the support of Congress for the project. Healy's reputation for fair treatment overcame the Chukchi's reluctance to part with some of their reindeer. Later, Jackson wrote that had it not been for Captain Healy, the project would never have succeeded.

Healy's reputation continued to grow for the next four years. His notoriety rested not only on his humanitarian and law enforcement efforts, but also on his personality. One U.S. Revenue Cutter Service captain described Captain Healy as "a hard man to serve under."[16] Interestingly, his officers bore the brunt of his hard-driving ways. If Healy allowed any leniency on board the *Bear*, only the enlisted sailors benefited from such generosity.

The trustees of the Sheldon Jackson Museum in Sitka, Alaska, voted to welcome Captain Healy when the *Bear* arrived in 1894. They wished to present him with their thanks for his donations to their museum. The local newspaper proclaimed it the event of the year. Mary Jane Healy again accompanied her husband. Later in the patrol, she noted in her diary that, in September, while in the village of Unalaska, the church bells had been rung in honor of Healy's birthday. This demonstration of affection made Mary Jane Healy proud of her husband.[17] Once more, however, the time had come for Healy to plunge to the depths of despair.

At the end of the 1895 patrol, Michael learned of the charges that resulted in the 1896 court-martial in San Francisco. Most early maritime historians end their stories of Michael A. Healy with the secretary of the treasury pronouncing him guilty and stripping him of his command. These historians point out that, while Captain Healy deserved the reputation of an excellent ice master and did care about the natives of the Far North, in the end, he should be judged just a very colorful failure.

Michael A. Healy died in 1904. He seemed destined to become only a footnote in the maritime history of the United States. One 1937 book, by naval officer and writer Frank Wead, covered Healy's old command, the *Bear*. In it, Wead depicts Healy as a great seaman and tells the story of the reindeer and some of Healy's rescues. He ends Healy's role in maritime history with the 1896 trial.

In 1949, U.S. Coast Guard officer Stephen H. Evans published his classic early history of the service, *The United States Coast Guard, 1790–1915*. Admiral Evans also stressed Captain Healy's great seamanship and his importance to the history of Alaska. Evans, however, did not even mention the trial, or attempt to delve deeper into Healy's life.

Meanwhile, when Admiral Evans' book came out, Fr. Albert S. Foley, SJ, was working on a biography of Bishop James A. Healy, Michael A. Healy's oldest brother, at the small Spring Hill College in Mobile, Alabama. In 1951, Father Foley wrote to Bessie Cunningham, a descendent of Michael A. Healy's oldest sister, Martha, with questions concerning Michael Morris Healy and

Eliza Clark's family. From her home just outside of Boston, the seventy-three-year-old Cunningham replied that she was "not anxious for my children to see the contents" of Father Foley's letters. "I can see no reason for delving back over a hundred years," she wrote. It would only make her children unhappy and do nothing but cause grief for the family. "We cannot go back a hundred years to right things, and it surely is not our fault that such things should have happened to our family." Bessie Cunningham wanted the Jesuit to forget the whole project. "Surely God will answer my many and heartfelt prayers to have the Healy family forgotten."[18]

As it turned out, other members of the Healy clan also resisted Father Foley's entreaties for information. In Santa Barbara, California, a cousin of Bessie Cunningham, also a widow, and her son wanted nothing to do with the Jesuit's questions. Foley later wrote that the California branch of the family expressed their fears "of even one word leaking out" about the family. The son displayed more anxiety than his mother. He feared his wife would leave him if the truth came out. His mother shrewdly devised a way to prevent Foley from writing about the family. She suddenly asked Father Foley to hear her confession. The Jesuit realized the woman wanted "to tie my hands by going to confession to me and getting the whole story under the seal of confession."[19] Hastily uttering an excuse, Foley fled the house.

Before beginning his own research, Foley learned a graduate student had earlier found Michael Morris Healy and Eliza Clark's family important. A senior professor, however, had strenuously disagreed, believing his student's research would "do no good." He had ordered the student to select another topic. "In a case like this," the professor ruled, "silence is golden."[20]

Father Foley, nevertheless, continued his quest. Foley's papers, now in Baltimore, Maryland, show his interest also focused strongly on Michael A. Healy. He felt the sea captain's life would make an epic movie. In a letter to the librarian of the U.S. Coast Guard Academy, the Jesuit related an unknown fact about Healy. Foley wrote that sometime in the 1950s, two screenwriters wanted to write a script based on the captain's life. Someone in the Healy clan directed the writers to a member of the family who had kept Healy's four large diaries. Foley, unfortunately, never mentioned the name of the person who held the journals. The screenwriters made an appointment to look at the contents of the diaries. The writers must have felt that their writing of the script would turn out to be a piece of cake, since four large diaries were certain to contain many of the captain's personal observations. The woman who kept the diaries apparently had never read them. What she subsequently read in the first volume caused her to take the journals outside and "burn them to ashes."[21] It seemed Healy's chance for fame perished in the flames of that terrible act.

What could Michael Morris Healy and Eliza Clark have done to cause such worry over a century after their deaths? Father Foley published his biography of Bishop James A. Healy in 1954. In it, he revealed to readers that Michael Morris Healy was an Irish immigrant and Eliza Clark was an African American slave.

Many people living in twenty-first century America fail to understand what a traumatic shock it would be for anyone in the mainstream American society of the 1950s to announce that they had an African American as an ancestor. When Foley made his revelation, the laws of racial segregation remained almost as strict as they had been before the Civil War. People regarded anyone with such a background to be "tainted," which was the actual word people used at that time to refer to anyone with African American ancestry. Foley later revealed that, after the publication of his first Healy book, someone vandalized a portrait of Patrick F. Healy hanging in Healy Hall at Georgetown University.[22]

Strangely, very few, if any, historians seemed to connect James and Patrick Healy with Michael A. Healy. Nor for that matter did anyone in the U.S. Coast Guard seem to make the connection. If, as is more likely, some of the historians and U.S. Coast Guard officers did know about Father Foley's work, they kept their own counsel.

In 1971, U.S. Army officer Robert E. Greene published *Black Defenders of America*. Greene also revealed the racial heritage of Michael A. Healy, drawing on Foley as his source. The time in which Greene's work appeared alone makes his book radically different from Foley's. By the 1970s, racial attitudes in the United States had changed. Public Information Officers of the U.S. Coast Guard now quickly proclaimed that no other African American had commanded a federal ship until at least World War II. Using very little research, they came upon Healy's nickname, "Hell Roaring Mike," which made great copy. Most information intended for the public followed the amateur historian's description of a colorful, tough, but humane, officer who brought help to those on a wild maritime frontier. The publicists of the U.S. Coast Guard, however, failed to further describe Healy as "a colorful failure" who suffered because of his drinking. Press releases and stories implied the "Hell Roaring Mike" nickname came from his boisterous voice on board ship when angry, not from his actions on the Barbary Coast. Most important, they did not mention that for Healy to succeed in the United States, he had to hide his racial heritage. In other words, the service very quickly began constructing a myth about Healy that stressed all the aspects of a great African American seaman and provided very little material about the actual man.

In 1987, Gerald O. Williams, a retired judge, wrote a lengthy unpublished master's thesis in history on Michael A. Healy, yielding the first scholarly study on the U.S. Revenue Cutter Service captain. While the study languished, the U.S. Coast Guard kept busy perpetuating the Healy myth, largely stressing his racial heritage. In 1988, James A. Michener published his novel, *Alaska*. His chapter on Capt. Michael A. Healy, which benefited from U.S. Coast Guard assistance, pictured the U.S. Revenue Cutter Service skipper as a larger-than-life historical figure. Nine years later, the service launched its newest polar icebreaker, the *Michael A. Healy*.

In 1999, an independent filmmaker, Maria Brooks, produced "The Odyssey of Captain Healy" for the Public Broadcasting System (PBS). Relying heavily on Williams' work, her production stressed how hiding his racial heritage largely contributed to Healy's alcoholism. This film, the first major effort to show Healy's drinking problem, also revealed something of the inner conflicts that drove the man. For instance, Brooks was also the first to reveal to a large audience that Captain Healy had attempted suicide late in life. In 2000, Prof. James M. O'Toole, of Boston College, wrote the first documented history of the family of Michael Morris Healy and Eliza Clark. Almost predictably, approaching a century after his death, and with his fame again rising, the threat of another plunge into obscurity lurked on the horizon.

Williams, Brooks, and O'Toole created problems for some in the U.S. Coast Guard. How could the service, many argued, name a ship after a man who not only suffered from alcoholism, but also faced charges in two trials? Some argued strongly for changing the name of the icebreaker.

Excepting the Healy biography by Williams and the works of Brooks and O'Toole, no treatment of Michael A. Healy's life has tried to see beyond the myth of the man, which was created largely after 1971. Part of the reason lies in the ashes of his destroyed diaries. The burning of the diaries and the passage of time makes understanding Healy's life extremely difficult. Take, for instance, two pivotal points in Captain Healy's life: the charges of drunkenness and the 1896 trial.

Historians and others have pointed out that alcoholism caused the end of Healy's good reputation. Very strong evidence exists to support this view; the few diaries and letters that do speak of Captain Healy all comment on his staggering about a ship or ashore. At various times during his career in the U.S. Revenue Cutter Service, Healy admitted to drinking to excess. Father Foley, who spent decades researching the lives of James, Patrick, and Michael Healy, however, argues that Captain Healy's staggering was not the result of strong drink. Foley believes Healy suffered from epilepsy and that the disorder caused the staggering. Father Foley, for some unaccountable reason, did not document where he obtained this startling information.[23] If, however, the information is correct, it changes many things about the man. It means that Healy had an additional psychological burden placed upon him. If so, Captain Healy must have known that if headquarters were to discover that he had epilepsy, then his days at sea were finished.

For unknown reasons, other than the willingness to simply accept Healy as a colorful failure, none of the early works on the sea captain ever closely examined the important 1896 trial. Even Father Foley failed to look deeply into what took place in the Appraisers Building in San Francisco. Apparently, these writers all believed Healy drank heavily, and this belief alone established his guilt. Delving into transcripts of the proceedings and newspaper accounts in the San Francisco Bay Area, however, reveals more than a simple case of exposing an officer as being guilty of overindulging in liquor. The trial has as many hidden layers as does Healy's life. Take, for example, the interesting testimony of Dr. Benjamin Sharp, a scientist from Philadelphia.

Captain Healy's reputation includes contributions he made to science during his exploration of Alaska. Yet, Dr. Sharp, Healy's guest on the *Bear* for part of the 1895 patrol, turned out to be one of the people adamantly opposed to Healy at the trial. The assistant secretary of the treasury ordered the trial delayed at one point so that Doctor Sharp could travel to San Francisco to testify against Healy. In his testimony, Sharp accused the captain of hindering his work. Sharp then switched his account to a personal attack against Healy's character. The scientist stated the junior officers in the *Bear* did not respect their captain because he did not act like a gentleman. His behavior, Sharp implied, resembled little more than that of a boorish common sailor. As an example, Doctor Sharp related that once, while at dinner, Healy mixed his mashed potatoes and gravy with his fingers and then commenced eating with his fingers as well. All testimony in the trial has to be treated as suspect, however, for, as a later account stated, there "was so much perjury on both sides that much of the testimony had to be disregarded in its entirety."[24]

But, what if Sharp's characterization of Healy and his method of eating mashed potatoes truly did describe the actions of a captain turned boorish sailor? Might not the elderly captain, in his own way, merely be showing his contempt for Doctor Sharp and the junior officers? Buried within the trial's transcripts, we find that Sharp testified that, in Healy's opinion, the whalers and merchant seamen ranked higher than the junior officers on the *Bear*.[25] Those researchers who had dug deep into the lives of Captain Healy and his siblings quickly learned that the offspring of Michael Morris and Eliza Clark Healy often had to act whiter than white people to hide their racial heritage. Just as he had to prove his whiteness, Captain Healy also felt the need, from time to time, to demonstrate his right to be called a sailor, his chosen profession. At the time of the trial, thirty-nine years of the captain's fifty-four years had been spent among tough deepwater sailors. Many sailors commit outrageous acts that seem to say, "see, only a sailor would do this."[26] Although Captain Healy had more than proved his abilities as a seaman, he needed, from time to time, to use the sailor's shock tactic to drive the point home.

Captain Healy also had justification for looking down upon some of his junior officers sailing in the 1895 patrol of the *Bear*. The transcripts of the trial contain the amazing revelation that some of the officers kept a written record of their captain's actions while in Alaskan waters. The very clear implication of a gentleman's mutiny ran throughout the trial transcripts. The official record also strongly implied that the officers would do their best to rid themselves of Healy.

The "discovery" of Healy's racial heritage fueled the imagination of the mythmakers. Now, people seemed to rush to prove Captain Healy's importance. Some believed Jack London based his character, Wolf Larsen, in his classic novel *The Sea Wolf*, on Healy.[27] One of the authors of this biography even heard a story told to children that had it not been for Captain Healy, Santa Claus would not have had reindeer.[28] During this resurgence of interest in Healy, none of the mythmakers asked why Healy's superiors in Washington, D.C., seven years after the 1896 trial, rescinded his sentence for being too harsh. Only one writer has covered Captain Healy's suicide attempts in 1900. And no one has yet explained why the service continued to keep Healy in command positions after these attempts.[29] Apparently this part of his life does not fit the myth. Even more likely, people find it easier to understand the myth than the truth.

The story of Michael Augustine Healy has never amounted to the simplistic tale passed down through the years. Captain Healy clearly does not resemble the man pictured by the myths initiated by the U.S. Coast Guard in 1971. From his earliest days in Georgia, Healy's family taught him that, if he wished to succeed in America, he had to hide his racial heritage. Such a heavy psychological burden had the potential to cripple many young boys. In Healy's case, his psychological burden only intensified with his failure to meet his family's expectations. The cruel sea further toughened Captain Healy in his early years, for as Joseph Conrad wrote, "the sea has no mercy."

In 1867, the United States' purchase of Alaska further shaped Healy's personality. Once he began working on the Alaskan maritime frontier, he participated in early conservation efforts as well as search and rescue, law enforcement, and medical efforts. During Healy's first patrol above the Arctic Circle, he saw firsthand at St. Lawrence Island many villages wiped out by starvation. The sight stayed with him and he attempted to do something to prevent further starvation. Captain Healy's life spans a period in which people began to think differently about working-class people, including sailors. The 1890 trial, in part, demonstrates that some felt sailors should have the same rights as workers on shore. Just as the 1890 trial in reality dealt with much more than the charge of drunkenness, so too did the 1896 proceedings. Above all, the Michael A. Healy story explains how one African American man, born in the time of slavery, dealt with race in America. The effects of this story still resonate in the twenty-first century.

Michael A. Healy's story does not need myths; it basically remains a sea adventure, marked by a large amount of tragedy. It presents a great seaman whose abilities should have brought him great fame. Life, however, constantly put forth episodes that snatched fame away from him. No matter how far he plummeted into despair after these episodes, Healy managed to regain his fame, only to repeat the cycle. Over a century after his death, the time has come to dispel the myths, to critically review the life of the former slave and judge whether he ranks as an Arctic hero or just as a colorful failure.

1

THE GEORGIA PLANTATION

The story of Michael Augustine Healy begins with the birth of his father, Michael Morris Healy, on September 20, 1796, in the tiny village of Athlone, some sixty miles east of Galway, in County Roscommon on the Shannon River in Ireland.[1] For reasons known only to him, Michael Morris Healy migrated to the New World in 1815, long before the great waves of Irish fleeing the potato famine.[2] Unlike the great majority of immigrants, Michael arrived in the United States with some money and education. He entered the bustling port of New York City, where, according to Fr. Albert S. Foley, the biographer of James and Patrick Healy, some of his sisters resided, and remained there for close to three years. When, according to tradition, a cousin living in Georgia wrote of the chances for wealth on the frontier, Michael immediately headed south, lured by the prospect of riches.[3]

On April 3, 1818, Healy appeared at the town of Clinton, Jones County, Georgia near present-day Macon. After walking into the county court house, Healy began the process of becoming a citizen of his new country. He filled out forms and took an oath. Healy testified that, since entering the United States, he intended "to become a Citizen thereof." When he signed the naturalization oath, Healy renounced forever any allegiance to any other nation and especially to "the Kingdom of Great Britain." Healy also swore that he had always "behaved himself as a person of good moral Character," believed in the principles of the federal constitution, and desired peace and good order. Upon signing the naturalization form, he became a citizen of the United States.[4]

As Healy received his citizenship, events in Central Georgia led to a major turning point in his life. By the 1820s, the pressure of whites upon the Native Americans of the area had caused the federal government to remove the Creeks and Cherokee. Whites divided the former tribal lands into two-hundred-acre parcels. "The names of free white males, widows with children, and minor orphans were placed in one lottery drum, with the numbers of the land lots in another. Local commissioners drew a name and a corresponding piece of land from each drum."[5]

With the proverbial "luck of the Irish," Healy won a substantial plot in Jones County in 1823 and won two more holdings in 1832. "Because it was random, however, the lottery system often produced a complex checkerboard of ownership, with one settler's fields scattered and broken up by those of others. Owners thus tried to consolidate their holdings."[6]

Healy found Central Georgia very "different from the cool and rainy land of his birth."[7] Extreme heat and humidity dominated its summer. The August temperature in his new surroundings averaged 86.4 degrees Fahrenheit in August, while those near his former home averaged 64.4 degrees Fahrenheit. Central Georgia had red clay soil and rolling hills covered with pine trees. The Georgia frontier caused one visitor from New England to write, "There is hardly a poor woman's cow" on Cape Cod "that is not better housed and more comfortably provided for than a majority of the white people of Georgia." The settlers were "coarse and irrestrainable in appetite and temper . . . almost imbecile for personal elevation." And yet, another visitor saw that as more people rushed into the area, the people improved: "Everything seemed new: there hadn't even been time to clear the tree stumps from the just-laid-out streets. All the houses 'looked as if they had been put up the day before,' a Scottish traveler remarked in 1829, and always in the air was the smell of the sawmill."[8]

New settlers eventually found cotton to be the best cash crop for this frontier. Earlier, Eli Whitney's invention of the cotton gin in 1793, a device that efficiently removed the seeds from cotton fiber, made the crop profitable. Seven years after the invention of the gin, the national production of cotton ballooned from around 3,000 bales to 73,000, and continued soaring upward after that.[9]

Although cotton provided a profitable crop, certain problems arose. The technology of the day made the growing of cotton a labor-intensive operation. After plowing the soil, "[s]eedlings were set in straight furrows by hand in March, and after about three weeks they took root. Next, they had to be thinned out and kept free of weeds, tasks that could only be done by hand and, worse, by constantly bending over. . . . By July, the hottest month of the year, the cotton began to bloom, and picking started at once. Bolls left on the plant too long popped open and were lost to the wind."[10] The more field hands a planter employed, the larger the crop and the quicker the harvest. Cotton also took a great deal out of the land. Planters grew corn or grass in the former cotton fields after two seasons and then plowed those crops under to help restore the soil. Thus, the planter with the most land held the advantage over a landowner with less acreage.[11]

The Georgia soil, a labor-intensive crop, hot weather, and the need for large plantations all combined to form the root cause of the tragedy of the Michael Morris Healy family. It also lies at the heart of two continuing problems in the history of the United States: slavery and race.

Cotton raised in the South prior to the Civil War came largely through the labor of black slaves. At first, the whites of Georgia resisted using slaves in their territory. The need for a large labor force, however, overcame this resistance. Eventually, even most of the clergy relented. In an attempt to soothe the consciences of some whites, lawmakers passed legislation limiting both the powers of masters and the providing of Christian instruction to those in bondage. Few, if any, whites ever faced charges under these laws. Whites even developed a theory that the biological makeup of black slaves suited them for work in hot climates, while whites lacked this in their biological makeup. This led to the reasoning that blacks not only worked best in the hottest weather, but that they actually enjoyed it. Slavery became entrenched and soon increased in Georgia. In 1790, for example, Georgia ranked fifth in slave population, but seventy years later, in 1860, only Virginia had a larger slave population.[12]

Michael Morris Healy began the hard toil of clearing land, building a home, and planting his crop. According to tradition, he erected a three-room log building, which stood on the "south side of a ridge about half a mile back from the [Ocmulgee River]."[13] This gave him a certain advantage, as a planter living near a river had good transportation for his harvested crop.

Healy came to the Georgia frontier with some cash. In 1822, for example, he loaned $200.00 to two men. Today, it would take $44,242.49 to have the same buying power as the $200.00. In other words, the loan amounted to a sizable sum. Three years later, the men defaulted and Healy went to court, recovering the money with interest. Ten times in his lifetime, he resorted to the courts to recover money others owed him.[14]

A dream of most people entering the United States centers on success and wealth for a family. Michael Morris Healy began his work toward fulfilling his dream of wealth as a twenty-two-year-old bachelor. Whom he selected as his partner made him "a social outcast by the people in [Jones County]" and began the tragedy of his family.[15] Healy chose as his partner Eliza Clark, an African American slave.

The origins of Eliza Clark Healy remain as unknown today as they were then. Years after her death, one of her sons hinted that she came from Haiti. A local Jones County historian suggested she came from the plantation of Samuel Griswold, who ran the state's first iron foundry. Another source described her as the slave of a Maj. James Smith, a surveyor in Macon. Yet another family tradition placed her in "Santo Domingo and [as being] brought in by French neighbors . . . who took refuge in Georgia from the West Indian revolutions and slave revolutions and . . . insurrections of the early nineteenth century." Another of the many "legends" to surface about Eliza identifies her as "the natural daughter of a French-Spanish father and a slave woman . . . with high cheekbones, black curly hair, and very fine features. . . . She looked Moohr or Hamltic. . . . Besides Oxonian English, she could also speak the Arabic languages of the Northwest Africa, also French and Spanish. . . . [Eliza Clark] wrote and talked about every subject under the sun as if she had a Ph.D." Her birth date, given as March 3, 1813, remains questionable. If true, it would make her seventeen years younger than Healy. From, at the latest, 1829 on, Eliza and Michael lived together faithfully.[16]

According to tradition, Eliza knew "all the plantation arts and crafts" and worked at being "a good homemaker." She quickly "transformed the log house into a snug and comfortable home."[17]

By living together, "they violated perhaps the most powerful taboo of nine-teenth-century America: marriage between persons of different races."[18] This taboo actually survived until at least the last third of the twentieth century. To understand this strong taboo, a person today needs to understand the concept of race in those years. Most people then believed that the blood that flowed in one's veins decided one's race "forever." This became known as the "one-drop rule." Put simply, if you had a Negro ancestor, or, as people in Healy's day would put it, blood, then, no matter how many other races intermingled in your family, the "biological 'fact' . . . could not be changed": you were a Negro.[19]

The one-drop rule came about because slavery in the United States had clear dividing lines—slaves were black, blacks were slaves—and it was necessary to maintain these distinctions. Despite these distinctions, however, the exploi-tation of female slaves by masters continued, being consistently condemned only in theory. The law sought to address this. Legislatures levied stiff fines on ministers who presided at weddings involving parties of different color. A free, white person involved in a sexual act with a person of color could face a fine or possible banishment. Georgia in 1750 became the first colony to pass a law making black-white marriages invalid. The law expressed the community's fear of the practice. It did not stop the mixed-race marriages, but it did make them rare.

To ensure the law imposed the strongest means of stopping mixed marriages, Southern states established the principle that children would always take the condition of their mother. A free man could not pass his freedom on to any child born of a slave. This acted as a form of racial control, ensuring that the white children of a master would always have a higher status than their mixed-race siblings.

Healy never took a white wife, thereby rejecting the practice of having two families, one white and one black. He also never formally married Eliza Clark; after all, the law forbade this. Instead, he simply chose to live as if legally married. Why he did so, we will never know. It may have been "a phenomenon that historians often overlook: love."[20]

Eliza's reasons for entering into this type of arrangement are easier to understand. She won a freedom, otherwise unavailable to her. This freedom, however, came at a price. Even though light-skinned, any children from this marriage, as per the "one-drop rule," would be considered black and therefore slaves. Should Michael die before she did, the law said Eliza and her children would remain chattels and would spend their lives as slaves.

Despite their status in Jones County, Michael and Eliza worked hard to succeed. Just because Healy took a slave as his wife does not mean he believed in abolition. At the time, he owned thirteen slaves. Healy, like his neighbors, still needed slaves to till his cotton fields. The mere fact that he could purchase this number of people in bondage indicated that Healy came to the frontier with money.[21]

Eliza bore children regularly and in two clusters. The first, James Augustine, arrived on April 6, 1830, and was followed by Hugh Clark, born on April 16, 1832; Patrick Francis, on February 27, 1834; Alexander Sherwood, on January 24, 1836; Martha Ann, on March 9, 1838; and Michael Augustine, on September 22, 1839. A baby, named Eugene, born on June 30, 1842, lived only a few weeks. The second cluster of siblings began with the birth of Amanda Josephine, on January 9, 1845, who was followed by Eliza Dunamore on December 23, 1846, and by a final sibling, another boy named Eugene, on January 23, 1849.[22]

The Healys' hard work on the plantation paid off. They had liquid assets, as evidenced by the loaning of money to neighbors. Healy eventually owned forty-nine slaves, with five men, twelve women, and thirty-two children of all ages. The oldest man was forty-five years old, the oldest woman fifty, and the children ranged in age from one month to sixteen years. In comparison, the average number of those in bondage in Jones County was fourteen. Of nearly five hundred slaveholders in the county, Healy ranked eighteenth in terms of number of slaves owned. Of the 412 property owners in Jones County, Healy, with 1,500 acres, ranked thirty-third in improved acreage and thirty-sixth in total land value.[23] By the standards of success then held in the antebellum South, the Healys' accomplishments put them in the upper reaches of society in Jones County.

But the matter of Eliza Clark Healy's race denied them this luxury. Many in the South overlooked mixed marriages, however, *if* the couples did not flaunt their arrangement. Michael Morris and Eliza Clark Healy had some advantages. They lived in an isolated area, kept largely to themselves, and did not flaunt their living arrangement.[24] Not known is whether Healy ever regularly brought Eliza into town. There is evidence, however, that he once brought her into a settlement to have a daguerreotype taken of her. Healy's ownership of wealth, land, and slaves excused him from many taunts. Nevertheless, his neighbors did not welcome him, or his family, with open arms. Two incidents reveal the underlining tensions that Michael Morris and Eliza Clark Healy faced. The first, according to tradition, involved an Ocmulgee River workboat that stopped by the Healy plantation one day. Healy offered the laborers some whiskey. One imbiber observed the Healy children at play. He then used a racial taunt, saying Healy's "yard children" would bring a good price at a slave auction in Macon. Michael responded by having Eliza turn the dogs loose on the man. The second incident concerns a notation recorded in a history of Jones County: "About 1845, a destructive storm blew through the county, and the locals immediately designated it 'the Healy storm,' almost as if it represented the judgment of heaven against the two of them—and against the county for tolerating this racial apostasy."[25]

Today, no one knows how the Healys raised their children. Events in the society they lived within, however, suggest they taught their family one fundamental lesson. As the slave population grew in the South, many whites began to worry about controlling the large numbers of slaves in their midst. Nat Turner's insurrection in Virginia in August 1831 did nothing to allay this dread. Fear led to legal actions. The first slave codes in Georgia before the American Revolution were less stringent than those of other colonies. The codes permitted freeing of slaves by masters and, in 1765, the colony even encouraged the immigration of blacks from elsewhere, providing for their naturalization. They could enjoy all the benefits of citizenship, except the right to vote.

After the American Revolution, however, the racial climate changed. In 1802,

Georgia outlawed the private freeing of slaves. Only the legislature had the right to grant freedom, and this right was exercised only in exceptional cases. At the time Michael Morris Healy signed his naturalization papers in 1818, Georgia further tightened its slave law by forbidding the freeing of slaves in last wills and testaments. Blacks could not own or carry firearms. Nor could masters teach them to read or write. "Slavery may have come late in Georgia, but once there, it took hold with no less force than elsewhere in the South."[26]

Even though the Healy siblings inherited various hues of skin color, people in Jones County knew about the family. Both Michael Morris and Eliza Clark Healy realized that racial attitudes in Georgia were unlikely to improve; indeed, it seemed more likely that such attitudes would worsen, with whites calling for even harsher measures against people of African ancestry. From the time their children could understand, Michael and Eliza taught them the consequences of their racial heritage. They would carry this lesson for the rest of their lives.

Despite the constant tension of race, Michael and Eliza did the best they could to make their children's lives as comfortable as possible on the frontier. The family never lived in a large mansion, with the large white columns so favored by novelists and Hollywood. Healy did not have the luxury of sitting on a large portico, sipping mint juleps with the delicate scent of wisteria in the air to relax him. The family lived in their original log house. Michael and Eliza's work, however, provided money enough for the luxury of carpets on the floor and wineglasses. Framed lithographs hung on the walls. A handsome birdcage held a bird to bring the joy of listening to natural music. Estate documents indicate that someone owned a fiddle, thus introducing other music into the home.[27]

Farming has always entailed the struggle to survive, even more so on an isolated frontier. The Healys had little time for anything but work. Their log home, however, held a library of over one hundred books. Whatever leisure time they managed to carve out of their day could be used in pursuit of the mind. The volumes ranged from practical works, cookbooks and medical texts, to adventure stories. A number of books told of exploits that took place in South America and Africa, while others offered the narratives of Lewis and Clark and tales of travels to far-off California. Edward Gibbon's *The History of the Decline and Fall of the Roman Empire* took up a large amount of shelf space, along with volumes by Shakespeare, Milton, Byron, and others.

Books on philosophy and religion also made up the library. Among these were a theological dictionary and a translation of the Koran, but, notably, no Bible. Three volumes on the Catholic Church also made up the collection.[28]

As early as 1837, Michael, now forty-one years old, recognized that a catastrophe loomed for his family. At the time, the average life span for a man living in the United States was under forty years. The hard life on the frontier could further shorten even this short life span. Early on, Healy recognized a simple solution that would save his children from slavery. Like many simple solutions, however, it required a great deal of anguish.

Contrary to modern-day popular opinion, racial attitudes prior to the Civil War varied little above or below the Mason-Dixon Line. Even in the supposedly enlightened North, people of color faced restrictions. The Healys' solution to the problem of their children's race "had to be a comparative one: where might their relative advantage be better than it was at home?"[29] In Georgia, no matter how light-skinned his children were, people in Jones County knew about Eliza Clark. In the North, his children's mixed racial heritage might not be recognized.

After deciding to send their children to the North, the Healys selected New York City, an urban area already familiar to Michael. Furthermore, as a successful planter, Michael had made trips to the city and befriended John Manning, a hardware and dry goods merchant in Manhattan. The businessman agreed to serve as guardian of the Healy children, becoming a surrogate parent to them. By placing his children under the care of a successful white businessman, Healy helped ensure that Northerners would accept his children as members of mainstream white society.[30]

The Healy library in Georgia indicates Healy's belief in education. Moving his children to New York City also offered them a chance at an education they could not obtain in the South. At first, Healy chose a Quaker school. Around 1837, Healy took his first son, James, then only seven years old, by ship to New York and enrolled him in the Quaker elementary school at Flushing, on Long Island.[31] From this point on, once Michael and Eliza considered one of their children to be ready, Michael brought the child north. More than a century later, this act of parental devotion by the Healys toward their children does not cease to amaze. Both parents knew their children could never again return home for, no matter how well-educated they were, they would always be considered slaves in Georgia. Furthermore, Michael Morris Healy risked facing legal action for educating slaves. Michael at least could make periodic visits to the North to see the children, but Eliza would never see them again. In other words, both parents, in effect, lost their nine children before they reached adulthood.

Michael Morris and Eliza Clark Healy paid a very high price to ensure their children had a chance at freedom. As the years passed, the children had to find other people, or institutions, to gain the support children need. Eventually, the children "almost never spoke of their parents." The less said of their mother the better. Tradition, however, has saved a story of Eliza's daguerreotype hanging in James' room in school, with a piece of cloth over it. Michael Morris Healy also had to be pushed aside; his presence would cause too many questions that would be difficult to answer. If the children wished to survive in white society, then they had to pursue the only option they perceived to be open to them: they must build a life and a life history that did not include their natural parents. The fact that the Healy children had to disavow their parents is one of the great tragedies of Michael Morris and Eliza Clark Healy's family.[32]

In 1844, seven years after Michael enrolled James in the Quaker school, there occurred a chance meeting that a romantic might call fate. While on the slow sea voyage to the North, Healy met and fell into conversations with a passenger from Boston, John Bernard Fitzpatrick, a Roman Catholic priest, who reminded his contemporary observers of Daniel Webster. Fitzpatrick was returning to Boston from Georgetown College, in Washington, D.C., after being consecrated an auxiliary bishop of Boston. The new bishop had two burning goals, the advancement of the church and the new opening of the church's college for young men. For whatever the reason, perhaps their Irish heritages, the planter from Georgia and Bishop Fitzpatrick spent long hours in animated conversation during the slow sea voyage.[33]

Michael Morris Healy probably did not practice the Catholic religion while in Georgia. Attending a church of his faith in the South of this time would have been extremely difficult, if not impossible. In 1820, for example, only two parish churches existed between Baltimore and New Orleans. A resident pastor did not arrive in Macon until 1841. Three years later, in 1844, the pastor withdrew to Savannah and only visited central Georgia once a month. While remaining "unchurched," the conversation between the Southerner and Bostonian made Healy realize that the new college and the church might offer his children security.[34]

At this time, the Catholic Church in New England was in a better position than it was in the South, but not by any great degree. A parish had been organized in Boston in 1789, and a resident Bishop appointed in 1808. The Boston diocese encompassed all six New England states, with few priests and small, scattered congregations. The large numbers of Irish immigrants arriving in the 1820s proved both a blessing and a curse. New parishes opened, but hostility grew toward the newcomers and their religion. The Pope's Day celebration during the colonial era, in which an effigy of the Pope was dragged through the streets and then set on fire, was suppressed during the American Revolution because of the alliance with France, but this hostility toward the papacy lay very close to the surface. In 1834, for example, a convent of Ursuline Sisters located in Charlestown, Massachusetts, just across the harbor from Boston, suffered the brunt of this hostility. Rumors quickly spread that lecherous priests had imprisoned the young nuns against their wills and subjected them to horrific indecencies. An angry mob attacked the convent, turned out the nuns, and burned the building to the ground.[35]

The church failed to recover the cost of the damages from the state of Massachusetts. The new college that Fitzpatrick mentioned to Healy during their conversations actually served as a part of the retrenchment of the Church. Bishop Benedict Fenwick had purchased a small academy at Worcester, Massachusetts, and proposed to focus its efforts on educating the sons of immigrants. The school took the name of the College of the Holy Cross, with a faculty made up of the priests of the Jesuit order. Located some forty miles from Boston, Bishops Fenwick and Fitzpatrick hoped the college would provide "a safe haven in which Catholic boys could pursue their studies undisturbed."[36]

The Healys decided to enroll their boys in the College of the Holy Cross. Today, the institution would be called a prep school in addition to a college. The four oldest sons—James, fourteen, Hugh, twelve, Patrick, ten, and Alexander (known always as Sherwood) eight—entered Holy Cross in the summer of 1844. Sherwood came directly from Georgia to the school.[37]

The year after his sons entered Holy Cross, Michael Morris Healy, recognizing his mortality and the dangers faced by his family, began putting his affairs in order. Most of the wealthier planters in Jones County simply drew up a legal document and instructed someone to carry out the terms of the will. Not so Healy. His will required a certain legal finesse. For example, the law forbade the mention of Eliza Clark. The same applied to his children. Healy shrewdly avoided both dangers, thus avoiding any possibility that the Georgian courts might forfeit his property to the state.

First, Healy astutely approached his will as if it were an ordinary document. He left his entire estate to his "beloved children in New York: James, Hugh, Patrick, Sherwood + Martha." Under Georgia law they could not inherit anything, but by placing them in New York, even though they actually resided in Massachusetts, and by designating his "worthy and trusted friend," John Manning, of New York, as their guardian, Healy achieved the appearance of legal correctness both in Georgia and New York. Healy instructed that all his property, with the exception of "Negroes," be sold and the money invested with Manning for the benefit of the children. The slaves were to be hired out every year "in the usual way." Only after the youngest child, Eugene, came of age would the slaves be sold, and the proceeds added to the estate. Healy next instructed that, when the children "now in Georgia shall arrive at the North," they would share fully in the estate. He further directed: "my trusty woman Elisa [sic], Mother of my Said children, . . . shall be removed to a free State when her Interest will best be consulted." The executors were to pay her $120 each year for the rest of her life. Eliza could be Healy's "trusty woman," but not legally identified as his wife. Nevertheless, Healy identified her as the mother of his children. Following the letter of the law, she inherited nothing, but would be supported for the rest of her life with a generous annuity. The $120.00 of 1845 translates to a $23,846.36 annuity today.

Healy also stated that the shares of his three daughters would go "to them and their bodily heirs only." This provision would prevent any unscrupulous suitor from marrying a daughter for her money. Interestingly, Healy designated several neighbors to act as his local executors, but New Yorker John Manning would be legally responsible for the children. Should Manning "pay the debt of nature," then Healy designated Fr. Thomas Mulledy, the president of the College of the Holy Cross, "to act as guardian" of his children and "to carry out the provisions" of his will. If Father Mulledy could not carry out this trust, then James, the eldest son, would serve jointly with "some discreet and proper person" of his own selection, most likely Bishop Fitzpatrick or Bishop Fenwick.[38]

Meanwhile, the four oldest sons thrived at Holy Cross. The boys recognized that Holy Cross offered them an identity that would help them avoid being dragged into bondage. The Healy family always faced the question of being black or white. They decided for themselves what they would be—Catholic. The four oldest boys were baptized on November 18, 1844.[39] Their choice had nothing to do with the Church's stand on slavery. In reality, the Church's stand on slavery, at best, remained ambiguous. Bishop Francis Kenrick, of Philadelphia, for example, wrote in 1861 that as long as masters treated their slaves kindly and according to "Christian principles," their identity as slaveholders was morally correct. A Catholic layman, Orestes Brownson, in the middle of the Civil War, wrote: "Why is it that you can scarcely get a single Christian thought into the negro's head and that with him religion is almost sure to lapse into a groveling superstition? Why, because he is a degenerate man, and a superstition is a degenerate religion."[40]

Entering the church "suggests" the children deliberately used "Catholicism at least in part to separate themselves from their African American heritage." The older children knew that to advance in the United States they had to be white. Learning very early in life that they must pass for white, they now needed an intermediary to make this difficult transition from black to white. In the nineteenth century, most Americans considered Catholics as white. The Healy children "made their identity simpler by making it more complicated."[41]

In truth, the older Healy brothers showed no sympathy for the abolitionist movement. Sherwood, as he grew older, defended the Catholic position on the ownership of slaves, but not on slave trading. He felt that many Protestant leaders of the abolition movement were very closely aligned with those in the anti-Catholic movement. "Hostility toward the abolitionist was . . . the normal, respectable opinion of most Americans during the 1840s."[42] By repeating the "respectable political opinion" of the time, the Healy children both distanced themselves from their mother's heritage and placed themselves within acceptable white society. For the rest of their lives, the siblings tried to prove themselves to be whiter than whites.

While the Healy sons excelled at Holy Cross, the rising crescendo over the unresolved domestic crisis of slavery swirled faster and stronger around their Georgia plantation home. Eliza Clark Healy's delivery of her last child, Eugene, in January 1849, might well have been the final straw that drove the family's father to a decision.

In any event, James recorded in his diary on July 25, 1849, that his father planned to visit "in the fall of the year, and will leave Georgia next spring."[43] Once the plantation and its holdings had been sold, Healy, along with Eliza and their three youngest children, intended to relocate to New York City, or perhaps Boston, and reunite their family. In the meanwhile, Michael and Eliza directed their energies toward preparing for the next year's crops and leaving the land they had labored on for the last three decades.

Then tragedy struck. Eliza Clark died suddenly on May 19, 1850. As was not uncommon for that time and place in the age of slavery, no explanation or cause of her death ever survived in either public or private records. The grief-stricken Michael Morris Healy now had three very young children—Josephine, five, Eliza, three, and Eugene, fifteen months—who needed his attention. According to tradition, he wisely borrowed their Aunt Nancy, his wife's slave sister, from Samuel Griswold's nearby plantation to care for them. The death of his faithful wife only further stiffened Healy's resolve to leave Georgia. With the new crop already in the ground, however, he, as a practical hard-working planter, felt a responsibility to bring in the harvest before departing for the North.

The summer of 1850 brought a heat wave that broke records for Jones County, with temperatures soaring to 104 degrees Fahrenheit. In New York that July, Hugh had met a friend of the family who told Hugh that his father was "enjoying excellent health."[45] On August 27, 1850, however, three months after Eliza's death, Michael Morris Healy died. He was fifty-three years old. Like his wife of so many years, his death went unrecorded by any of his children, or anyone that knew him. The combination of heat, worry about the crop, and, mainly, worry about his remaining children in Georgia may have contributed to his death. Or, perhaps the romantic notion that Michael Morris Healy died of a broken heart over the passing of his beloved wife of at least twenty-one years might be closer to the truth. Very quietly, he was laid to rest next to Eliza Clark Healy.[46]

The death of the elder Healys brought an end to their little-known love story. Even in death, however, their parental concern for their children continued. Michael Morris Healy's masterfully crafted will ensured both the education of his sons and daughters in the North and a tidy sum with which they could begin their lives.[47]

2

DOWN TO THE SEA

Shortly before turning eleven years old, Michael Augustine Healy said good-bye to his mother. After their emotional parting, his father escorted him to Worcester, Massachusetts, where he would attend the College of the Holy Cross. The elder Healy then said farewell to his sixth child and returned to Georgia. Nothing is known about the young Healy's early childhood and very little is known of his time at Holy Cross. Any chance of understanding Michael Augustine Healy's formative years on the Georgia plantation went up in smoke when the four large diaries he kept later in life were burned.[1]

Not long after the young Michael left Georgia, his mother died, which placed an additional psychological burden upon the boy. This burden doubled within two months of his beginning school at Holy Cross when his father died, leaving all nine children orphans.

The story of the Healy family might well have ended with the deaths of Michael Morris and Eliza Clark Healy. The nine orphans, however, received a legacy left by their parents that, combined with their natural intelligence and drive, helped them to succeed in life. By 1850, James, the eldest child, had entered a seminary in Montreal, Canada. The responsibility of settling the affairs of their father, Michael Morris Healy, therefore fell to the next oldest son, Hugh, who was now living in New York City, and to John Manning. Hugh realized that traveling back to Georgia entailed the risk of being captured as a runaway slave. He and Manning, therefore, initially had to depend upon three of the Healys' neighbors in Jones County who had been designated as executors of the will: Robert Hardeman, William Moreland, and Charles McCarthy. Luckily for the Healy orphans, the three respected attorneys carried out their duties in a trustworthy manner.[2]

The sale of the plantation and items associated with it, with the exception of the Healys' slaves, added $13,200 to the estate. Tuition at Holy Cross totaled a very steep $150 a year, the equivalent of the entire annual wages of a farm laborer. This first installment to the estate, therefore, ensured that the Healy children did not suffer any immediate financial difficulties.[3]

Slaves proved to be the Healy estate's most valuable commodity. This fact involved the Healy children in one of the most tragic ironies of the family: the children of African American descent, their own mother a slave, would secure their financial futures by becoming slaveholders themselves. The Healys' situation, however, was not unique. Unbeknownst to many, some free African Americans held slaves in the antebellum South. The African American historian Carter Woodson accounts for more than sixty of these owners in Georgia in 1830.[4] For the Healy children, becoming slaveholders enabled them to further distance themselves from their racial heritage. First, they declared themselves white. Then they joined the Catholic Church, which effectively provided additional distance between themselves and their racial heritage. Now, as slaveholders, they had one more means of denying their heritage.

In his will, Michael Morris Healy ordered that his slaves be hired out until all of his children had completed their studies or were old enough to care for themselves. Six months after Michael Augustine Healy entered Holy Cross, his father's estate received the money from the hiring out of forty-nine slaves. The planter William Westmoreland, for example, hired the slaves David and Vina for $140. In 1852, the estate drew an income of $1,537, less the two and a half percent commission owed to the agent that negotiated the transaction, from the hiring out of the Healy slaves. In other words, the Healys' children inherited the financial wherewithal to live their lives comfortably until such time as they decided their own course in life.[5]

Meanwhile, someone would have to make the journey to Jones County to bring the three youngest Healy children out of the South. James, as the eldest, should have made the risky journey, but, apparently, he felt his work at the seminary could not be interrupted. To put the best possible spin on James' decision, we can grant that he may have felt it was faster to travel to Georgia from New York City than from Montreal. In any case, the dangerous task fell upon Hugh. Congress had just passed the Fugitive Slave Law. In the eyes of Georgia law, Hugh would fit the description of a runaway slave. All it would take was a neighbor reporting him to authorities or to a professional slave catcher, who could legally go to New York City and arrest Hugh there, for Hugh to be taken back to Georgia as a slave. If captured, Hugh would need to prove his free status, which he could not do. Furthermore, some people, including some in the North, ran a lucrative criminal business of providing white witnesses to indict a free African American as a runaway slave. These false witnesses then shared in the profit of the slave's sale. The law also levied stiff penalties on anyone sheltering runaway slaves. This meant that any friends or neighbors of Michael Morris Healy that had agreed to provide a haven for his children until Hugh arrived risked punishment under the law for their act of kindness.

Somehow Hugh managed to enter Jones County undetected. Just as amazing is the fact that he found Josephine, Eliza, and Eugene being cared for, according to tradition, by their Aunt Nancy. Circumstantial evidence suggests that Hugh took the time to visit the graves of his parents, for the records show that he paid a workman in Jones County to erect a stone wall around their graves. He then returned to New York with the three youngest children. By 1851, all of the orphaned Healy children resided in the North.[6]

In the meantime, while all of this occurred, Michael Augustine Healy labored through his first year of study at Holy Cross. The pressure of beginning in a new environment, combined with not knowing the fate of his younger siblings, weighed heavily upon the young boy as he studied Latin Grammar, Geography, English Grammar, Bible History, Latin and English Exercises, and Arithmetic. In 1851, Holy Cross suffered a major fire and classes did not resume until 1853. Michael stayed with John Manning's family during this unplanned vacation. Where, or if, he attended school during his stay in New York City is unknown. In September 1853, *The Matricula of The College of the Holy Cross* recorded a Michael A. Healy, of Georgia, entering the school for "the second time."[7]

When the young Healy reentered Holy Cross, he faced the daunting reputation of his older scholarly brothers. James, for example, earned a place in the school's annals as its first valedictorian. In addition to academic honors, three of the older Healy brothers as well as their sister Martha Ann wished to pursue a religious life in the Catholic Church. With their outstanding academic records, the older Healy brothers, plus the faculty of Holy Cross, expected great things from the young Michael. In addition, Michael's older brother Patrick had also returned to Holy Cross, this time as a teacher.

On November 23, 1853, shortly after the young Michael A. Healy resumed his studies at Holy Cross, Patrick F. Healy wrote to Fr. George Fenwick, who had served as a mentor to all the older Healy brothers: "Placed in a college as I am, our boys are well acquainted either by sight or hearsay with me & my brothers, remarks are sometimes made (though not in my hearing) which wound my very heart. You know—to what I refer. The anxiety of mine caused by these is very intense. I have here with me a younger brother Michael. He is obliged to go through the same ordeal. . . . [W]e shall always be subject to some such degrading misfortune. Providence seems to have decided this."[8] Patrick's "anguished complaint to Father Fenwick was as close as he or others [in the family] ever came to speaking of their dilemma."[9]

If the remarks caused "anguish" for the mature Patrick, then it does not take a large amount of training in psychology to imagine how it may have struck the teenaged Michael. Furthermore, research suggests that sibling rivalry can cause even gifted children to underperform at school. In other words, Michael Augustine Healy entered his formative adolescent years carrying a very large psychological load. Not too surprisingly, the fourteen year old began rebelling. Tradition has it that he started running away.

One year after Patrick wrote his distressed letter to Father Fenwick, he wrote again to his mentor, this time about his younger brother. Michael, he wrote, was "a source of great anxiety" for both himself and James, who now served as the patriarch of the family.[10] Sherwood apparently deepened the tension that existed between the older brothers and the teenaged Michael. In a letter to Patrick, dated March 10, 1854, Sherwood writes, "I am sincerely sorry and heartily ashamed of my conduct toward Mike, asking the Almighty Dispenser of all things to let me feel, rather than him, the effects of my negligence of him may have produced."[11] Although the cause, written or otherwise, of Sherwood's need to seek his younger brother's apology remains unknown, it probably involved Sherwood's frustration with his younger sibling's lack of academic interest or his attitude toward authority. James now felt he must take action. He chose to send his fourteen-year-old brother to a seminary in Douai, France. As James explained to Father Fenwick, he did not want "to make a priest of [Michael], but to give him a chance to redeem his lost time and character." James added that "his conduct has not corresponded to my hopes."[12]

Douai lies in flat country along the banks of the Scarpe River. The town is located 13 miles southwest of the Belgium border, 24 miles south of Lille, and 121 miles northeast of Paris. Founded by William Allen in 1568, the English College at Douai is remembered for those of its members who began preparing for Catholics an English translation of the Bible known as the Douay-Rheims Version.[13]

James' plan for Michael seemed a perfect way to force a restless boy "to redeem his character": Michael would undergo a long ocean voyage, travel to a little-known region of France, and benefit from the regimentation of a seminary. The conflicting currents that ran through the young Healy upon learning of his older brother's decision can only be imagined. Even today, many young boys who know only home and school might quail at such news.

James, however, miscalculated his brother's temperament. Michael looked upon his new surroundings in France as a challenge to his abilities to run away. According to tradition, just before his sixteenth birthday, Michael A. Healy somehow made his way to the docks of Liverpool, England. There, he signed on board a merchant ship as a "boy," the lowest rating in the sailing merchant fleet. Michael had turned sixteen by the time his brothers learned of his latest adventure. They were forced finally to accept the inevitable fact that their brother needed to steer his own course in life.

Why did a boy from rural Georgia, a boy who grew up miles from the sea and knew only the shelter of home and school, choose the sea? Three important reasons spring immediately to mind. Michael Morris Healy's library contained many books that told great tales of adventure. The elder Healy read some of these books to his children. These early stories from childhood may well have planted the seed of adventure in the young Michael. Two aspects of Michael's experience at Holy Cross, however, offer the greatest insight into his decision. Michael showed no interest in academic pursuits or in a life with the Church. As a result, the older brothers felt anxious about his character and looked upon him as a failure. This alone could drive any teenager to rebellion. More important, however, is the fact that Michael saw his older brother, Patrick, a noted scholar and teacher at Holy Cross, stung by whispered rumors. It did not take much imagination for the young Healy to recognize what lay in store for him. Perhaps at sea he could still the whispers.[14]

In the nineteenth century, the sea seemed to many a young man a way to escape perceived injustice, and, most important, offered a sure path to adventure. Most of these young men, however, had no idea of what awaited them on a deepwater sailing ship. Even the few who did have family members at sea really had no notion of what life at sea was like. Frederick Pease Harlow's brother, a mate on a deepwater ship in the 1870s, wrote home saying: "Do not let the boys follow the sea. At best, it's nothing but a dog's life." Harlow ignored his brother's dire warning.[15] Young boys did not know about tainted food, long periods of monotony, often brutal officers, and the many other dangers of life at sea. Healy, and others, instead "pined in happy ignorance, for the yo-ho-ho of life at sea. . . . [It']s easy to dream fondly of the heaving deck, the gouts of freezing spray, the struggle with . . . fifty knots of wind, because nothing like that" had ever happened in their daily experience.[16]

The College of the Holy Cross, even in the early nineteenth century, lay close enough to Boston for an adventurous boy to reach the city's busy docks. Or one can imagine that while he lived in New York City, the nearby docks may have beckoned to the young Michael. In any case, some time during the many times he ran away before being sent to Douai, Michael surely watched sailors along the wharves, just returned from ports throughout the world. These swaggering men seemed so much freer than the people at Holy Cross. The impressionable Healy also saw many black sailors who seemed on equal footing with their white shipmates. Later, Healy learned that this equality applied only to those who "sailed before the mast," the old salts term for an ordinary sailor. Only whites served as officers in ships. (By the end of the nineteenth century, African Americans at sea suffered the same discrimination as those on shore.) Whatever the reasons, by 1855, Michael Augustine Healy had decided to follow the sea. It was to be a calling he would never abandon.[17]

Healy became a deepwater sailor in the hard and dangerous sailing merchant marine. The young lad possessed the same drive and determination to succeed as his older siblings did. Although he may have thought the sea offered a path to equality, Healy quickly learned that, in reality, the tight confines of a sailing merchant ship simply reproduced the racial tensions of life on shore, and oftentimes enforced an even harsher version of that life. A ship in the Age of Sail reflected a rigid class structure. (This continues, albeit to a lesser extent, today.) The ordinary sailors lived in the most forward section of the ship, in an area ahead of the masts known as the forecastle—hence the nautical expression "sailing before the mast," which designates those below the rank of officer. Those in charge who ranked below the captain, known as mates in the merchant marine and as officers in the U.S. Navy, lived in the after portion of the ship, or aft, located in the stern of the ship. Even on the smallest deepwater ship, the two locations signified an enormous gulf in terms of the treatment the ship's various ranks received and affected everything from food and living conditions to punishment. In the U.S. Navy of the period, the gap was absolutely unbridgeable. The merchant marine, however, allowed some to make the crossing. The very difficult transition from being one who served before the mast to being one who served as mate involved untold hardships for those who attempted it.[18] Many shipmates of the sailor who achieved mate status, for example, did not understand why anyone cared to move "aft" and often shunned the man. On the other hand, many mates looked upon the sailor as bringing the attitudes and manners of the forecastle aft. In other words, these sailors were betwixt and between.

Today, one finds it difficult to understand just how brutal life could be at sea in the nineteenth century. This should come as no surprise, for few people living on the beach even during the Age of Sail understood what took place upon the trackless ocean. Living conditions at sea were often abominable, with death always lurking nearby. "Generally, [the ordinary sailor] died young. Fevers took far too many of his shipmates. The sea took others. Sometimes a whole watch might be lost over the side. . . . Men who fell from aloft had little chance, whether they fell on deck or into the sea."[19]

Captains held positions of authority that sailors, without a hint of irony, described as being "next to God." There was no deviating from a skipper's decision. A mate held a somewhat lower position than the captain, but the captain always backed up his mates.

In today's world, the punishments meted out to sailors in the nineteenth century seem, at best, cruel. One method of breaking a sailor that has come down through the years is flogging, or whipping, a sailor for some misdeed, which often amounted to something trivial. The instrument used for flogging sailors, known as a "cat of nine tails," or simply, a "cat," gained its infamous name from its nine straps, each of which ended in a small lead ball, or knot, that tore into the sailor's flesh. Sailors received lashes from the cat in front of the entire crew. Witnessing the impact of such an instrument on a bare back made many strong men sick. The cat became a common means of punishment used by officers against sailors. On the USS *Columbus*, for example, between September 2 and September 24, 1845, the punishment log shows that twenty-five sailors received a total of 177 lashes, with four men receiving twelve lashes each. William E. Tucker, one of the sailors who endured twelve lashes, received his punishment for "committing a nuisance on Berth Deck."[20]

Besides flogging, captains had other corporal means at hand for punishing a sailor who wished to test their authority. Tricing up, for instance, quickly broke a man without cutting his back. The master at arms, responsible for enforcing order in a ship, placed the sailor's hands behind his back and manacled his wrists. Manacles consisted of iron bracelets connected by a chain that were applied to each wrist, much like modern-day handcuffs. Sailors called the restraining device "irons." Someone designated by an officer then ran a line (rope) through the chain between the irons and rove the line through a ring on the mast high above the deck. Next, a group of sailors hoisted the recalcitrant sailor upward, with his hands still behind his back, until his toes just touched the deck. This forced the sailor's head downward, wrenching his arms upward from his back. The intense pain made a muttering seaman quickly change his mind about disobeying orders. Traditionally, corporal punishment only applied to ordinary sailors. Officers, who were considered gentlemen, presumably did not need such means to keep them in line.

One sailor in the Age of Sail described how captains and mates wielded their power without the use of formal corporal punishment. "The third day out we went aft in a body and complained about the food[,] which was the very worse any of us had ever had. The Captain told us the food was good enough for a bunch of wharf rats, and he said some other things that I cannot [say], ordered us forward, and as we did not move fast enough to suit the mates[,] they waded into us with belaying pins [wooden devices to tie line shaped like clubs] and beat us up plenty. If we hit back, that would be mutiny, of course."[21]

Masters of merchant ships rarely, if ever, were questioned by shipowners about their methods of running a ship. On those rare occasions when they were asked about their methods of punishment, skippers pointed out that the nature of sailors decreed strong disciplinary methods. Those before the mast, captains argued, came from all over the world and from the lower rungs of society. Such men understood only strong, swift, and unbending discipline, masters explained. Officers felt the measures kept the men at their tasks and prevented mutiny. Captains were certainly right about the international diversity of deepwater crews. One ship, for example, "had twenty-four able seamen and . . . there were at least fifteen nationalities among them." Most "were articulate only among their own kind. Quite a number could not read or write, and that was little loss to them. None wrote books."[22] (Seamen in coastal ships, however, tended to come from one area.) In the end, the reason why seamen continued to receive harsh treatment and had little recourse to defend themselves against such treatment is that owners cared only for profits and people on the beach had no understanding, nor any reason to care, for those at sea. Deserting from a "hell ship" proved to be a sailor's only means of escaping intolerable conditions on board. Many did just that.

Despite the existence of some "hell ships," many captains treated their crews humanely. Not too surprisingly, the so-called "wharf rats" reacted well to this type of master. It is probably the case that more captains treated their crews decently than not, but a sailor never really knew what lay ahead of him when he signed aboard a ship. True, salts talked among themselves, warning each other against certain skippers, but this information did not always prove reliable. Even when a sailor was lucky enough to sign on board a ship with a good captain, he was unlikely to gain a master that coddled his crew. Those few men who actually sailed in large sailing ships, and wrote about it, describe their captains as tough. Although many captains had wives and children on board, the presence of domesticity did not necessarily gentle them. Indeed, some of these wives proved equally tough enough to take over command of a deepwater sailing ship when their husbands became disabled.[23]

One of the most persistent stereotypes of a sailor is that of a person who is almost childlike when on land, a person who drinks heavily and spends his money freely. The expression "spending like a sailor" peppers the English language. Sailors themselves recognized some truth in the landsman's hackneyed description of them. Certain sailor chanties (songs) depict a fictitious sailor by the name of Jack Tarr as someone forever being taken advantage of by the machinations of those on shore.

Deepwater sailors held one of the lower positions in society. Most claimed the sea as their only home. Very few, if any, respectable women wanted anything to do with the ordinary sailor, although this attitude did not necessarily translate to officers and mates. Deepwater ships rarely tied up in areas of what might be called cultured living. "Crimps," runners who worked for sailors' boarding houses, usually met the ships when they entered port. They welcomed the sailors with drink and promised them women and anything else that would get them to their boarding house. It took a strong individual to resist these temptations after a long sea voyage. Once at the boarding house, the sailor received more drink and typically awoke later either on another ship outward bound, with no money, or in the boarding house with a hangover and no money. Left with nothing, the sailor's only solution was to sign on board another ship.

The teenaged Michael Augustine Healy entered this tough, unforgiving world of the sea. And, like his older brothers at Holy Cross, Michael thrived in his chosen profession.

Every sailor of that time knew that death awaited he who went down to the sea. Such knowledge shapes a personality, giving one a pessimistic outlook on life. The young Healy began at the lowest level before the mast. According to tradition, the short, slight, light-skinned Michael grew a moustache as soon as possible in hopes of hiding the shape of his lips, which he feared might give away his racial heritage.[24]

While in his formative years, Healy may, or may not, have had excellent shipmates. To paraphrase Rudyard Kipling, however, men crammed into a ship's forecastle do not plaster saints make. Landsmen, and even sailors themselves, classified some in the forecastle as dangerous men. There is little doubt that Healy did not mind reinforcing the stereotype of the drunken sailor. If he did not drink, he risked inviting his shipmates to regard him as different, and few in the forecastle wanted to be considered different. Some "different" sailors became known as "Jonahs." Jonahs were considered jinxes capable of causing bad things to happen. Sailors treated Jonahs harshly, sometimes even killing them. Much later in life, Healy wrote, "I am not much of a Christian."[25] While his brothers threw themselves into the study of theology and the Church, Michael began to "come up through the hawse pipe" and finally earned the rank of officer on a sailing ship. Making the difficult transition from forward to aft required not only toughness, skill, and intelligence, but an intangible factor, too, a personality that allowed officers to notice an exceptional sailor. As a mate, Healy now had to supervise those in the forecastle. He applied the same hard discipline as any mate did: anything else could be construed as weakness by those watching from either side of the mast.

Most sailors in the nineteenth century, as is still the case today, carried two sea bags: one physical, the other mental. The physical bag contained their meager possessions, while the mental one comprised what sailors called "sea stories." The stories offered a way for unlettered men to pass on their experiences, weaving an oral history for those whose lives rarely appear in the annals of history. The yarns also made for precious diversion between watches. The few surviving sea stories from that age offer a glimpse into a way of life now long forgotten.

In developing his seaman's personality, Healy became a master of telling sea stories. Some sea stories are especially interesting because they reveal more about the storyteller than they do the story. In 1899, forty-four years after Healy began his career at sea, he could still captivate an audience of cronies and a San Francisco reporter. Healy, wrote the reporter, "hitched up his starboard leg, which he gracefully threw over the arm of a chair" and began to recite his tale.[26]

"Well, I was mate on the brig *Boomerang*, Captain Spain, loading at Port McQuarrie for Melbourne. Just when the vessel was about to receive the last consignment there stepped up to me a tall, lanky and delicate looking Australian, asking for passage to Melbourne. I told him we carried no passengers, but the man insisted, saying he was willing to pay anything provided we would take him. I said I would see the captain and let him know. I went forward and found the captain and said,

"'Captain, there's an Australian on the dock who wants to go to Melbourne.'

"'He can't go,' said the Captain.

"'He says,' I persisted, 'that he will pays what we ask, and I don't think he'll live two days.'

"'How's that?' asked the captain, very much interested.

"'He can't live two days. He has the wasting consumption,' I replied.

"'Poor chap, poor chap,' sighed Captain Spain, sympathetically. He gave such violent sighs that I began to fear he would blow his heart out by the strength of those great gusts of sympathy.

"'Take him aboard, Mr. Mate: take him aboard. As a Christian man I could never again enter the house of prayer if I let a man die in the God-forsaken land. Charge him this,' he added, naming a pretty steep figure. 'And he's miner, eh? Well, well, Mr. Mate, remember that a charitable act has its reward, when you least expect it. Remember that, Mr. Mate, and you will have success in life.'

"We will say the passenger's name was Smith. He was nearer dead than alive, but he hoped the sea trip to Melbourne would revive him. He was a miner, and in a basket which was carried aboard for him was [8,000 English pounds], or about $40,000 and over, worth of gold dust. This basket was placed in his cabin, he saying at the time he feared he would not live to enjoy his money. He was liberal, paid the captain the sum asked for the passage, fed the steward handsomely, and was an uncomplaining sort of person.

"When off Flinders Island the second day out and early in the morning the steward came to me and said:

"'Passenger's dead sir. I took him his cup of coffee as usual and tried to awaken him. I thought he was asleep. But he's dead, sir.'

"'Are you sure, Steward?' I asked. 'He was all right last night.'

"'Dead, sir; dead as a doornail.'

"I went with the steward to the cabin, and catching Smith by the shoulder, shouted, 'Helloa, Smith, wake up!' I placed my ear to his heart and satisfied myself he was dead.

"'Cover him up, steward,' I ordered, and went to the captain's room and knocked at the door. The captain called out:

"'Who's that?'

"'The mate, sir.'

"'Are we making land?'

"'No, sir.'

"'Then why in the name of Hades do you disturb me?'

"'Passenger's dead, sir.'

"'The _____ he is!'

"'Dead as a mackerel.'

"'Oh, no, he ain't. He's only very low,' and Captain Spain came running out, pulling on his trousers, and being in a greater hurry that I ever saw that admirable man in before. He went straight to the passenger's stateroom, and called out excitedly:

"'Mr. Mate, he's not dead. But he's very near dead. In fact, he's so near dead it's no joke. We must have everything in order, Mr. Mate. So go get your log book, and be damned quick about it, or he may go off any moment.'

"I ran for the log book, and seated myself with book on my knee and pen in hand. The steward was also present. The captain was by the bed, and placed his arm under the passenger's head, and, whispering low in the man's ear, said:

"'I, John Smith, about to die on the brig *Boomerang*, do hereby make my last will and testament. Is that right, Smith?' and the head of the passenger slowly rose from the pillow, acknowledging the captain's words.

"'Did you see that, Mr. Mate?' said the captain, growing more and more excited. 'For God's sake, write faster. Don't you see the man is dying. He can't hold on much longer. God, this is rough work for a Christian man to do. You've got that down, Mr. Mate, have you? Well, well, you're damned slow Healy, you are; damned slow. Now are you ready?'

"'Yes,' I said, for I felt sick over the horrible farce. There was the man, dead cold, stiff and stark, and here was I, a party to as ghastly a fraud as was ever perpetrated. But the captain again bent down and commenced:

"'Do I understand you to say that for all the kindness and goodness I, Captain Spain, have shown you while on board as a passenger, that you give me the champagne basket and all its contents?'

"And again the head slowly rose from the pillow. 'He says, 'Yes,' said the captain, excitedly. 'For heaven's sake, hurry, Mr. Mate, or he'll be dead.'

"I wrote down this lying declaration. The humor of it was beginning to strike me.

"Here was a dead man making his will, and giving up his hard-earned wealth to a man who had never spoken to him, and the will being entered in a log book in all proper form, no court would throw out. Certainly I began to think it was rather selfish of the captain to take the whole $40,000; but we, the steward and I, were helpless.

"Again the captain bent his head and said, 'Do I understand you to say that for all the kindness and goodness shown you by Mate Healy that you give him all your clothes?'

"Again the head rose from the pillow. 'He says, 'yes!' screamed the captain. 'He gives you all his clothes.'

"'A scurvy joke,' I thought, as I penned the words conveying me the precious gift of a lot of tuberculous old clothes, not worth one dollar, while the captain had snugly bagged $40,000. But I had to write.

"'For Lord's sake, hurry. Don't you see he is dying and he's just aching to say something more?'

"I really could not see any anxiety on the part of the dead man to speak, but discipline is discipline, and so I said, 'Ready!' and again the captain put his head down.

"'Do I understand you to say that because of the goodness and kindness of the steward you give him all the loose change there is in your clothes?'

"The steward started and smiled. He, too, began to appreciate the ghastly joke. The head of the man rose in answer.

"'Have you it all down?' asked the captain.

"'Yes, sir,' I answered.

"He let the head fall with a thud, got up from his knees, and said:

"'The son of a gun is dead as a herring. Throw him overboard.'

"The captain got his money through the courts, the steward the loose change amounting to two shillings, and my part of the will I threw over board after the corpse. Now, . . . did you ever hear of a stranger will?"

From the age of fifteen until he turned twenty-six in 1865, Healy sailed in the deepwater merchant fleet. He began in a British East Indiaman and eventually sailed throughout the world. By the end of his first decade at sea, he had risen to Second Mate and sailed regularly between Boston and the Mediterranean.

Meanwhile, news of the Healy family reached Michael. Hugh, one of Michael's four older brothers, had died in 1853 as the result of a tragic accident. The remaining three—James, Patrick, and Sherwood—had each entered the Church and studied in Canada and Europe. Michael's sister Martha, soon to be followed by Josephine and Eliza, had entered a convent in Montreal, while Eugene remained in New York.[27]

James became the secretary of Bishop Fitzpatrick of Boston and was appointed chancellor of the diocese in the early 1850s. Thus, he began his steady rise in the Church. Patrick and Sherwood gravitated toward scholarly pursuits and promised to occupy important roles in the Catholic Church.[28]

What allowed these amazing siblings to move up in the world is directly traceable to the foresight, hard work, and sacrifice of their parents, Michael Morris and Eliza Clark Healy. Their parents' estate gave the Healy siblings an opportunity denied to many in the United States. Now, the Healy children grown, the stipulation that the Healy slaves be rented out until the children could manage their own affairs had expired. The first slaves from the former Healy plantation entered the Macon slave auction on January 3, 1854. A slave by the name of Daniel, who had been appraised at $400, brought in $1,200. A woman by the name of Caroline, along with her three children, one an infant, sold for $1,500. At the end of the sale, even with some slaves remaining to be sold, the estate received the large settlement of $30,000. Consider that in 1850, a farm laborer in the United States earned an average salary of $130.20 per year.[29]

In January 1856, the Macon slave auction began to sell off the remaining slaves. Another tragedy marked this sale, which already does not reflect well on the Healy siblings. A woman named Margaret and her four children—William, Julia, Violet, and, interestingly, Martha Ann, the name of the oldest Healy daughter—numbered among this group of slaves. A year before the auction, Margaret had initiated a suit against the Healy estate in the hopes of winning freedom for her and her children. On what grounds Margaret based her claims is unknown. Did Margaret witness Eliza's children escaping to the North and decide to try to win the same freedom for her family? This question cannot be answered. The result of Margaret's suit, however, is a matter of historical record. Predictably, Margaret lost. She and her children entered the auction block along with the other slaves. Worse, each of her children sold to a different master, no doubt as punishment for the trouble she had caused. Unable to obtain freedom for her children, Margaret suffered the loss of her family so that the Healy children could avoid a similar fate. Had it not been for Michael Morris and Eliza Clark Healy's careful planning, their children would surely have suffered the same sad fate that Margaret's children did.[30]

One last story remains concerning the slaves of the Healy family. In 1860, four years after Margaret's bid for freedom, a record book in Jones County, Georgia, reports that Samuel Griswold, a wealthy plantation owner, sold "a Negro woman, Nancy, of yellow complexion, also a Negro girl named Nancy, of yellow complexion" to a neighbor. The record then shows that these women were sold again, this time to "James A. Healy, of the State of Massachusetts, city of Boston." Why did James buy these two women? A local historian of Jones County suggests that Eliza Clark Healy originally came from the Griswold plantation. It is possible that the elder Nancy was Eliza's sister, thus making her an aunt to the Healy children. It is also possible that Nancy kept the youngest Healy children safe until Hugh was able to reach them from New York City. While no one has provided documented proof to explain why James A. Healy bought these two slaves, it can be presumed that Healy freed them. What became of the women remains unknown. Perhaps this act helped assuage the consciences of the elder Healy children.[31]

The final settlement of the estate of Michael Morris Healy came in October 1859. The executors transferred at least $51,000 from the Macon Branch of the Mechanics Bank of Augusta to John Manning in New York City. At this time in the United States, a laborer in an urban area could expect to earn $374.92 a year. One historian suggests that each antebellum dollar would equal approximately fifteen dollars today. This values the Healy estate at over three-quarters of a million in today's dollars. In other words, through the efforts of Michael Morris and Eliza Clark Healy, their children received the possibility of financial security for the rest of their lives.[32]

How the Healy children divided their inheritance is not recorded, but a reasonable supposition is that James, now the family patriarch, managed the family's financial affairs. James purchased a home in West Newton, Massachusetts, for $7,500 in 1861. As a family, the children, since leaving Georgia, had enjoyed no real home. The house provided for this need whenever members of the family passed through the Boston area.[33]

By the end of his first decade at sea, Michael Augustine Healy, through intelligence, skill, personality, and perhaps some financial influence, had risen through the ranks from ordinary sailor to second mate, the third highest rank of officer on a merchant ship. The slight, short, twenty-six-year-old sailor's piercing blue eyes brooked no nonsense. Coming up as he did through the hawse pipe, Healy learned not to question orders. As an officer, he expected no less from those he commanded. As was evident in the sea stories he told, Healy believed that "discipline is discipline." In other words, Healy proved to be no different than any other sailor who managed to come aft from before the mast.

What drove Healy to sea, however, would weigh on his mind and remain a fundamental part of his identity for the rest of his life. Healy craved the recognition of his older, scholarly brothers. He never fully received this recognition, no matter how hard he tried. Ultimately, Healy's brothers looked upon him, at best, as a mere sailor, complete with all the negative connotations associated with that nautical stereotype. To compensate for his brothers' lack of respect for his chosen profession, Healy constantly tried to demonstrate his importance and, indeed, from time to time, he did not hesitate to embellish the stories that catalogued his exploits. As many storytellers do, especially those who tell stories of the sea, Healy wrapped a kernel of truth in the fabric of tall tales and exaggeration. Nevertheless, Healy could never bury deep enough in story the most profound and important part of his psyche. His racial heritage remained a fact that he could not dismiss. Healy knew that if anyone ever found out about his mother, at best it meant a speedy return to the forecastle. Very few mates would wish that sentence upon anyone. While there is no evidence that Healy received the nautical nickname of "bucko mate," a term reserved for mates who always stood ready to impose harsh discipline, sailors in the forecastle, given the opportunity, sometimes treated disrated (demoted) mates harshly. One salt recalled a skipper that disrated a bucko second mate and sent him forward. When "a couple of the boys got through with him he wasn't worth picking up."[34] Given the racial attitudes of the time, first among them the basic law that blacks did not command whites, there is no question that a captain who learned of Healy's racial heritage would quickly demote him and send him forward with no chance for appeal. There is also little doubt of Healy's fate in the forecastle among some of the white crew sailors when they learned they had taken orders from an African American.

By hiding his racial heritage, Healy seemed destined to achieve, in the nautical world, the rank next to God: that of a master of a sailing merchant ship. At the age of twenty-six, however, Healy, like many sailors before and after him, fell in love. Unlike many sailors, however, Healy chose to marry.

3

LOVE AND THE SAILOR

By 1864, Healy was regularly setting sail from the port of Boston. The Waltham Street house Rev. James A. Healy had purchased in West Newton, Massachusetts, became extremely useful to the young officer. Newton was an easy commute by train into Boston. This allowed the sailor to enjoy a real home while in port, a luxury not available to many of his shipmates. The Healy home also removed him from the normal sailor haunts. Just as important, it permitted Second Mate Healy to witness the growing importance of his older brothers in the Catholic Church and, along with that, their rising political influence in Boston and Massachusetts.

Sometime in 1864, while ashore in Newton, or Boston, Second Mate Healy did what many a sailor before and after him has done: he met a woman and fell in love. Just how the two met is unknown.

Mary Jane Roach's father, John, born May 10, 1811, immigrated in 1830 to the United States from Dublin, Ireland. He arrived at Eastport, Maine, and made his way to Boston. There, in 1833, he married another Irish immigrant, Margaret Lee, in the Cathedral of the Holy Cross by, interestingly enough, a Rev. Michael Healy. John worked for many years as a laborer and waiter. The couple had two daughters, Mary, born January 3, 1834, who died young, and Mary Jane, born July 27, 1836. John Roach demonstrated as much drive as Michael Morris Healy. He purchased a boardinghouse in 1858 at 13 Beacon Street, located in the West End of Boston and known then as the "shady side of Beacon Hill," the fashionable area of the city. Irish and African Americans dominated the ethnic groups in Roach's neighborhood. When Mary Jane Roach met Healy, she had spent most of her life helping her family, especially after the purchase of the boardinghouse. It is not unreasonable to imagine that Mary Jane and Michael met either at the Cathedral of the Holy Cross or at the Roach's boardinghouse.[1]

Even today, families of sailors realize that their husbands and fathers will be absent for long periods of time. During Healy's years of sea duty in the merchant marine, voyages lasting several hundred days were not uncommon. Healy knew better than most what it meant to grow up without a parent nearby. He wished to continue to advance in his profession, but he also wanted a stable home. As Second Mate Healy considered the ways he might overcome this problem, he took note of the small government ships patrolling the approaches to Boston Harbor. He knew that the ships checked merchantmen for evidence of smuggling activities. Healy realized that while the ships did travel offshore, they remained close to the ports they patrolled and seldom remained at sea for long stretches of time. Surely these vessels needed experienced seagoing officers. These were the circumstances and logic that led Second Mate Michael A. Healy, of the U.S. Merchant Marine, to join the U.S. Revenue Cutter Service.

The U.S. Revenue Cutter Service was officially established in 1790, seventy-four years before Healy turned his thoughts to the service. As the break between England and the colonists in the future United States loomed, many felt that one means of fighting back against the homeland would be to foil England's collection of taxes on imported goods. Smuggling goods in from the sea is an ancient practice, but the American Revolution added a patriotic justification to the enterprise.

After the formation of the new United States of America, one of the first acts of Congress in 1789 was the establishment of tariffs on imported goods. The tariffs provided much-needed revenue for the fledgling nation and offered some protection to newly established industries. Many citizens, however, saw little difference between a tariff imposed by the United States Congress and taxation imposed by England. To some, the new United States meant yet another challenge to overcome in their desire to escape taxation.

The first secretary of the Treasury, Alexander Hamilton, recognized that a substantial amount of badly needed revenue was being lost to smuggling. To remedy the situation, he proposed the establishment of a seagoing police force that would enforce the customs laws. Hamilton sought funds from Congress to build ten small vessels and station them along the coast from New England to Georgia with the express purpose of intercepting the bootleggers. Congress authorized Hamilton's request on August 4, 1790.[2]

The new organization, housed in the Treasury Department, struggled to find a recognizable name. Over the years, it was called a system of cutters, Revenue Service, and Revenue-Marine. "Congress first referred to the service as a named organization in a law passed in 1863, in which the term 'Revenue-Cutter Service' received official sanction."[3] In 1915, the U.S. Revenue Cutter

Service was merged with the U.S. Life-Saving Service to form the U.S. Coast Guard.

None of the first ten small ships of the new service measured over sixty-five feet in length. They had been built either in the areas in which they would operate, or as close to their future homeports as possible. The *Massachusetts*, for example, was built in Newburyport, Massachusetts, and operated out of Boston from 1791 to 1792. Constructed by William Searle, the new seventy-ton vessel measured sixty feet, nine inches overall, with a seventeen-foot, eight-inch beam, and a shallow draft of seven feet, eight inches. The ship carried four swivel guns to enforce the customs laws. The *Massachusetts*, commanded by John Foster Williams, shipped four officers, four enlisted men, and two boys.[4]

These American ships became known as cutters, named after the small vessels that navigated the English Channel. They were schooner rigged, as this was a type of sailing vessel that most American seamen understood. Early schooners had fore and aft sails, and some had a square sail near the top of either the foremast or main mast. Another advantage of the schooner-rigged cutter was that it provided both speed and seaworthiness. Their shallow draft, moreover, enabled the cutters to operate in areas close to the beach, where smugglers operated. Even after the service shifted their sailing vessels from sail to mechanical propulsion, the vessels kept the title of cutter.[5]

The primary duty of the early cutters was to intercept and board merchantmen inbound or outbound from harbors. Officers would board the vessels and check their papers, ensure that all cargoes were properly documented, seal the cargo holds of incoming vessels, and seize those ships in violation of the law. To prevent smuggling, the cutters needed to sail away from their home harbors and intercept any ship approaching the coast. Usually, smuggling goods in from the sea took place out of sight of land. The bootleggers only sometimes unloaded their goods directly onto the beach, and more often unloaded them onto smaller craft that would then transport the goods to shore. The small cutters, therefore, had to be fast and agile enough to operate both close to shore and in the open sea. Unlike merchantmen and naval vessels, they usually did not operate away from their home port for extended periods of time.

Crews of the cutters of the new seagoing service were small and differed significantly from those of naval ships. Training for officers in the U.S. Navy, for example, centered on operating large fleets, often during combat, and thus stressed gunnery and naval tactics. The U.S. Navy also required officers to supervise large numbers of sailors. Revenue officers, on the other hand, operated to a large extent by themselves. This meant that commanding officers had to possess the ability to carry out missions with little direction from higher command. In other words, lower-ranked revenue officers made crucial decisions that naval officers of a similar rank would not usually be given to make. To intercept and board ships, these cutter officers needed great proficiency in seamanship. They also had to have training in gunnery and law enforcement. Only twice in the history of the U.S. Revenue Cutter Service did its decision-makers feel it would prove more cost-effective to use naval officers in the cutters, and both times the experiments proved "unsatisfactory." Crewmen on cutters, much like the officers that commanded them, had to be sailors that could undertake a wide variety of duties. Unfortunately, few accounts of early revenue officers and fewer still of the ordinary sailors that shipped with them have survived in maritime history.[6]

As the U.S. Revenue Cutter Service grew, it soon acquired other missions not necessarily envisioned by its founder, Secretary Hamilton. Two such early tasks dealt with pirates and human "contraband."

Pirates operated throughout the Gulf of Mexico in the early nineteenth century. One of the most notorious pirates, Jean LaFitte, for example, operated out of New Orleans. The Florida Keys provided another area of operation for the freebooters. Piracy interfered with and seriously damaged trade, thus prompting the decision that the U.S. Revenue Cutter Service would carry out combat missions against pirates. The primary cutters involved in this struggle were the newly constructed *Alabama* and *Louisiana*. Built in 1819, both measured fifty-seven feet in length, had a beam of seventeen feet, a shallow draft of six feet, and displaced fifty-six tons of water. Their home port was New Orleans.[7]

On August 31, 1819, the *Alabama* and *Louisiana* fought it out with one of LaFitte's lieutenants, who commanded the pirate ship *Bravo*. Capt. Jarvis Loomis, commanding the *Louisiana*, ordered the cuttermen to board and seize the ship. They accomplished their mission only after using cutlasses against the pirates in hand-to-hand combat. The next year, the two revenue cutters put a landing party ashore to break up a pirate's den.[8]

As early as 1794, the Treasury Department instructed revenue cutters to prevent the importation of new slaves ("contraband" in revenue terminology) from Africa to the United States. New laws passed against the foreign slave trade in 1807 advanced this mission. Before the Civil War ended, cutters had captured numerous slavers and freed almost five hundred slaves.[9]

Many other duties fell to the small cutter force. The cuttermen, for example, enforced the quarantine regulations and laws of the day. They also enforced

President Thomas Jefferson's unpopular embargo of 1808. Cuttermen even helped prevent the logging of live oaks in naval reserves in Florida. They participated in ensuring that navigation laws were effective, improved the chances that shipwrecked sailors would be saved, and provided transportation for government officials, to name but a few of their growing responsibilities.

Soon after the founding of the small service, the cuttermen found themselves taking on a military role. Cutters participated in every major war and military skirmish of the United States, including actions against Native Americans in Florida and in the Pacific Northwest.[10]

The U.S. Revenue Cutter Service, however, was fraught with two main areas of weakness: its administration and its recruitment of personnel. On the surface, the service's method of recruiting its officers seems an ideal way to grow a marine police service. Most of the officers were former mates in the merchant marine. They were commissioned and directed by the local collector of customs. Mates in the merchant marine brought with them a great deal of sea experience, which was sorely needed in the cutters. This method of recruitment had a bad side, however. The collectors of customs held their positions through political appointments. In the days before civil service, the collectors, operating under what has come to be known as the spoils system, could be replaced every time a new party came into power. Thus, officers, because they were commissioned by collectors, held onto their commissions according to the whim of politicians. Many politicians did not hesitate to command revenue officers to transport them in their cutters for official and unofficial reasons. By the end of the Civil War, the service seemed bound for becoming bogged down in a morass of politics and used as little more than a yacht service for office holders and their friends. This, then, was the small organization that Second Mate Michael A. Healy considered joining. Early on, he recognized the importance of political influence to obtaining a commission in the service.[11]

On Thursday, October 13, 1864, Healy penned a letter to the secretary of the Treasury applying for the position of third lieutenant in the U.S. Revenue Cutter Service. He claimed to "have been to sea for nine years" and to have "been three times second officer and once first-officer of a brig for eight months." Healy mentioned that he could "bring a considerable number of recommendations" to show himself "fit for the position."[12]

Assistant Surgeon R. Burke, on Friday, January 13, 1865, wrote to Capt. Stephen Cornell, President of the Board of Examination, that he found the new applicant physically qualified for the duties of a lieutenant in the "Revenue Cutter Service of the United States." Six days later, Captain Cornell wrote,

"Michael Healy has passed his examination for the grade of 3rd Lieutenant, rating No. 5 in Navigation & No. 7 in Seamanship."

As part of the application process it was suggested that the applicant write an autobiographical account of his sea experience. On Wednesday, January 18, 1865, Healy mailed his account. It constitutes the first written record of how Michael A. Healy made his way through his career by twisting the facts of his life so that his racial heritage would not be recognized. Furthermore, the future myth of Michael A. Healy stems from the contents of this letter. When, in the 1970s, his life eventually became a topic of discussion, some quoted the letter as evidence of his early years at sea.

Healy began his short letter by stating that his "parents" placed him in "The English College at Douai in France": "Being an unruly boy[,] my Parents in order to punish me for my misconduct, procured for me a birth [*sic*] as boy on board an East-Indiaman called the *Jumna*." By the time Healy went to sea, of course, both of his parents had been dead for close to five years. His brother James sent him to Douai. Perhaps in Michael's mind James was a surrogate father, or perhaps Michael felt this sounded better on a job application. Many years later, however, one of the obituaries published upon Healy's death states that he ran away to sea, suggesting that Healy did not mind promoting this romantic notion.[13]

Healy next briefly outlined his career at sea, noting that although "I have been near ten years at sea my life has been comparatively easy, having never yet suffered actual shipwreck, though I have at different times lost spars, sails, &c." He pointed out that, having "now been a long time at sea, my friends wished and advised me to come to some definite determination to my future life. Having never obtained a birth [*sic*] beyond Second Mate, and once or twice mate of a fruiter, I was advised to apply for a situation in the U.S. Revenue Cutter [Service]." He closed his two-and-a-quarter-page letter by stating that he had reported to New York to take the required written examinations, but was "sorry to say" that he did himself "little or no credit."

At best, Healy's brief autobiography should be looked upon as a sailor's written sea story. The truth is buried within it, but it is surrounded with embellishment. The kernel of truth is that sometime around 1855 Healy turned to the sea. For the next nine years, he practiced his trade. Whether he ran away to sea, worked before the mast, sailed around the world, or watched as his captain extracted a will from a dead man, is open to debate: each scenario sounds interesting and adds a dash of salt water to his persona. But, the important truth is that he did go to sea and he did convince the U.S. Revenue Cutter Service that he possessed the knowledge required to fill the position of third lieutenant. With his ability to weave a story that seems credible, it should come as no surprise that Healy successfully kept his racial heritage a secret.

The examining board next turned to Healy's letters of recommendation. The most influential letter came from John Albion Andrew, the Republican governor of Massachusetts who was described as the state's "most celebrated governor of his generation."[14] Andrew's letter of November 19, 1864, shows just how much Michael depended upon James for political support. The governor remarked, "I do not know [Michael] Healy myself, but I am well acquainted with his brother, Rev. James A. Healy, the Secretary of the Bishop of this Diocese; and if one can argue from the qualities of a clergyman to those of a sailor, and the two brothers are alike, I should say that you would have few brighter and more capable young officers in your Revenue Marine than Healy if you shall appoint him."

Letters from people who actually knew Michael, coming from those associated with the sea, contained less flowery language. The master of the bark *Limuel*, Andrew Burantt [?] wrote, "Mr. Michael Healy served in my vessel as Second Officer and discharged his duty to my satisfaction during the voyage and it gives me pleasure to testify to the same." The owner of the brig *Nicholas Riggio* [?] stated: "we have found him perfectly competent, trustworthy and industrious, and of good habits, and we cheerfully recommend him to the office of 3rd Lieutenant in the Revenue Service."

Thirteen days after submitting his autobiographical letter to the U.S. Revenue Cutter Service, Michael Augustine Healy, twenty-five, married Mary Jane Roach, twenty-eight, on Tuesday, January 31, 1865. The groom's oldest brother, Fr. James A. Healy, married them in the Cathedral of the Holy Cross, Boston. Healy's older sister, Martha, is listed as one witness. Another person, who attended the ceremony and the dinner afterward, said the marriage was "a most happy and agreeable match on both sides." The newlyweds moved into John and Margaret Roach's home, at the time a logical choice. If Healy continued his career as a seagoing officer, then Mary Jane could continue to help her family. The same would hold true were Healy to receive a commission in the U.S. Revenue Cutter Service.[15]

Almost a month after his wedding, a James M. Dolliver, of Boston, wrote to the Treasury Department stating that Healy had "passed his examination for a 3rd Lieut. in the Revenue Service": "He has been waiting orders here a month. If you could get him in Active Service, you would do him a great favor, and oblige a great many Friends." Ten days later, on March 7, 1865,

Michael A. Healy received a commission as a third lieutenant in the U.S. Revenue Cutter Service, for which he would receive a salary of nine hundred dollars a year.[16]

Where an officer numbered on the seniority list, generally known as "the list," determined when he would be promoted to the next higher rank. That is, an officer positioned at number three would be promoted before an officer positioned at number eighteen. Other factors also entered into this system. One punishment for an infraction that could befall an officer was to be demoted to a lower number on the list. On the other hand, officer selection boards had the prerogative to select a very promising officer positioned lower down on the list over those positioned much higher. This prerogative, however, was rarely exercised. In other words, an officer's placement on the list held great importance, a fact that continues to this day. Charting an officer's rise, and sometimes fall, on the list is one means of determining how an officer's career is progressing. Initial determination of where a new officer might be placed on the list of U.S. Revenue Cutter Service officers resulted from a combination of when an officer received his commission and other factors, such as the results of the applicant examination. As an officer stayed on in the service, his position on the list eventually was determined by his time spent in the service, his ability to perform his duties and, unwritten in any regulations, his political allies and even the financial state of his family.

A total of twenty-six third lieutenants, including Healy, entered the service on March 7, 1865. Of these twenty-six new officers, Healy placed seventeenth. The U.S. Revenue Cutter Service officer's register for September 1865 shows Healy as joining in Massachusetts and lists him as number eighteen of forty-eight third lieutenants in the service. Thus, in terms of future promotion, Healy placed respectably on the list.

Positioned at number thirty-nine on the list was Calvin L. Hooper, a man who would figure prominently later on in Healy's career. Born in Maine on July 7, 1842, Hooper like Healy had served in the merchant marine before entering the service in California. He received an acting third lieutenant's commission, before obtaining his permanent commission on June 6, 1866.[17]

Nearing the very bottom of the list of third lieutenants, at number forty-five, was Leonard G. Shepard, another important person in Healy's career. Shepard was born at Dorchester, Massachusetts, on November 10, 1846. Shepard first went to sea at the age of sixteen and had received a "full course of instruction in navigation at the Boston Nautical College." He served in the Civil War on board "one of the supply ships, and was present at the fight at Fort Fisher." He entered the U.S. Revenue Cutter Service as a third lieutenant on September 18, 1865, from New York.[18] Both of these men saw hard service in the Arctic and their careers overlapped or intersected with Healy's many times.

The U.S. Revenue Cutter Service often rotated its junior officers among the many cutters at the beginning of their careers. Every port patrolled by the service presented different challenges. Transferring young officers to a number of ports gave them a good chance of gaining a wide range of experience. At the time, most cutters had home ports along the East Coast, the Great Lakes, and the Gulf of Mexico. Healy's first nine years in the service illustrate this constant movement from one cutter and one geographical location to another.

Third Lieutenant Healy reported to his first cutter, the *E. A. Stevens*, at New York City on April 27, 1865. This 120-ton, 101-foot ship began as an experimental naval ironclad. Built in Hoboken, New Jersey, the *Stevens* ended up in the U.S. Revenue Cutter Service in 1862. Earlier known as the *Naugatuck* and informally called the "Stevens Battery," the ironclad was a semisubmersible, needing only fifteen minutes to take on enough water ballast to sink almost three feet. It could then enter battle with only its turret above water, within which was mounted a one-hundred-pound Parrott rifle. The cutter had participated in actions against the Confederate *Virginia* and at Drewry's Bluff, Virginia. After being repaired in New York City, the cutter remained there as a guard ship. Healy served on board the *Stevens* for only a few months in order to obtain his new uniforms and begin the process of learning how to board and examine vessels for potential violations of customs laws.[19]

Later that year, Healy reported to the *Chase* at Ogdensburg, New York, on the St. Lawrence River, where he continued the routine of examining cargoes. The 170-foot cutter had a schooner rig and displaced 477–530 tons. It was during this same year that Healy received the sad news that his first son, John James Healy, born on November 5, 1865 at 13 Beacon Street, had died the day of his birth. Shortly after the death, John and Margaret Roach purchased a new boardinghouse at 83 Brookline Street, and Mary Jane Healy moved with her parents to the new house.[20]

In winter, heavy ice slowed shipping in the Great Lakes region. Most of the cutters stationed on the lakes kept only a skeleton crew on board during this season. The officers then took periods of leave, or found themselves assigned to other duties. Third Lieutenant Healy's service record shows that on January 13, 1866, he received a leave of absence for three weeks.

On June 8, 1866, Healy received a promotion to second lieutenant and, among the thirty-three officers of the same rank, earned the position of number ten on the list. His pay increased to $1,500 a year. In the meantime, Calvin L. Hooper and Leonard Shepard remained on the third lieutenant's list at the positions of number five and number nine, respectively. Hooper and Shepard subsequently advanced in their own careers at a good pace, although not as fast as Healy did.[21]

Meanwhile, at 83 Brookline Street Mary Jane awaited the birth of their second child. In light of the loss of their first son, Michael felt he should be present with his wife for the event. On October 12, 1866, Second Lieutenant Healy received ten days of leave. Nevertheless, the boy, whom they named Eugene, decided to enter the world on November 1. The memory of his first son's death must have weighed heavily on Healy. His concern caused him to seek what the service now calls a short humanitarian transfer in order to be near his family. That December, the transfer took him to the 138-foot, 350-ton topsail schooner *Pawtuxet*, at Boston. He remained at his new assignment in Boston from December 1866 to May 31, 1867.[22]

During the period Healy served on board the *Pawtuxet*, events in far-off St. Petersburg, Russia, became extremely important to the way Healy's life would unfold in the late 1860s. In 1725, Russian Czar Peter the Great sent the Danish explorer Vitus Bering east of St. Petersburg to seek out the easternmost coast of Asia. After traveling across Siberia, Bering constructed ships at Kamchatka. He sailed through the strait that now bears his name in 1728, proving that Asia and North America were two separate continents. He returned to St. Petersburg in 1730.

In 1733, Bering initiated another expedition with the purpose of mapping Siberia and the western coast of North America as far south as Mexico. He managed to sail past Kodiak Island before his ship wrecked on an isolated island, where he died in December 1741. Bering's work led to other expeditions, and the Russian occupation of the North American continent eventually extended as far south as Fort Ross, California, just north of San Francisco.[23]

By the early 1800s, Americans had begun pushing into the Pacific Northwest region, finding rich natural resources, as well as Russian explorers and traders. The Imperial government never had the resources to support any type of strong military or trading establishments in the Pacific Northwest or Alaska. None of the permanent locations they settled ever numbered over four hundred people. Russia's defeat in the Crimean War (1854–1856) further decreased the Imperial government's interest in the region.

In 1859, in a move to offset some of Great Britain's designs in the Pacific, Russia offered to sell what is now Alaska to the United States. The approaching

American Civil War put the purchase on hold. On March 30, 1867, however, when Russian Minister Edouard de Stoeckl once again offered to sell Alaska to the United States for $7.2 million, Secretary of State William Seward agreed. The Senate approved the purchase on April 9, and President Andrew Johnson signed the treaty on May 28, 1867.[24]

Most Americans saw no sense in the purchase. Newspapers quickly drummed up terms such as "Seward's Wallrussia" to express the public's displeasure. Given the state of geographical knowledge in the mid-nineteenth century, the outpouring of resentment toward the purchase is understandable. With very little knowledge of the vast northern region, Americans felt foolish about investing in a land that would surely be covered with ice and snow throughout the year. What could such an icebox contribute to the growing nation? To help the nation, and themselves, understand the new purchase, the federal government in 1867 dispatched the cutter *Lincoln* of the San Francisco-based U.S. Revenue Cutter Service to survey the coastal areas of Alaska.[25]

Very few, if any, officers of the U.S. Revenue Cutter Service, or officials of the Treasury Department for that matter, recognized the importance of the *Lincoln*'s voyage. With the passage of time, however, the purchase of Alaska would cause a radical change to ripple throughout most of the service. Prior to 1867, the cutters continued their traditional work near their home ports. Alaska, however, required that the service operate away from their home ports and for long periods of time, much like U.S. Navy ships. As time passed, the demands of Alaska also helped initiate a change in the command and control structure of the service. If Healy and his brother officers joined the service in order to remain close to home, Alaska caused a rude change in the trajectory of their lives. The course of Healy's life began to change just over two months after President Johnson signed the treaty to purchase Alaska.

After his short tour of duty on board the *Pawtuxet*, Healy reported in June 1867 to the schooner-rigged 90-foot, 120-ton cutter *Active*, in Philadelphia, Pennsylvania. Within two months, he received orders for a major change of cutters.[26]

Second Lieutenant Healy's next assignment took him to a newly built cutter called the *Reliance*, at Baltimore, Maryland. The service granted him three days leave before reporting on board on August 1, 1867. He needed the three days for putting his affairs in order and saying his farewells to Mary Jane and Eugene. His new duties entailed helping to place the new cutter into service and then making the long voyage to its new home port of San Francisco.

Earlier that year, the John F. Fardy & Brothers Shipyard of Baltimore had received a contract to construct two topsail schooners for the U.S. Revenue Cutter Service for a total cost of $89,000. The service accepted the 110-foot cutters, the *Reliance* and the *Vigilant*, on June 3, 1867, at the builder's yard, which was located at the foot of Montgomery Street near what is now Federal Hill Park and within a half mile to the east of the Baltimore Orioles' baseball stadium at Camden Yards.[27]

The logbook of the new cutter *Reliance* shows Second Lieutenant Healy reporting for duty on August 1. On this typically hot, humid summer day in Baltimore, Healy found the crew of the cutter busy with the normal duties of getting a new wooden sailing vessel ready for sea. Entries in the logbook over the next ten days, for example, record new crewmen reporting on board, supplies arriving, and the crew holystoning the vessel's decks. (Holystoning involves cleaning a wooden deck with a soft sandstone brick by pushing the brick back and forth in a scrubbing motion.)[28]

The *Reliance* carried four commissioned officers. Capt. John A. Henriques, the first commanding officer of the new cutter, entered the service from Connecticut as a third lieutenant on March 27, 1863, and received his captaincy on June 6, 1866. Second Lieut. Thomas B. Mullett, the second in command, entered the service from Ohio, having been promoted on May 29, 1866. Mullett's seniority by two numbers made Healy the third senior officer on the cutter. Third Lieut. Lemuel C. Cowan entered the service from Pennsylvania on July 20, 1867, and had the dubious distinction of being the junior officer. Captain Henriques assigned Healy the important duty of navigation officer on board the *Reliance*.[29]

The enlisted crewmen of the U.S. Revenue Cutter Service did not join for a specified period of time as is the case in today's service. Rather, they signed on much like merchant sailors did, that is, they signed on for a single voyage. Most of the sailors came from the world's major ports and thus the crews formed a polyglot of nationalities. Almost no historical evidence has survived about these early sailors.[30]

In 1867, there were two ways for a sailing ship to reach San Francisco from Baltimore. The easiest way—traveling around Cape of Good Hope at the southern tip of Africa—also proved to be the longest. Most captains chose to sail the shorter route, which took them around Cape Horn at the southern tip of South America. Some romantics say Poseidon (known by the Romans as Neptune) exacted a toll for taking a short route. Even today, many Americans who have little experience with the sea, recognize the name Cape Horn. Sailors still speak about the dangers of this region.

A sailor's lexicon from the sailing ship era gives us some idea of what awaited the crews off the southern tip of South America. As a sailing vessel proceeded southward from the United States, it passed through treacherous lines of latitude; at 40 degrees South latitude, the ship entered the "roaring forties," next came the "furious fifties," which were followed finally by the "screaming sixties."

Cape Horn is located at 55 degrees 59 minutes South latitude by 67 degrees 16 minutes West longitude. The cape itself is a pyramid of rock jutting 1,394.4 feet into the air at the southernmost tip of South America. With no landmass to the west of the Horn to break up the winds that sweep across the globe, the region is subject to furious lashing gales. Jutting northward from Antarctica, the Palmer Peninsula further complicates matters, causing a narrow gap, known as the Drake Passage, to form between the frozen continent and South America. Unchecked gale-force winds howl through the narrow passage, forming mountainous seas. One shipowner offered the following warning to his captains bound for the Horn: "It is nearly always very bad. . . . The winds blow almost continuously from the west, and although gales do not last so long in summer as in winter, they are more frequent and stronger. On the other hand, the winds are more variable in winter, the cold is bitterer, and the hours of daylight are much reduced—lasting from nine to three—and there is mist and snow to make things even worse. In short, navigation is nowhere more difficult than in these waters."[31]

Many books about seafaring give various boundaries for the region of the Horn. For sailing ships, the best description of the boundary around Cape Horn is from 50 degrees South latitude in the Atlantic to 50 degrees South latitude in the Pacific. For a ship traversing the Atlantic toward the Pacific, however, a captain usually steered well into the Pacific once clear of the Horn. This prevented the ship from being driven by westerly winds onto the lee shore of Chile. The owners of some ships required their captains to run at least two hundred miles into the Pacific before turning northward—a total of 1,200 to 1,500 extra and very hard nautical miles to sail. In foul weather, those 1,200 to 1,500 nautical miles often took weeks to sail. As late as 1908, the sailing ship *Denbigh Castle* fought the Horn for three weeks before its master finally gave up and ordered his ship to come about. The ship then ran east halfway around the world to Fremantle, Western Australia, arriving there after a total of eight and a half months at sea. Old salts understood that nobody relaxed south of 50 South latitude.[32]

In waterfront bars in New York, Baltimore, Liverpool, San Francisco, and any other port where deepwater sailors gathered to drink and swap sea stories, some old salt eventually bragged about the number of times he had rounded the Horn: the greater the number of passages, the higher the status of the sailor. Sailors who had made the rounding against the westerly winds held the highest bragging rights. To be sure, rounding against easterly winds never came close to resembling a leisurely sail on a lake, but most sailors understood that the real fight came to those traveling from the Atlantic to the Pacific.

On August 17, 1867, with a light breeze and drizzle prevailing, the little *Reliance* "stood down the river" at 3:15 p.m. and passed Fort McHenry, the defense of which during the War of 1812 inspired Francis Scott Key to write "The Star-Spangled Banner." Less than five hours later, Third Lieutenant Cowan recorded in the log that the *Reliance* "came to anchor in 5 fathoms water off Magothy [Magoty] River, with 15 fathoms of chain on Port anchor," approximately eight miles north of Annapolis, Maryland. While anchored, Dr. John C. Carter, the cutter's doctor, reported on board.

At 5:00 a.m. the next day, Healy recorded that the *Reliance* weighed anchor and beat down the Chesapeake Bay in light winds. The cutter continued slowly down the large bay until Tuesday, August 20, when Healy wrote, "1 PM Cape Henry [, Virginia,] bore NW by W distant 7 miles from where we take our departure," or approximately seven miles to the northeast of present-day Virginia Beach. In "clear and very warm weather," Healy and the *Reliance* began the long sea journey to San Francisco. For old salts, the best indication that a cutter had actually begun a deepwater voyage of any great distance is the notation in the log recording that the officers had "placed all hands on an allowance of one gallon of fresh water per day." Deepwater sailors lived with strict rationing of fresh water. Officers forced sailors to use this small allowance both to clean themselves and their clothing.

The *Reliance*'s crew quickly settled into a routine of taking in, or resetting, sails, maintaining the cutter, and standing their watches. Seldom did sailors have the luxury of a holiday aboard the cutter. On Sundays, for example, Captain Henriques inspected the crew and the ship. After the inspection, an officer read the crew the regulations and defined the punishments for breaking the regulations. Salts called this the reading of the "rocks and shoals."

Six days after their official departure a record was made in the logbook, placing Seamen James Chick and George Cooper on the sick list. This kind of entry marks another classic routine on board a military deepwater sailing ship: the constant shuttling on and off the sick list, both for minor and major medical problems.

On September 2, when the cutter was approximately five hundred miles northeast of San Juan, Puerto Rico, Healy recorded "strong breezes, heavy head seas." A gale continued until the next afternoon, when the weather changed to "moderate breeze, clear and pleasant."

Ten days later, when the cutter was almost eight hundred miles east of San Juan, Healy's entry in the log illustrates the kind of friction that can easily build in the gritty atmosphere of a small cutter on a long sea voyage. "James Chick (Sea[man]) put in irons," Healy wrote, "and triced up for striking the gunner, refusing obedience and using threatening language to the officer of the watch." For many years, one of the great fears held by officers of naval ships centered on an uprising—in a sailor's lexicon, a mutiny. Most of the officer corps believed that the uneducated lower classes that comprised those who sailed before the mast needed to see harsh punishment meted out to keep them in line. This is the first recorded incident of Healy applying this method of controlling crewmen. Whether or not he ever employed this punishment before remains unknown.

Thirty-five days after leaving Baltimore, another incident took place on board the *Reliance* that happened all too frequently to sailors who worked directly with the sails. On Saturday, September 21, the cutter had reached a position east of Port of Spain, Trinidad. At 9:10 a.m., the cabin boy, William H. Howard, was at work on the Martingale back rope, one of the lines that help hold the bowsprit, which is the mast that extends out from the bow of a sailing ship. The executive officer recorded that, in an instant, heavy seas "washed [Howard] overboard." The crew quickly threw "some floatation [device] for a buoy." Almost immediately after the device went over the side, the executive officer "sent 2nd Lieut. Healy in the boat to pick up the boy." Tragically, the sea swallowed Howard before Healy and the rescue boat could reach him. Two days later, the log reveals that an officer gave the cabin steward, James A. Howard, "all the effects of his brother Wm. H. Howard (Cabin Boy) lost-at-sea on the 21st inst."

From September 23 to October 21, the logged positions of *Reliance* chart the slow track-line of the cutter's progress southward. Log entries record a sailor injured, a petty officer demoted to seaman for "disobedience," and a few men shuffling off and onto the sick list. On October 9, at five hundred miles offshore from the Brazilian city of Fortaleza, Healy recorded his sighting of a peak on the island of Fernado Noronha. Twelve days later, the log shows the *Reliance* "making entrance to Santa Catherina [Catharina]," Brazil, located 450 miles southwest of Rio de Janeiro. The cutter came to anchor at noon the next day.

This marks the only Atlantic port of call made by the cutter during its long voyage southward.

As per custom and regulation, Captain Henriques wrote a letter to Washington describing the voyage thus far. "We were 49 days from Capes of Virginia to [the] equator[, with] a fine run from the equator to St. Catherine[, which] took only 14 days." The cutter averaged "140 miles per day, some days 200 miles to 240," despite a "sharp gale of 30 hours [that] delayed it. Vessel very dry, didn't ship one barrel of water."[33] Despite the optimistic tone of the letter, Captain Henriques did mention the loss of William H. Howard. Henriques, however, failed to mention any problems with personnel, such as the tricing up of James Chick. Perhaps Henriques considered such details too trivial for his senior officers in Washington; more likely he omitted the reference because captains rarely, if ever, cared to call attention to any disorder on their cutters.

The *Reliance* remained a few days in port at Santa Catharina. On October 23, Healy recorded the port watch section of the crew remained on liberty until sunset, while the starboard watch transferred fresh water to the cutter. The officers and enlisted men of the crew sampled whatever pleasures they could find on their first break away from their cutter. On October 24, the logbook recorded that James McColloch had been placed "in double irons by order of Commanding Officer for drunkenness and Riotous conduct." The next morning, an entry noted that John Kialy had been placed in irons for "drunkenness and using disrespectful Language to the Officers." In the afternoon, McColloch found himself again confined in double irons, this time for using "threatening language to the Master at Arms."

Wednesday, October 30, found the crew of the *Reliance* engaged in the formal firing of a seven-gun salute as the United States Consul, Mr. Lindsay, visited the cutter. The next day work began in earnest on preparations for the hard voyage ahead around Cape Horn. Captain Henriques discharged troublemakers James McColloch and George Chick, while Doctor Carter deemed George Cooper too sick to continue.

The discharge of two disorderly crewmen did not mean the end of personnel problems, however. On November 2, for example, two men found themselves confined for drunkenness. Three days later, the *Reliance* began its passage toward the Cape Horn region.

Six days later, Healy logged that the *Reliance*'s crew were busy preparing sails for the Cape Horn passage. The next day, as if to give the cuttermen a taste of the weather to come, the officer of the deck recorded "rain, cold, gales, heavy sea," and the watch "found deck leaking badly[,] damaging [the] provisions."

Prior to the *Reliance*'s departure from Santa Catharina, Captain Henriques gave his navigator, Second Lieutenant Healy, the proposed strategy for rounding the Horn. His orders called for Healy to navigate the cutter through the Straits of Le Maire, which lay between Tierra del Fuego and Isla de los Estados. Once into the Drake Passage, they would maneuver to nearby the Horn and then shape a course southwestward until arriving to the west of the small island of Diego Ramirez. Somewhere in the vicinity of the island, the plan called for turning up toward San Francisco. Plotting the positions of the *Reliance* close to a century and a half later, it is amazing how close the small cutter stuck to the plan as it advanced across one of the deadliest bodies of water known to mariners in the Age of Sail.

On November 14, approximately two hundred miles off the Argentina coast, with a moderate breeze and clear and pleasant weather, Healy reported that "Roland Basker (2nd Class Boy) fell from the Main Mast, severely injuring himself." Fortunately, unlike many sailors who fell from aloft, Basker did not die from his injuries, but remained on the sick list until December 8.

At 1:30 p.m., on November 20, 1867, Healy recorded the *Reliance*'s position some twenty miles from the southernmost point of Isla de los Estados, "from which we take our Departure" around the Horn. Thus began the cutter's short, but tough, war with the Horn.

The next day, the cuttermen sailed into the grip of the Horn's infamous weather. Strong gales lashed the *Reliance*. At 7:30 a.m., the officer of the deck logged "took in Fore Topsail and double reefed Main sail." A half hour later, the winds "carried away" part of the jib sail. Throughout most of the first day in the Drake Passage, the crew of the *Reliance* endured heavy squalls of rain, snow, and hail. The cuttermen kept busy taking in, or reefing, sails. Over an eighteen-hour period, the cutter averaged 2.9 knots per hour. At one time, however, the weather slowed the *Reliance* to such a degree that for two hours it progressed only a single knot.

The following day, Friday, November 22, began with moderate weather, and the watch piled on more sail. By 3:40 p.m., moderate gales again howled down the Drake Passage and the crew again reefed the sails. From 8:00 p.m. through midnight, the small cutter progressed only one knot.

At 1:00 a.m. on Saturday, November 23, Healy logged "frequent and severe squalls" and, at 3:30 a.m., "made Horn Island bearing NW1/2W, distance about 15 miles." This is as close to Cape Horn as the cutter ventured. The *Reliance* now turned onto a more southerly course before making the westerly turn for Diego Ramirez Island. All of this was executed in "heavy head seas," but slackening wind.

Sunday found the cutter still making a southerly course in bad weather. The next day, the *Reliance* headed southwesterly, battling strong gales, snow, hail, and heavy head seas. The cutter's speed for most of the day fluctuated between two and three knots, with one short burst of seven knots per hour. On Tuesday, at 190 miles southwest of the Horn, the *Reliance* reached the southernmost point in its battle through Drake Passage, and the following day, on November 28, the cutter began its long voyage northward to San Francisco. A few more days of severe storms and high seas yet had to be endured, but Healy and the *Reliance* had weathered the worst of the passage. Despite enduring eight days of unrelentingly bad weather, the cutter incurred very little damage and, most important, lost no cuttermen to the Horn.

On December 17, having safely entered the Pacific Ocean, the *Reliance* sailed into the beautiful surroundings of the port of Valparaiso, Chile. Another ship's captain described the approach that Healy observed: "[T]he bay is studded by elevated and broken land, which changes its dark shades with ridge and cliff; and at its head the picturesque city rests on the naturally terraced, rocky hillside, reflecting its quaint beauty in the undulating waters whose constant surf whitens along the shore. . . . The distant view from seaward reveals the Andes in all their grandeur."[34]

Here, Healy and his shipmates sampled the delights of the "picturesque city." After stocking up on provisions such as "raisons [*sic*], butter, cheese," Captain Henriques ordered the anchor weighed, and the *Reliance* resumed its journey northward to San Francisco.

The Pacific Ocean portion of the voyage may have seemed a bit anticlimactic to Healy after the excitement of rounding the Horn. His log entries over the next 5,300 nautical miles indicate nothing but routine duty at sea. At 10:30 p.m., on January 27, 1868, the *Reliance* sailed into its home port of San Francisco, 163 days after departing Baltimore.

The next day, Captain Henriques wrote another letter to Washington. He praised his officers for their hard work on the long voyage. When it came to the seaworthiness of the cutter *Reliance*, Henriques gushed, "We made the run from Saint Catherine, Brazil, to Valparaiso in 43 days," even though they hove to in gales off Rio Plata and to the west of Cape Horn. "Little thing really spread herself," Henriques wrote, "making the most extraordinary run of 37 days and eight hours."[35]

Captain Henriques noted the cutter arrived "safe and sound at its destination, sound as a dollar—not a spar lost—not a boat gone." Henriques apparently chose to forget the injury of Richard Basker. Interestingly, on the same date as the captain's letter, an entry in the log records "Francis Cliner released from irons and discharged for insubordination and abusive language to officers."

Despite being in the port of San Francisco and away from the confined atmosphere on board a small cutter, problems with the crew continued to plague the *Reliance*. On January 31, Healy wrote in the logbook: "Richard Brooks put in irons and triced up for drunkenness, fighting, and disorderly conduct." Two days later on Sunday, February 2, First Lieut. Edward B. Fairlong submitted a report to Captain Henriques that recorded: "John Riley discharged for drunk and disorderly conduct, insulting and indecent language to officers. Robert Long for absent without leave, Charles Brown for inattention to duty, Robert Denneark (Gunner) for absent without leave. James McCulloch was discharged because the quartermaster had tried at times to take the life of the master at arms and was a dangerous man to the crew. A vicious, incorrigible upon whom punishment had no effect, a 'bully' detested by the whole crew and using obscene language." The report went on to tell of the dismissal of "George Cooper, [with] a loathsome mass of corruption through a venereal disease called Secondary siphylis [*sic*]. He endangers the health of the rest of the crew by his presence on board." The report also bore the signatures of Healy, another officer on board, and the doctor, John C. Carter.

So little is known about the early crews of the U.S. Revenue Cutter Service that it is difficult to judge the *Reliance*'s crew as being any better, or any worse, than any other during this period. The log entries do show, however, that Second Lieutenant Healy and other young officers of the service expected obedience from their crews and did not hesitate to apply draconian measures to enforce discipline. One of the duties of cutter officers entailed commanding boarding parties sent out from cutters to ships to put down grumblings in the forecastle. Young officers, both on board the *Reliance* and other cutters, later applied the strict discipline they learned from their own superiors early in their careers. Upon reaching command rank, it should not be surprising that the future captains expected their junior officers to unquestionably obey any order given them and to squash any outbreak of disorder with swift, strong measures.

Meanwhile, in Boston, Fr. James A. Healy decided to undertake a cruise to the Mediterranean. As his two youngest sisters, Amanda Josephine and Eliza

Dunamore, took care of the house in West Newton, he included them in his plans. Father Healy also included in the party two older women as chaperones: Mrs. Thomas Hodges, who acted as "mother" to the youngest brother, Eugene, and Mary Jane Healy. Thus, as her husband's cutter neared its new port of San Francisco, Mary Jane departed Boston on her own sailing adventure right after New Year's Day 1868. She left their son, Eugene, in the care of her parents.

As Mary Jane was soon to learn, January on the Atlantic can be stormy. The crossing proved how badly a ship can ride in high seas, and the travelers suffered severe seasickness. Once in the Mediterranean, however, the party settled into a pleasurable voyage. In February, they viewed the Parthenon in Athens through binoculars. On warm evenings, they lounged on deck, either reading Shakespeare aloud or indulging in conversation.

The travelers also enjoyed a six-week layover in Sicily and Southern Italy. James, who had studied in Europe, guided the women to landmarks and museums and escorted them to the opera several times. The travelers did not return to Boston until the middle of May. Such a voyage must have seemed a great adventure to the daughter of an Irish Catholic immigrant, whose husband served a continent away from her and their son.[36]

"In 1867 our 'fathers' at Washington got the idea that smuggling was being carried on at this port," Augusta Barrett Sherman, a schoolteacher in San Diego, wrote in her diary. "I never knew what it was that was being smuggled. So they sent the revenue cutter *Reliance* for our protection. She sailed around the Horn and arrived here early in 1868. The vessel remained here a number of months, but finding that there was nothing for them to do, she was ordered to Alaska."[37]

On Saturday, February 15, 1868, nineteen days after Healy arrived in San Francisco, and while Mary Jane cruised the Mediterranean, the *Reliance* raised anchor and began the voyage to San Diego, stopping at only a few places en route. At Santa Barbara, the officer of the day recorded in the logbook that, on February 22, cuttermen "Boarded schooner 'Alert' with armed boat crew[.] [F]ound most of foremast hands drunk & had been fighting. Mate badly cut in several places. [Placed in irons the] ringleader brought them on board cutter & confined them" in a hold. Two cuttermen remained on board to guard the schooner. A wardroom steward later journeyed over to the *Alert* with bandages for the mate. The next day, Captain Henriques ordered the prisoners returned to their ship's captain.

On February 24, the *Reliance* continued on its voyage to San Diego, arriving there two days later on a clear and pleasant Wednesday, and anchored in seven fathoms of water in San Diego's harbor. The cuttermen began their anti-smuggling efforts the next day by boarding a whaling ship and a sloop.

As Augusta Barrett Sherman pointed out in her diary, from February 27 until April 2, 1868, the crew enjoyed an almost idyllic existence in the warm climate of San Diego, with few duties to carry out beyond routine maintenance of the cutter. This all came to an end, however, when the *Reliance* weighed anchor on April 2, and started the very slow trip northward back to San Francisco, arriving there, after a few stops, on May 2, 1868. Over five months later, as a result of the United States' purchase of Alaska, Second Lieut. Michael A. Healy took his first step on the journey that would inaugurate the myth of "Hell Roaring Mike."

4

EASTERN INTERLUDE

Michael A. Healy's first foray into Alaskan waters was the result of the Congressional Act of July 27, 1868 (15 Stat. 240), which not only extended to Alaska United States laws regarding navigation and commerce, but also created a customs district in Sitka. The secretary of the treasury ordered Captain Henriques to take the *Reliance* from San Francisco to Sitka and help enforce the customs laws in Southeastern Alaska. On Thursday, October 30, 1868, under clear skies and light winds, the cutter *Reliance* departed San Francisco.

Seventeen days later, nearing their destination, Healy and his shipmates found themselves in heavy seas and gale-force winds. The storm forced the small cutter to lie off the Sitka harbor for seven days. Finally, on November 23, Captain Henriques selected an officer who could safely take a small boat and its crew into the harbor to obtain a pilot. The captain wisely chose Healy, for the second lieutenant brought the small boat safely into the harbor and the pilot out to the *Reliance*. Once on board, the pilot brought the cutter to anchor, arriving in Sitka's harbor at 9:00 p.m.[1] Michael A. Healy had just received his first welcome to the territory amid weather that would typify his forthcoming years of sailing in Alaskan waters.

Healy soon learned that certain aspects of duty on this far-off maritime frontier differed greatly from those of other ports. In the afternoon on Tuesday, December 1, for example, the "Chief of the Chilcal [Chilkat] tribe" came on board the cutter for a visit. Captain Henriques turned out the crew in the chief's honor.

Very soon after their arrival, the officers of the *Reliance* began boarding vessels and searching their cargoes for contraband. On December 14, an officer received orders to relieve the customs official on board the steamer *Otter*. Two days later, Healy took over this duty. On December 17, U.S. Revenue Cutter Service officers seized the schooner *General Harmony*, from San Francisco, for transporting illegal whiskey.

The isolation and rainy winter weather in Sitka proved too much for many of the sailors serving in the *Reliance*. One of Healy's entries in the logbook states that he placed a man in the hold in irons for being drunk and disorderly. This episode proved to be the first of many occasions in which drinking caused the crew to run afoul of their officers in these northern climes.

The crew of the *Reliance* welcomed the new year of 1869 in a manner unusual for sailors. The officer of the deck recorded: "Received news from the shore of a disturbance with the Indians[.] [C]alled all hands to quarters. Shotted guns & sent boat to the [U.S. Navy ship] USS *Saginaw* to inform them. Armed crew and trained guns on the Indian village." The disturbance must have passed uneventfully, since no further record action appears in the log for this day.

Nevertheless, at 1:30 p.m. the next afternoon, the officer of the deck recorded, "The authorities on shore wishing to capture a chief of the Chilcot[Chilkoot] tribe of Indians who was secreted in the Indian village abreast of the vessel and fearing resistance on the part of the . . . Indians, trained the guns on the village and made all arrangements to cooperate with the army in furthering the ends of justice. The chief gave himself up[,] piped down from quarters[,] but kept an armed watch . . . for fear of a further outbreak."[2] No further problems with the natives are recorded in the cutter's journal.

On January 10, Healy wrote to headquarters: "Having been now nearly two years from home and family, I would most respectively beg to be transferred to the Atlantic coast."[3] Problems among the officers on board the *Reliance* may also have played a part in Healy's request, for in the event that he could not be sent to the East Coast, Healy asked that he be transferred to another cutter. The isolation of life on the cutter in the Alaskan frontier must have felt like extended sea duty to many of the officers on the *Reliance*. Close quarters on a small cutter can quickly cause friction within a crew.

As his request for transfer made its slow journey eastward—not to mention its even slower journey through the bureaucracy of the Treasury Department—Healy continued a monotonous routine. For the rest of January and all of February, the entries in the cutter's logbook reflect the continued inspection of ships and other craft, plus the confinement of a number of crewmen as punishment for trouble ashore. One entry near the end of February does record the return of an unnamed third lieutenant from an "exploring expedition." No doubt there were times that Healy and other officers and crewmen of the *Reliance* ventured beyond the area of Sitka.

The routine changed for Healy on March 4. The day started for the cutter's crew with a normal request for help. The collector of customs at Sitka ordered

Captain Henriques to seize the ship *James Crawford*. Henriques, in turn, delegated an officer with a boat crew to carry out the orders. Later that evening, at 5:30 p.m., the officer of the deck recorded that the watch "noticed the Ensign of [schooner] 'Legal Tender' set [flying] union down. [This is the international signal for distress.] Sent an officer and armed boat crew to ascertain the problem. [Found] that a portion of the crew had been engaged in a fight during the absence of the Master[,] but as he returned to the vessel and expressed himself able to quell the disturbance without assistance[,] recalled the boats at 6 PM."

Six days later, Healy, along with a quartermaster and seaman from the *Reliance*, received orders to sail on board a seized ship as a prize crew bound for San Francisco. On March 12, 1869, the ship cleared the harbor of Sitka. Thus ended Healy's first exposure to Alaska.

Like most naval officers who request orders to a new station, Healy must have frequently wondered about the progress of his request. His official record states that on Friday, July 2, 1869, the Treasury Department ordered him to be transferred to the East Coast. By the time these orders reached San Francisco, however, Healy had already sailed, once again, to the north. Indeed, this second voyage north is nowhere to be found in Healy's official service record in Washington, D.C. The correspondence relating to this voyage is unfortunately no longer available and its existence must be surmised from the muster rolls and the cutter's log entries.

On September 1, 1865, the U.S. Revenue Cutter Service received a new 165-foot cutter built by John F. Fardy & Brothers of Baltimore. The *Lincoln* retained a fore topsail schooner rig, but also came powered by steam. Plans called for the cutter to sail around the Horn to Port Angeles, Washington. By April 18, 1869, the cutter had sailed out of San Francisco and was headed north.[4] The muster rolls for May of 1869 show a "Second Lieutenant Healy" on board. One of the likeliest reasons for his service on the cutter is the fact that Capt. John A. Henriques commanded the vessel. By this time, Captain Henriques knew Healy's abilities as a seaman and it seems only logical that he would request him to serve on his ship.

Healy sailed on board the *Lincoln* until it returned to San Francisco in November. This little-known voyage of Healy's is important to his career for three reasons. First, it advanced his reputation as a sailor who could handle the difficult waters of the north. Second, prior to this voyage, Healy had generally sailed only in the waters of Southeastern Alaska. During this patrol, however, he traveled as far as Kodiak, and on Sunday, May 16, 1869, when the *Lincoln* entered Unalaska's harbor, Healy began his first duty in the Bering Sea. The cutter sailed to the Pribilof Islands and into Bristol Bay, among other locations, acquainting Healy with yet more of the Alaskan frontier. Third, Second Lieut. Calvin L. Hooper sailed with Healy as a shipmate on the voyage. Thus began a long friendship between the two men, one in which Hooper would help to guide Healy's life.

Once the *Lincoln* returned to San Francisco, Healy departed for Boston. The joy of returning to the East Coast, however, soon turned to sorrow. On January 5, 1870, Michael's second son, Eugene, died from the "croup." This must have been doubly hard for Healy, who, having departed the East Coast less than a year after Eugene was born, had little time to get to know his son. As is usual in these cases, the service allowed Michael an extended period of time to grieve and to help Mary Jane cope with her loss. It was some time before Healy reported to his next cutter.[5]

Meanwhile, on July 20, 1870, Healy received a promotion to first lieutenant. The new rank increased his pay to $1,800 per year. Just as important, Healy's first lieutenancy put him in line for billets as either an executive officer (second in command) of major cutters, or a commanding officer of smaller vessels.[6]

The newly promoted First Lieut. Michael A. Healy reported to the 137-foot, 240-ton schooner-rigged cutter *William H. Seward* at Wilmington, North Carolina, on August 5, 1870. How Healy felt about being stationed so close to Georgia is not recorded, but it must have made him uncomfortable. His service record shows that Healy received fifteen days leave beginning on September 15, 1870.[7] He requested the time away from the cutter because of the imminent birth of his third son, Frederick Aloysius, which took place on October 5, 1870. At the time, Michael and Mary Jane lived at 24 Upton Street, in the south end of Boston. Mary continued to care for her father, John, and invalid mother, Margaret. Mary Jane and her family felt that Frederick might not survive infancy and quickly scheduled his baptism on the same day of his birth. The baptismal certificate records Fr. Alexander Sherwood Healy, the fourth oldest son of Michael Morris Healy and Eliza Clark, as Frederick's godfather.[8] On October 21, 1875, within five years of attending the baptism, Fr. Alexander Sherwood Healy died, the third of Michael A. Healy's older brothers to die young.[9]

On December 5, 1870, less than two months after the birth of Frederick A. Healy, First Lieutenant Healy reported on board the 110-foot, 227-ton topsail schooner-rigged cutter *Vigilant* in Boston. The *Vigilant* and her sister cutter, the *Reliance*, have the distinction of being the last cutters that completely relied on sails.[10] It is possible that Frederick's poor health resulted in this assignment, with the service allowing Healy, for the sake of his family, a short tour in Boston.

In any case, Healy took up the duties of his new assignment while he tried to learn the responsibilities of being, for the third time, a new father. As it turned out, Healy had little time to master either duty. Just over nine months after reporting on board the *Vigilant*, he received orders to report to the 104-foot, 192-ton cutter *Moccasin*, at Newport, Rhode Island. This assignment marks the first time Healy served on board a steam-powered cutter. Whoever within the Treasury Department was responsible for transferring officers may well have thought that Newport was close enough to Boston for Healy to avoid undue upset about his sudden move.

Healy reported on board the *Moccasin* in September 1871.[11] His rank of first lieutenant made him second in command of the cutter. Third Lieut. Albert Buhner, born in Germany on June 2, 1842, also served with Healy. Buhner, having entered the U.S. Navy on November 20, 1861, served during the Civil War as a Master's Mate. He received an honorable discharge on July 13, 1866. Buhner officially entered the U.S. Revenue Cutter Service on March 6, 1871, from South Carolina, as a third lieutenant. He had served only a short tour on the cutter *Gallatin*, at Buffalo, New York, before reporting on board the *Moccasin* on October 30, 1871. Buhner would serve again with Healy in the future.[12]

Duty at Newport proved hectic. On Monday, November 13, 1871, for example, Healy noted in the logbook that the officers and crew boarded twelve ships. The cutter's log contains many similar entries, along with other entries recording a few cases of helping ships in trouble, a few seized illegal cargoes, and all instances of bad weather: the standard logbook entries of any U.S. Revenue Cutter Service cutter operating near a busy port.

At 9:30 a.m., on December 10, 1871, however, Second Lieut. A. D. Littlefield penned the following in the journal: "mustered the crew & inspected the ship. By order of the Hon. Secretary of the Department reprimand of Lieut. M. A. Healy, bearing date of 2nd inst. was read in presence of the ships company, Lieut. Healy being present in person."[13]

Buried within the large journals in which clerks handwrote the service records of the officers of the U.S. Revenue Cutter Service is a November 2, 1871, entry about First Lieutenant Healy, which states: "Charges of gross intoxication performed + directed to forward defense." Eighteen days later, the clerk made an additional entry confirming that Healy acknowledged the "truth of [the] charge, begs clemency of [the Department] + promises to abstain in [the] future."[14]

On December 2, S. W. Macy, the collector of customs at Newport, received a letter signed by George S. Boutwell, the secretary of the treasury, who had enclosed an additional letter concerning Healy. Boutwell instructed Macy to personally "hand" the letter to Healy's commanding officer on the *Moccasin*. Boutwell further instructed that the crew and officers attend a special muster and that, with Healy present, the contents of the letter be read aloud.

The letter began by acknowledging that Healy had written and confessed his guilt on charges of "intoxication and conduct unbecoming an officer and gentleman . . . preferred by the Collector of Customs at Newport, R.I." Boutwell went on to state that he "deeply regretted" that Healy "occupying . . . [a] trusted and honorable position in the service should be so far forgetful of his duty to himself and his obligations to a service which he should constantly strive to adorn, as to permit himself to dishonor both in the unseemly and disgraceful manner you admit yourself to have done." Boutwell wrote:

> [Healy's conduct] merits the severest punishment within the power of the Department to inflict, but as this [is] understood to be your first offense, the Department, in view of your apparent appreciation of the deep disgrace your indiscretion has brought upon yourself and service, the promise of deep contrition expressed in your letter, and the promise of amendment in the future by taking and keeping a solemn pledge never again to taste intoxicating liquors, has concluded to pass over for the present, your offense with this reprimand but your continuance in the service must depend upon your maintenance of that course of conduct which best comports with the character of an officer and gentleman, for any departure there from, coming to the knowledge of the Department, officially or otherwise, will be followed by your instant dismissal.

Brother Patrick's intercession may have helped Boutwell reach his decision to issue a reprimand instead of a dismissal.

Lastly, Boutwell stated that Healy should consider himself detached from the *Moccasin* and placed on waiting orders.[15] In the nineteenth century, awaiting orders meant one of three things for an officer. If no suitable billet for an officer's rank remained open at the time of a transfer, he could be deemed awaiting orders. Likewise, an injured or sick officer could be said to be awaiting orders until he had recovered. In both cases, the order meant that the officer stayed ashore, at reduced pay, until either a billet became available or the officer recovered and returned to duty. The third use of awaiting orders was to provide punishment short of summarily dismissing an officer from the service. In other words, the officer remained ashore at reduced pay until a higher authority in the U.S. Revenue Cutter Service allowed him to return to full-duty status.

The next entry in Healy's service record, also made on December 2, states simply, "[R]eprimanded for drunkenness."[16] These three words mark the gathering of a cloud that hangs over Healy's name to the present day. The event that brought all this about took place on September 28, 1871, at a hotel in Newport. An investigation revealed that Healy had drunk to excess and caused such a disturbance that police officers had "to convey" him back to the cutter. Once there, he required confinement to prevent him from "harming the officers and crew."[17]

By Monday, December 4, Healy's status of awaiting orders ended with the reading of Boutwell's reprimand. Shortly thereafter, he received orders to report to the 90-foot, 120-ton, schooner-rigged cutter *Active*, in New Bedford, Massachusetts.

Healy's actions in the short time he served on board the *Moccasin* changed the shape of his life in two major ways. First, in the very small maritime organization, the charge of drunkenness quickly circulated among the officer corps. Second, prior to his transfer to the *Moccasin*, Healy's career had spiraled steadily upward. Within six years of joining the service in 1865, Healy held the second highest officer rank, first lieutenant, in the U.S. Revenue Cutter Service. Among thirty-four first lieutenants in the service, he ranked at number nineteen on the list.[18] After the events on the *Moccasin*, however, officers that once ranked below Healy began to rise above him. By May 1, 1873, for example, Leonard G. Shepard, who had previously ranked below Healy, now placed at number sixteen, while Healy ranked at nineteen, and Calvin L. Hooper twenty. By 1876, the change had become even more pronounced. Of thirty-four first lieutenants, Shepard had risen to number two, while Healy remained at number nine, and Hooper ten. Four years after that, Hooper ranked higher than Healy. Clearly, the drunkenness charge slowed the trajectory of Healy's career.[19]

From January 1872 to July 1874, Healy served on board the *Active* as second in command. He performed the routine duties of boarding ships and examining cargoes. The whaling industry in New Bedford had passed its peak by the time Healy arrived in the Massachusetts seaport. His assignment, however, allowed him to meet and befriend the owners of the remaining whaling ships as well as many of the ships' captains. Healy understood these tough men who spent their lives pursuing whales.[20]

On July 13, 1874, Healy received orders to report to the cutter *Richard Rush*. The *Rush*, built by the Atlantic Iron Works in East Boston, Massachusetts, had a schooner rig, but also boasted a compound expansion steam engine, a coal-fired boiler, and a single propeller. The 140-foot cutter—which had a draft of eight feet, ten inches, displaced 180 tons, carried a crew of forty, and was armed with two 6-pound guns—cost the Treasury Department $79,000. One of three cutters in the *Dexter* class, it was the second to bear the name *Rush*, in honor of the eighth secretary of the treasury. Once again, Healy found himself a member of the first crew on a new cutter, a position known among sailors as "a plank owner." Other interesting parallels to Healy's earlier service on the *Reliance* greeted the first lieutenant. Like Healy's assignment on the *Reliance*, his new assignment ordered him back to San Francisco. Even stranger, his former commanding officer, Captain Henriques, now commanded the *Rush*. Those who assigned officers in the U.S. Revenue Cutter Service searched for the right person to command and serve in the important position of executive officer. In other words, the assignment of Healy to the *Rush* seems inevitable.[21]

On July 13, Healy departed for the *Rush*, and the next day Captain Henriques received authorization to hire a crew. Henriques reported that the new cutter had been placed in commission on July 21, 1874.[22]

Michael and Mary Jane realized that she had to stay in Boston. Mary Jane needed to take care of four-year-old Frederick, as well as her aging father and infirm mother.

On July 27, Captain Henriques received orders to sail the *Rush* to New York City, where the crew would outfit the ship for the long voyage to San Francisco. The cutter dropped anchor at Hoboken, New Jersey, on August 11, then moved briefly to Staten Island, and finally moored at Pier 39 on New York City's East River. There, the cuttermen prepared their vessel for the long sea journey to the West Coast.

On the breezy, late Sunday afternoon of August 30, the routine preparations received an unexpected jolt. Someone from the cutter had spotted a boat with four men in it capsizing. The officer of the deck quickly ordered the cutter's small boat cleared away. "Dennis Murly coxswain[, and his crew]" recorded Second Lieut. N. B. Rogers, "succeeded in rescuing all of the men, and made an attempt to tow the boat ashore, but owing to the strength of the tide was obliged to let her go." The boat crew landed the rescued men in New Jersey and returned to the *Rush*.

Finally, in the afternoon on Tuesday, September 15, under partly cloudy skies and a moderate breeze, the 140-foot cutter cast off from Pier 39 and began its passage to San Francisco. Unlike their earlier sail around Cape Horn in the *Reliance* in 1867, Captain Henriques and First Lieutenant Healy benefited from new maritime technology. Henriques now had a steam engine with a single propeller (screw) to supplement the sails of the *Rush*. The service, however, according to their normal penny-pinching ways, continued to use the sails whenever possible to save on the cost of coaling the cutter. The cutter's new means of propulsion allowed Healy, as a seaman, to investigate regions very difficult to reach in vessels powered only by the wind.

The *Rush* made good time on its passage south, encountering only a few gales en route, and arrived in the harbor of Rio de Janeiro, Brazil, in the evening on October 28. There, the crew of the *Rush* viewed the beautiful city replete with sandy beaches and tall green peaks dominated by the granite peak of Corcovado. They also sampled more earthly delights. The abstracts of the *Rush*'s logbook generally contain excellent penmanship. For the three days the cutter remained in Rio de Janeiro, however, scrawled entries abound, as if the writer did not want to waste time on paperwork while Rio called. In any case, the *Rush* departed Rio de Janeiro on the evening of November 4, 1874, and continued southward. Once out to sea and heading for the Cape Horn region, the quality of the penmanship greatly improved.

The new technology allowed for a relatively safe route around one of the most dangerous waters for sailors. Using their steam engine, the crew on board the *Rush* did not have to do battle with the Horn. The cutter entered the Straits of Magellan via the V-shaped entryway on the Atlantic side of Argentina on November 15. The steam-driven vessel passed by the present-day city of Punta Arenas, Chile, and then continued down the Smyth Channel to the Pacific. Even though it made its way through relatively protected waters, the cutter faced stiff winds during its passage and had to anchor every night. By December 2, Healy had seen for the second time the hills surrounding Valparaiso, Chile, as the *Rush* came to anchor.

On January 8, in light winds and fog, the *Rush* passed Fort Point, and, at 10:00 a.m., moored to a buoy in San Francisco harbor. Almost immediately, Healy received a message from Mary Jane that her father, John, lay on his deathbed. Mary Jane needed help. Her father near death, she had to care for a sickly infant and an infirm mother. Healy received permission for thirty days of leave, beginning January 29, two days after the death of John Roach.[23]

Shortly after Healy's arrival at 24 Upton Street, he and Mary Jane learned the contents of John Roach's will. Like Michael Morris Healy, John Roach managed to leave his family in better straits than many at a time when being an Irish Catholic immigrant in the United States meant second-class citizenship. John Roach's will stated that he bequeathed the house at 24 Upton Street, valued at $8,000, to Mary Jane, along with the $10,000 insurance policy he had purchased on September 6, 1866. In addition, he left "all of the bonds of the United States that I now hold at my decease (amounting now to five thousand dollars) and a note or notes amounting to three thousand dollars and interest secured by my mortgage upon house and land numbered eighty-three (83) Brookline Street in said Boston." At the time, the average annual wage of a person living in a city amounted to $423.[24]

Healy took an additional thirty days to get his affairs in order at home. Nearing the end of close to sixty days of leave, Healy decided he needed even more time at home, and was awarded awaiting orders status on March 16, 1875. The combination of family matters requiring immediate attention, his brother's poor health, and the thought of being once again a continent away from Mary Jane and Frederick brought about the delay in Healy's return to the *Rush*.

Nevertheless, by June 10, 1875, Healy had reluctantly returned to San Francisco and the *Rush*.[25] Interestingly, the new cutter did not see service in Alaska for its first two years on the Pacific Coast. Rather, the *Rush* departed San Francisco and worked its way south to Monterey, Santa Barbara, and San Diego. Shortly after returning from a southern patrol, the cutter worked north to Crescent City, California. Between patrols, officers and crew boarded ships in San Francisco's harbor, checking manifests and cargoes. They also saved lives. On August 8, and again on August 26, 1876, for example, a small pulling boat crew from the cutter rescued a total of four men whose boats had capsized in the harbor.

Before the end of 1876, Captain Henriques received orders to report to another cutter. This left First Lieut. Michael A. Healy in temporary command of the service's newest major cutter.[26]

Shortly after taking temporary command, Healy received orders to sail northward to Astoria, Oregon. He safely navigated the *Rush* across the dangerous Columbia River Bar, an area known as the "graveyard of the Pacific," and anchored off Astoria on January 6, 1877. There, Capt. John White came on board for transportation to Portland, Oregon. The next day the *Rush*'s engineers got steam up, and the cutter proceeded up the broad Columbia River, arriving at Portland on Monday, January 8.

At Portland, the *Rush* came alongside the newest cutter in the service and the first to be built on the West Coast, the *Thomas Corwin*. Captain White left Healy's cutter and took over command of the *Corwin*. Healy also transferred some cuttermen over to the new vessel to help sail it south to its home port of San Francisco. By January 23, Healy had also brought the *Rush* back into San Francisco's harbor.

In February, Healy's duties took his cutter to Crescent City in Northern California before returning to its home port. In March, he commanded the cutter when it made its return passage between San Francisco and San Diego. At the end of March, however, Capt. George W. Bailey took command of the *Rush*, and Healy resumed his duties as executive officer.[27]

In May 1877, the cutter began its first voyage in Alaskan waters. The *Rush* and her cuttermen proved a welcome sight to the Alaskan inhabitants, for no government cutter had ventured northward during the previous and momentous year of 1876—the service's busy schedule during the one hundredth anniversary of the new American republic prevented a northward voyage. Healy's knowledge of the region proved helpful to his new commanding officer on their first stop in Alaska at Sitka on May 20. Sitka continued to develop as the major port on the northern Pacific coast and served as the capital of the territory. The capital grew slowly from "a civilian population of 391, of whom 10 were saloonkeepers and 29 professional prostitutes" in 1869 to a population of 444 by 1880.[28]

After a two-day stay in Sitka, the *Rush* left for Kodiak. Departing Kodiak, Captain Bailey had orders to stop at Ounga [Unga] and Belkofsky [Belkofski] to distribute circulars on new regulations concerning the hunting of sea otters. A growing fear that these valuable fur-bearing sea mammals would be hunted to extinction prompted new laws that prohibited white hunters from pursuing the mammal. Bailey informed the Treasury Department that while heavy weather prevented him from entering Belkofsky, members of the Alaska Commercial Company had promised to send the regulations to the settlement. The cutter arrived at Unalaska on June 19 and then sailed northeastward for the Pribilof Islands.

As seas go, the Bering Sea is shallow and small. Its surface temperature hovers between 48.2 and 53.6 degrees Fahrenheit in August, with colder temperatures recorded above the Bering Strait. Any sailor washed overboard without proper survival gear has about fifteen minutes to live in such frigid waters. Needless to say, the sailors of the U.S. Revenue Cutter Service did not have access to the type of equipment that would allow them to survive in such cold water. The Bering Sea also has the dubious distinction of lying in the path of low-pressure systems that traverse the North Pacific Ocean, and its shallow waters can quickly build to mountainous seas. It is a rare day that the sea is calm. When Healy sailed into the area, it was sparsely charted, a danger compounded by the fog, drizzle, and rain that dominate the weather. In other words, the Bering Sea marks the entrance to the dangerous world of sailing in high northern latitudes.

A natural counterbalance to these dangers for sailors even today is the amount of marine life in the Bering Sea. Pelagic birds numbering in the hundreds of thousands dive into the cold waters after fish, while whales spout in the distance and other marine mammals in great numbers swim nearby. Despite this grand display of fauna in the Bering Sea and Arctic Ocean, however, few sailors in Healy's day took the time to marvel at these wonders.

First Lieutenant Healy soon found that his former duties inspecting the cargoes of ships on the Great Lakes, the East Coast, and the Pacific, including his assignment in Southeastern Alaska, only minimally prepared him for life on the Bering Sea. Interestingly, it would be a marine mammal, *Callohinus alascanus*, the Alaskan fur seal, that would determine Healy's fate and, to some extent, that of the nation.[29]

Had he wished, Secretary of State Seward might well have pointed out to his distracters that the thick pelt of the sleek marine mammal alone helped justify the purchase of Alaska. As early as 1869, decision-makers in the United States recognized the fur seal "as the source of the only revenue income" from the territory. Realizing this, Congress set aside the Pribilof Islands, the only breeding grounds of the fur seal, as a special government preserve. On April 1, 1870, the Treasury Department granted a twenty-year lease to the Alaska Commercial Company, with authorization to kill seals on the islands. In return for the lease, the company paid the government an annual rent along with a tax on each skin taken. During the lease period, the Alaska Commercial Company took in 1,977,277 skins and paid the Treasury Department $6,020,153, an amount just under the purchase price of the huge new territory. Obviously, any threat to such a productive source of national income would receive immediate attention. Soon, just such a threat loomed on the horizon.[30]

The sealing industry in the Bering Sea began in 1706 when the Pribilof Islands came under Russian domination. Five islands make up the Pribilofs: St. Paul, St. George, Otter Island, Walrus Island, and Sea Lion Rock. The largest two islands, St. Paul and St. George, have large fur seal rookeries. By the mid-1840s, the Russians had already begun the leasing method and controlled the size of the herd by harvesting only surplus males. The lessee, moreover, could only kill the mammals on land. This arrangement meant that only extra animals were taken, and the government strictly controlled the killing.[31]

The Alaskan fur seal is the largest of the pelagic fur seals. From December to May, the seals live entirely at sea, ranging as far south as the latitude of southern California. The animal is both highly gregarious and polygamous, demonstrates a limited intelligence, and is possessed by an instinct that allows nothing to stand in its way. It "exhibits no . . . ability to learn from its experience." This inflexibility played a key role in the animal's future.[32]

Around the first of May, the great bull seals begin to come ashore in the Pribilof Islands and stake out their territories in the rookeries. Weighing more than a quarter of a ton, the huge animals take possession of an area covering six to twelve square feet and fiercely defend it. The choicest locations are those closest to the water's edge, where the bulls have the greatest chance of attracting the cows, which usually arrive in the first week of June.

The cows arrive pregnant and must give birth to their pups on land. Before the cows and their pups leave the island for their long stay at sea, the bulls entice the cows into their harems and mate with them. The bulls continue their frenzied sequence of enticing, mating, and defending for more than six weeks, all without leaving their territory for food. The cows, however, usually leave the rookery to feed.

Bulls that are not strong enough to defend their own territory and attract a harem, called bachelor bulls, are driven to an area of their own. This isolation usually lasts for about six years. Bachelor bulls, like cows, leave the island for food. Once in the sea, it is difficult to distinguish a male from a female. The land method of harvesting fur seals eliminates this confusion because the bachelor bulls are easily identified as those animals driven to an area away from the other seals. The natives then kill the bachelor bulls with clubs. Thus, if properly controlled, this system poses no real danger to the herd, for the breeding bulls and cows are left unharmed.[33]

Because no one knew anything about the fur seal, the secretary of the treasury appointed a young artist-naturalist, Henry Wood Elliott of the Smithsonian Institution, as a special agent to conduct a study of the animals. He began his studies by trying to obtain an estimate of the seal population. During his first six weeks on St. Paul Island in the Pribilofs, he also somehow found the time to court and marry the daughter of a former Russian official.[34]

Thus began the work Elliott would labor over for at least fifty years. By the time Healy entered the Bering Sea, Elliot had estimated the fur seal population at three million breeding seals. Elliott felt that the "highly polygamous nature of the breeding bulls would allow the fur company to take one hundred thousand bachelor seals each year without injury to the natural increase of the herd, '*provided no abnormal cause of destruction occurred.*'[35] Perhaps officials of the Treasury Department realized that such a lucrative source of income located in an isolated region would naturally attract the interest of those who wished to grow wealthy without worrying about the consequences of their actions. In any case, Washington possessed only one federal organization that had the legal right to enforce federal law upon the sea: the U.S. Revenue Cutter Service.

As early as 1868, the cutter *Wayanda* sailed northward "for the purpose of preventing the killing of fur-bearing animals." Early the next year, the service ordered Lieutenants Robert Henderson and Winslow B. Barnes to the Pribilof Islands "to prevent illicit traffic and the violation of the revenue laws, with particular reference to . . . the killing of fur seals."[36]

Eventually, the cutters assigned to the Bering Sea received many "tack on" duties, such as providing medical care to isolated settlements and conducting search and rescue missions. Nevertheless, except for 1876 when no cutters sailed northward, the primary duty of every cutter in the Bering Sea region, from 1868 to 1911, was protecting the fur seals from poachers. First Lieutenant Healy's foray into the Bering Sea in 1877 provides an example of this work.

Captain Bailey, as per custom and regulations, wrote as regularly as possible to the Treasury Department of his work in the Bering Sea. He usually sent out his reports when the *Rush* arrived in a port substantial enough to suggest that his communication would reach Washington, D.C., in a reasonable amount of time. In most cases, mail went out when the *Rush* reached Unalaska and again when it reached home port. Some of the reports handwritten by commanding officers in the Bering Sea detail in crabbed penmanship the worst of everything that had happened to a cutter. This is understandable, as most of the cutter fleet comprised aged ships. Furthermore, as is often the case among a group of different people, the writing styles varied from very poor to very good. Captain Bailey's case proved exceptional in that he had a brand-new cutter; thus he made no mention of cutter-related problems in his reports. His writing style over his first venture into the Bering Sea proved very concise, almost to the point of being terse. Despite the captain's brevity, however, his reports make evident the nature of the work in the Bering Sea.

After departing Unalaska, the *Rush* stopped at the Pribilof Islands to check for illegal sealing. Captain Bailey ordered Healy to detail an officer and two crewmen to remain at St. George Island as guards against poachers. The cutter then worked northward to St. Lawrence Island, arriving there on July 15, 1877.

The island, located southwest of the Bering Strait and closer to Siberia than to Alaska, proved a natural stopping point for cutters headed for the northern reaches of the Bering Sea.[37]

The *Rush*'s track line next took the crew to St. Michael, a small settlement near the mouth of the Yukon River. On Tuesday, July 17, the officer of the deck made the following entry in the cutter's journal: "At the request of all the white inhabitants of St. Michael's, took on board an Indian by the name of Konigan for passage to San Francisco[,] he being accused of the murder of a white man by the name of Edward Boyle, said Konigan to be turned over to the proper authorities at San Francisco where several parties from this place would appear against him."[38]

From St. Michael, the *Rush*, now transporting an alleged criminal, worked southward, stopping once again at St. Paul Island to check for illegal sealing, and returned to Unalaska on July 29. After a few days of "rest" and refitting, the cutter again made preparations for continuing on its journey. Indeed, "resting" and "relaxing" are two words that do not convey the reality of a sailor's life in the small settlement of Unalaska in the Aleutian Islands.

First, the cutter needed to take on more coal. No enlisted person that coaled steam vessels for the U.S. Revenue Cutter Service or the U.S. Navy ever left records of their fond memories of the dirty manual labor. Large naval ships often employed a band to help pass the time, but on board a small cutter only the curses of men and the rustling of coal pierced the air. Depending on the commanding officer, if the cursing got too loud, the men received punishment. Coal dust settled in every nook and cranny on board a cutter. Surviving photographs taken of crews after coaling show just how completely the coal dust covered the men. Once coaled, the cutter then needed a thorough cleaning. The only thing the crew had to look forward to after coaling at Unalaska was the plentiful fresh water to wash up in. After this intense manual labor, the routine maintenance of the cutter, such as scraping paint, continued.

The only recreational activities available to the enlisted men involved hiking in the local area. A tradition eventually developed for members new to the patrol to hike to the top of Mount Ballyhoo and place their names and comments in a logbook kept there in a metal container. As the years passed, and Unalaska's size increased, officers acquired special recreational buildings. It is not known whether the enlisted men had the same type of facilities. No doubt many among the enlisted found someone with illegal liquor.[39]

Before the *Rush* departed Unalaska, Captain Bailey informed Washington that he had handed his prisoner over to officers on board the steamer *St. Paul*, which was bound directly for San Francisco. As for the captain's future plans, he intended to cruise to Attu, an island at the far western end of the Aleutian Chain, and remain in the Bering Sea region, as he put it, "as long as the weather will permit and my provisions hold out." He pointed out that no illegal vessels cruised near the Pribilofs.[40]

Cruising along the Aleutian Islands, the crew found themselves within the area used for hunting sea otters. Captain Bailey pointed out that Attu and Atka "are the only two settlements of natives" that lie to the west of Ommiak, which is the island west of Unalaska. While the Alaska Commercial Company maintained a store at Attu, the sea otter hunt proved so poor that the company felt it might have to close its doors. "If they should," wrote Bailey, "the natives will suffer for tea, sugar, + flour which seem to be the actual necessities of life among the Alleutions [sic]." At Atka, Captain Bailey and First Lieutenant Healy found "upward of 200 inhabitants who seem to be in better circumstances, as they get more otter, or enough to keep them in tea, sugar, etc."[41]

By September 1, the *Rush* had returned to the Pribilof Islands. Finding no illegal activity, the crew returned again to Unalaska and remained there for ten days before setting off once more for the islands. Captain Bailey felt that the lack of evidence of seal poaching from the previous trip meant he could now order the return of the guards he had placed on the island. When the *Rush* returned the second time, however, Bailey learned of a schooner nearby that seemed very interested in finding out whether a revenue cutter still patrolled the area. After discussing the situation with Healy, his executive officer, Captain Bailey decided to remain in the area. Despite "very bad weather," Bailey kept the *Rush* on patrol until October 12. Feeling confident that the impending bad weather would put an end to the poachers' activities, Bailey shaped a course back to Unalaska.[42]

On November 8, 1877, back at home port in San Francisco, Captain Bailey wrote his final report on his activities in the Bering Sea region. Just before leaving Unalaska for the south, Bailey had reported on four white men, who had married native women and had families, settling on [Sanak?] Island. Bailey had earlier interviewed two of the men. They already knew of the new law against white men killing fur-bearing animals of the sea and had sent the other two men to San Francisco to petition the government for a dispensation. They felt that as long as they were married to native women, they should have the same rights as the natives. Bailey agreed, but could do nothing about the situation.[43]

Ultimately, Captain Bailey's report devoted a mere thirteen handwritten pages to his entire patrol of Alaskan waters, which lasted from May to November. Despite its brevity, the report highlights the unique character of those who sailed in the Bering Sea and Arctic regions. Every report contained information on law enforcement. As far as now can be determined, none of the commanding officers, and few, if any, of their junior officers had any scientific training. Yet, because they labored in such an isolated and uncharted region, their reports contain anthropological, meteorological, oceanographic, zoological, ornithological, and geological information. If one looks closely at the captain's brief report, one finds evidence of concern for the natives of the Far North, as well as for the area's wildlife. True, some of the captain's concern comes from the knowledge that to hunt some of these mammals into extinction was to end a source of income for the United States; yet the captain's report also contains a glimmer of concern for the potential loss of a species, in and of itself.

First Lieutenant Healy's experiences with both Captain Henriques and Captain Bailey honed his ability to compose useful reports. Using his natural intelligence and training, Healy became a master at this duty.

On November 8, the day Captain Bailey penned his final report, Healy received a communication that ordered him "home." The orders included the opportunity to report "to [the Treasury] Department[, Washington, D.C.,] for examination" for the rank of captain. Healy successfully completed the examination on January 14, 1878, and immediately reported to the 99-foot, single-screw cutter *William E. Chandler* at New York City. The harbor cutter was to be First Lieut. Michael A. Healy's first permanent command.[44]

Any revenue officer in command of a cutter in the nation's busiest harbor faced the constant routine of boarding ships and checking cargoes. During the month of July 1878, for example, Healy's crew spent twenty-six days under way, boarding 409 vessels, and seizing 155 of them for violations. This work did not include the hard labor needed to keep the cutter properly seaworthy. The maintenance and boarding alone proved a large amount of work for a crew of only two officers and nine enlisted men.[45]

A commanding officer in New York City also faced official visits from any government dignitary visiting the city. On July 11, 1878, for instance, Healy logged, "Hon. John Sherman, [secretary of the treasury], and party, came on board. [On the] 13th Secretary + party left the vessel." While sometimes an onerous duty, Healy, like his older brothers, knew the value of cultivating good relations with high officials. Throughout his career, Healy showed a strong interest in affairs concerning the officer corps and did not hesitate to write to politicians he met while commanding the *Chandler* to share his concerns.[46]

By 1880, First Lieut. Michael A. Healy had spent over two years command-ing the *Chandler*. At that point in his career, these years proved the longest period of time that Healy had been stationed relatively close to Mary Jane and Frederick.

That same year, across the continent, Capt. Calvin L. Hooper, command-ing the cutter *Corwin* at San Francisco, pondered his orders. Hooper had just received a special mission to the Arctic. The Treasury Department gave Hooper the choice of whom he wished to serve as his second-in-command. Captains in the U.S. Revenue Cutter Service knew, either by personal observations or by reputation, those officers senior enough to fill the important billet of ex-ecutive officer. In 1880, Captain Hooper, after serving in four cutters on the West Coast, including duty at Sitka, knew of only one first lieutenant for the position. Healy and Hooper had both served in the *Lincoln* in 1869 as second lieutenants. Hooper's choice of Michael A. Healy as his executive officer for the special mission changed Healy's life and led to his first brush with fame.[47]

5

HEALY'S POLAR PASSION

Upon learning of his special orders to report to San Francisco, Michael and Mary Jane Healy discussed how this assignment would affect their family. For almost three years, Michael and Mary Jane had enjoyed the closest thing to a regular homelife that they had ever experienced in their fifteen years of marriage. Because Healy's orders mentioned only a special assignment, it appeared the duty might be temporary. Nevertheless, even if the family traveled by the newly available transcontinental train, Healy's latest assignment meant a long and difficult journey for Mary Jane and ten-year-old Frederick. Libby Beaman, for example, who accompanied her husband on a transcontinental train ride to San Francisco in 1879, described the journey as a "harrowing trek": "the engine [belched] black smoke that covered us so that we looked more like Negroes than ourselves. The engine also spewed live coals that at one time set the baggage car on fire and, on another occasion, caused two bags of mail to burn."[1] Furthermore, it was possible that Michael would spend only one or two years on the West Coast and then be able to return again to the East. Mary Jane and Michael decided together that she and Frederick should remain on the East Coast until Michael learned about his next set of orders. Therefore, for part of 1880, Mary Jane and Frederick lived in Portland, Maine, close to the patriarch of the Healy family, Bishop James A. Healy.[2]

Captain Hooper's decision to request First Lieutenant Healy to act as his executive officer on board the *Corwin* seemed a logical one. Two changes slowly taking place in the Bering Sea and Arctic regions, however, would come to affect revenue officers of this time. Healy, caught up in a succession of transfers, probably did not recognize the importance of these changes. In 1880, however, both Captain Hooper and First Lieutenant Healy faced the results of the new currents in the regions.

The first change came many years before on July 24, 1848, when Capt. Thomas Roys strained to see through the dismal and enveloping cold fog of the Bering Strait. Captain Roys had many things on his mind that Monday, not least among them the safe navigation of his small 275-ton whaling bark, the *Superior*. Of equal concern to the whaling captain was his own decision to press forward on a voyage of discovery into an unknown region for whalers, the Western Arctic. Three years earlier, he had learned from a Russian officer in Petropavlovsk, on the Kamchatka Peninsula, of strange whales sighted north of the Bering Strait. Roys determined that he would investigate these sightings at his first opportunity.

The tough full-bearded, one-handed master—Roys later lost his left hand in 1858, during an experiment with a rocket harpoon—had concealed from his crew both his plan and his destination.[3] Even the owners of the *Superior*, the Grinnell Minturn Company, knew nothing of their captain's plan. Years later, Roys wrote, "There is heavy responsibility resting upon the master who shall dare cruise different from the known grounds, as it will not only be his death stroke if he does not succeed, but the whole of his officers and crew will unite to put him down."[4] When the officers and men of the *Superior* learned, on July 20, of their captain's plans, fear swept the ship from stem to stern. Indeed, "The first mate burst into tears." Close to mutiny, the crew moved slowly to carry out Roys' orders.[5] But then, as if the entire journey had been scripted by an adventure writer, the *Superior* broke out of the fog. From that moment, "Roys knew he had made the greatest whaling discovery of the century."[6]

Whales in huge numbers surrounded the *Superior*. On July 25, Roys, who bore the scars of a fighting whale, took charge and ordered a boat lowered to go after their first whale. His crew, who, up to that moment, had "never expected to see home again," realized they had encountered a species they had never seen before. They took their first bowhead whale (*Balaena mysticetus*) three miles north of Big Diomede Island in the Bering Strait. Roys' crew became the first commercial hunters to kill a whale north of the Aleutians. Roys' discovery completely changed the American whaling industry and led directly to some of the most important moments in Michael A. Healy's life.[7]

By the time Healy reported on board the *Corwin* in 1880, American whaling had radically changed. In the first half of the nineteenth century, the industry had boomed. There was a constant search for new hunting grounds. The strong market for whale oil, which was principally used as an illuminant in lamps, ensured large profits for the whaling shipowners. (The wealth, however, did not necessarily trickle down to all of the members of the whaling crews.) In addition, baleen, used by some species of whale to strain plankton, became as important a resource supplied by the sea mammals as their oil. Baleen "was the only material available in the nineteenth century that approximated the properties supplied by spring steel, celluloid and flexible plastics of the twentieth."[8] After the American Civil War, the fashion industry became the largest consumer of baleen, using it to manufacture corset stays and skirt hoops.

For decades, whaling required little in the way of expensive technology. Shipowners had the luxury of a steady market that demanded no large outlays of capital for improvements. After 1750, for example, "when tryworks were first put aboard ship for rendering oil at sea, the only changes in technology or methods were minor ones."[9] The changes that did take place—which mainly concerned the perfection of harpoons, darting guns, and bomb-lance shoulder guns—were inexpensive and "merely reduced the losses of whales already struck."[10]

The market began to change for the worse in 1865. First, the American Civil War caused a rapid shift in energy demands from whale oil to petroleum. Furthermore, naval battles during the war destroyed a great many whaling ships. By 1875, whale oil was selling for just 65.25¢ per gallon, whereas ten years earlier a gallon had sold for $1.45.[11] The 1870s marks the decade when many American owners of whalers tried to counter this decline in the industry by fitting their ships with auxiliary steam as an extra power source.

Roys' discovery of the bowhead fishery, however, brought about great changes in the whaling industry. The bowhead whale is a large, docile, slow-moving mammal and is easy for whalers to take. Each mammal yielded an average of one hundred barrels of oil and fifteen hundred pounds of baleen. The new whaling grounds "became the most productive source of whale products in the industry" for at least sixty years.[12] One source estimates that from 1849, when Roys made his discovery, until 1914, when the fishery died, a total of 18,650 bowheads were killed from a stock estimated at between twenty to thirty thousand whales.[13]

Whalers after the bowhead worked from the Bering Strait northward, and then generally turned eastward along the northern coast of Alaska, sometimes traveling as far east as Herschel Island, near Canada's Mackenzie River delta. Some whaling also occurred out of shore-based stations and native villages.

Whaling was a dangerous profession. Working above the Bering Strait entailed additional dangers. The season generally lasted from April to October. Any later than October, ships risked being caught and crushed by the polar ice. The movement of the ice pack, which usually floats not far offshore even in the summer, is capricious, governed by the wind and the currents. Even during the normal hunting season, a sudden gale could trap a ship in the deadly pack ice. In 1871, for example, thirty-two whalers were abandoned to the ice on the northwest coast of Alaska. Five years later, twelve more were lost, while ten others were lost in the Arctic itself. After 1876, steam power seemed at least one solution to the dangers faced by sailors aboard these ships. This type of propulsion allowed the vessels a means of maneuvering that did not depend upon the wind. What kept the ships in this dangerous area after 1875 was the incentive of rising prices for baleen in the fashion industry. The completion of the transcontinental railroad also increased the value of whaling in this region, for baleen could now make its way faster to Eastern markets. This development also changed a whaling tradition that had lasted for more than three decades.

From at least the 1840s on, whalers departed New England ports in the autumn on voyages that lasted two to three years. They journeyed to the West Coast around the Horn, or sometimes around the Cape of Good Hope, and began working in the warm areas of the Pacific. The whalers arrived at the Hawaiian Islands around March to refit. After a short period, they sailed northward seeking right whales (*Eubalaena glacialis*) in the Gulf of Alaska and bowheads in the Sea of Okhotsk and, after 1848, moving to areas above the Bering Strait. In October, at the end of the season, the whalers would head south again to the Hawaiian Islands for refitting and then into the warm areas of the Pacific only to land once again in the islands in March. They continued this cycle until returning to New England.[14]

The transcontinental railroad, however, made owners see the advantage of having whalers stop at San Francisco instead of Hawaii. Once whalers began moving farther east into the Arctic, steam whalers became more popular, and it was more efficient to operate out of San Francisco. By 1880, the whaling industry had built a strong center in San Francisco.[15]

The second current that precipitated change in Healy's duties began when, during the early decades of the nineteenth century, there developed an intense interest in the Arctic and specifically in the North American Arctic. Some of the curiosity stemmed from commercial desires to find a northern maritime route through the Western Hemisphere to the Indies. Down through the years, this quest has become known as the search for the Northwest Passage. A number of explorers perished in the Arctic region while on this quest. Sir John Franklin's expedition, for example, set sail on May 19, 1845, in search of the route, and all 128 men disappeared into the vastness of the Canadian North.[16] Even beyond the commercial advantages of finding the Northwest Passage, the Arctic became a literary and artistic theme, with painters creating fantastic scenes from the drawings of those who ventured into the frigid north. John Barrow, the secretary of the British Admiralty, led the way in promoting Arctic exploration. Barrow felt such endeavors were "in every way worthy of a great and prosperous and enlightened nation."[17]

For years after 1845, leaders of expeditions to the Far North stated two primary reasons for penetrating the polar regions of North America. The explorers usually said their first goal was to locate the remains of the Franklin Expedition. Adventurers gave as a second reason the advancement of scientific knowledge of a largely unknown region. A deeper examination shows, however, that national prestige had entered the picture. According to Farley Mowat in *The Polar Passion*, by the mid-nineteenth century, the "North American Arctic was very much a reality to people of every walk of life. It had become real [to the people of that time], and it stayed real for them because men of their kind were venturing into its remote fastness unprotected by the elaborate mechanical shields that we now demand whenever we step out of our air-conditioned sanctuaries."[18] This led to a worldwide "polar passion" that eventually focused on the attainment of the North Pole.

In 1878, James Gordon Bennett, owner of the *New York Herald*, proposed an expedition to explore the Arctic. A year earlier, Bennett and his newspaper had sponsored the search for the lost missionary, Dr. David Livingston, by Henry M. Stanley. An expedition to the Far North, they reasoned, might help bolster readership even more.

Lieut. George Washington De Long, of the U.S. Navy, received the nod to lead the expedition. He had gained his first experience in the polar regions during the 1873 search and rescue of the members of the *Polaris* Expedition in Greenland. De Long's first comments upon viewing the Arctic in the Greenland area seem less than enthusiastic. "I never in my life saw such a dreary land of desolation," he wrote, "and I hope I may never find myself cast away in such a perfectly God-forsaken place." Emma De Long, the lieutenant's wife, however, later wrote that the "polar virus was in his blood and would not let him rest."[19]

His statement about the Arctic aside, De Long contacted Bennett about sponsoring a naval expedition to the North Pole. The naval lieutenant based his plan to reach the pole by ship upon two theories that were then much in vogue. Capt. Silas Bent, a naval hydrographer, felt that a branch of the Japan Current swept up through the Bering Strait and cut a swath straight to the North Pole. The other theory came from the German geographer August Heinrich Petermann, who theorized that an extension of Greenland extended to Wrangel Island, just above the northern Siberian coast. If these two theories proved correct, De Long felt there would be little danger in working his ship through the ice.[20]

The *Pandora*, an English ship built in 1861 at the Pembroke Dockyard in Wales as a gunboat for the Royal Navy, became the vessel that Sir Allen Young would use for two private expeditions to the Canadian Arctic. Young had the hull strengthened and reworked the engine so that it could provide two-hundred horsepower at about sixty revolutions per minute. Prior to Bennett's purchase of the ship for the expedition, the *Pandora* had crossed the Arctic Circle six times. The ship was 146 feet in length, with a beam of twenty-five feet. Fully loaded and rigged, she drew approximately fifteen feet of water and registered at 244 gross tons. Bennett, after spending more than $50,000 in six months of preparation, renamed the vessel the *Jeannette*. Historians of polar exploration now refer to De Long's quest as the *Jeannette* Expedition. Although the modifications and refitting were not without conflict and compromise, most considered the ship and its crew of thirty-three "more sturdily fortified for ice encounter than any previous exploring ship."[21]

Before his departure, De Long held a conference of whaling captains in San Francisco to obtain their views on the success of his expedition. De Long learned that not all of these tough seamen held high hopes for the venture. Capt. Ebenezer Nye, of New Bedford, Massachusetts, and master of the *Mount Wollaston*, hesitated to give his opinion. After continual prodding by the naval lieutenant, Captain Nye replied, "Put her [the *Jeannette*] into the ice and let her drift, and you may get through or you may go to the devil, and the chances are about equal."[22] As fate would have it, Nye's own ship also played an important role in the 1880 patrol of the cutter *Corwin*.

De Long and his crew set sail from San Francisco on July 8, 1879. The *Jeannette* carried enough supplies for three years of work in the Arctic. Lieutenant De Long's tactics called for touching in at Herald Island. Upon reaching the island, he proposed building a cairn and depositing a record of their progress. From there, they would continue on along the coast of Wrangel to the North Pole, leaving similar cairns at twenty-five mile intervals.

By the spring of 1880, no word of the expedition had reached the United States. Although this caused some uneasiness, no one yet expressed fear for the crew. At about the same time, however, two New Bedford whalers, Captain Nye's *Mount Wollaston* and another ship, the *Vigilant*, had gone missing.

With three ships missing in the Far North, the civilian head of the U.S. Revenue Cutter Service within the Treasury Department, Maj. Ezra W. Clark, recognized certain advantages for the service. (Perhaps to command a certain amount of respect when dealing with the officer corps of the U.S. Revenue Cutter Service, Clark, then a civilian employee of the Treasury Department and in charge of the service, kept his Civil War military title of major.) First, there was the chance for publicity. Just as important, this publicity might allow the service to gain control of the operations of the cutters in Alaska. At the time, the cutters' movements remained under the command of the collector of customs of San Francisco. Clark thus began a lengthy correspondence with Captain Hooper over the captain's orders for the 1880 cruise to the Arctic.[23]

"I have given a great deal of thought and attention to the subject of this cruise," Clark wrote in a letter to Captain Hooper. "I think it offers a good opportunity to make history. . . . If you have the opportunity to plant the Revenue flag on land where no flag has ever been planted before . . . [I] know you will do it. If you are the first to inform the world [that Herald Island] is a part of Wrangel Land, you will get the credit." He ordered Hooper to submit a report of the voyage in a form "as full and complete as possible." Clark also suggested that Captain Hooper encourage talented members of the crew, meaning officers, to supplement the report with drawings. To help encourage a detailed and well-written report, he even promised Hooper sole authorship of the published report.[24] In another letter, Clark wrote, "Healy is sent to you, as being your choice. He is a very good man. . . . [He] has had great experience and is level headed. He will not fail you in an emergency." With this, Clark concluded that he had given Hooper "everything you have asked for."[25]

Capt. Calvin L. Hooper and First Lieut. Michael A. Healy's 140-foot topsail schooner, *Corwin*, also had an inverted cylinder steam engine with a single propeller. The cutter normally carried eight officers and thirty-three enlisted men. For firepower, the *Corwin* carried three guns. The cutter's construction ideally suited her for work in the Arctic. The *Corwin*'s heavily timbered frame of Oregon fir meant the cutter could withstand ice pressure. Australian ironwood also reinforced the cutter's bow. In addition to Captain Hooper and First Lieutenant Healy, other officers listed for the 1880 cruise were: Second Lieut. Edmund Burke, Third Lieut. C. D. Myrick, Third Lieut. J. Wyckoff, Chief Eng. James Wayson, First Ast. Eng. A. L. Broadbent, Second Ast. Eng. John G. Balls, and Second Ast. Eng. F. E. Owen. Of the men, First Assistant Engineer Broadbent would play an important role in Healy's later career.[26]

Although those cutters of the U.S. Revenue Cutter Service that ventured into the Arctic had been reinforced for duty in the ice, they were not true polar icebreakers. Polar icebreakers are heavily reinforced. They make their way through the ice pack by pushing aside the ice whenever possible. When the sea ice becomes too thick, they use their great power to ride up upon the ice and crush it with their weight. The icebreaker then backs off and repeats the process until it can make its way through. Not until World War II did the U.S. Coast Guard receive its first true polar icebreaker.

In contrast, when the *Corwin*, like later cutters of the U.S. Revenue Cutter Service, entered the ice it attempted to dodge the ice floes. When the pack ice began to consolidate, the cutters attempted to push some of the ice aside with their small steam engines. As the ice thickened, the cutters faced real danger of being crushed by the ice, better known by those who worked in the polar region as "being nipped." A captain of any cutter that worked in the ice needed excellent seamanship skills and the judgment to know when to beat a retreat. Once beset, there were only two ways to free a ship: let it drift until, with any luck, it found open water; or hope the wind opens a lead—an opening in the ice pack—and follow it to safety. All those who commanded ships entering the ice in the nineteenth and early twentieth centuries needed a large amount of maritime experience. (Some captains did try blasting the ice with explosives, the usual result being simply a blackening of the surface of the sea ice.)

The *Corwin* departed San Francisco for the Far North at 3:30 p.m. on Saturday, May 15, 1880.[27] Despite its peaceful name, the North Pacific in late spring and again in fall feels the influence of most of the low-pressure weather systems entering North America. Winds of fifty to sixty knots pile up seas of forty feet and higher, along with horizontal rain and snow.

After twelve days of "stormy, disagreeable weather," the *Corwin* reached the small settlement of Unalaska. Hooper's report from Unalaska noted that the *Corwin*, "although deeply loaded and driven hard to make a good passage, proved herself an excellent seaboat and in every way staunch and seaworthy." Healy and the crew of the cutter, even on June 7, found the "hills . . . still covered with snow, and the air . . . raw and cold." Healy oversaw the fitting "out [of] the crew with clothing of all kinds required for the cruise—rubber boots, underclothing, socks, mittens, blankets, coats, etc." Hooper wrote to headquarters that it had been difficult obtaining a crew due to the scarcity of sailors in San Francisco. Some came on board, Hooper wrote, "with only one suit of clothes, and no money to buy more; they are now, however, comfortably provided." The nature of the mission meant that the *Corwin* had a real chance of being beset in the ice for the winter. Guarding against such an eventuality, Hooper ordered ninety gallons of cranberries taken on board from the Alaska Commercial Company at Unalaska, as he felt they made an "excellent antiscorbutic." He also ordered extra food. To further justify this extra expense to the penny-pinching U.S. Revenue Cutter Service, Hooper pointed out that, if they found the missing whalers, he could transfer the extra supplies to them. If "these things are not used," he further added, "they will be turned over to the company on our return and no charge made for them."

The next day, June 8, Captain Hooper ordered a course shaped for the Priblilof Islands. Unlike Healy's former commanding officer, Captain Bailey, Hooper's written reports were lengthy and detailed. Of course, Hooper realized his writings might end up in print.

By the time the cutter departed for the Pribilofs, the crew of the *Corwin* had started to learn about their new executive officer. They saw a slightly built, short man, with dark straight hair, kept shorter than the normal style common to that day. He had a moderately broad nose. Healy wore a medium-sized, somewhat unruly, mustache with the ends extending well below the corners of his lips, a style sometimes known as a walrus mustache. His hands appeared small, but showed the wear of rugged work on the deck of a sailing ship.

Healy made up for his size in three ways. First, no one ever questioned his knowledge of seamanship. Those before and aft the mast recognized Healy as an excellent man of the sea.

Second, First Lieutenant Healy, by 1880, had perfected what today's military likes to call a "command presence." His deep-set piercing blue eyes, combined with his loud voice, perfected over the years of working on the decks of sailing ships, made subordinates quail.

Third, because of his experience, Healy did not brook disobedience. He expected immediate and unquestioning obedience to any order he gave. Any sluggishness, or the slightest suggestion of disobedience, on the part of an officer or enlisted man, caused those blue eyes to bore into him and that stentorian voice to echo in his ears.

After delivering the mail at St. Paul on June 9, Hooper ordered a device known as an icebreaker rigged onto the bow of the *Corwin*. At 8:00 p.m., the navigator plotted a course for Cape Romanzof, Alaska, near the Yukon River delta. Interestingly, near Cape Romanzof are two locations named after early U.S. Revenue Cutter Service officers who worked in Alaska. Approximately twenty miles to the south of the cape is the settlement and bay of Hooper, named after Capt. Calvin L. Hooper, and approximately eighteen miles to the east of the cape is the town and bay of Scammon, named after Capt. Charles Scammon.[28]

Two days later, in the early morning hours, a lookout reported spotting "ice blink" to the east. In the polar regions, skies are usually overcast with low, grayish clouds. In the right conditions, whenever the sun breaks through the clouds, its rays will reflect off the ice and create a lighter spot on the clouds. Many times this is the first indication a navigator has that ice is nearby. (Water sky, another phenomenon of the ice pack, is useful to navigators while moving through the ice. In this case, a darker spot on the clouds appears if there is open water some-where within the ice.) Soon the *Corwin's* lookouts spotted grease ice, which looks like oil upon the water and is usually the first ice encountered near the pack. Pancake ice follows next and finally the pack itself. Hooper ordered the cutter to follow the edge of the pack. "Seeing no prospect of getting around the ice to northward," Hooper ordered the *Corwin* eastward. A sudden gale struck, shoving the sea ice into a tighter pack along their proposed track line. Hooper decided to retreat to Nunivak Island, which lies off Alaska's southwestern coast, and in the early afternoon dropped anchor in a protected harbor.

Hooper recorded that the island's inhabitants, having never seen a steam ves-sel, shied away from the strange thing belching smoke in their harbor and ran into the surrounding hills. Later, they returned to the beach and, reluctantly, some of the braver ones came on board the *Corwin.*

On June 13, with calmer weather on their side, Hooper again ordered the *Corwin* to sea. All went well, as the cutter made its way through a lead, with the ice thickness "two to eight feet above the water to twenty-five to thirty feet under the water." The notoriously thick Bering Sea fog drifted over the cutter. Nevertheless, despite the ice and fog, the cutter made "acceptable" time in the opinions of Hooper and Healy and soon lay forty miles off the coast of Cape Romanzof.

On June 15, however, all progress stopped. What at first seemed like a minor delay turned more serious. A crewman near the bow of the *Corwin* sounded the water with a lead line. (This process involves throwing a rope [a line], which has a weighted lead on one end and measurements along its length, over the side of the ship to determine the depth of the water. The leadsman calls out the depth to the officers on the bridge.) The leadsman's reports showed that the cutter was not in deep water surrounded by ice, but was, in fact, in water that measured only five fathoms (thirty feet) deep. Concern began to seep into Hooper's mind that the ice might cause them to run aground. Indeed, the *Corwin* did receive "some pretty sharp nips." At one point, the cutter found itself "lifted bodily up several feet, and held suspended for some minutes." To add to the danger, the ice jammed the rudder hard over, carrying away the steering gear. Captain Hooper described his crucial repair solution to Healy, who then supervised the work. All hands piled sacks of coal on the *Corwin's* forecastle to shift the weight of the bow forward and thereby raise the stern. One of the worst enemies of anyone working in the northern latitudes is moisture on the skin. The crewmen of the *Corwin*, working on a cold, damp deck, with wet material, could not avoid getting their hands drenched. This caused hands already numb to suffer more pain. Despite these hazards, however, the crew managed to repair the rudder and fix it so that it "could be taken in, out of the way of danger, in a few minutes."

The *Corwin* continued to drift according to the caprice of wind and ice. On June 18, the wind finally shifted the ice sufficiently to permit the cutter to escape the pack. Once free, the navigator shaped a course to near St. Lawrence Island.

In 1879, Healy's former commanding officer, Capt. G. W. Bailey, who was still in command of the *Rush*, had reported stories of "the wholesale starvation of the natives" on St. Lawrence Island.[29] Hooper's orders directed him, if possible, to investigate these claims. As the *Corwin* passed along the northern side of the island, Capt. Hooper stopped at four villages. In three of the four villages, all of the inhabitants had died of starvation. The cuttermen found some survivors at a fourth settlement. Captain Hooper estimated that at least four hundred natives on this island alone had died of starvation over the previous two years. Hooper laid the problem squarely on the shoulders of maritime traders and whalers. He reasoned that the people of the island had spent more time obtaining furs and ivory for the sailors than providing for their families. Furthermore, what the natives usually received for their trade goods was illegal liquor. "So long as the rum lasts they do nothing but drink and fight." The revenue captain ended his report with the conclusion that, "unless some prompt action be taken by the Government to prevent them from obtaining whiskey, they will in a few years become extinct."

Healy, of course, also witnessed the grisly scenes on the island, and they affected him deeply. Eight years later, for example, when interviewed by a reporter in New York City, Healy still recalled the "horrible example of the effect of the illicit trade in whiskey." He began thinking about how to stop such mass starvation.[30]

Finished with his work on St. Lawrence Island, Captain Hooper ordered the cutter to the Siberian coastline. The cutter first touched at Plover Bay [Bukhta Provideniya] and then again at St. Lawrence Bay [Zaliv Lavrentiya], the last known location the *Jeannette* had visited to coal the ship. The *Corwin's* track line next included the Diomede Islands, located in the narrow confines of the Bering Strait. Captain Hooper kept working his cutter eastward along the pack's edge toward Kotzebue Sound. Whenever the lookouts shouted out a vessel in sight, the cuttermen boarded and asked about the missing whalers and the *Jeannette*. Finding Kotzebue Sound covered in ice, Hooper decided to head south through the Bering Strait to St. Michael to coal and clean the boilers.

While at St. Michael, Captain Hooper investigated charges that the American schooner *Leo* had traded with the natives, selling them whiskey, arms, and ammunition. The *Corwin* departed on July 10, after firing a few volleys from their guns "for the benefit of the natives," in search of the traders. Hooper finally caught up with the schooner on July 13 in Kotzebue Sound. Captain Hooper called away a boarding party of "officers and seamen." A search of the *Leo* revealed much whiskey in boxes labeled "Bay-rum," "Jamaica ginger," "pain-killer," and "Florida water," along with five breech-loading Henry repeating rifles. Hooper seized the *Leo* and detailed Second Lieut. W. H. Hand to sail the schooner back to San Francisco. Interestingly, Healy had a connection to the *Leo*. In its previous life, the ship had sailed as the former cutter *Reliance* that Healy had served in as navigator around the Horn from Baltimore to San Francisco.[31]

Captain Hooper continued working along the Alaskan coast, still seeking information about the missing whalers and the *Jeannette*. On July 14, the lookout on *Corwin* spotted the whaler *Helen Mar*. When Hooper questioned the master, George Bauldry reported last seeing the two whalers forty miles southeast of Herald Island. The master also told of his crew's own trouble being trapped in an unusual October freeze. Such a freeze in calm weather can form six inches of sea ice overnight. The *Helen Mar* barely escaped the ice. Later, Captain Bauldry said of his experience: "No human being can imagine what we had gone through, or what anxiety of mind I suffered with all these lives dependent upon me. Neither the mate, Mr. Carter, or myself had had a bit of sleep for five nights or days, and I feared he would die, he was so nervous. To induce sleep, I gave him a large amount of laudanum, and he lay with both eyes wide open, yet in the deepest sleep. Had there been fifteen miles more of ice to go through, we certainly would have gone to the bottom." It is no wonder that Captain Bauldry informed Hooper that he felt the crews of the two whalers "will never be heard of again."[32]

Near Cape Lizbourne, above the Arctic Circle, a party from the cutter located veins of coal. The veins, discovered earlier by the cutter's ice pilot, Capt. E. E. Smith, proved useful to the cutter. The Corwin coalmine can still be found on twenty-first century navigational charts of the Arctic.

Besides searching for the missing vessels, Hooper's instructions ordered him to record soundings, chart corrections, and other hydrographic observations. Quite naturally he delegated this responsibility to Healy, who had a "natural interest" in the task. In 1880, the maritime Arctic had few accurate charts, and Healy would continue the work he began on the *Corwin* over the next fifteen years. Some of the more unusual hazards that Healy faced in charting came at Chamisso Island, in Kotzebue Sound. The surveying party went onto the island in an attempt to obtain an accurate latitude and longitude with a sextant. There, they met one of the smallest but most obnoxious denizens of the Arctic. Healy, in attempting to use the sextant, found the "air so filled with mosquitoes that it was . . . impossible [to use the device;] they covered the lenses of the instrument and the artificial horizon, and attacked the observers with such vigor and in such numbers that they were compelled to give up the attempt."[33] On the top of the island, someone had erected two monument poles bearing the names *Blossom*, *Plover*, and *Herald*, all ships of early explorers to the area. Hooper ordered the *Corwin*'s name carved into the monument.

The search for the missing whalers and the *Jeannette* continued, both along the Alaskan coast and out toward Herald Island. By August 3, the *Corwin* lay thirty-five miles from the island. Hooper ordered a lookout at the masthead in hopes of seeing some sign of smoke or human habitation. The cutter could get no closer to the island, as the ice had thickened and a fog began forming. Hooper retreated to open water.

After continuing the search in the open sea, Hooper decided to return to Herald Island. This time, the *Corwin* approached to within three miles of the island's high cliffs. Convinced that none of the whalers or the *Jeannette* party had reached the island, Hooper retreated again from the ice. He tried passing south of Herald Island and, following the edge of the pack, reached Wrangel Island. But again, a combination of fog and ice forced him to retreat.

Hooper then ran eastward to Alaska and eventually came to an area off Point Barrow, the northernmost native settlement in Alaska, earning the distinction of commanding the first government ship to reach this village. After a brief stay, Hooper ordered the *Corwin* westward. Along the way, he seized another vessel, the *Loleta*, for trading in illegal firearms and ammunition. This time, the task of taking the vessel back to San Francisco fell to Lieut. John Wyckoff.

Captain Hooper then made one more attempt to reach Wrangel Island. Early in September, he again shaped a westerly course, following the southern edge of the ice pack. As the *Corwin* passed near Herald Island, the temperatures plunged below zero. The lookout soon reported the high hills of

Wrangel Island: ice encircled the island, while the land showed a fresh coat of snow. The cuttermen came to within twenty-five miles of their goal.

Even though it appeared that ice encircled the island throughout the year, Hooper felt that the strongly built *Jeannette* might have bulled its way to a sheltered harbor and sent parties ashore. Nevertheless, with new ice forming, Captain Hooper felt it was time to retreat. "Even to remain in sight of [the island]," he wrote, "was to expose the vessel to great danger of becoming embayed in the ice, as the large quantity of drift ice which lay outside of us, was likely to close in at any minute and compel us to remain all winter." Reluctantly, Hooper ordered the *Corwin* to the south.

In his report to the secretary of the treasury, Captain Hooper stated confidently that he had done everything in his power to locate the *Mount Wollaston*, the *Vigilant*, and the *Jeannette*. He felt that both the *Mount Wollaston* and the *Vigilant* had been crushed by the ice and speculated that none of their crews survived. Even though the ice prevented the *Corwin* from landing a search party on Herald Island, Hooper felt the island was too inhospitable for any castaway sailor to survive on it. "Herald Island is inaccessible to all but birds of the air," Hooper wrote, "and even were it possible for men, poorly provided for such work as they were to reach the island, or find shelter on it, starvation would be sure to follow." As it turned out, Hooper's assumptions proved largely correct: the ice indeed crushed the *Mount Wollaston* and the *Vigilant*, and the cold and exposure killed all survivors.

In the case of the *Jeannette*, however, Hooper remained optimistic. Even though he had received no reliable sightings of the exploring expedition, he felt the crewmembers of the *Jeannette* were far better equipped to survive the rigors of the Arctic than the whalers had been. "I have no fears for the safety of the *Jeannette*," Hooper reported. "The fact that they have not been heard from seems to indicate that the vessel is safe, and that they consider themselves to be able to remain another year at least. Should they be compelled to abandon the vessel and cross over to the mainland, they would have no difficulty in reaching Plover or St. Lawrence Bay [in Siberia], where they would be well cared for by Tchukchis [Chukchis] as, in fact, would be the case at any place on either the Asiatic or Alaskan coast."

When Captain Hooper and the crew of the *Corwin* returned to search the Arctic again in 1881, they learned the fate of the crews of the two whalers. Officers from the cutter discovered that in the autumn of 1880 natives on the north shore of the Chukchi Peninsula had located a dismasted ship close to shore. The natives boarded the ship and found its masts had been cut away to provide firewood. Venturing cautiously below deck, they found "four blackened, emaciated corpses." The natives gathered a few items and retreated, planning to return the next day. The wind shifted, however, and the ship drifted away. Officers from the *Corwin* examined the few items and, from the description of the vessel, identified it as the *Vigilant*.[34]

The *Vigilant* had carried enough food for its crew to winter over at Point Barrow. The officers of the *Corwin* theorized that both whalers were beset by pack ice farther north than the *Helen Mar* had been when it ran into trouble. At least some, if not all, of the crew of the *Mount Wollaston* had made it to the *Vigilant*. Among the items recovered by the natives were the spectacles of Capt. Ebenezer Nye, the man who had warned Lieutenant De Long of the dangers of the ice. Some members of each crew remained on board the *Vigilant*, while others made the desperate choice to try to make it over the ice to land and died a cold death in the attempt.[35]

Hooper also proved to be right about many details concerning the *Jeannette*. Caught in the ice in September 1879, the exploring ship sprung a leak. Lieutenant De Long never succeeded in freeing his ship from the pack. Even as the crew of the *Corwin* searched in 1880 for the *Jeannette*, it drifted deeper into the Arctic. The exploring ship remained at the mercy of the pack ice until June 12, 1881. The ice finally crushed the *Jeannette* some 150 miles north of the New Siberian Islands. The crew loaded supplies into boats and sleds and started the long haul over the ice to the Siberian coast. Sometime during this march, a gale divided the expedition into two parties. Chief Engineer George Melville led twelve survivors to safety at a Russian village on the delta of the Lena River, but De Long and twenty other crewmen perished some 1,200 miles west of Wrangel Island.[36]

Despite not finding the three ships, Captain Hooper had reason to feel a good measure of pride in his accomplishments on this first official mission of the U.S. Revenue Cutter Service north of the Arctic Circle. He had enforced U.S. law in a lawless place. His report, published by the U.S. Government Printing Office, is also full of descriptions of the flora and fauna of what was then a little known region of the world.

Some of Hooper's most interesting observations concern the people of the Far North. His writings reveal the U.S. Revenue Cutter Service crews' ambivalence about the natives they encountered. Healy's feelings mirrored Hooper's when it came to observations about the Eskimo and what actions were needed to help them. Hooper penned some observations that are typical of nineteenth century elitism toward other cultures. When describing the natives of Alaska, his report is sprinkled with words like "dirty," "dull looking," and "lazy." And yet, other parts of the report read as if they were written in the late twentieth, rather than the nineteenth, century. Hooper noted, for example, that using the word "Eskimo" in his report went against his better judgment. He pointed out that, according to one source, "the name 'Eskimo,' . . . was given to the natives of Southern Labrador as a term of derision by the inhabitants of Northern Labrador, and means 'raw fish eater.' The name with which they refer to themselves and each other is 'Inuit.' They know no other name. It would seem much the better way to drop entirely the term of reproach applied by one tribe to another, and use the name properly belonging to them, rather than to soften down the former by a change in spelling."

Although he rigidly enforced the ban on the sale of firearms and cartridges to the natives of the Far North, Hooper felt that the law caused "a source of great hardship to the natives of Arctic Alaska." Hooper reported: "Many had purchased their arms prior to the enactment of the law, and still have them, but can procure no ammunition. Having used these rifles for several years, they have become accustomed to them, while, through long disuse, they have lost much of their former skill with the bow and arrow and depend entirely upon their guns for subsistence. This is particularly the case with those who hunt reindeer [caribou]. They buy cartridges occasionally from the [Chukchi] at fabulous prices."

Hooper sounded his greatest complaint against those selling illegal liquor to the natives. He felt that if this practice continued in the Bering Sea and Arctic regions sure destruction would lie ahead for the native people.

When the *Corwin* cleared the ice in September, Captain Hooper shaped a course to San Francisco, making a few stops in Alaska along the way. After a "most favorable" passage that allowed for a "remarkably quick run," the *Corwin* arrived at her home port on Tuesday morning, October 12, 1880.

Major Clark's expectations about the value of the special cruise above the Arctic Circle proved more than correct. Normally, cutters came and went out of San Francisco with hardly a mention in the newspapers of the Bay area. Not so with the *Corwin*. The studio of Bradley and Rulofson on Montgomery Street photographed the cutter's officers individually and as a group arranged in a semi-circle around an image of the *Corwin*. (The photograph of Healy is the earliest known picture of him in uniform.) Indeed, the cutter's crew were received with a curiosity equal to that later reserved for astronauts returning from the moon. Questions about their adventures pelted the officers and crew. The publication of Captain Hooper's report in 1881 helped satisfy some of the public's desire for information.

San Francisco editors, however, wanted information for their readers immediately. Healy helped provide it. Upon docking, the crew, led by Healy, began "a long roistering binge along the San Francisco waterfront." Reports indicate that the event, even in a sailor's town, proved memorable. Unlike his fellow senior officers, Healy did not mind extolling his exploits. Reporters knew a good source when they found one. Years later, any reporter charged with trying to describe Healy mentioned his ability to tell sea stories. In 1888, for example, one journalist wrote, "To spin a yarn acceptably, without backing and filling, yawing and sheering from the true course, is a gift usually accredited to the tarry toiler of the sea. . . . The reputation of reeling off a 'cuffer' in 'shipshape and Bristol fashion' is maintained by Capt. M. A. Healy." This willingness to tell sea stories, while well lubricated by drink, is the genesis of his nickname, "Hell Roaring Mike," which he carried for the rest of his life. No one, however, ever dared call him that to his face.[37]

As the years passed, Healy became known for his volatile ways. He was quick to strike out at any perceived slight. At first glance, the pairing of First Lieutenant Healy with Captain Hooper on board the *Corwin* might well seem destined for a great deal of friction. Up until the incident on board the *Moccasin* in 1877, Healy had been senior to Hooper. Finding himself under the command of an officer who had previously ranked below him seemed sure to anger Healy, given his reputation labeled him a firebrand. Yet, the arrangement seemed an amicable one. No extant document suggests that the two senior officers of the cutter worked together any way but harmoniously during the 1880 patrol. Indeed, it appears that in the coming years Hooper and Healy mutually respected each other's abilities in the Far North.

After the patrol, Captain Hooper wrote to Major Clark about Healy's abilities. "Lieutenant Healy has carried out his duties to my complete satisfaction, and has demonstrated his skill in navigation and seamanship," Hooper said of his second in command. "Few officers of the service have a superior knowledge and ability to command a vessel in these dangerous waters."[38]

Given Healy and Hooper's good working relationship, as well as the success of the 1880 patrol, Clark may well have intended to keep the two men on the same cutter for yet another search for the *Jeannette* in 1881. As is usual in Healy's life, however, fate stepped in.

While Healy sailed with Captain Hooper, Healy's former commanding of-

ficer, Capt. George W. Bailey, the first revenue officer to write about the mass
starvation on St. Lawrence Island, continued in command of the *Rush* in the
Bering Sea. On October 16, during the patrol of 1879, Captain Bailey, not feeling well, went out on deck for some air and never returned. Captain Bailey has
the dubious distinction of being the only senior officer lost on Bering Sea Patrol
during the U.S. Revenue Cutter Service's years of operation (1867–1914).[39]

Captain Hooper recommended to Major Clark that First Lieutenant Healy
receive Bailey's command of the *Rush*. At the time, this seemed a logical recommendation. Healy was very close to making the final step toward his captaincy.
With an exciting mission under his belt and a good recommendation from
Captain Hooper, Healy should have had no problem receiving command of
the cutter. Nevertheless, a familiar specter raised its ugly head. In a letter to
Healy, Major Clark wrote: "On your return from the Arctic, I had determined
to transfer you to the *Rush*. I was pleased when I received a letter from Captain
Hooper recommending that you be given a command. . . . But I have received
a report of your drinking habits which have placed you in some disgrace and
warranted a reprimand from the Department."[40]

Clark expressed his willingness to listen to Healy's version of events. Were
the charges to be true, however, Clark admitted, "I should feel much embar-
rassed if called upon to make a recommendation on your behalf."[41]

Healy confessed to the charges. Contritely, he promised to take a vow of
"total abstinence" from alcohol.[42] Not for the last time in Healy's life did
someone in command take him at his word. Major Clark wrote, "Your statement . . . quite dispels the solicitude I had felt in regard to the matter and I am
prepared to dismiss [the comments]."[43]

On November 1, 1880, First Lieut. Michael A. Healy acknowledged his orders to report to the cutter *Rush*, his first independent command in Alaskan
waters. He made one cruise in the *Rush* before acknowledging, on February 24,
1882, orders to relieve his former commanding officer, Capt. Calvin L. Hooper,
and take over command of the cutter *Corwin*.[44] All of First Lieut. Michael A.
Healy's experiences as a sailor served as a prelude to this command. The short
man with the piercing blue eyes and stentorian voice now began some of his
greatest years at sea.

James A. Healy, the oldest brother of Michael A. Healy, in 1855. He became Bishop of Portland, Maine, in 1875. Photograph courtesy of Archives, Archdiocese of Boston.

Patrick F. Healy, SJ, who became the second president of Georgetown University.
Photograph courtesy of Archives, Georgetown University.

Mary Jane (Roach) Healy. Photograph courtesy of Thomas Riley.

Frederick A. Healy. Photograph courtesy of Thomas Riley.

Michael A. Healy, 1880, after the search for the *Jeannette*. This is the earliest known image of Healy in uniform. Photograph courtesy of Archives, College of the Holy Cross.

The cutter *Bear*, foreground, helping another ship in the ice. Photograph courtesy of U.S. Coast Guard.

Left to right: Mary Jane Healy, Michael A. Healy, and Matrona Salamatov, ca. 1892, on board the *Bear* at Unalaska. Matrona was an Aleut daughter of the priest at Belkovski, Alaska. After the priest's death, Sheldon Jackson and Rudolf Neumann arranged for her to attend school in California. She was the assistant teacher at Unalaska in 1892–1893 and 1896–1897. Photograph courtesy of U.S. Coast Guard.

Background left to right: Mary Tuck, John Tuck [?], Michael A. Healy, Mary Jane Healy, and an unidentified man. The young women are probably from the Jesse Lee Home for orphans in Unalaska. John and Mary Tuck were the first missionaries sent out to supervise the home. Mary Jane befriended Mary Tuck and helped by donating clothing to the home. Photograph courtesy of U.S. Coast Guard.

Cuttermen capture a reindeer, while members of the Chukchi, two U.S. Revenue Cutter Service officers, and an Imperial Russian government official look on. Photograph courtesy of U.S. Coast Guard.

Captain Healy prepares to harpoon something from the flying jib area of the cutter *Bear*. Healy was no longer a young man when this photograph was taken and this shows his toughness into his later years. Note the figurehead of the *Bear*, now in the Mariner's Museum, Newport News, Virginia. Photograph courtesy of U.S. Coast Guard.

After purchasing reindeer from the Chukchi, U.S. Revenue Cutter Service crewmen took the animals to the small boats of the *Bear* for transportation to the cutter. Photograph courtesy of U.S. Coast Guard.

Drawing in San Francisco *Chronicle* (1895) newspaper of Lieut. Chester White and Mabel Howe.

Once the small boats from the *Bear* brought the reindeer alongside the cutter, the crew hoisted them on board and placed them in pens built on the deck. Photograph courtesy of U.S. Coast Guard.

The commissioned officers and warrant officers of the *Bear* in 1895, many of whom brought charges against their captain in the 1896 trial in San Francisco. *Standing left to right:* Dr. Bodkin, Engineer Coffin, Lieutenant Daniel, Lieutenant White, Lieutenant Emery, and unidentified warrant officers. *Sitting left to right:* Chief Engineer Schwartz, Healy, Engineer Dory, and Lieutenant Buhner. Healy shows his age in this photograph. Photograph courtesy of U.S. Coast Guard.

Part of the enlisted crewmen of the *Bear* in 1895. Some of the men defended their captain during Captain Healy's 1896 trial, even at the risk of being charged with mutiny. Photograph courtesy of U.S. Coast Guard.

Healy served as Capt. Calvin L. Hooper's executive officer during part of 1880. Hooper watched over Healy's career and testified for him at the 1896 trial. Hooper, with full beard, is at the center of the seated officers. Note in the background the young Frederick A. Healy, Captain Healy's son. Photograph courtesy of U.S. Coast Guard.

Clay Young, the great-grandson of Michael A. Healy, his wife Ania Samborska, and their daughter Nina, the youngest descendant of Capt. Michael A. Healy. Photograph courtesy of Clay Young.

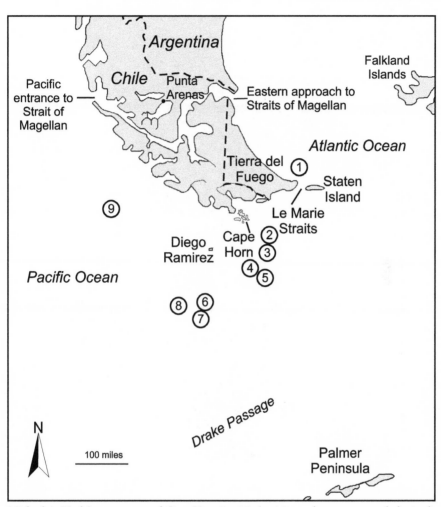

Michael A. Healy's voyage around Cape Horn in 1867 (positions taken at noon and obtained from dead reckoning). Map by Susan Browning.

Alaska below Bering Strait, showing major locations that Healy visited. Map by Susan Browning.

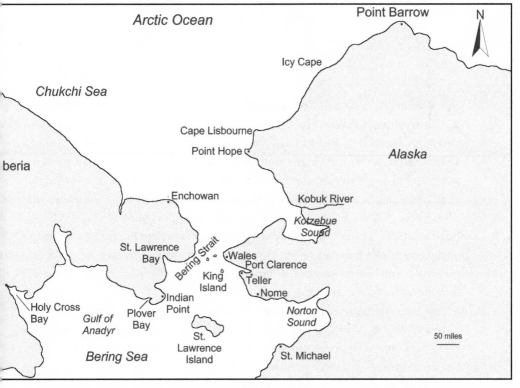

Bering Strait area and Arctic, showing major locations that Healy visited. Map by Susan Browning.

6

CANNONS, EXPEDITIONS, SHIPWRECKS, AND REINDEER

Michael A. Healy's first patrol in 1882 as commanding officer of the *Corwin* might have shaken a lesser officer. In Angoon, Alaska, Healy took part in what Rep. James H. Budd, of California, described as "the greatest outrage ever committed in the United States upon any Indian tribe."[1] Representative Budd was guilty of a selective memory; either that, or he possessed a poor knowledge of the ongoing American Indian Wars. He failed to recall either the events at Sand Creek, Colorado, in 1864, or at the Washita River, in what is now Oklahoma, in 1868.[2] His comment might simply have been a politician's hyperbole, or the efforts of a member of the Democratic Party to embarrass a Republican president. For Native Americans, however, Healy's actions in 1882 reverberate into the twenty-first century.

The 1882 voyage to Alaska started off routinely. On April 12, Healy received orders to sail "to Alaska, and the Seal Islands." He set sail from San Francisco eight days later only to be ordered the next day to instead "proceed to Cape Serdze, [Siberia.]"[3] Healy's previous adventures during the search for the ill-fated *Jeannette* would once again intrude into his life.

Several years before, upon joining the search for the *Jeannette*, the U.S. Navy had purchased the 138-foot, 490-ton steam whaler *Mary and Helen*. Built by Gross, Sawyer & Packard at Bath, Maine, in 1879, the builders meant the ship for Arctic work. Heavily reinforced for working in the ice, the whaler, powered by a steam engine, could reach speeds of eight knots in open waters. The U.S. government paid $100,000 for the *Mary and Helen* and the navy renamed it the USS *Rogers*. On November 30, 1881, while locked in pack ice at St. Lawrence Bay, Siberia, the crew of the ship heard the dreaded cry of "fire!" The *Rogers* burned to the waterline. Fortunately, the crew made it to shore, where they spent the winter with natives. Healy's new duties entailed collecting the survivors and transporting them to San Francisco. Healy returned to San Francisco with the sailors on June 23 and, after making repairs to the *Corwin*, again departed for Alaska on July 15.[4]

Work in the Bering Sea proved routine. In October, Healy shaped a course toward Southeast Alaska, expecting to make a normal journey through the Inside Passage, and then head home. Instead, what happened at Angoon would become part of the legend of Michael A. Healy.

Angoon is located on a peninsula of land along the western side of Admiralty Island and is accessible to both Chatham Strait and Kootznahoo Inlet in Southeast Alaska. It is approximately sixty miles to the southwest of Juneau. Historically, Admiralty Island has been home to the Kootznoowoo Tlingit, the indigenous people of Southeast Alaska. Their location, among the many islands of the Southeast Alaska region, made them "neither oriented as strongly toward the open sea as are the more maritime Tlingit groups, nor as exclusively toward the rivers and inland bays as are the mainland tribes." Their location, however, made the inhabitants of the village "accomplished boatmen."[5]

From the 1700s into the mid-1800s, fur trading was the primary money-maker for the village. In 1878, the Northwest Trading Company established a post and a whaling station on nearby Killisnoo Island. Whaling, along with a Bureau of Indian Affairs school and a Russian Orthodox Church, attracted some from Angoon to Killisnoo.[6] What took place at Angoon is usually interpreted as a "misunderstanding between whites and natives, that is, ignorance of each other's ways," and a culmination of a long series of misunderstandings.[7] Added to the mix was the neglect of Alaska by the United States government since acquiring this northern land in 1867.

Alaska's great size—twice that of Texas—and wide range of topography and climate made it a different type of frontier. With a coastline covering more than forty-seven thousand miles, Healy truly served on a maritime frontier. Most of the land's original inhabitants lived at, or near, the coast, or along rivers. Until the gold rushes drew people north, the territory had few inhabitants, which perhaps explains why lawmakers in far-off Washington, D.C., neglected this newest possession. Despite this apparent indifference, however, decision-makers did see something they recognized: "the Indian problem."[8]

One of the recurring themes in the history of the United States is how the country dealt with its native inhabitants. The record of lawmakers on the subject is not one of lasting glory. It should come as no surprise that the same fate awaited the Native Americans of Alaska.

Today, most people realize that the majority of Native Americans in the nineteenth-century American West lived a nomadic life based around the horse and hunting opportunities in the vast open spaces. Much of their lives were spent in the constant search for food. The original inhabitants of Southeast Alaska, however, lived in a far different environment than the Native Americans in most of the traditional frontier regions of the United States did. The tribes of this region occupied an archipelago, whose geographic features shaped their habits in ways different even from those in other regions of Alaska. Angoon, situated in the Alexander Archipelago, enjoyed an environment blessed with an abundant supply of food. Not for them was the constant migration in search of sustenance. The sea provided Pacific salmon, halibut, cod, herring, and other food. While early settlers on the Great Plains were forced to forage buffalo "chips" for a fuel supply, those in the Alexander Archipelago had access to abundant reserves of smelt or "candle fish," creatures so loaded with oil that when dried they burn like candles. With a ready supply of most of the food they needed, the people in this region developed a village way of life. Furthermore, the cyclic nature of fishing placed a premium on periods of intense labor and preservation of the catch, which, in turn, led to periods of leisure.

The Native American population of Southeast Alaska at the time outsiders began to appear has been estimated at no more that twenty-five thousand people. The slow influx of Europeans—in numbers estimated at less than one thousand—did not prove "impossible to accommodate."[9] An anthropologist who worked in the region in 1880 observed that the Native Americans "are not adverse [*sic*] to changes in [their] mode of life" and "do not flee at the approach of whites; on the contrary they leave their village site to settle nearer the trading posts, the salmon fisheries, the gold mining or other places where there are opportunities for easy gain."[10]

Nevertheless, there had been sporadic clashes between outsiders and Native Americans in Southeast Alaska. In 1857, before the departure of the Russians, Sitka was almost destroyed by an attack. The deadly encounter, however, "was the spurt of a dying flame."[11] What, then, led to the "dying flame?"

As was the case with most native populations in the Western Hemisphere, the introduction of new diseases caused the greatest devastation. By 1882, however, the native populations of Southeast Alaska also had the introduction of strong drink to reckon with. The introduction of liquor to native populations is directly related to the federal government's hit-and-miss efforts to bring government to the new territory.

Between 1867 and 1885, there "was literally no government of any sort in Alaska."[12] A few U.S. Army garrisons dotted the landscape of Southeast Alaska, but these had been withdrawn by the summer of 1877. The only remaining representatives of the federal government were a customs collector at Sitka and deputy collectors at such locations as Wrangell and Tongas, both in Southeast Alaska. As a result of living near government garrisons and white settlements, the Native Americans learned how to distill liquor. Indeed, the word "hootch" entered our language from natives who "learned how to distill a kind of rum called 'hoochenoo,' so-called because they had originally been taught by an ex-soldier at Killisnoo."[13] Others called it "squirrel whiskey, because it [obsessed] the consumer with a desire to climb a tree."[14] More than one observer of the time felt that the effects of liquor alone could mean the total extermination of the Native Americans of Alaska.

Once the U.S. Army pulled out of Alaska, fear began to take hold of whites remaining in Sitka, the largest settlement in Southeast Alaska. M. P. Berry, the Collector of Customs at Sitka, reported to the secretary of the treasury, "the Indians immediately assumed an arrogant bearing, and plainly informed us that there was neither gunboat nor soldier; therefore they had no fear."[15] Berry went on to describe in detail the gutting of the hospital and the destruction of the stockade by unruly "Indians."

The Treasury Department continued to periodically send revenue cutters through the area. Cutters, however, could only sporadically patrol the region. Soon rumors began to fly among the residents of Sitka that a massacre of whites was in the making. Yet, in the summer of 1877, Captain John L. White, of the U.S. Revenue Cutter Service, reported that, "After diligent inquiries and careful observation since our arrival here, I have not discovered any breach of the public peace, nor has my attention been called to any particular act, save a few petty trespasses committed by the Indians, half-breeds, and white men as well."[16]

Nevertheless, unease increased among the whites whenever a cutter left Sitka. The years 1878 and 1879 are marked by a growing panic among the white settlers. The memory of the deaths of Lt. Col. George Armstrong Custer and his entire immediate command at the Little Bighorn River in Montana in 1876 was fresh in the minds of most Americans. The deaths of whites by Native Americans still induced fear in most non-natives, no matter where they lived. After all, Americans had been fighting Native Americans since the 1607 Jamestown settlement. Over the centuries, fear and hatred of the Native Americans had become a part of white culture in the United States. Perhaps the public's long-standing horror of a massacre led by Native Americans can best be summed up by the advice given by Western frontiersmen and troopers: "Save the last cartridge for yourself."

Remaining Russians in Sitka even petitioned the Czar to send help, and a Russian man-of-war soon cruised in British Columbian waters. The inhabitants of Sitka next appealed to the British for help. The HMS *Osprey* answered their call. Finally, after much inattention on the part of Washington, D.C., the USS *Wolcott* arrived. By mid-June 1879, the USS *Jamestown* had taken up a permanent station at Sitka. The navy ruled Alaska, or at least Southeast Alaska, until 1884, when the territory received its first organic act and appointed a governor. Clearly, the two cultures of the area did not understand each other: a circumstance that created a tinderbox that simply awaited a catalyst. That catalyst was not long in coming.

Capt. Leslie A. Beardslee commanded the *Jamestown*. Beardslee felt that if he was to play a role in preventing any clashes between white settlers and the Native Americans of the area, he should study "the customs, laws and superstitions of the Indians, in order that I might be able . . . to reduce the hostility which had arisen between them and the whites, and to bring the two races into harmonious relations." Captain Beardslee was among the few whites to say that the Native Americans "are not naturally savage."[17] The captain's "reputation of fair dealing . . . spread among many Indian groups, for he was able to establish friendly relations[,] even with the fierce and arrogant Chilkat, but . . . whites felt that his policies were too lax."[18]

One important native custom Captain Beardslee noted was that if "an Indian dies while in the house of another, or is killed while in the employ of another, the house-owner or employer is responsible. The Indians seldom fail to yield to this, the very foundation of their laws, and a refusal to make equitable settlement is always a cause of war."[19] Further, the Tlingits did not make a distinction between accidental deaths and negligence. The law remained the same in either case. If the naval officer who succeeded Beardslee had heeded this observation, then, perhaps, the incident at Angoon would never have happened.

In 1882, Comdr. E. C. Merriman replaced Captain Beardslee in a customary naval change of command ceremony. The new naval officer presented "a great contrast" from his predecessor, a fact that "was welcomed by the whites, but all the more irritating to the Indians who had known Beardslee."[20] The events at Angoon actually began with a logging incident at Killisnoo.

A native was killed in the process of felling a tree for the Northwest Trading Company near Killisnoo. Officials stated that the native "was warned of the danger," but kept at the task.[21] As was the custom of the Tlingit, immediately "a certain number of blankets were levied as a fine upon the company by his relatives, and payment demanded."[22] The company refused to pay. Events remained at an impasse.

Commander Merriman then appeared on the scene. The USS *Adams*, the navy's new station ship, touched at Killisnoo on the way to Sitka. The superintendent of the Northwest Trading Company made a complaint to Merriman. The Collector of Customs at Sitka, William Gouverneur Morris, later wrote a detailed account of the events leading up to the actual incident at Angoon. His account is the basic material most writers have used to relate what took place in Southeast Alaska. Morris described how Commander Merriman "informed the Indians that in the future no such payments should either be demanded or enforced as far as white men were concerned; that if they persisted in such course he would punish them severely, and that in this instance the company would and should not pay."[23] Collector Morris wrote that the natives "submitted with bad grace."[24]

A few days later, on October 22, 1882, while hunting whales for the Northwest Trading Company, a native crew had a gun explode; a crewman, who was also a shaman, was killed. Morris's version of what led up to the Angoon incident states that the natives in the crew then overwhelmed the whites on board and took control of the craft. Other natives soon seized "nets, whaling gear, and [the] steam launch of the company, . . . and demanded payment of two hundred blankets for the dead man. The white men were kept close prisoners. A plan was formed to murder the engineer of the launch," but he managed to escape.[25]

At just this time, the *Corwin* was coaling at Sitka. Later, First Lieutenant Healy filed a brief account of the incident. He reported that the Northwest Trading Company refused to pay, and that the natives were threatening to destroy the store, other buildings, and boats and to kill the two white men they held captive.[26]

The superintendent of the company's trading post, J. M. Vanderbilt, gathered his family, fled to the company's tug, the *Favorite*, and made his way to Sitka to seek help from the U.S. Navy. Healy, knowing the deeper draft of the *Adams* prohibited the larger naval ship from entering the shallow waters off the villages on Admiralty Island, volunteered to transport the naval commander and his naval landing party aboard the shallow-draft *Corwin*. Commander Merriman readily accepted the offer. Customs and courtesy of the naval services almost demanded that Healy offer his services. Furthermore, Healy may well have remembered that, during his previous service in Sitka on board the cutter *Reliance* in 1869, unrest among the Native Americans quickly subsided with only a show of force.

Commander Merriman, in charge of the force, placed a howitzer cannon and a Gatling gun, an early type of machine gun, aboard the *Favorite*, along with fifty men and twenty marines, under Lieut. C. W. Bartlett of the *Adams*. The *Favorite* departed Sitka at 3:00 a.m., on October 24. The *Corwin*, carrying Commander Merriman and Collector Morris, as well as additional sailors and marines from the *Adams*, departed four hours later. The *Favorite*, meanwhile, picked up a surveying launch, along with additional men, and took it into tow. With its greater speed, the *Corwin* overtook both craft and took them into tow. Bad weather hampered the cutter's speed, and the three vessels arrived in the area on October 25. For the time and place, this improvised naval force, augmented with a cannon, a Gatling gun, and marines, ranked as a formidable flotilla.[27] Against this force, the Native Americans mustered only spears and bows and arrows, with clubs, axes, and knives for hand-to-hand combat.

Upon reaching the scene, Commander Merriman, according to Collector Morris, arrested the two native leaders and brought them on board the *Corwin*. The naval commander demanded the release of the two white men. He also informed the two leaders that he placed "a fine of four hundred blankets, payable the next morning, under the penalty of having their canoes destroyed and principal village [Angoon] shelled and burnt."[28]

Collector Morris clearly reveals his feelings about Captain Beardslee's earlier efforts to understand the Native Americans of the area in his appraisal of the situation: "So temporizing has been the policy pursued within the past two years by the Navy toward the Siwashes [a derogatory word for Native Americans] that they evidently thought this a game of bluff. They were surly and impertinent, and affected not to think that Commander Merriman would put his threat into execution. They, however, took precautions to make use of the intervening night in taking to a place of security their large canoes and valuables."[29]

Commander Merriman called First Lieutenant Healy and his other officers together and laid out his tactics. Lieutenant Bartlett would take the *Favorite* and the surveying vessel behind the village via the inlet. Merriman reasoned that the natives, upon seeing the tug, would think the only people on board were employees of the company and would therefore try to take it over. Bartlett was to "treat the Indians kindly if they show a peaceful disposition. . . . Should the Indians show fight[,] attack them vigorously."[30] Furthermore, the landing party was to get "possession of every canoe" it could and "get all the Indians to come to the white settlement if possible." Merriman further instructed: "Should the Indians forcibly resist after knowing your intentions, do not hesitate; open fire at once, and I will immediately come to your support in the *Corwin*. Use all diplomacy first, however."[31]

In the meanwhile, the *Corwin* would steam up the Chatham Strait side of Angoon. Merriman would signal in the event an attack was beginning. Whichever party gave the signal would receive the support of the other during the attack.

Shortly after coming to rest off Angoon in the *Corwin*, Commander Merriman ordered Healy to open fire on the village. According to Merriman's confusing account of the action, the naval commander might have ordered cannon fire before Lieutenant Bartlett had freed the captives. Perhaps Merriman was "far more concerned with fining and punishing the Indians" than with freeing the hostages.[32]

After the *Corwin* began raking the village with cannon fire, the *Favorite* commenced firing the howitzer. Merriman reported that the men aboard the tug had "previously destroyed the canoes and the principal houses in the lagoon." Merriman further explained, "I purposely spared some houses, although apparently accidentally, sufficient to house the Indians for the winter." After the cannon fire lifted, the marines entered "and fired the village, sparing five additional homes."[33] In his description of the action, Healy related that forty canoes were destroyed, but the houses of friendly Tlingits were spared. Rumors circulated that the shore party not only burned, but also looted.

The Tlingit version of events is markedly different. One young resident of Angoon who witnessed the events later said:

The people [continued working after the man was killed] and [then] tied up the boat. They wanted the boat to stop whaling until the dead man was buried.

The white people at Killisnoo got scared and sent word to Sitka that the Indians were preparing for war. This was not true. They only wanted the boat quiet for two days until they buried him. He was an important man. The Tlingit didn't know what the whites wanted until the Coast Guard [Revenue Cutter Service] came out and they heard the shells and saw the smoke. . . . Six children died from the smoke.

[The attacking force] went up Favorite Bay after they burned the village and got all the people's canoes and chopped them up. The people stayed where they were. They couldn't move down, and everything they had at Angoon was gone. People lived that winter on oil they had put up, and went hunting, and caught fish in the streams. They suffered plenty.[34]

Villagers of Angoon for years believed that they were "grievously wronged" and "entitled to compensation for their sufferings."[35] Some accounts imply that Healy is the one responsible for the destruction of Angoon. A close look at the events, however, reveals that the revenue cutter officer was acting under the orders of Commander Merriman. Traditionally, the U.S. Revenue Cutter Service assisted other branches of the U.S. armed forces. Healy had no choice but to follow the orders of the senior naval officer present, in this case Commander Merriman. Collector of Customs Morris, who also commanded Healy, permitted the revenue officer little leeway in his actions. Clearly, Morris preferred Commander Merriman's tactics. Furthermore, Healy, as mentioned, may well have felt that a show of force would likely defuse the situation. First Lieutenant Healy found himself in a situation that demanded he follow orders despite any personal feelings. All of Healy's service had conditioned him to follow orders given by higher command. It should not come as a surprise to anyone that he, in turn, expected such unquestioning obedience from those he commanded.

The remainder of the 1882 patrol may well have felt anticlimactic to Healy after the events at Angoon. On November 15, the *Corwin* finally returned to San Francisco.[36]

March 3, 1883, proved to be a memorable day for Healy. After a long wait, Healy finally received orders to sew onto his uniform the shoulder straps containing an oak leaf, which signified the rank of captain in the U.S. Revenue Cutter Service. Ten days later, he took the oath of office. Eighteen years after entering the service, he now held the highest rank available to a revenue officer.

The cutters of the U.S. Revenue Cutter Service, working as they did in the relatively unknown regions of the Bering Sea and Arctic Ocean, provided natural platforms for scientists and expeditions to study and explore this vast new territory. Meanwhile, the increasing number of whalers pursuing the bowhead led to additional search and rescue cases. During Healy's next two patrols, exploration, search and rescue, and other such duties claimed much of the captain's attention, while, at the same time, the seed of a humanitarian idea began to take root.

In 1883, the year after the incident at Angoon, Healy took on board the *Corwin* Lieut. George M. Stoney, of the U.S. Navy. Lieutenant Stoney's mission was to bring to the natives of St. Lawrence Bay, Siberia, gifts for helping the crew of the USS *Rogers*. Once his mission was completed, Stoney had to remain on board the *Corwin*, with no duties, until the cutter returned to the United

States. Bored, the lieutenant did what many in the military are usually loath to do: he volunteered for another mission.

Stoney's boredom came at the perfect time for Healy. The *Corwin* was anchored near Hotham Inlet, most of which lies just north of the Arctic Circle on the northern portion of Kotzebue Sound. The sound, in turn, borders the northern side of Alaska's Seward Peninsula. Captain Healy instructed Lieutenant Stoney to load one of the *Corwin*'s small boats with supplies, select one crewman from the cutter, and make an exploration of the inlet. As a result of this exploration, the naval lieutenant and the cutterman discovered the Kobwak [Kobuk] River. They ascended the river in an easterly direction, some forty to fifty miles. They did not, however, reach the headwaters of the Kobuk. Lieutenant Stoney reported the results of his journey not only to Captain Healy, but also to the U.S. Navy. Therefore, both Healy and Stoney received credit for the discovery of the river. The expedition unexpectedly piqued the interest of Stoney who, using inter-service rivalry as a means of leverage, managed to obtain naval funds to mount further expeditions up the river.[37]

The discovery provided Healy with an opportunity to test a private theory that he had pondered for some time in the captain's cabin of the *Corwin*. Any cutterman who worked in the Arctic knew that, in heavy ice conditions, a revenue cutter could not bull its way to Point Barrow. With more and more whalers hunting the bowhead whale in the Arctic, Healy knew that eventually some ships would fall prey to the region's crushing ice. How, the captain wondered, would a cutter be able to rescue those in distress near Point Barrow? Not too surprisingly, given his knowledge of the Arctic, Healy turned his attention inland. Captain Healy knew that the Colville River emptied into the Arctic Ocean just east of Point Barrow, while the Koyukuk River, located in approximately the same longitude, ran south into the Yukon River. The Kobuk River lies midway in latitude between the mouths of the Colville and Koyukuk Rivers and empties first into Hotham Inlet and then the Chukchi Sea, just north of the Bering Strait. Healy had heard reports from the natives of the Alaskan coast of a large inland lake. Perhaps the headwaters of all three rivers lay in this lake. If that were true, perhaps these rivers could be utilized as escape routes for whalers trapped in the ice near Point Barrow.

To test his theory, Healy eagerly sought permission from Washington to launch a U.S. Revenue Cutter Service expedition up the Kobuk River in 1884. He argued that, even if his theory were proven incorrect, such an expedition stood to improve scientific and geographical knowledge of, and maybe even commercial interests in, the region. The fact that Lieutenant Stoney now had the Navy's permission to mount such an expedition, however, proved the strongest selling point of Healy's proposal. Should Stoney make the discovery, the work of the U.S. Revenue Cutter Service would evaporate. Major Clark, the Treasury Department civilian in charge of the service, felt that beating the Navy and winning the fame for the discovery of the headwaters had priority over the other reasons and, on that basis, approved the expedition.[38]

Meanwhile, a young officer, Third Lieut. John Cassin Cantwell, reported for duty on board the *Corwin*. Born on January 9, 1859, in Raleigh, North Carolina, Cantwell began his career differently than most young revenue officers of the 1880s. He first entered the service as an enlisted man on January 9, 1879. After serving a year in the enlisted force and rising to the rating of boatswain, the ambitious youngster took the competitive examination for cadet at the service's new School of Instruction, which eventually became the U.S. Coast Guard Academy. He received his appointment on June 7, 1880, just as Healy prepared to depart San Francisco as the executive officer of the *Corwin*'s search for the two missing whalers and the *Jeannette*.

Cantwell served two years as a cadet, before taking and passing the examination for the rank of third lieutenant and receiving his commission on July 8, 1882. Like all new officers of the service, Cantwell served in a number of cutters during his first two years as an officer. On March 26, 1884, he received orders to report to the *Corwin*.[39]

On July 7, 1884, the *Corwin* neared the mouth of the Kobuk River. With permission secured from headquarters, Captain Healy selected Lieut. George H. Doty to lead the expedition. When Doty was badly cut in an accident, Healy replaced him with Third Lieut. John C. Cantwell. Captain Healy may well have selected Cantwell because he, like Healy, had come up through the ranks. Healy might have believed that Cantwell's enlisted experience, combined with his formal training in classrooms and practical training on three other cutters, made him an officer able to operate independently. Chosen to accompany Cantwell were Second Asst. Engineer Samuel B. McLenegan; Quartermaster Horace Wilbur; Fireman Frank Lewis; James Miller, a miner; and Andre Fernda, a guide and interpreter. Cantwell was ordered to take the *Corwin*'s steam launch up river. The launch would tow two smaller boats carrying additional supplies and camping equipment. Among his many instructions to Cantwell, Captain Healy enjoined him not "to excite [the] cupidity or awaken [the] distrust" of any of the natives the lieutenant might encounter. If a "collision" could not be avoided, Healy instructed Cantwell to "try and make good your retreat without bloodshed. If, however, this be impossible, act with firmness, decision, and moderation."[40]

The expedition departed on July 8, and Lieutenant Cantwell did not come alongside the *Corwin* again until August 30, after traveling 1,104.9 miles. "We are pioneers of the river," boasted Captain Healy to the secretary of the treasury.[41] He did point out, however, that neither Stoney nor Cantwell had reached the headwaters of the river; thus far, neither man had proved nor disproved his theory.

Undeterred, Captain Healy sought and gained approval for a second U.S. Revenue Cutter Service expedition. Prior to arriving in the Kobuk River area in 1885, Captain Healy, while on St. Paul Island in the Pribilofs, met a trained naturalist from the Smithsonian Institution, Charles H. Townsend. The U.S. commissioner of fisheries had sent Townsend to Alaska to gather data on seals, fish, and other wildlife. After meeting Healy, Townsend requested permission to accompany the *Corwin*. Healy quickly grasped that having Townsend on the expedition "would be of great value to science and of much interest to the public." He promptly offered to let the naturalist accompany Cantwell, and Townsend accepted with alacrity. "The opportunity of accompanying the *Corwin*, afforded through the courtesy of Captain Healy," Townsend later wrote, "was one which I gladly availed myself of, as it enabled me to visit a remote and usually inaccessible region." Also included in the expedition were Seaman William G. Marsh; Fireman Frank Lewis; and Myninck, an interpreter. The expedition began on July 2, 1885. At the same time, Healy dispatched Engineer McLenegan and Seaman Nelson on an expedition up the Noatak River.[42]

While the expeditions made their ways up the Kobuk and Noatak Rivers, Captain Healy left the area to rendezvous with the whaling fleet before it attempted to work into the Arctic. The *Corwin* being the only cutter suitable for Arctic work, Captain Healy bore the extra burden of providing search and rescue assistance for those above the Arctic Circle. During the 1885 patrol, forty-two whaling ships worked in Arctic waters, eighteen from New Bedford, Massachusetts, and the rest from San Francisco. Five of the forty-two ships were totally destroyed. One, the *Napoleon*, was crushed by ice and the entire crew reported as lost. The remaining thirty-seven whalers also incurred some damage from the ice and storms during the season.[43] No wonder Healy had such a strong interest in his Kobuk River expedition.

Beginning with his service in the cutter *Active* at New Bedford in 1872, Healy had grown to respect the captains and officers of whalers. At first, these tough seamen distrusted the U.S. Revenue Cutter Service officer who enforced federal laws in the north. When the search for bowheads moved deeper into the Arctic, however, the whaling masters and officers grew "to [love] him; he was tough and brave and capable and profane and bibulous as they were—if not more so."[44]

Despite the personal importance of the Kobuk expedition to Healy, the captain reported August 10, sixteen days before the end of the expedition, as "the most eventful [day] of the season" that "will long be remembered by the whaling fleet and the crew of the *Corwin* as a day of calamities."[45] The events of August 10 took place near Icy Cape, approximately 140 miles to the southwest of Barrow, Alaska.

At least thirty whalers lay at anchor that day awaiting better ice conditions before pushing farther into the Bowhead whaling grounds. After a beautiful Arctic summer morning, the weather, as is usual in the region, turned. The wind "hauled" gradually to the south, and squalls swept the area. The wind increased "in force every moment." Around noon, a small boat brought on board the *Corwin* from the bark *Abraham Barker* eagerly awaited mail. As the boat pulled away, a heavy squall struck the craft and capsized it, throwing the crew of six into the frigid waters. The *Corwin* quickly called away their small boat, and the boat crew pulled the shivering men to safety.

By two in the afternoon, the storm had increased to gale force. The whalers could not hoist their anchors because of the seas and strong winds. A majority of the ships, "working under short sail," got underway by either slipping or cutting their cables (anchor lines). An hour later, the bark *George and Susan* cut one of its cables and began to drag its other anchor. It ran afoul of the anchored bark *Mabel*, causing the *Mabel* a great deal of damage.

The *George and Susan* then ran ashore, striking hard on the beach. In less than three hours, the master found seven feet of water in his ship's hold. Some of the ship's crew, in a panic, cleared away two boats and made for shore. To reach the beach, however, they had to pass through a zone of heavy surf. Both boats swamped, drowning three of the crew. The survivors of the two boats managed to reach shore exhausted and semi-conscious.

Captain Healy set out to help the ships in the fleet. Observing that the *Mabel* was in "an extremely dangerous position," Healy gave orders to the helmsman to take the cutter into the breakers (breaking waves) near the beach. Even in the twenty-first century, mariners enter surf zones with trepidation. In extreme conditions, "pressures in excess of one ton per square foot have been measured in breaking waves, while wind pressures rarely exceed 10–12 pounds per square foot."[46] Captain Healy, however, possessed the seamanship to judge that, with his skill and a little luck, he might be able to help the crew of the *Mabel*.

Under Healy's orders, the *Corwin* drew near the *Mabel* and dropped anchor in four and a quarter fathoms (25.5 feet), letting out ninety fathoms (540 feet) of anchor chain. Heavy waves began to break all over the *Corwin*, with one "very heavy sea over her starboard quarter which swept clear forward to the forecastle."

Captain Healy picked the best seamen in his crew and placed them under the command of the pilot, Mr. Douglass, for the next harrowing maneuver. The chosen men clambered into the *Corwin's* small boat, which, along with the crew it carried, remained on board the *Corwin*. Healy then ordered the cutter to steam ahead on its anchor chain until it passed ahead and to windward of the *Mabel*. Into this tempest, Healy ordered the launching of the small boat. Douglass and his crew paid out a light line (rope) from the *Corwin* to the *Mabel*. Healy reported that, despite a "heavy sea and strong wind and tide, [Douglass] succeeded in running the line in a most admirable and seamanlike manner." The crew of the *Corwin* tied the light line to a heavy towing hawser and signaled the crew of the *Mabel* to start pulling the thick rope to their ship in preparation for towing. As the whaling crew worked at heaving the line to their ship, the *Mabel's* anchor cable parted, and the ship struck heavily on the beach. In "less than thirty minutes," the *Mabel* "became a total wreck."

Unable to help the crew in such weather, Captain Healy ordered the *Corwin* to a better anchorage and, after the storm slackened, sent a boat ashore with the doctor to help the castaways on the beach. The *Corwin's* crew kept busy throughout the night and into the next morning helping any ship in distress. In all, Captain Healy received credit for rescuing fifty-four crewmembers of the wrecked whalers.

With this harrowing work finished, Captain Healy shaped a course to rendezvous with the two exploring parties in Hotham Inlet. The two parties returned on August 27, and although Captain Healy's theory, in the end, did not prove correct, the work accomplished by the explorers proved of immense value to science and to the geographical knowledge of Alaska. (Stoney competed with Cantwell during 1884 and 1885. Although better equipped than the U.S. Revenue Cutter Service officer, unlike Cantwell, the naval lieutenant failed to reach the headwaters of the Kobuk River.)[47] Cantwell gave his commanding officer the credit he deserved for suggesting the expedition. "Much, if not all, of the honor of being pioneers at the headwaters of the [Kobuk]," Cantwell wrote to Healy, "is due directly to your forethought, and the example you set me of well-sustained and indomitable energy."[48]

Another important thread in Captain Healy's career began in 1880 during the *Corwin*'s search for the two missing whalers and the *Jeannette*. Along with his commanding officer, Captain Hooper, Healy witnessed the mass starvation on St. Lawrence Island. As mentioned earlier, viewing these horrendous sights greatly affected Healy. Hooper and Healy, along with other revenue cutter service officers, believed that as more outsiders pushed into the northern regions of Alaska, the native population would move closer to the brink of extinction. Healy and others felt that whalers and maritime traders interrupted the Eskimos' normal hunting life by causing them to hunt animals not for food but for furs, which they traded for liquor. Although many of Healy's reports indicate that, at least on the western and northern coasts of Alaska, the constant patrols by the service held much of the illegal liquor trade in check, the specter of mass starvation still loomed.[49] The large harvests of whales and walrus by outsiders further interfered with the normal balance of native life in the Far North. Despite countless long hours of pondering the question of how to save the native Alaskans, a solution to the problem eluded Healy.

Years later, John C. Cantwell remarked that, on his 1885 expedition, he noticed the similarity between the vegetation of the upper reaches of the Kobuk Valley and that of areas away from the Siberian coast. Cantwell recalled a group of people who lived in that area of Siberia, the Chukchi. Like the Laplanders of Finland, the Chukchi herded reindeer. The animals provided them with most of the material they needed to survive in their harsh climate. Cantwell discussed with Townsend whether the flora of coastal and inland Alaska could support reindeer, a mammal not native to North America. If so, the herding of reindeer might provide a solution to the Alaskan Eskimo by eliminating the need to hunt for food. During their expedition, Cantwell and Townsend discussed this idea at length. After his examination of the Kobuk River region, Townsend felt the vegetation would indeed be suitable for reindeer. Upon their return to the *Corwin*, Lieutenant Cantwell and Townsend took their idea to Captain Healy.[50]

Healy felt the plan had merit and agreed to an examination of the coastal plain that runs from the Yukon River delta to the Arctic Ocean. Again, Townsend reported that he found the area suitable for raising reindeer. While others, including Captain Hooper, had proposed the reindeer as a solution to the Inuit's food problems as early as 1880, it was Healy, Cantwell, and most importantly, Townsend's botanical survey that showed the animals could survive in Alaska. Were it not for Captain Healy's understanding that a scientist could enhance Cantwell's efforts, Townsend's scientific stamp might never have justified a social engineering project that sought to help the native people of northern Alaska.[51]

Captain Healy, like all commanding officers working in the Far North, sent reports to the Treasury Department. As the "polar passion" continued, however, decision makers in the Treasury Department saw Healy's operating area as a possible source of publicity. They felt that the commanding officer of the *Corwin*—with ready access to scientific observations of Alaska's flora and fauna, plus news on expeditions, rescues, and the little-known people of the Far North—had the potential to produce exciting reading. Most importantly, if such reports were printed by the Government Printing Office and distributed among the legislature, then, perhaps, more funds for further exploration might be in the offing. Capt. Michael A. Healy did not disappoint the Treasury Department. While comparing anyone's writing style with that of another is inevitably subjective, the authors believe that most readers would find Captain Healy's printed reports on his 1884 and 1885 cruises in the *Corwin* far more riveting than those written by Captain Hooper. Healy's two reports contain observations on many subjects, ranging from birds to natives. They contain details about expeditions and rescues, including drawings and photographs of these and many other subjects. In other words, Healy's reports contain plenty to indulge the public's insatiable appetite for material on the Far North.[52]

Healy's reports reveal him as a man who by any standard, then or now, easily wears the title "ice master." As a report-writer, however, Healy may have been a little too good for the bureaucrats in the Treasury Department. Captain Healy never hesitated to point out to the Department the problems associated with service in Alaskan waters. Although couched in the flowery bureaucratic language of the nineteenth century, his reports reflect his thoughts on the nature of duty in the Far North. In his 1884 report, for example, Healy detailed one of his growing concerns. He pointed out that the U.S. Revenue Cutter Service's duties in Alaskan waters actually had two "theaters of action" that were a "thousand and more miles apart."[53] One area stretched north from the tip of the Pribilof Islands to above the Arctic Circle. The second "theater of action" contained the Pribilof Islands and extended southward. As Healy correctly pointed out, it was "simply impossible for one vessel to prevent illicit trade and succor distressed seamen in the Arctic, and guard the seal islands and stop the illegal taking of otter and [the] introduction of arms on the coast of the Alaska Peninsula and among the adjacent islands."[54]

Healy wrote that, "as nobly as this little vessel [the *Corwin*] has accomplished the work placed upon her," the cutter could not adequately perform all the duties expected of her. Without mincing words, Captain Healy stated that building another vessel "as large as a man-of-war" and using only that cutter in Alaska, as some had proposed was "an absurdity that only requires a comparison of the duty to be performed with the territory requiring attention to make it manifest."[55] Healy clearly saw the solution. The service needed two cutters in the Bering Sea region, one cutter for the northern theater and the other for the southern theater.

While the 1884 and 1885 reports contain well-written narratives with good illustrations, Captain Healy never authored another report printed by the Government Printing Office. Perhaps leadership in the Treasury Department tired of Healy's constant commentary. More likely, the 1884 and 1885 publications accomplished what the bureaucrats wished, and they then wished to move on to something else. In any case, between 1885 and the absorption of the U.S. Revenue Cutter Service into the U.S. Coast Guard in 1914, the service saw the publication of only two additional reports on its operations in Alaska, one in 1899 and the other in 1902.[56]

The U.S. Revenue Cutter Service's tenure in the Treasury Department was one of penny-pinching and making do with whatever was available. Purchasing officers sought solutions that cost little, or could be had at no cost. While the service recognized as valid Healy's request for another cutter, the Treasury Department's solution to the problem should come as no surprise.

7

THE CAPTAIN AND THE IMMORTAL *BEAR*

Old salts know that ships are living entities and have souls. If a ship has a good reputation, then it takes on an almost mystical persona. In 1935, sixty-two years after she moved down the ways at Dundee, Scotland, the steam barkentine *Bear* maneuvered to the dock at her home port of San Francisco. In the milling crowd on the dock that day was naval officer and writer Frank Wead, who struck up a conversation with an old Arctic veteran while the two men waited for the mooring lines to snake over the side of the ship. Looking at the *Bear*, the old sailor said: "Too bad she can't talk. She'd tell some yarns. There's one in every timber she's got. If you put 'em all together landlubbers'd call it a fairy tale."[1]

Capt. Michael A. Healy had assumed command of this long surviving cutter forty-nine years earlier. The experienced ice master immediately began adding to the yarns that the sturdy Arctic vessel was destined to carry "in every timber she's got." The U.S. Revenue Cutter Service, meanwhile, apparently had come to accept the wisdom of Healy's earlier proposal to divide the Bering Sea region into two separate theaters of operation, each with its own cutter. At about the same time, the U.S. Navy decided that it no longer needed a ship designed to work in sea ice.

Previously, in 1881, as a part of the United States' polar passion, the U.S. Army had dispatched a scientific expedition to establish a base camp at Lady Franklin Bay in Northeast Ellesmere Island, Canada. More than likely, it was the army's resentment over the navy's total monopoly on U.S. publicity in the polar regions that sparked this mission of discovery, rather than a desire to expand the frontiers of science. Army Lieut. Adolphus W. Greely's orders directed him to push northward from his base camp as far as possible. The army lieutenant reached Lockwood Island to the north of Greenland at eighty-three degrees and twenty-four minutes north latitude, a record for that time.

Lieutenant Greely had counted on a supply ship reaching the base camp in 1882. The ship, however, could not penetrate the ice. The final blow to the army's expedition came on July 23, 1883. Not only did the relief ship sink, its naval escort retreated without leaving behind any provisions. Lieutenant Greely, however, had planned for the possibility of a severed supply line. His plan involved a steam-driven launch and three whaleboats that had been deposited by the ship that brought the expedition to Ellesmere Island. The steam launch would tow the whaleboats and their occupants to safety. In reality, a storm capsized two of the boats, and the survivors just managed to make land near Cape Sabine, Ellesmere Island, with only a few provisions among them. Unaware that their relief ship had sunk, the men awaited rescue. It wasn't long before the Americans began rationing their food. After the food gave out, some of the men starved to death. Some of the survivors resorted to cannibalism.[2]

Meanwhile, back in the United States, newspapers clamored for the assemblage of another party to search for the missing Greely Expedition. The U.S. Navy heeded the call and mounted the Greely Relief Expedition, which comprised a rescue flotilla of four ships under the command of Comdr. Winfield S. Schley, who insisted that each vessel carry its own ice pilot and steam-powered launch. One of the ships—the collier *Loch Garry*—carried the fuel for the other ships. Great Britain assisted the expedition by donating the *Alert*, which, being the slowest boat least suited for work in the ice, became the reserve vessel. Commander Schley placed his trust in two steam vessels, both purchased by the U.S. Navy, to successfully rescue Lieutenant Greely's expedition.[3]

Designed as a steam whaler, the 1,250-ton, wooden-hulled *Thetis* was built by Alexander Stephen and Sons of Dundee, Scotland, and launched in 1881. The *Thetis* measured 188½ feet in length and 29 feet in the beam, with a draft of 17 feet, 10 inches. The navy purchased the *Thetis* expressly for the Greely Relief Expedition, and Commander Schley chose the former whaler as his flagship.[4]

The expedition's other important ship, the *Bear*, also began its life in the Scottish shipyard. Built for Walter Grieve, of Greenock, Scotland, and launched eight years before the *Thetis*, the *Bear* had a length of 198 feet, 4 inches; a beam of 30 feet; a draft of 17 feet, 11 inches; and a displacement of 703 tons. This steam barkentine had been built for the tough Newfoundland seal trade.

To prepare the *Bear* for work in dangerous ice fields, the shipyard lay her ribs of Scottish oak close together. (The closer together the ribs, the stronger the ship.) In addition to sails, a Scotch boiler and engine provided propulsion to a two-bladed screw (propeller). The screw "could be stopped with the blades vertical in the wake of the keel and so offer little resistance to passage through the water when cruising under sail alone." Above and below the waterline, the *Bear*'s sides were sheaved with Australian iron bark, "the toughest wood known." The bottom of the ship was covered in yellow pine, which in turn was covered with a coat of copper paint and an anti-fouling mixture to stop the boring Teredo worm and inhibit sea-growth and barnacles. The foremast and mizzenmast were made from Norwegian pine, while the largest mast, the mainmast, was made of a hollow iron tube. Three shillings were placed where the masts would sit, "heads up for luck, to pay for the passage of her crew to Charon and across the River Styx in case she was lost at sea."[5]

With his four-ship relief expedition assembled, Commander Schley set out for Greenland. He allowed the two ships that could make the best time through the ice, the *Bear* and the *Thetis*, to move at their own rapid pace.

Lieutenant Greely recorded in his journal:

> By the morning of the 22nd we were all exhausted, and it was only through the energy of [Sgt. Julius] Frederick or [Sgt. David L.] Brainard, I do not remember which, that we obtained, around noon, some water. That and a few square inches of soaked seal-skin was all the nutriment which passed our lips for forty-two hours. . . . Near midnight of the 22nd I heard the sound of the whistles of the *Thetis*, blown by Captain Schley's orders to recall his parties. I could not distrust my own ears, and yet I could hardly believe that ships would venture along that coast in such a gale.[6]

Commander Schley found only seven men, out of the Greely expedition's original twenty-six, still alive. The doctor in the relief expedition later stated that not one member of the small group of emaciated men could have lasted more than a few days longer.

The relief expedition carrying the survivors arrived at Portsmouth, Virginia, amid a tumultuous welcome. The U.S. Atlantic Fleet that lay at anchor in Portsmouth greeted the expedition, "having dressed ship with every available flag and pennant."[7]

For their outstanding work, the navy rewarded most of the ships of the expedition by selling them off. The *Thetis*, however, did not suffer this fate. The U.S. Navy laid her up in the New York Navy Yard until 1887, then reactivated and assigned the *Thetis* to naval duties in Pacific waters.[8]

The same act of Congress that purchased the *Bear* for the relief expedition, however, also ordered that the ship be sold immediately after the expedition's return. By this time, new nautical technology was causing the beginning of the end of wooden ships in the navy, and the *Bear* became an anachronism over-night, no longer fit for naval service.[9]

Around the same time the Greely Relief Expedition was fighting its way through Greenland's ice, Captain Healy's request for another cutter to work in Alaska made its rounds within the Treasury Department. By 1885, rumors had begun circulating throughout the service that, true to its penny-pinching ways, the Treasury Department had come upon a deal for a ship that had proven itself in the ice. More important even than its record in the ice, the ship meant the Treasury Department would not have to undergo the expense of building a new cutter. Healy, responding to the rumors, wrote, "It is generally under-stood that the *Corwin* is to be relieved by the *Bear* for Arctic duty. If such a change is contemplated, before it is made I would respectfully call the serious attention and consideration of the Department to the fact that nineteen feet of water, which I understand is the draught of the *Bear*, is altogether too great to make her an effective cruiser on the shore of the Arctic Ocean. With such a draught, all effectiveness as a cruiser against contraband trade and as an aid to vessels that might become stranded would be seriously impaired if not totally destroyed."[10]

Captain Healy felt a shallow draft vessel was best for Arctic work. Using his best bureaucratic wiles and language, he ended his 1885 report with the observation that since he had "cruised for a number of years in every portion of Alaska, from Sitka to Point Barrow, and among all the islands, and served on this duty much longer than any other person under the Government, I should understand the needs of the country in this respect; therefore the foregoing suggestions are made as a matter of duty only, and with becoming deference and hesitation."[11]

Even as Healy penned his reservations, the U.S. Revenue Cutter Service obtained the *Bear* in 1885. After Captain Healy reported to his new command in 1886, he began to modify his views about the cutter.

Over the coming years, Captain Healy's cruises to the north in the *Bear* followed a general routine. Around April, officers and crew reported on board and began preparing for the months ahead of them. Orders, mail for the iso-lated areas of Alaska, and supplies for the crew started arriving. During the first year that Healy commanded the *Bear*, three cutters made the long voyage north. The area of operations for each of the cutters closely followed Healy's suggestion of dividing the region into northern and southern areas. The *Cor-win*, Captain Healy's former command, worked south of Bering Strait, along with the newer *Rush*. Both cutters concentrated on protecting the seal herds.

The *Bear*'s main patrol area encompassed the northern section of the Bering Sea and into the Arctic. The cutter also made a stop at the Pribilofs on its way north and again after turning south toward Unalaska.

Every year that Healy sailed northward, his orders included special duties related to tasks that can broadly be defined as either humanitarian or scientific. On his first cruise in command of the *Bear*, for example, Healy searched for any trace of the whaling ship *Amethyst*. The ship had not returned to her home port of San Francisco after the 1885 Arctic whaling season.

Captain Healy began his first cruise in the *Bear* by ordering his navigator to shape a course from San Francisco to Departure Bay, British Columbia, where they would stop for coaling. After the crew's hard, dirty labor of heaving coal, the *Bear* sailed through the beautiful Inside Passage to Sitka. After a brief stay, the cutter made its transit across the Gulf of Alaska to the harbor of Unalaska.[12]

By this time, Healy had over thirty years of sea experience. He began his career in the age of sail and now worked during the slow transition from sail to steam. One third of his three decades at sea had been spent in the dangerous waters of the Bering Sea and Arctic Ocean. Now, following a short visit at Unalaska, Healy would sail his new command, the *Bear*, for the first time into the Bering Sea.

As the *Bear* began to work northward, many a Bering Sea Patrol sailor subscribed to a bit of doggerel penned by someone who sailed in the patrol:

Hear the rattle of the windlass as our anchor comes aweigh;
We are bound to old Point Barrow and we make our start today;
Keep a tight hold on to your dinner, for outside the South wind blows,
And unless you are a sailor, you'll be throwing up your toes.[13]

Although in 1886 Healy's area of operations was officially north of the Pribilofs, the captain briefly patrolled the islands looking for poachers, as well as inquiring about the missing whaler *Amethyst*. Hearing no news of the missing ship, and finding no evidence of illegal sealing, he ordered his navigator to shape a course northward.

When the *Bear* encountered the ice pack, the cuttermen began observing the pack's movement and looking for leads in the ice, information that might prove useful to them later. Healy then ordered the cutter southward to locate the whaling fleet. When he encountered the ships, they were working their way northward along the Siberian coastline. He informed their masters of his ice observations, then sailed back to Alaska's Arctic coastline where Healy and his crew began escorting whalers through the ice and helping any that ran afoul of the pack. During the years that Healy commanded the *Bear*, the cutter usually met the whaling fleet somewhere near Port Clarence, which lies northwest of Nome and just south of the Bering Strait. There, he sent small boats ashore to obtain fresh water in large wooden casks. As the whaling fleet and the *Bear* awaited the opening of the pack, their crews passed the time "gamming," visiting and talking with each other.

In 1886, once the whalers were on their way to the bowhead whaling grounds, Healy visited a number of villages along the northern coast of the Bering Sea, checking for illegal liquor, providing medical aid, and asking around for any sign of the *Amethyst*. Eventually, the cutter made its way to Barrow. According to the few old salts who sailed in the Arctic region, the Eskimos had names for everything. Carrying on a tradition that began with the *Corwin*, the natives called the *Bear* the *Oo-mi-ak-puck pe-chuck ton-i-ka* (no whiskey ship). If Healy allowed anyone ashore at Barrow, he ordered the *Bear* moored to shore ice and used dog sleds to make the trip to the beach.[14]

The *Bear* then cruised among the whaling fleet along the northern shore of Alaska. The cuttermen helped any whaler having trouble in the ice, while the cutter's doctor ministered to the sick and injured. Whenever Healy spoke with a whaler, he asked if the ship's master had sighted the *Amethyst*. With not a single villager from along the Bering Sea and Siberian coastline or any ship's master reporting a trace of the missing ship, Healy reasonably concluded that the whaler, along with its crew, had been lost to the sea. Healy followed the old whaler's belief that the *Amethyst* was now assigned to the "legendary armada of the Arctic; [where] ghostly vessels, gripped fast in the pack, manned by frozen, soulless corpses, circle endlessly around the Ice Pole of the north. The Eskimos believe that their masts grow into icicles, extending to the skies, up which the souls clamber to Heaven."[15]

As the bowhead hunting season drew to a close, the *Bear* began working southward. Once again, Healy's cutter patrolled around the Pribilof Islands, looking for any late-season poachers. Finally, the *Bear*'s bow pointed southward and began the long journey back to San Francisco.

Homecoming fell on October 17, 1886. Upon arrival, the crew received their pay, and most of the enlisted crew struck out for the tender mercies of the Barbary Coast. There, they mixed with the likes of Calico Jim, who was "reputed to have reached the zenith of his career when he shanghaied six policemen, sent one after the other to arrest him." The officers of the *Bear* "were placed on 'waiting orders' or temporarily to duty on other cutters," while the *Bear* remained out of commission, watched over by a skeleton crew until the following spring. During the patrol, Michael A. Healy passed his forty-sixth birthday.[16]

Captain Healy's general routine while sailing in the north varied little from his first patrol. Most old salts agree, however, that while sea duty may consist of many days of routine monotony, one never knows when that monotony will give way to something unusual. Probably the best description of Captain Healy's career in the north is that his routine consisted of nothing routine. For example, in 1885, in his last report as commander of the *Corwin*, Healy wrote that thirty-three whalers visited the Bering Sea and the Arctic, the majority of which were "more or less damaged by ice." In addition, Healy reported five of these whalers as missing. Among the missing, Healy listed the bark *Napoleon*, commanded by Capt. S. P. Smith, of New Bedford, Massachusetts. It was during Captain Healy's second patrol in the *Bear*, in 1887, that the saga of the *Napoleon* unfolded.[17]

At 7:10 p.m. on Tuesday, May 5, during a gale, the bow of the *Napoleon* slammed into a large piece of ice. The bark shook with the force of the impact. Almost immediately, the crew, some of them only half dressed, spilled out of the forecastle as water gushed knee-deep into the crew's quarters. On deck, freezing sea spray flew over the ship. Captain Smith faced a hard command. He had to give the order to abandon ship.[18]

Smith managed to maneuver the sluggish *Napoleon* into a position that protected the small boats from the advancing ice as they were lowered into the frigid water. Within fifteen minutes of striking the ice, all of the bark's crew had huddled in the boats. Shivering from fear and cold, they watched as the *Napoleon* slowly listed and then capsized. The events that led to the sinking of the *Napoleon* happened so fast that its crewmembers had scrambled into their boats with only the clothes they were wearing. Stored in the lifeboats they discovered only a small supply of ship's biscuits to sustain them. The whalers now faced an Arctic storm, hundreds of miles from any source of rescue. Yet another danger confronted the survivors: the ice had begun to close in around them.

Eventually, the four boats struck out for shore, two of which were rescued by another whaler. The other two boats managed to reach the Siberian coast carrying only four survivors, among them boatsteerer James B. Vincent, of Martha's Vineyard, Massachusetts.

In the end, only Vincent survived. An elder of the Chukchi adopted him and taught him how to survive in the harsh climate. Vincent was accepted as a member of the elder's small village of about 125 people. He dressed the same as everyone in the settlement.

At some point around January 1, 1887, Vincent carved a message into a block of wood. He gave it to some passing natives who were traveling to the coast. "He had little hope that it ever would get to anyone from the outside world."[19]

On June 8, 1887, the whaler *Hunter*, off Indian Point, Siberia, welcomed a group of natives aboard for the purpose of trading furs. Two stories exist as to what happened next. Herbert L. Aldrich, who was on board the *Hunter*, recalled: "One old deersman produced a piece of wood carefully wrapped up, on which were letters crudely carved. After some study, we read the following on one side, '1887. J.B.V. Bk. Nap. Tobacco. Live'; and on the other side, 'S.W.C. Nav. M. Help. Come.'"[20]

Aldrich later claimed that the officers deciphered this message. They decided to pass it through the whaling fleet until the report reached the *Bear*.

The second story has Captain Healy receiving the message while anchored at Port Clarence with the whaling fleet. This account maintains that Healy translated the message to read: "1887. James B. Vincent. Bark *Napoleon*. Give tobacco to the native bringing the message. Alive ten miles southwest of Cape Navarin."[21]

No matter which version one chooses to believe, Captain Healy quickly had the *Bear* underway to Cape Navarin. He ordered all possible speed for the entire four-hundred-mile voyage. On the second day out of Port Clarence, however, the *Bear* entered a thick fog. Healy slowed the cutter and navigated by dead reckoning, which involves estimating a position by taking into account the course, speed, and time already traveled. The next morning, the cutter broke out of the murky fog to find "that the course of the ship had been so correctly maintained that she was resting one or two miles off the cape."[22]

Cruising along the Siberian coast, Captain Healy searched for a village. Upon finding one, he obtained a guide, headed in the direction roughly given on the block of wood, and found Vincent. A newspaper reported that it was only through the "indomitable perseverance and zeal of Captain Healy, added to his familiarity with northern waters, that the rescue of the castaway was finally accomplished." Healy distributed gifts to the villagers for their help in taking care of Vincent. Later, Vincent said: "No man can imagine how overjoyed I was when my attention was attracted by the shouting of the natives, and I looked up to see a white man, and to find myself at last rescued. The officers of the revenue cutter *Bear* were exceedingly kind to me, not only while I was on board, but particularly when I landed in San Francisco, alone and penniless."[23]

The Vincent case illustrates what all those who went to sea in whalers knew: they stood a very good chance of becoming shipwrecked. The hunt for the bowhead whale north of the Bering Strait further decreased the chances of survival for those cast adrift. When the hunt carried the whalers eastward across the northern coastline of Alaska, their chances plummeted still lower, even in summer, and dropped to almost zero by autumn. Capt. Thomas W. Roys, who discovered the bowhead grounds in 1848, recognized this danger and thought someone should make provisions for anyone in distress in the area. The result was a hastily planned government station, "staffed expediently," that gave little aid, and abandoned the effort after only seven years of operation. Less than a year later, a major incident left more than one hundred whalers destitute on the Arctic shore, not far from the former Point Barrow Refuge Station. "But if the station's brief history was a model of governmental mismanagement and irresolution, its establishment also displayed governmental responsiveness—albeit dilatory—to deteriorating conditions in the whaling industry."[24]

Captain Roys' prediction that whalers in the Arctic region would suffer significant losses proved accurate. In 1871, thirty-one ships met their end in the ice, fortunately with no loss of life. Five years later, however, thirteen ships went down, taking the lives of forty sailors with them. Nevertheless, the profits from whaling kept owners of whalers sending their ships into danger, despite the lack of shoreside help. The U.S. whaling companies noted that the British government laid in supplies along the Arctic coast to aid those searching for the lost Franklin Expedition. Taking their lead from the British, in 1880 the U.S. whaling companies unsuccessfully petitioned Congress for money to cache supplies at various points along the frozen coastline.

Two years later, the New Bedford steam whaler *North Star* met her end near Point Barrow. Luckily for those cast adrift, the government had established a weather station at the point, and the men sought shelter at the station until other ships arrived in the area. The next year, 1883, the weather unit closed down operations and the Pacific Steam Whaling Company of San Francisco rented the building from the government for use as a trading post and a shore whaling station. The government made a provision that if any wrecks happened nearby, the company would provide care for the sailors.

In 1884, Captain Healy wrote to Sumner I. Kimball, the General Superintendent of the U.S. Life-Saving Service, about establishing a lifesaving station at Point Barrow. Captain Healy felt the risk the *Corwin* took by remaining near the point in late autumn was unacceptable. Following up on his suggestion in a letter to the secretary of the treasury, Healy pointed out that a crew at such a station could also help control the illegal liquor trade. A group of ninety-six whaling ship owners, agents, and captains then petitioned the secretary in support of Captain Healy's plan. Josiah N. Knowles, managing partner of the Pacific Steam Whaling Company, even offered to provide Kimball with the money to build and staff the station. Despite this incentive, however, the proposal languished until another crisis occurred.

On August 2, 1888, thirty whaling ships lay at anchor just west of Point Barrow. Toward evening, a breeze sprung up that within three hours increased to a screaming Arctic gale. The ships upped anchor and sought shelter to the east of the point. By 6:00 p.m. on August 3, the intensifying wind had veered west, and the seas in the shallow anchorage had built. The bark *Eliza* parted her cable, setting off a series of collisions that sunk or damaged several ships. Meanwhile, other vessels also experienced difficulties. After the wind and the seas calmed, 110 sailors found themselves in perilous surroundings. Fortunately, the cutter *Bear* and the U.S. Navy's *Thetis* stood nearby and prevented a large loss of life. This, however, did not end the terrible year of 1888. East of Point Barrow, near Herald Island, a fleet of at least thirteen whalers narrowly escaped entrapment in the ice.

Newspaper headlines throughout the United States stirred the public's outrage about the many dangers facing the Arctic whaling fleet. The New Bedford Board of Trade lent its strong voice to the growing clamor for government help by sending a petition to President Grover Cleveland. While most of the whalers wanted a series of stations at which they could seek refuge in times of trouble, the House of Representatives' Commerce Committee sent a bill to Congress for a paltry $15,000, enough to build and equip only one station at Point Barrow. The bill passed.

Captain Healy transported precut lumber in the *Bear*. On August 1889, near Cape Smyth, about eleven miles south of Point Barrow, Healy detailed Third Lieut. David H. Jarvis to supervise the construction of the station by the cutter's crew and carpenters from nearby whalers. The Point Barrow Refuge Station measured thirty by forty-eight feet, with a twenty-ton coal bunker on one side and a central room with bunks for fifty men along the walls. Its storeroom was stocked with enough provisions to sustain the survivors that would fill its fifty beds for more than a year. While the construction went smoothly, the staffing and operation of the new station can only be described as Byzantine and need not be recounted here. Suffice it to say, the "chaotic tenure" of the station's first superintendent, Gilbert B. Borden, a retired whaling captain, and lack of rescues "caused the station's supporters to lose interest." Even Captains

Hooper and Healy suggested closing the station.[25] Knowles, once the strongest advocate of the station, also joined in falling for its closure. Part of Knowles' change of heart may have stemmed from a chance his company had to buy the station cheap and use it to replace their crumbling whaling station. As it happened, the Pacific Steam Whaling Company did receive the deed for the station on December 29, 1896.[26]

Meanwhile, Captain Healy returned in the *Bear* and divided his time between the Bering Sea and his family home. On September 21, 1888, however, he received orders "to report to the [Treasury] Department and to travel via Central and Union Pacific Railroads from San Francisco to Council Bluffs, [Iowa.]"[27] The reason for the orders is no longer available, but we can surmise that Healy's expertise might have been sought concerning the fate of the refuge station. After finishing his work in Washington, D.C., Captain Healy received twenty days leave.

By this time, Capt. Michael Augustine Healy had at least three decades of sea duty under his belt. He had sailed around the Horn at least twice and worked as a mariner throughout the world. From 1874 onward, he had worked in two of the most unforgiving environments for sailors, the Bering Sea and the western Arctic. Unlike some in the naval services of today, except for very brief periods of returning for temporary duty to Washington, D.C., Michael spent most of his time away from home on board ships for long periods of time. The normal routine of the Bering Sea Patrol, for instance, ensured that he would be away at sea for at least seven months of the year. Once the cutters cleared the area of the Inside Passage to Alaska, there was little in the way of any place for rest and relaxation. The two ports of call where he could relax somewhat were at Unalaska and Nome. Even today, neither of these ports can be considered mainstream American towns. In 2000, for example, Nome's population was 3,505 and Unalaska's was 4,283, and both towns are located in isolated areas. In the early twenty-first century, while sailing a few miles off shore along the Alaskan coastline above the Bering Strait, sailors still see very little, if any, signs of habitation until the tall radio towers of Barrow heave into view. In other words, the land remains as isolated now as it was in Healy's day.

Healy celebrated his forty-sixth birthday on his first Bering Sea Patrol in command of the cutter *Bear*. Along with the isolation, eleven years in the Bering Sea above the Arctic Circle can take its toll on even the strongest person. Above the Arctic Circle, the winds are never warm and at times the cold seems to penetrate your very soul. In addition, the wind and reflection off the ice can quickly burn your skin and even cause snow blindness. The nineteenth century had no handy sunscreen to rub on your skin, or special dark glasses to protect your eyes. Even dressed in furs and gloves, working in the maritime Arctic one never seems to be able to keep dry and warm, two states vitally important to survival. Hands exposed to the cold, once held near heat, hurt as they begin to warm and even when they are finally warm, still ache. Those working in such an environment know that they must face constant pain.

When modern-day icebreakers work in the ice pack, the officer of the deck maneuvers the ship through the ice—known as conning the ship—following the precedent set by early Arctic navigators, such as Healy. Most good ice navigators know they must get as high as possible on the mast in order to see over pressure ridges and hummocks in the ice. Today, ice conning stations high on the mast are warm, enclosed spaces. Captain Healy, however, recorded many shifts of up to seventy hours in the crow's nest, facing the full fury of the Arctic weather. Healy aptly described the toll placed upon captains who dared to navigate in the largely uncharted Arctic waters. The "exposure to the severity of the climate," he wrote, "soon ages a man and breaks down his constitution."[28]

As the 1880s drew to a close, changes began to take hold in Captain Healy. He recognized he had a drinking problem and asked Mary Jane to accompany him on his voyages in 1883, 1884, and 1885. While she remained on board, Healy seemed fine, but his volatile temper was apt to flare up at any moment. Healy recognized his own "Irish disposition," but his experiences at sea intensified his rage. Brother Patrick, when he sailed with Michael in 1883, confided to his diary that he witnessed in his brother "exceedingly unpleasant" moments of rage that sometimes even included those closest to him. While at sea, Patrick realized that his brother's moodiness caused him to throw himself "back upon himself and his grievances." Patrick witnessed on one occasion after returning home from sea, a heated argument between Michael and Mary Jane, during which Michael stomped out. He returned four days later, contrite and begging forgiveness.[29]

It was known that the Far North took its toll upon Michael A. Healy, but most did not realize just how much. Mary Jane, of course, recognized his moods, but out of loyalty she did not publicly seek help.

For the most part, Healy was able to control his moods and only reveal what he wanted people to see. For example, before departing for San Francisco from Washington, D.C., Healy visited New York City and his first command, the *Chandler*. While aboard the cutter, a reporter from Joseph Pulitzer's newspaper, *The World*, interviewed him. Never one to hide his exploits from the press, Healy made great copy for the journalist.[30]

The then unknown reporter first informed readers of Healy's qualifications: "The reputation of reeling off a [sea story] in 'shipshape and Bristol fashion' is well maintained by Capt. M. A. Healy, the dignified commander of the revenue cutter *Bear*." The journalist reported that Healy had been detained in Washington "on urgent Department business," but "seized the opportunity to again look in upon his friends before bidding them a final adieu and departing for the land of the setting sun, where he has been ordered."

In response to a question about duty on board cutters in the Arctic, Captain Healy replied, "Well, it is a mighty sight pleasanter to be sitting in these cosy [*sic*] quarters of my friend here and talking about it than to stand for forty hours on the bridge of the *Bear*, wet, cold and hungry, hemmed in by impenetrable masses of fog, tortured by uncertainty, with the good ship plunging and contending with ice seas in an unknown ocean."

Healy then gave a short description of his career:

I held the rank of third lieutenant when for the first time I viewed the rough and desolate shores bordering on the cruel, mystic Arctic. The very name carries with it a suggestive thrill, a shudder of horror.

I was attached to the revenue cutter *Corwin* when she made her cruise after tidings of the whalers *Vigilant* and . . . *Wollaston*, with instructions to communicate with the *Jeannette* and De Long if possible. It was in June when we struck the ice which forms a perpetual barrier around Wrangel Land. The outline of the land loomed up and was well denned, about twenty-five miles distant. The furtherest point north reached was about 71 degrees 50 minutes, which record has not been beaten by any United States vessel. . . . The ice we encountered was something terrible, and the sharp bows of the *Corwin* were sadly battered from forcing her way through the thick fields. We visited St. Lawrence Island and there found a horrible example of the effect of the illicit trade in whiskey. Out of 700 inhabitants, over 500 were found dead of starvation.

At one point during the interview, Captain Healy said, "It has been my fortune to have a great deal of this extreme northern work to do. . . . I am now a captain, at the top of my profession, so far as the Revenue-Cutter Service is concerned." As he left New York City to return to the *Bear* in San Francisco, Capt. Michael A. Healy's comment did not seem so much the braggadocio of a sea dog, as it did the truth.

"Monster Healy"

On Tuesday, March 8, 1889, R. W. Bartleman, Secretary of the Massachusetts Humane Society, mailed a letter to the Treasury Department. Bartleman requested a "statement of the services of Captain M. A. Healy" in "rendering assistance to wrecked or disabled whalemen in the Arctic Ocean; also, . . . his place of birth."[1] Founded in 1786 to save those in danger of drowning, the Boston-based volunteer organization carried enough importance in the nation's capital to receive a reply in only eight days from I. H. Maynard, the Assistant Secretary of the Treasury.[2] The typed, eight-page return letter detailed Healy's service for the years 1882 to 1888. Maynard concluded that the *Corwin* and the *Bear*, "while under the command of Captain Healy, were instrumental in rescuing two hundred and fifty-six shipwrecked sailors, one hundred and eighty-six of whom were transported to San Francisco."[3] Not surprisingly, Maynard included the rescue freshest in the public's mind, that of boatsteerer James B. Vincent, the whaler shipwrecked in Siberia whom Captain Healy had rescued in 1887. Maynard informed Bartleman that Captain Healy's record gave Georgia as his place of birth. Bartleman's letter, sent prior to the *Bear*'s 1889 cruise, marked a movement among whalers and others to honor Healy for his years of helping the whaling fleet in the Arctic.

Only a few of those who served or rode as passengers on the revenue cutters into a little-known region, unfortunately, ever bothered to leave diaries or letters describing their impressions of, or duties, adventures, or experiences in the Arctic areas. As a result, a scarcity of accounts exist that detail day-to-day life aboard these cutters.

During the patrol of 1889, however, Dr. James Taylor White, a surgeon, served as the doctor on board the *Bear*. The son of Capt. John W. White, of long service in the U.S. Revenue Cutter Service, Alaska and along the West Coast, James' father still remained on the active list, but on detached duty as an inspector in the U.S. Life-Saving Service on the West Coast.[4] Doctor White, in other words, knew something of the service. White's importance to our understanding of Capt. Michael A. Healy, however, resides solely in the fact that he kept a diary.

Doctor White recorded that the *Bear* departed San Francisco on Monday, June 10, 1889, at 9:15 a.m. On board were eight other officers, a crew of forty-four men, and two passengers in the cabin. First Lieut. Albert Buhner served as executive officer and Engineer Horace Hassell as chief engineer (hereinafter referred to as "chief"). Second Lieut. John C. Cantwell held the important position of navigator. Captain Healy had previously served with both First Lieutenant Buhner and Second Lieutenant Cantwell.

Almost immediately after getting underway, White began recording the quirks of his brother officers. Writing of their departure, he observed that the poor "chief seems rather excited and to steady his nerves, he imbibed rather freely in some spirits which he kept corked up in a one gallon demi-john."[5]

Two days out of San Francisco, White recorded that he held an inspection of the berthing decks and, finding them damp, "remarked about it being unhealthy to sleep in such damp places." Lieutenant Buhner's reply set the tone for the relationship between the two men. "There you go, just like all the other doctors. Now this deck has got to be kept clean and when I want to wash it [,] I will and I will dry it when I please."

Later in the day, White wrote that Cantwell "has grave designs on [Hassell's] whiskey." The doctor recorded that he heard a conversation between the two men:

"Ain't it about time, Chief?"
"Shouldn't wonder."
"Siz'er up."
"That's right."
"Pretty good stuff."

Doctor White wrote that there was a method behind this design to rid Hassell of his personal whiskey supply. Cantwell wanted the supply gone, so the Chief would have to "buy from the wine mess" and thus help the officer's wardroom fund.

Almost two weeks later, while in Unalaska, White visited the other cutters in port. He remarked that he could not "help noticing the difference in the atmosphere on the 'Rush' and 'Bear'": "it all comes from having two men at the head who are gentlemen. You go on board [the *Rush*] and everything is lively. You are not afraid to laugh and look pleasant, while here you are afraid to do any thing for fear of getting a blowing up. So far Capt. Healy has been very pleasant, at least to me. The only one complaining is Mr. Cantwell but I don't think Mike is at all partial and we will all have our turn. The only trouble I have had is with Mr. Buhner (6/20) and since then he has only spoken to me in an official way."

On June 24, Doctor White mentioned taking a walk near Unalaska and stopping on his return to board a whaler. There, he found "Mr. Buhner on board and thirteen of the men in irons." White wrote, "Of all the dirty holds I ever saw this vessel beats all and, they tell me, all whalers are alike."

In this short passage, White deals with the sight of sailors placed in irons. This observation is the best illustration of a relatively common punishment inflicted upon sailors in the Bering Sea.

While in Unalaska, Doctor White began commenting on Healy's drinking. He remarked that Captain Healy "over loaded" once and that "three decanters of *medicine* have already gone in to the cabin." (White's emphasis.)

June 29, White recorded that "three men from [a nearby coal bark] laughed at [Captain Healy] and he had them placed in double irons and ordered them 'triced up' but the officers *did not hear* the order." As explained earlier, placing a sailor in irons refers to snapping manacles connected by a chain onto his wrists, on the order of modern-day handcuffs. To be placed in "double irons" means to have manacles placed on both one's wrists and ankles. Tricing up, the reader will recall, refers to putting a sailor's arms behind his back, placing his wrists in irons, running a line run through the chain of the wrist irons and up to a ring high on the mast, and finally hoisting the sailor until his toes barely touch the deck.

Later, Captain Healy invited some of his officers to accompany him on a picnic. White mentions that the junior officers did not care to go, and "[Third Lieut. David] Jarvis succeeded in breaking the affair up."

Doctor White recorded that he felt Healy's behavior grew more erratic the longer the *Bear* remained in Unalaska. As an example, he noted an incident concerning Second Lieutenant Cantwell. It began when Healy, without advance planning, came out on deck and ordered the cutter to get underway for a short distance and anchor in the harbor. Earlier, Doctor White had confined Lieutenant Cantwell to his bunk owing to sickness.

After the *Bear* anchored, Healy noticed that Cantwell was not at his anchor detail station. When he asked about Cantwell, Healy learned that White had placed Cantwell on the sick list and responded, "The doctor must either report the case or Mr. Cantwell come on deck." Doctor White then made a written report.

Upon receiving the doctor's report, Healy said, "What's the matter with him?"

"Neuralgia."

"You may order him to go ashore. Tell him he's not worth a damn. I'll tell him so."

"Shall he go on shore to stay or is he to come back when this is over with?"

"Tell him to take the first steamer to San Francisco. He's not worth a damn any way. I'll tell him so. I'll tell him he's not worth a damn."

White noted: "Damn was as strong a word as he could find just then. His tongue was so thick that it would hardly work."

Doctor White mentioned that most of the officers in the wardroom agreed that Lieutenant Cantwell was "playing off and has fooled me badly." Later, Healy ordered White to go ashore, find Dr. Samuel J. Call, of the Alaska Commercial Company, and hold a medical survey on Cantwell. White recorded that he felt a great sense of relief when Doctor Call reached the same diagnosis. The officers of the *Bear*, however, still believed that Cantwell was malingering. "Mr. Jarvis," White recorded, "told me he thought Cantwell was shamming for he knew the man and knew it was his nature." Rumor in the wardroom had it that Healy wrote a letter to Washington in which he accused his lieutenant of being a "fraud," "deceitful," and of "no earthly account as an officer."[6]

Finally underway in the Bering Sea, Doctor White went on to record incidents in which he believed Captain Healy was drunk. He also mentioned that Healy had difficulty sleeping.

On Monday, July 8, Doctor White recorded, "Capt. Carrigan of the 'Wanderer' came over to tell us his crew had mutinied and wished our aid. Mr. Buhner went over with the master at arms and a lot of irons and about 9 P.M. I was sent for in great haste as one man had fainted. When I reached the bark I found that twenty-one men had been placed in double irons and 'triced up.' One man had fainted and I was to see whether he had been injured or not. I considered his a case of fright and as this is his first cruise I don[']t think he will come to sea again."

Five days later, Doctor White again recorded officers of the *Bear* going to the aid of a whaling captain. "This morning three men on the Bk 'Tom Pope' were placed in irons for refusal of duty. There was also trouble on another vessel but nothing serious."

One of the many reasons the officers and crews of the U.S. Revenue Cutter Service earned the respect of those in isolated areas was the medical care they provided for both sailors and natives. Doctor White's diary entry on Saturday, July 6, for example, records that a "sailor from the 'Narwhale' was sent on board for surgical treatment, and in the evening [I] operated on him." On the same day, White wrote that he "was occupied administering to the medical wants of the natives."

Without a doubt, the crews cared for the native people. At times, however, the officers seemed to look upon native customs as being unworthy of respect. On Saturday, July 13, White reported that, while out hunting, he and his companion, Mr. Carrigan, one of the *Bear*'s passengers, came upon some graves. "I found the graves more numerous than the game and to me more interesting. Carrigan soon caught the fever and so guns were laid aside and a hunt for curios commenced. We were quite successful, finding stone & bone implements in the old graves. I found some pieces of pottery, the first I have ever heard of among these natives." Seventeen days later, near Point Barrow, White wrote, "I took a walk through the grave yard. Here they bury different from the Point Hope natives. Their older graves are all underground but the more recent ones are on top. The body is wrapped up in skins and secured to the ground by pegs. We opened two but found no trinkets of value."

Toward the end of the patrol, Doctor White wrote his strongest passages on Captain Healy's drinking. On Friday, July 26, for example, White wrote that the captain, upon finding little trade from a group of villagers in their boats, "got mad and drove them off, throwing coal at them and even going so far as to point a gun at them."

> He says he is not coming up here next year and wants to fix it for the next fellow.
>
> The Capt. appears about crazy and is almost blind. He has drunk only four gallons of my whisky besides his own and as much more from the whalers, beer and wine not counted. This makes four weeks of continuous drunk.

White continued his comments on Healy's drinking sporadically throughout the rest of the cruise.

On Wednesday, July 31, Doctor White noted that the day marked the "first time any of our men have been placed in irons. A man, Jones, became rather impudent and was placed in the coal bunkers for his trouble."

Despite White's many comments about Healy's drunkenness, he did record on August 27 that while off the mouth of the Yukon River most of the officers and crew of the *Bear* were sent to help the crew aboard the grounded steamer *Yukon*. Captain Healy, with a skeleton crew, including the doctor, were able to successfully work the *Yukon* free and tow it safely to St. Michael. Doctor White's diary ends on Sunday, September 29, with the *Bear* moored once more at Unalaska.

Dr. James T. White's diary is extremely important because it is the first major historical document to portray Captain Healy's drinking to excess for long periods of time while on duty. At this time in naval history, it was permissible for officers to drink while on board a ship at sea, but they were not to drink so much that it interfered with their duties. White's diary establishes beyond doubt that drinking was an accepted routine for the officers of the *Bear*.

The *Bear* returned to San Francisco on October 21, 1889. The crew received their pay and departed, while the cutter's officers resumed their normal routines in port.

On December 13, 1889, Michael and Mary Jane were met in the lobby of the Occidental Hotel by a delegation of whaling captains. The couple was escorted to a special room for a banquet. Presiding over a gathering of at least 150 representatives hailing from San Francisco and the whaling and the shipping industries was Capt. William H. Kelly of the bark *Jane Gray*. On behalf of the whaling and shipping industries, Captain Kelly presented Michael with a beautiful testimonial and a watch for all his years of service in the Arctic.

Less than one month later, however, pedestrians in San Francisco received handbills calling for them to attend an "indignation mass meeting" at the Metropolitan Temple on Fifth Street, at 8:00 p.m., Saturday, January 11, 1890. The notice blared, "Healy! Healy! Healy! The monster of the U.S. Revenue Marine Service! Come and Hear of the Horrible Deeds Committed by that Fiend in Alaskan Waters."[7]

On Saturday evening, members of the Coast Seaman's Union, led by a band and dressed in uniform, marched through the streets of San Francisco to the Metropolitan Temple. The musicians led the sailors into the gathering. Carrying an American flag, the sailors paraded to the platform and "placed [the flag] on the stage behind the speaker's desk." A few minutes later, members of the Brewery Workers Union "forced their way through the crowd and found places on the platform for their principal officers. They carried a transparency displaying the picture of a triced-up sailor and the words, 'The Tortures of the Inquisition Revived by Captain Healy.'"

Unlike those who gathered at the Occidental Hotel in honor of Healy's award, this large audience comprised working-class men. The San Francisco *Call* observed that very "few of the gentler sex" attended. On stage to make the required oratory, sat "the Hon. Charles Sumner, Rev. J. A. Cruzan, ex-Judge Robert Ferral, Herman Guttstadt, Rev. Richard Darcout, D.D, W. J. B. Mackay, Thomas Finnety, Andrew Fursyth, Alfred Fuhrman, H. Whitman, and members of the Coast Seaman's Union in uniform, and the Brewery Workers in regalia." The program began with the distribution of an affidavit by a seaman named Alfred Holben. "A lively air by Professor A. J. Smith's band" helped prepare the audience for the evening of speeches. What drew a crowd that "thoroughly tested" the seating capacity of the Metropolitan Temple was the condemnation of "the tricing-up of three American seamen named Alfred Holben, Otto Daeweritz, and Roy Framsden at Oonalaska [Unalaska] by Captain Healy of the United States Steamship BEAR."

Mackay, editor of the Coast Seaman's *Journal,* read Holben's affidavit and told the audience that American ships "are known throughout the world as the most barbarous afloat. They are barbarous because such men as Healy are given authority." The pastor of the Third Congregational Church, Reverend Cruzan, intoned: "men were once tortured upon the land and the day has come when they must no longer be tortured on the sea. . . . The man who can rule on sea or land is the man who can rule himself. He who cannot control himself cannot control others."

Sumner declared that harshness had no place on the deck of a naval vessel. He declared that he had sailed around the Horn in 1850 before the mast: "during that voyage of six months I never saw a man struck or heard one sworn at. I never heard an oath from an officer or anything that could be considered ungentlemanly." One wonders what ship Sumner sailed in—one from the Papal navy?

Herman Guttstadt claimed that conditions in the American merchant marine were inferior to those of the British. "Congress," he said, "should be urged to repeal all laws which give to officers the power to treat sailors as Captain Healy had treated the sailors who complained against him."

Former judge Robert Ferral felt that Healy had operated outside of the law. He called for a trial on charges of cruelty and inhumanity to seamen. Ferral praised the intervention of the new seaman's union in this case.

The last speaker, Alfred Fuhrman, Statistical Secretary of the Council of Federated Trades, compared Healy's actions to the burning of the witches at Salem, Massachusetts. "Thank God we know that the strong arm of a strong government will make the repetition of such acts impossible," he said. "If, after full investigation, the general Government did not accord the vindication sought, the people could display their sovereignty at the ballet box." The crowd loudly proclaimed the resolutions proposed by Fuhrman and called upon the Secretary of the Treasury to investigate the case. Henry H. Spicer, a sailor who had served on board the cutter *Bear*, gave his eyewitness report of the incident. James Hughes, the master at arms serving in the *Bear* at the time, and the man who had triced up the sailors, accused Captain Healy of being constantly drunk while at sea.

Mackay forwarded the resolution to Washington, D.C., on January 25. While the document made its way across country, Mrs. Rosamond R. Johnson, President of the California Woman's Christian Temperance Union (WCTU), wrote to William Windom, the Secretary of the Treasury, requesting action against Captain Healy. Mrs. Johnson quoted a judge, whom she did not identify, as stating, "It is difficult to imagine how a gentleman on land should be transformed to a demon at sea." Mrs. Johnson supplied the Secretary of the Treasury with the not too surprising answer, "The habitual use of intoxicating drink is proven to be the transforming agency."

Sixteen days later, on January 29, Mrs. M. B. Eden, identified as the Superintendent of Work Among Sailors of the California WCTU, wrote a letter to Secretary Windom. Her strongly worded missive told of how she worked on "behalf of our Arctic Sailors, and whalers whose sufferings you have it in your power to lessen very much by giving the U.S. Steamer ship, which yearly goes north for the protection, in part at least, of our whaling fleet, into the command of a temperate, and humane man." Mrs. Eden continued, "I am reliably informed that Captain Healey [*sic*], the present commander, is while at sea, an inebriate, being often in a drunken state for days at a time, and while in that condition, has been guilty of great cruelty toward the men on board the whalers, and some of the merchant vessels." Further, she claimed that Healy "endangered the lives of the crew of the 'Bear' by running it aground, while too drunk to navigate, and also the lives of the men on the whaling bark 'Logodo' while towing the latter vessel out of Oonalaska [Unalaska]." Mrs. Eden went on to point out that Captain Healy had triced up twenty-three men on the bark *Wanderer*, causing one sailor to faint and another to go into convulsions, and the doctor from the *Bear* had had to attend to the sailors. She also pointed out that Healy's drinking led to his "brutality." Mrs. Eden concluded, "had Captain Healey [*sic*] been a sober man, I doubt if any of these cases of cruelty, and neglect of duty would have happened, for he was undeniably and dreadfully drunk on each occasion."

Not all accounts, however, seemed to weigh against Healy. One newsletter said the mass meeting "was called by the Coast Seamen's Union, at which a little red-nosed demagogue spoke, assisted by a sensational preacher, who has no standing in the community north of Market Street." This newsletter actually characterized the mass meeting as being "presided over by men who know nothing of the facts of the case, or else they are political panderers. It was no place, at least for a preacher of the gospel, to sit in judgment on a man who has the respect of the mercantile community, and adjudge him guilty without any positive knowledge of the subject."

Reacting to the adverse publicity, Secretary Windom did what many bureaucrats do when placed in embarrassing circumstances by the press: he appointed a board of inquiry composed of three members. Appointed president of the board was Capt. John W. White, father of Dr. James T. White. Also on the board were Collector of Customs T. G. Phelps of San Francisco and Surgeon T. H. Bailhache. Phelps had sailed to Alaska early in his career, and Doctor Bailhache "was familiar with the medical results of long Arctic cruising."[8] The task of defending Captain Healy fell upon Maj. E. B. Stonehill, while attorney H. W. Hutton represented the three seamen who accused Healy of the cruel acts.[9]

The New York papers began covering the story as early as February 28, 1890. The *Times* reported, "the merchants of San Francisco are extremely desirous to see Capt. Healy retained in the service from the fact he has rendered their whaling interests incalculable aid. The Seaman's Union and the citizens of San Francisco not interested . . . in the whaling trade demand, on the other hand, the expulsion of Capt. Healy from the service. In well-informed Revenue Marine circles the opinion is expressed that Capt. Healy will escape with a light reprimand."

The hearing took place in Room 25 of the Appraisers Building in San Francisco. On Monday, March 3, testimony began. The three seamen—Albert Holben, Roy Framsden, and Otto Daeweritz—the prosecution's star witnesses, filed in. Under questioning, they told a strange tale of being crewmembers on board the coal bark *Estella*. En route to Unalaska, Capt. E. O. Avery and his first mate became so drunk that the ship was endangered. At times, the three seamen refused to obey what they considered to be absurd, drunken orders from Avery. Then, Captain Avery's drunken actions caused the bark to run aground. Unaided by any officers, the crew managed to work the vessel afloat and anchor it overnight. Wary of the bark's perilous position and fearing it would sink that night, the three seamen took their belongings ashore. Finding their bark still afloat the next morning, they returned on board.[10]

Eventually, the *Estella* arrived at Unalaska. Shortly thereafter, the cutter *Bear* came alongside it to start coaling. The thirty-three-year-old Holben, with fifteen years of sea experience, related how his "Mate called me out of the hold," where he was busy shoveling coal. "Here is Captain Healey [*sic*]," Holben reported the mate as saying, "he wants to see you." Since Holben claimed he had never seen Captain Healy, he asked, "Where is the man that wants to see me?" Holben testified that Healy simply looked at him and remarked, "Alfred, you are very tricky." Holben replied, "What did you say that to me for?" Captain Healy, according to the seaman, sternly answered, "Not another word, but go forward." The sailor obeyed, complaining, "I don't know what you have got to do with whatever." According to Holben, nothing further happened until a few days later.

Holben proceeded to testify that after he and Framsden finished with their part of coaling the *Bear*, they received orders to let go the mooring lines of the revenue cutter. After casting off, the two seamen returned to their own ship and stood by the rail, where Framsden asked his shipmate, "Where's our captain?" Overhearing this remark, Captain Healy asked, "Are you talking?" Framsden replied, "Yes, sir." Captain Healy then called for his master at arms, James Hughes. Upon Hughes' arrival, Captain Healy pointed at Framsden and ordered the master at arms to "put that man in irons right away." Hughes quickly went below to get the irons.

According to Holben, in the meanwhile, another sailor on board the *Estella* had joined his shipmates at the rail. "Why don't you go forward and get out of sight," the newly arrived sailor advised Framsden, "so that he will not see you?" Framsden promptly followed this advice. When the master at arms returned on deck, therefore, Captain Healy could not see the offending sailor and told Hughes, "never mind, he is gone."

The advice-giving sailor then said to Holben, "I don't see what he [Captain Healy] has got to do with you." Holben replied, "No, I don't think he has got anything to do with me." According to Holben, Captain Healy overheard this remark and quickly replied, "No, haven't I [?] Master-at-Arms, put that man in irons, never mind the other one!"

Hughes, with an unidentified revenue officer in tow, rushed over to the bark's forecastle, where Holben had taken refuge. "Young fellow," the master at arms quietly explained, "you have to come, if he wants you, he is going to have you too." Holben then turned to the revenue officer, asking why he was being punished. The officer replied that he had been ordered to put him in irons and trice him up. The sailor next asked, "What are you doing it for?" In reply, the *Bear's* officer truthfully said, "I have to obey orders."

The master at arms then triced up Holben twice: once for seven or eight minutes and a second time for about fifteen minutes. After that, Hughes put Holben's arms around a stanchion and shackled them with irons. This forcibly seated the sailor so it appeared that he was hugging the stanchion. Holben remained in that position for over four hours before being released. The master at arms then ordered him back to his ship, with the warning that it would be "better" for him, if he did not say anything about it to his shipmates. "This is nothing," Hughes said, "the next time you will be treated a damned sight worse."

During the questioning, the New York *Herald* reported that Captain Healy "walked up and down the floor, never asking a question or otherwise taking part in the proceedings." The transcript of the trial, however, shows that he did question the witnesses. Healy asked Holben, for example, whether or not he and the other two sailors had argued with the master and the mate of the *Estella*. He followed that up by asking if the mate had tried to strike Holben and if the other two sailors instead had struck the mate. Only after additional questioning did Holben admit that both the mate and Framsden showed bruises and cuts indicating a fight.

Captain Healy proceeded to his next set of questions. He began: "You state you never saw me before, and that I called you 'Alfred'?"

"No, I never saw you before."

"How do you suppose I got your name [?] How could I know your name?"

"The Captain told you my name, or the Mate told you my name."

"I said that you were full of tricks?"

"Yes sir."

"Did I not say to you that the Captain and the Mate had made very serious reports against you, and cautioned you to be more careful?"

"You did not say such a thing. The only words were the words I say that you spoke to me."

Roy Framsden, a sailor with five years of experience in American ships, basically confirmed what had happened up to the point when the master at arms placed Holben in irons. He related that he then sought out Captain Avery and asked why Holben had been taken away. Avery replied that it was none of his business and implied that Holben "was no good, he was no sailor." Captain Avery next called Framsden a "God-damned Hoodlum." When Framsden protested, stating the captain "had no occasion to call me a hoodlum," Avery promptly called for his mate and gave orders that sent the mate rushing over to the *Bear*.

In short order, the mate returned with an officer and the master at arms from the *Bear*. "As I was going aft over the gang-way," testified Framsden, "Otto Daeweritz asked Captain Healy . . . what he was putting me in irons for, as he had no occasion at all [to do this.]" Captain Healy first replied, "It is none of your business." Then, for whatever reason, Healy gave the order, "Put that man in irons." As the two sailors got into the small boat that would take them to the cutter, Framsden remembered Captain Healy shouting new orders, "Put those men in irons and trice them up good."

Otto Daeweritz, with six years of experience on American ships, confirmed Framsden's account of how the two came to be triced up. The twenty-three-year-old Daeweritz proved the least talkative of the three sailors. Surprisingly, he seemed almost apologetic about testifying against Healy. Captain Healy, meanwhile, did not interrupt his pacing to question either Framsden or Daeweritz. Shortly after hearing the two sailors' testimony, the trial adjourned for the day.

James Hughes, the *Bear*'s master at arms and a ten-year veteran of sailing in British ships, led off the testimony on Tuesday, March 4. He had shipped as an ordinary seaman on May 4, 1889, and was rated by Healy as a master at arms eight days later. After Hughes seated himself, reported the New York *Herald*, Captain Healy stopped his pacing "long enough to take a good look at Hughes' face and then resumed his walking."

The master at arms repeated the testimony already given that detailed how he came to be called by Healy to place Holben in irons. He then told the three members of the board how he and Lieutenant Cantwell had boarded the *Estella* and entered the crew's quarters in the forecastle. "Young fellow," Hughes reported Cantwell said, "you might as well come quiet, for come you will have to." The two revenue cuttermen and their prisoner then returned to the *Bear*, where Hughes promptly triced up Holben.

According to Hughes' testimony, after the mate of the *Estella* came on board the *Bear* and talked to Lieutenant Cantwell, the lieutenant quickly ordered

Hughes to go back aboard the bark, place Framsden in irons, and bring him back to the cutter. As Hughes escorted Framsden in irons to the small boat that would transport him to the *Bear*, Daeweritz approached Captains Avery and Healy and asked, "Captain, what are you putting the men in irons for?" Regardless of which captain the unfortunate sailor questioned, the response came immediately from Captain Healy. Wheeling about, Healy ordered the master at arms "to take him too." The remaining testimony relates to the tricing up incident followed by stories told by the three sailors subjected to the punishment.

When questioned whether or not he had ever seen Captain Healy drunk, Hughes retreated from his earlier remarks at the mass meeting. "I cannot swear," the master at arms said under oath, "that I ever saw Captain Healy drunk." Upon closer questioning, Hughes testified that Healy might have had a drink of liquor, but, in his opinion, his captain "was able to do his duty."

Hughes testified that he had never seen tricing up used on English ships. When asked whether he had seen cuttermen inflict this punishment again on another occasion, the master at arms described an incident he had witnessed on board the bark *Wanderer* near Port Clarence later in the cruise. Hughes related that, in this case, upon boarding the ship, he had seen "a chain stretched along her deck": "I think there were seven men that were in irons, and the chain passed through their irons, and the other seven were made fast with a small line, and there were five or six more up aloft."

Once on board, the revenue lieutenant with him "called these men down from aloft, and he told me to take the irons off the men that were ironed around the chain, and told me to put them on behind their backs." Hughes could not remember whether they triced up twenty or twenty-one sailors. The coxswain from the *Bear*, who had been in charge of the boat that brought them over to the *Wanderer*, assisted him in this task; they "triced them up on board in the same position as on board the 'Bear.'" Hughes continued: "They were left there, I am not able to tell how long, but there was one man fainted in the lashings. We lowered him down and the first lieutenant sent the boat back for . . . Doctor White of the 'Bear.'" Hughes recalled that it took "twenty minutes from the time the man fainted until he came to" and reported that he did not know the reason for this mass disciplinary action.

The president of the board, Captain White, then asked Hughes how Captain Healy treated his own men on board the *Bear*. Hughes replied, "Very well."

Next, Healy asked another series of questions. This time, he began: "How many men were punished on the 'Bear' during that trip?"

"One man."

"Jones?"

"Jones, that is all."

"Did you make any report against any of the men?"

"I reported two men, but they were not punished."

Hughes explained to Captain White that he had reported the men for making noise after hours, but Captain Healy merely "cautioned them and told them not to let it happen again."

Further questioning by the board revealed that Healy had demoted (disrated) Hughes just before they left Unalaska and embarked on their return trip to San Francisco. Healy did not give Hughes a reason for his demotion. Shortly after returning to San Francisco, Hughes reported sick. He was given an honorable discharge and sent to the hospital.

After Hughes testified, the *New York Times*, under the headline "The Terror of the Arctic," noted that San Francisco "has a strong stomach in matters of nautical brutalities." The article continued: "these repeated complaints of Healy's severities have attracted comparatively little attention until this year. But at last the public is beginning to realize that where there is so much smoke there must be some fire." The unknown reporter pointed out that Healy had cruised in Alaska for many years. "Every year his return has been heralded by the complaints of the whaling and other crews with whom he happened to be brought in contact." Trying to understand why Healy appeared so cruel, the reporter pointed out: "sometimes the complaints [against him] have been unjust, and have been known to be so, and that fact, until this year, has given Healy the reputation of a persecuted man. Encouraged by impunity, he has apparently allowed his domineering instincts to carry him beyond all bounds."

The reporter also contended: "Healy is not by any means a fiend. He is simply a natural despot whose autocratic temperament has been developed by a long course of unrestrained sovereignty in regions in which the commander of a revenue cutter is a Proconsul whose whims are law." Furthermore, the article claimed that the "divine right of a Captain to get drunk and maltreat his crew has been one that has [been] upheld with especial enthusiasm."

The article went on to report that everyone agreed that Captain Healy treated his own crew humanely, but singled out the crews of whalers for special treatment. Finally, the reporter closed by pointing out that it was "unfortunate" that "none of the other revenue commanders who have cruised in the Behring

[Bering Sea] and the Arctic have [not] been subjected to the charges of cruelty, while such accusations drift home with his ship as regularly as his [Healy's] annual cruises."

The following witnesses essentially repeated the description of the tricing up incident on board the *Estella*, along with comments about Healy's lack of sobriety. The first non-sailor witness, Dr. F. Bass, detailed the toll tricing up took on the human body. Mrs. N. B. Eden, who wrote to the Secretary of the Treasury about Healy's drunkenness, was the next non-sailor to testify. Before she could deliver her testimony, however, the attorney for the three sailors, H. W. Hutton, made an unusual statement before the board.

Hutton told the board that he had initially taken the case on the understanding that he would represent the three seamen in their suit against Healy, based on Healy's alleged mistreatment of them. After arriving at court, however, "a number of people spoke to me and asked me to take general charge of the matter, and said they would produce abundant evidence to sustain all the charges. That was the first time I knew anything about drunkenness or insobriety on the part of Captain Healy." Hutton then agreed to take on the case "for the time being, but they had to furnish witnesses to sustain the charges, as I knew nothing about them." The people urging Hutton to attend to Healy's drinking habits said they had a number of witnesses from many vessels to support these accusations. Nevertheless, Hutton explained: "they have failed to furnish them. At their request I asked for a continuance for two weeks. Now they tell me their witnesses are not here, and they are not ready to proceed. That is my position so far as the insobriety is concerned. I don't know anything about whether Captain Healy was sober or not. They have failed to furnish me with the witnesses, and consequently I wish to disclaim any further interest in that part of the case at all. They have failed to keep their part of the contract, and I do not consider it binding on me."

When Mrs. Eden came under questioning, she gave as her source for the charges against Captain Healy a seaman named Henry Spicer, who had served on board the *Bear*. Despite having known Spicer for less than a year, Mrs. Eden had invited him into her house and considered herself "well acquainted with him." Under close questioning, however, Mrs. Eden admitted that she could only recall two men from the *Bear* who had spoken about Healy's drunkenness. She then testified that the drunkenness charges were based upon hearsay evidence, but could not recall the names of those who gave this evidence. Mrs. Eden remembered the names of only two men: Henry Spicer and William O'Connor.

William O'Connor, at the time of the trial, was serving in the cutter *Rush* at San Francisco. While O'Connor told the trial board that he knew Captain Healy "was a drinking man," he testified, "I can't say that I did see him intoxicated." O'Connor went on to say that Healy treated his crew with consideration and kindness. In O'Connor's opinion, Healy treated merchant crews more harshly than he did his own.

Next to testify was Lieutenant Albert Buhner, the executive officer of the *Bear*, who claimed that the *Estella* incident began when Captain Avery sent word to Healy that his crew was mutinous. The twenty-five-year veteran officer said that "three men had pounded the mate, and he pointed out the mate, and showed his face had been pounded." Buhner testified that his instructions from Captain Healy were that, given the difficulties that had transpired on board the bark, "if any more occurred, to go on board and take the people that made the difficulty out of her and put them in irons."

Buhner testified that he later noticed Healy speaking to the sailors, one of whom was using "some very profane language to Captain Healy." Buhner stated, "I was very astonished and looked wondering why Captain Healy would permit such language." Buhner then went on to describe the tricing up of the three sailors. Buhner, however, said that his instructions from Captain Healy "were to frighten them only [,] more than pain them. That was the idea."

In reference to the large number of men triced up on the *Wanderer*, Buhner said that the crew had once refused to work and then, when the ship was in a dangerous position, they again refused to work. The crew was therefore triced up and let down as "soon as they requested to be let down and promised they would resume their duties."

Buhner testified that he had witnessed many cases of tricing up while serving in the navy during the Civil War. He did admit that the navy had abolished the punishment in 1863, but went on to point out that tricing up was not a routine punishment in the U.S. Revenue Cutter Service either, but was only used "in such cases as the 'Wanderer's' crew—when crews are rebellious enough and they resist proper authority, it is often necessary to bring them to their senses of their duties by harsh measure upon themselves." Buhner felt that tricing up was "very much more effective and . . . considerable less trouble" than placing men in irons.

The last three witnesses to testify at the hearing were Henry H. Spicer, Mrs. Eden, and Healy. At the time of the *Estella* incident, Spicer testified, Healy was drunk. Moreover, Spicer claimed that throughout the cruise he had observed the captain in an intoxicated state. Major Stonehill and the board, however, attacked Spicer's testimony on two counts. When a board member observed the seaman looking at some papers while he testified, he asked what Spicer was reading. The sailor replied that he had kept a diary of the weather and the courses the *Bear* ran during the patrol. The board then pursued a line of questioning that tried to get Spicer to admit that he had kept the diary for the Seaman's Union, which intended to use it against Captain Healy. Spicer strongly denied this. Next, the board's questioning turned to whether Spicer had stolen a pistol from a shipmate on the *Bear*. Again, the seaman adamantly denied that he was guilty of such an act.

Mrs. Eden now took her turn in the witness chair. Major Stonehill asked her if she had sent a letter to O'Connor. In the letter, dated March 14, Mrs. Eden admitted she was disappointed that O'Connor had not kept his word to her about testifying against Healy. She felt that if "Captain Healy is removed it will be a check on drunkenness & cruelty in the future, and will be a long step toward seeing better treatment for the men of our Merchant Service." Mrs. Eden admitted to sending the letter, and Stonehill excused her from the witness chair.

Following the advice of his attorney, Captain Healy, after hearing the testimony of forty-four witnesses, took questions from the board. Healy began by saying that upon his arrival in Unalaska, he had consulted with Capt. Leonard Shepard of the cutter *Thetis* about the construction of the refuge station at Point Barrow. During this conference, Captain Shepard said that Captain Avery of the *Estella* had continuously complained about the mutinous behavior of his crew. Shepard had put the matter off, hoping the problem would go away. The *Thetis's* skipper felt Healy could face the same problem.

As soon as the *Bear* came alongside the *Estella* to take on coal, Captain Avery began with a constant stream of complaints. Healy informed him that, since most of the incidents he complained about had already happened, Healy could do nothing about them. "I endeavored all along to smooth the matter over without taking any positive action," explained the accused captain.

One day, when Captain Healy and Captain Avery were standing on the *Estrella's* deck overseeing the discharging of the coal, the mate came to report to Captain Avery. "The men swear and curse at me," said the mate. "Every word I say is answered with oaths and insults. . . . I can't say a word but I am told to go fuck myself." Healy advised Avery that the "best thing you can do is to put the men on the beach." Avery said he would not have enough men to work his ship if he did that. Avery wanted Healy to either punish the three men who were the ringleaders, or swap them for three of his men and bring the ringleaders on board the *Bear*. Healy refused. The complaints continued, but, according to Captain Healy, he "endeavored all along to avoid complications."

On the day the coaling was completed, Captain Avery again approached Healy and told him "that the men had abused the mate, and threatened him, and he wanted me to take some notice of it." Healy testified that he said, "If you will send the ringleader here, I will talk to him, perhaps that may answer."

When the man reported to him, Healy told him, "The captain and the mate have made serious complaints against you, and I want you to behave yourself. I warn you that if you do not behave yourself I shall take notice of it."

The sailor replied, "Is that what you called me out of the hold for."

"Yes, I want to warn you that if you do not behave yourself I shall take notice of it."

"You can go to hell."

"Go forward."

Healy said the sailor turned to go away, but said, *sotto voce*, "That son of a bitch better not bother me." Healy did nothing about the comment.

Shortly after this confrontation, Healy related that the following interaction occurred as the lines between the *Estella* and the *Bear* were being let go: "One of the men let go the wrong line. I called to him and said, 'What did you let go that line for?' He says, 'Shut up, you have nothing to do with us.' I called for the master at arms to put him in irons, but the man ran away." By the time the master at arms returned, Captain Healy told him that the man had run away and to never mind. Healy admitted to saying something to the other man who was standing near the man who ran away. The sailor replied, "There is a bucko Captain, we want no bucko skippers here." (A bucko skipper is one who is harsh, or brutal, to his crew.) Captain Healy ordered the master at arms to put the sailor in irons, but did not mention a tricing up.

After the *Bear* was moved and moored to a buoy, Healy went ashore and visited the whaler *Bertha*. While there, the mate of the *Estella* came on board and said to Captain Healy, "I want protection from my men."

Healy replied, "What is the matter now, why can't you manage your crew[?]"

The mate replied that two men, Alfred Holben and Otto Daeweritz, had threatened him for having reported the conduct of the crew to Captain Healy and "swore they would cut his guts out." As to why he could not manage his crew, the mate said that Captain Avery was an old man and the mate had "no backing whatever in the ship."

At this point, Healy explained to the board, he called Lieutenant Buhner to the whaler *Bertha* and gave him orders to go to the *Estella*, collect Otto Daeweritz, take him on board the *Bear*, "and put him in irons." Healy then told the board that as his executive officer took Daeweritz off the bark, Holben demanded to know where his shipmate was being taken. "To the *Bear*," replied Buhner. Holben immediately insisted upon going also.

Healy, who had returned to the *Bear*, overheard Holben and warned him, "If you do, I will trice you up." Holben continued with his demand. Captain Healy then ordered Buhner to take Holben to the *Bear* and trice him up once he got him aboard the cutter. "I told the Lieutenant subsequently, as he was going over [to] the vessel," testified Healy, "Don't be severe to them; frighten them more than you hurt them." After being informed that the men had been triced up, Healy told his executive officer to keep the men in irons until "knocking off time."

The board next turned to the *Wanderer* incident. Captain Healy related how the skipper of the ship, Captain Corrigan, "reported that his crew had knocked off duty, and that he wanted assistance." Healy promptly dispatched his executive officer over to the whaler with an armed boat crew. Upon his return, Lieutenant Buhner reported to his captain that the seamen "had absolutely refused duty." Despite the fact that Lieutenant Buhner had spoken to the sailors and even threatened them with prison, they still refused to work. Finally, Buhner told the mutinous sailors that he would return after dinner to see if they had changed their minds.

Captain Healy firmly insisted that he had given his executive officer no specific orders, only that the crew of the *Wanderer* "must turn to." When later that evening Buhner returned to the *Wanderer* as promised, he decided on his own to trice up all of the mutineers who still refused to work. In Captain Healy's opinion, this was the only option left to his executive officer, since there "was no jail, or authority whatever in Port Clarence."

Healy then launched into a list of other cases in which whaling skippers had called for his assistance with managing their unruly crews. In one case, off Point Hope, he lectured the captain that "he could not work his men all day." Healy said: "the men must not be worked like animals, but like men; a regular time for rest, and a regular time for work and a regular time for meals. I told him I did not want to hear any more complaints [from the crew.]" Healy went on to explain that while he did give out punishment, he also offered shelter to those who were sick and destitute.

When asked whether it was customary to trice up sailors, Healy responded:

"It is not customary treatment except on frontier places. We are empowered by Congress to suppress mutinies. We have no right to exercise magisterial functions. Our functions are such as exercised by policemen. We must suppress mutinies. A policeman does not sit in judgment on a man before he acts. That is our position."

When asked whether there was a list of punishments published by the service, Captain Healy continued:

We are not governed by Naval rules at all. If a mutiny occurred in San Francisco, to quell the mutiny or disturbance we would go and arrest the man, and turn him over to a policeman. But up there, where there is no jail to bring him to, that is the last resort, to trice men up. . . . In doing what I did I thought I was doing my duty. I have gone through a trial such as this before, and I reported the case to the Department. I asked them about my action, but they have never replied. I took it for granted, under those circumstances, that I was perfectly justified. . . . I never punished a man in anger, or on the spur of the moment.

Despite Healy's reference to having "gone through a trial such as this before," a search of the National Archives shows no record of Healy facing a hearing, or trial, on any charge prior to the trial of 1890.

Healy went on to point out that, in twenty-six years of service in the U.S. Revenue Cutter Service, he had "triced up two or three crews." Healy further explained, "We never do it when we are within the jurisdiction of magistrates or policemen." After hearing Healy's testimony, the board adjourned on March 20 to reach their decision.

On March 26, the board published their findings. The board found that the three sailors serving in the *Estella* were guilty of mutiny, that Captain Healy had "used every reasonable effort to persuade the men to cease their insubordination before resorting to the extreme measure of punishing; that they retorted only with insulting language; and that their punishment was, therefore justifiable." In the case of the *Wanderer*, the board also found in favor of Healy, noting that no sailor from the ship came forward to testify against the action. Although the board acknowledged that discipline must be enforced, even in frontier locations, they felt that tricing up should "be discontinued, by order of the Department, as a punishment in the future, as its infliction is liable, in the opinion of the Board, to result in injury to the person upon whom it is inflicted."

Next, the board addressed the charges of drunkenness leveled at Captain

Healy. Writing for the board, Captain White noted that all the whaling captains interviewed testified to Healy's sobriety. Each of the twenty-one witnesses for Healy claimed that he was never drunk on duty. On the other hand, only two people testified as to his drunkenness.

Finally, the copy of the findings, now housed in the National Archives, records the board as stating that the "testimony goes to show that Captain Healy has been a particularly intelligent, zealous, and efficient officer in the discharge of his difficult and perilous duties in the Arctic; that he is humane and kind to his men, and to shipwrecked sailors and unfortunates whom he has [relieved] and who have, in many instances, been thrown upon his personal bounty. . . . We recommend that Captain Healy's long and arduous service in the Arctic be duly recognized by the Department."

The tricing up and drunkenness issues, however, were not yet settled as far as Mrs. Eden was concerned. On March 24, 1890, she again wrote to Secretary Windom. Mrs. Eden noted that the board was made up of "undoubtedly estimable men, who, it is only fair to suppose, desired to see the truth brought to light, and justice done to all concerned, but it was scarcely possible that they should not have felt a considerable sympathy with another Revenue Officer placed before them in circumstances so trying." She felt that the prosecution was not allowed enough time to gather witnesses willing to testify against Captain Healy. She claimed that hearsay evidence was admitted for the defense, but not for the prosecution. This, according to Mrs. Eden, caused the attorney for the prosecution to become so frustrated that he withdrew from the case. Mrs. Eden also objected strenuously to Healy's earthy language, as she and other members of the WCTU were in the room.

Mrs. M. F. Gray, also of the WCTU, wrote a letter to Secretary Windom endorsing Mrs. Eden's claims. She wrote that the three women of the WCTU who attended the hearing "were made to feel that we were not wanted and the minister in charge of the Mariner's Church was requested in behalf of the defense to use his influence to have us 'let up on Capt. Healy.'" Mrs. Gray also felt Captain Healy's language "was *too vile* to repeat under *any* circumstances & a person guilty of committing such obscenity in a public place could be lawfully arrested & made to suffer the penalty therefor—yet this 'Board of Inquiry' *never* rebuked him in any way whatever!" (All emphasis is Mrs. Gray's.)

Mrs. Gray also leveled charges at Captain Healy's attorney. He "was both uncivil & unjust in his treatment of us women." In a postscript to her letter, Mrs. Gray let the secretary know that there were "several persons in Washington who know me quite well if you wish references."

The attorney for the three seamen, H.W. Hutton, also complained to Secretary Windom. Covering some of the same ground as the women of the WCTU, Hutton focused his attack on the admission of hearsay evidence and the use of affidavits about Healy's good character. Hutton clearly felt the board exhibited sympathy for Captain Healy and, on that basis, had excused his actions.

None of the letters swayed Secretary Windom, however, and the board's findings stood. Capt. Michael A. Healy was free to prepare for the 1890 patrol.

9

The Czar of the North

With the traumatic experience of his trial behind him, Captain Healy began preparing for the 1890 Arctic cruise. Although she had sailed with him in 1883, Mary Jane did not enjoy either the isolation or the danger of the Far North. Writing to her brother-in-law, Father Patrick, during the earlier cruise, she admitted, "the ice, the awful ice has struck terror to my heart and soul" and vowed, "no more Arctic for me."[1] Nevertheless, when Michael asked her to accompany him in 1890, Mary Jane agreed, confiding to her diary, "my husband needs me."[2] She gathered together her necessities for the long months at sea, left Room 8 of the Occidental Hotel, and joined Michael on board the *Bear*.

In the new decade, Captain Healy faced new forces swirling about the Alaskan Maritime Frontier. As a result, the years 1890 through 1894 brought Healy face to face with unusual events, even by Bering Sea Patrol standards. On Independence Day, 1890, two missionaries landed near Cape Prince of Wales to begin their work. The cape is the point of Alaska that juts out into the Bering Strait and points like a finger westward to Siberia. This seemingly banal incident inaugurated an important movement that would flow throughout the maritime frontier of Alaska.

Ultimately, two men would play key roles in a humanitarian effort on the Alaskan maritime frontier. Captain Healy's role in this effort elevated him to the status of a giant in the forty-ninth state's history. At first glance, the other man was hardly a giant in stature, but he, too, would eventually cast a long shadow across Alaska's history.

Born on May 18, 1834, in the village of Minaville, New York, to parents who regularly attended church service, Sheldon Jackson, as a schoolboy, was described as "a lad of slight build, physically small, a sufferer at times from poor health and weak eyes." Before graduating in 1857 from the Princeton Theological Seminary, Jackson applied to the Presbyterian Board of Foreign Missions for an assignment to either Siam in Southeast Asia or Colombia in South America.

The board, however, primarily because of their doctor's report, did not consider "him as a fit subject in the foreign field." Apparently, the board believed that the twenty-four-year-old Jackson, who stretched to just over five feet tall, lacked the physique necessary to perform the arduous duty of overseas missionary work.

At least, Jackson thought the board felt this way. "They thought I was not strong," he later responded to a newspaperman's question, "but I had an iron constitution, with the exception of dyspepsia." For the rest of his life, Jackson labored to become "foremost," if he could not be "first," among men. The board finally accepted him, but "limited his field of labour to the Indian tribes within the territories of the United States."[3]

Jackson traveled almost a million miles in pursuit of his missionary work. He established over a hundred churches and missions, including the first Presbyterian churches in Wyoming, Montana, Utah, Arizona, and Alaska. On three separate occasions, newspapers prematurely reported his death, and one newspaper went as far as printing his obituary while he was still alive.

Jackson has earned the reputation of being "egotistical and often tactless, but persistent and aware of how to apply political pressure," making him a controversial figure. His strongest supporters admitted that he was no angel, and even his severest critics conceded their amazement at what he managed to accomplish.[4]

One of Sheldon Jackson's solutions to the problem of the perceived decline in the Eskimo population was to provide schools and teachers for the natives. Jackson contacted Presbyterian, Episcopalian, and Congregational mission societies and asked them to provide teachers "in return for government subsidies and proselytizing privileges."[5] By these means, Jackson hoped to raise the natives "from the condition of hunters to herders . . . a long step upwards in the scale of civilization."[6] Teachers would have the double duty of Christianizing the natives while changing, and thereby advancing, their culture. Jackson felt that missionary teachers who attacked drunkenness, poverty, and disease among the natives would improve the lives of the Eskimo through cultural change.

Two men were charged with the task of establishing and administering the school at Wales in 1890. At age thirty-two, Harrison Robinson Thornton, a Congregationalist, was the older of the pair. A resident of Farmville, Virginia, he had failed to finish law school because of an "indisposition [which] took the form of a severe depression."[7] Unemployed for two years, he then held a series of jobs, teaching, clerking, mining, and newspaper reporting. He was again unemployed when offered the position of assistant teacher in Alaska.

The other missionary, William Thomas Lopp, was born on June 21, 1864, at Valley City, Indiana. Lopp worked for six years as a teacher and principal "in various Indiana schools." He obtained a B.A. from Hanover College, Indiana, in 1888, and two years later answered an advertisement in a religious magazine seeking "Christian teachers for mission schools" in Alaska. Lopp received the position of head teacher, while Thornton would serve as his assistant. Lopp's "quiet strength and peaceful nature buoyed the mission work."[8]

Despite Jackson's perception of a declining Eskimo population, the village in which Thornton and Lopp began their work—called Kinugumut by the natives, but now known as Wales—was anything but weak. The village was, in fact, "a thriving and healthy community."[9]

The villagers, also known as Kinugumuts, had earned a reputation both as "ferocious warriors" and as maritime traders of "impressive ability, a fact that kept whites from dominating them."[10] They also provided natives living in the interior with marine animal oils, while those in the interior provided the Kinugumuts with caribou hides. The Kinugumuts also conducted a brisk trade with the reindeer people of Siberia. But most of all the Kinugumuts relished trading for rifles and whiskey.[11]

Those sailing in the Bering Strait area, however, called the Kinugumuts "a band of hypocrites and shylocks, possessing a large share of brazen effrontery."[12] Capt. Calvin L. Hooper, Healy's commanding officer during his early years in the Bering Sea Patrol, considered there to be no "worse [natives] on the coast" than the Kinugumuts, whom he called "great bullies" that traveled "in large numbers compelling smaller bands to trade with them at their own terms."[13] Another senior officer of the U.S. Revenue Cutter Service, Capt. George Bailey, said the Kinugumuts were "a bad set, fond of rum."[14] Edward William Nelson, an ethnographer, wrote, "on several occasions the villagers of Cape Prince of Wales fairly took possession of vessels with small crews, and carried off whatever they wanted."[15]

On July 5, 1877, the small trading brig *William H. Allen* departed the Siberian shore and sailed eastbound across the Bering Strait. An unusual change in the weather becalmed the brig in fog halfway between the Diomede Islands and Cape Prince of Wales. Capt. George Gilley, described as a "half breed Kanaka" from the Bonin Islands, had his small crew of twenty-four Hawaiians drop anchor to keep from drifting onto the Prince of Wales shoals.[16]

Three craft containing Kinugumut villagers approached the *Allen* and signaled that they wished to come on board to trade. "The chief," Captain Gilley later reported, "was about six feet five inches tall, by far the most powerful native we had ever seen. I knew he was a murderous villain, and that his followers would do just what he told them to."[17] A confusing series of events, including gunfire, unfolded on board the *Allen*. In the end, thirteen native Kinugumuts, including the chief, lay dead, along with one crewman from the ship. Over the years, these deaths would haunt the Kinugumuts.[18]

When Lopp and Thornton arrived at Cape Prince of Wales in 1890 they found a "bold, confident, and boisterous" people. They also found that they had landed at the site of not one, but two villages, one established near the beach and the other on a hill. Although the villages were spaced only seventy-five yards apart, a wide gulf separated the temperaments of the two groups. Those nearest the sea were "the most aggressive" and were "feared by the hill villagers and the residents of other smaller settlements from Kotzebue to the Yukon."[19] As a result, the two settlements had become bitter enemies.

Sensing the tension, the two missionaries tried to build their combination dwelling and schoolhouse in a way that demonstrated their neutrality. They miscalculated, however, and ended up building on land held by the hill people, thus inflaming the beach people. Healy assigned crewmen to help with the construction of the buildings.

As the *Bear* lay off shore during the construction, Michael and Mary Healy invited Doctor Jackson to take a sponge bath in the Healys' sleeping quarters, saying they both planned to remain in the chartroom area or about the deck.

Once he had finished his bath, Jackson, without checking with Captain Healy, invited Thornton to also take a sponge bath. Forty-three years later, Tom Lopp, in a memorandum concerning his memories of Wales, wrote, "Healy came below before [Thornton] had finished, entered the bed room, and made some uncalled remarks. Of course there was no excuse for Healy's conduct. But Jackson should have insisted on assuming [the] entire responsibility for it."[20] Captain Healy, who was never known to forget what he perceived to be a wrong, from that moment on had little respect for Thornton.

Once the *Bear* departed, Lopp and Thornton passed an unpleasant summer, being, for all practical purposes, barricaded within their building. They put up with drunken people from the beach community, who still harbored resentment for the Gilley incident. Some broke into the house, tore up furniture, and shattered windows. Thornton, following Jackson's advice, reached on these occasions for either a pistol or a rifle. Lopp, however, believed that defending oneself with weapons was "not the advice" that should be followed.[21]

The fact that the beach people had no headmen who could stop the attacks on the missionaries complicated the problem. The leadership of the beach village resided in the hands of those handling the maritime trading craft. These leaders, known as *umealit*, had grown wealthy plying their trade. As smugglers of whiskey and rifles, they did not want the missionaries in their midst. After the whiskey ran out during one drunken session, Lopp and Thornton asked the umealit to come to their building. The two men told the village leaders that they had plenty of arms and ammunition and would not hesitate to use them. They then delivered their best threat. If the two missionaries were harmed, "the revenue cutter would return and destroy the villages with its guns." The umealit quickly understood, their attacks on the missionaries ceased, and an uneasy truce came into effect.[22]

Upon reaching Wales, Jackson, who had received permission to travel on board the *Bear* to inspect the schools, listened to Thornton and Lopp's problems with the natives. They cited the continual problems of drinking among the natives and the tensions caused by this drinking. After being apprised of these problems, Healy called many of the Kinugumuts on board the cutter. He lectured them about drunkenness and interfering with the mission. Healy then ordered the firing of three shells from the *Bear*'s guns to reinforce his meaning. The Kinugumuts cowered on the cutter's deck. The cutter departed shortly thereafter for work further north, where Healy would face yet another serious incident involving the clash of two cultures.

Many years after his death, one aspect of the myth of Captain Healy focused on his duties as a law enforcement official of the federal government. This myth paints Healy as a colorful and unorthodox lawman, enforcing federal laws, or modifying them, as he saw fit. When William Kjellmann, at Teller, for example, questioned the legality of Healy's ruling concerning salvage rights of a wrecked ship, Healy shot back, "If it isn't the law, I make it the law."[23] The problem with the myth, however, is that it does not take into account just what Captain Healy faced as the sole representative of the federal government in the Far North.

Traditionally, one of the primary duties of all officers of the U.S. Revenue Cutter Service was the enforcement of federal laws. As an officer in the U.S. Revenue Cutter Service on the isolated Alaskan maritime frontier, Healy faced an additional challenge. Until the gold rush of the 1890s drew large numbers of people into the northern regions of Alaska, "the only evidence of law and sovereignty of the United States north of the Aleutian [Islands] was the annual journey of a single revenue cutter during the three months of summer."[24] The vastness of Alaska meant that cutters could visit outlying villages perhaps once a year. Until the large influx of would-be miners to the region in the 1890s, the law north of the Aleutians was Eskimo law.[25] To be sure, the natives respected the *Bear*'s cannons, and Captain Healy made sure to offer demonstrations of this power from time to time. The thought of being raked by cannon fire no doubt helped to keep the peace between many groups of natives.[26]

Mary Jane's diary entries reveal how Captain Healy enforced the laws with the Eskimos during the 1890 patrol. On July 16, shortly after Thornton and Lopp landed at Wales, Healy was notified that a native, known only as Isaac, and his wife were drunk. Captain Healy sent his executive officer, Lieut. Albert Buhner, ashore to bring Isaac and his wife on board the *Bear*. Once on board, Healy brought the two natives to the pilothouse where, according to Mary Jane, "the Captain read them a lesson" and told them he might take them to San Francisco and place them in prison. "The poor things were frightened to death." Healy kept Isaac and his wife on board the *Bear* until eight o'clock that evening. He then told the couple that he had decided to release them, but only if they promised not to drink or take liquor in trade. Furthermore, Healy told them he "would keep his eye upon them and make inquiries about them in the future and if he found they drank any more he would not let them off." Healy then sent Isaac and his wife ashore.[27]

Earlier, Captain Healy had waited at Port Clarence for the ice to open before proceeding to Point Barrow. Capt. S. P. Smith of the schooner *Mary W. Thomas*, of San Francisco, took advantage of this delay to inform Healy of the criminal actions of one of his seamen. Not only had "Richard Price, [Smith's] colored steward[,] . . . stabbed Wm. Noonan, seaman," the merchant captain explained, but he had also "threatened the life of the first mate." Smith had ordered Price put in irons and confined below deck. Upon his inspection of the imprisoned man, Healy found him "in the hole, in a place where he could hardly have lived for the season and in a wretched condition." At the earnest request of both the African American and his captain, Healy subsequently reported to the secretary of the treasury, "I removed [Price] on board the 'Bear' where he was liberated, given a ration, and will be set at work when able."[28]

The gold rush of the 1890s further complicated law enforcement in the Far North. At St. Michael, in the Yukon River delta, and at Nome, the nonnative population ballooned from "ten to twelve times the population of the entire Bering Strait [region] in the space of a year."[29] Given the racial attitudes of the nineteenth century, this meant Captain Healy had to deal with how to enforce serious violations of American law by natives against whites. Again, the vast area of Alaska made it "difficult to bring the offender to justice" when courts and jails were thousands of miles away.[30]

Charles D. Brower, the white whaler and trader who, beginning in 1884, lived at Barrow for over fifty years, detailed in his autobiography an incident in 1890 that illustrates the clash of the two cultures. According to Brower, a native woman and a white man named Portuguese Joe had been living together in Barrow. The woman had previously lived with a native in a distant village. One day the native man, while in Barrow, saw Joe and the woman talking and came over to them. According to later testimony by the woman, the conversation between Joe and the native man was friendly, and Joe told the man to take the woman and go back to their village. Joe then got up and began walking away. The native man then shot Joe in the back, walked up to him, and administered a coup de grace with his rifle. After that, the native calmly took his sled and two dogs and headed inland.[31]

One major difference between the Alaskan maritime frontier and the frontier in the contiguous United States was that whites did not create their own settlements, but instead lived as minorities in Eskimo villages.[32] Brower recalled that had the incident "been Eskimo against Eskimo" they could have "left it to the natives to settle": "This was far more serious. Nobody knew if the Eskimos would back us up in punishing the murderer, or stand together against us."

Brower went on to describe how the white men of the village came together to discuss what action they should take. Eventually, Brower said to the group: "The way I look at it, this is the time for a firm hand. I don't know how they're going to take it, but I do know what they're going to think of us if we let this murderer get away with it."

The whites decided they must punish the murderer. The group of whites called in the two headmen of the village. Brower and his companions said they were going to capture the native and punish him. While the headmen offered no objection, they refused to help, "pointing out the dead man was not one of their kind."

Eventually, the whites captured the murderer outside of the village. When Brower and another man brought the native into the village, all the Eskimo inhabitants had disappeared. Brower sent for the headmen to witness the "trial," and the woman who had witnessed the killing was brought to testify. She repeated her account. The native man agreed with what the woman said, but added that if the white men "let him go he would never kill another white man." Not too surprisingly, the whites found the man guilty and sentenced him to death.

The headmen, at first balking at the sentence, finally agreed that if the Eskimo had killed another Eskimo, they too would have sentenced him to death.

However, the headmen also thought that since the woman was at the root of the problem, she too should die. Brower wrote, "we wouldn't consider" this suggestion.

The whites wanted the Eskimos to carry out the sentence, but they refused. One white man then proceeded to load half of the rifles slated to kill the native with ammunition and the other half with blanks. He then shuffled the rifles so no one would know who fired the fatal shots.

After burying Portuguese Joe, Brower spent many hours working on a document that explained what happened. They knew that Captain Healy and the *Bear* were due at any time. Brower wrote of the group of whites that went aboard the *Bear* to present their document: "we hoped [it] would enable the authorities to justify our action as clearly as we did ourselves. The result was somewhat different from what we had expected."

> Said Captain Healy, severely: "I don't want your damned report."
> "But, Captain,—it explains—"
> "You men had a perfect right to shoot that fellow on sight."
> And tearing up the report, Captain Healy tossed the pieces overboard.

Healy realized that certain residents in Alaska would not rank any law enforcer high on their list of favorite people, especially those living in isolated, lawless regions. In his seaman's brusque manner of speaking he stated, "I do not care."[33] To Healy, his duty remained his sole concern.

While traveling on the *Bear* during the event-filled 1890 patrol, Jackson and Healy carried on long conversations. The talk between the tough sea captain and the determined missionary naturally turned to the fate of the Alaskan Eskimo. It was during one of these conversations that Healy revealed something to the missionary that had occupied his thoughts since at least 1880.

In his 1880 report, Captain Hooper mentioned that he felt it was the federal government's responsibility to look after the Eskimos. Writing many years after his service in the Bering Sea and the Arctic, retired U.S. Coast Guard officer John C. Cantwell pointed out that even the removal of the Eskimos from their "settlements along the coasts of the Arctic Ocean" was discussed. Cantwell honestly admitted that the action was "unthinkable," not least because to do so "would make it impossible to utilize their assistance to white men who might be cast away on the shores of the Arctic Ocean."[34]

Those who journeyed to the Bering Sea and Arctic Ocean reported that the Chukchi of Siberia, like the Lapps of Norway, herded reindeer (*Ranger tarandus*). The animals provided their herders with some of the means necessary to survive in a hostile environment.

Healy also informed Jackson of the discussion between Lieutenant Cantwell and naturalist Townsend about the reindeer and their ability to survive on the vegetation in Alaska. With the question of an available source of food for the reindeer solved, the captain contended, three other problems presented themselves. The Chukchi who herded reindeer lived inland, so the first problem was how to contact these inland natives. However, the Chukchi annually drove their herds to the Siberian coast, especially to an area around the East Cape, which was an easy sail for any cutter, or ship, from the coast of Alaska's Bering Sea. Realizing that the Chukchi's herds spent part of the year on the coast seemed to solve the first problem, but a larger problem remained: Could the Chukchi be convinced to sell some of their animals?

While both men pondered how to convince the Chukchi to sell their reindeer, their discussions turned to yet another problem—finances. Lastly, the two men discussed who would tend the animals until the natives could learn to herd them? Given his background, that Jackson became enthusiastic about such a project seems almost preordained. In fact, perhaps "enthusiastic" is too mild a word to convey Jackson's reaction. As Dorothy Jean Ray states in *Eskimos of the Bering Strait:* "A less determined or thick-skinned man would have wilted a thousand times during his affiliation with the project."[35]

The two men hammered out a simple, but effective plan. Jackson's strength lay in promoting the plan, and administering it. He also had considerable influence in the halls of Congress and could thereby secure federal funds to finance the reindeer importation. Captain Healy, upon receiving permission from the Treasury Department, would transport the animals from Siberia to Alaska.

Eventually, Captain Healy began working the *Bear* south of the Point Barrow region. Soon after, Michael and Mary Jane Healy and the *Bear* began the slow journey southward toward Unalaska and San Francisco. As the cutter sailed to San Francisco, missionaries Thornton and Lopp opened their new school at Wales. The patrol finally ended on November 30, 1890, when the cutter dropped anchor at its home port.

After settling the official U.S. Revenue Cutter Service matters that always took up time upon return from a patrol, Captain Healy penned a letter to W. D. Harris, the U.S. Commissioner of Education in Washington, D.C., about the reindeer plan. After "he watched with pleasure" the arrival of missionaries among the native people of the north, Healy pointed out the perceived "exhaustion of the native food supply."[36] He then mentioned his many discussions with Jackson about the necessity of introducing reindeer to the region and teaching the Eskimos how to herd the animals. Healy noted that as the "Indian" boy in the Dakotas received training by the Bureau of Education to raise stock, "so in the industrial schools of Alaska it is proposed to teach the Eskimo young men the raising of tame reindeer." "A few thousand dollars now [spent] in the establishment of this new industry," Healy advised, "will save hundreds of thousands hereafter."[37]

After Jackson returned to Washington, D.C., however, his enthusiasm and lobbying for the project failed to sway congressional leaders. Although bills were introduced to fund the project, Congress rejected them. Jackson faced stiff opposition. Many legislators cited the same three reasons why the project was impossible: the reindeer could not survive the sea voyage, the Chukchi would not sell their reindeer, and the costs for the project were too high.

Balked by Congress, Jackson next appealed to the general public for funds to save the Eskimos. Although individual contributions were small, the determined missionary succeeded in raising $2,146, enough to buy barter goods. Jackson planned to sail with Healy in the *Bear* during 1891.[38] Congress did not supply the money Jackson desired, but the federal government did help in other ways, the most obvious being the use of the cutter *Bear* at no cost to the missionary.

On the patrol of 1891, Mary Jane again accompanied her husband. As one of his first duties, Captain Healy had orders to transport a witness to a trial being held in Juneau, in Southeastern Alaska. The Treasury Department also wished him to transport, while en route to Juneau, Prof. Israel C. Russell, of the U.S. Geological Survey, and his exploring party to Mount Saint Elias, also located in Southeastern Alaska. Healy was ordered to drop the expedition off in the best possible location to begin their trek and then continue on to Juneau.

Captain Healy had the *Bear*'s navigator shape a course first to Yakutat, Alaska, and then on to Icy Bay, the closest approach to Mount Saint Elias. Once at Icy Bay, the cutter's small boats would transport the expedition's men and supplies to the beach. As an expert seaman, Captain Healy realized that open beach landings posed one of the greatest dangers to small boat operations. If breakers swept the shoreline, Healy knew, the danger doubled. Later, Healy wrote an unofficial letter to Capt. Leonard Shepard about what took place at Icy Bay. Captain Healy confided that he could "speak more plainly to you in this letter than I would like to do in an official document."[39]

Healy wrote that, before sending the *Bear*'s boats into the beach, he climbed to the masthead to gain a better view. "[W]ith glass [telescope] in hand," Healy wrote, "to survey and select a suitable and convenient landing for the Professor to make his way across the country, my solicitude being to land his party and outfits especially without getting them wet, as I did not wish any miscarriage of his expedition to be laid to the Cutter Service."

Healy ordered Lieut. David H. Jarvis, who had eight years of commissioned service experience, to take a boat crew closer to the beach to better judge the breakers close up. Healy carefully watched through the glass as Jarvis examined the approach to the beach. The lieutenant returned and reported that he "thought that everything could be landed without damage."

On the basis of Jarvis's report, Captain Healy ordered three boats lightly loaded. Lieutenant Jarvis received orders to lead the way. Healy stressed to the individual officers in charge of each of the three boats "to take no risk and if there was danger of spoiling the outfits not to attempt landing but to return on board." Healy also ordered Third Lieut. Leonidas L. Robinson and Second Lieut. Howard M. Broadbent to follow the more experienced Jarvis to near the line of breakers. He repeated that Robinson was "not to land until he ascertained how Mr. Jarvis made out. . . . [E]ach officer was to survey and judge for himself the feasibility of getting his stuff ashore without damaging it."

In a letter to Bishop James A. Healy, Healy's oldest brother and the patriarch of the family, Mary Jane wrote: "The first boat landed and did not take on water, but the second boat regardless of the orders that Captain reinterated [*sic*] again and again [before] they left the vessel's side, followed too near the rollers and before they actually got into the surf she rounded broadside to and upset and all were drowned, except one man[.] [H]e saved himself by seizing a bag of flour and holding it before him, the breakers would strike it every time and carry him higher on the beach, until he was where they could rescue him, and when they could rescue him, he was nearly gone."

Mary Jane continued: "You can imagine the suspense and anxiety on board, for we could not tell the result of the accident. The Captain said I am afraid all in the second boat are lost, but hoped against hope. . . . [W]e could not reach them or get news from those all that day and night[.] [E]verybody on board were straining their eyes trying to count the men on shore, but next day we learned the sad news that Lieut. Robinson and six men were drowned, one man was of the exploring party."[40]

The next day, Lieutenant Jarvis and his boat crew rammed their boat into the surf and safely passed through the breakers. Once Jarvis reported there was no danger, three boats again received their cargo and started into the beach, this time landing safely. As the boats pushed off for the return trip to the *Bear*, Mary watched as one of the craft's sweep oarlocks broke and the boat capsized. Mary wrote in her diary: "I screamed that the boat had gone[.] [T]he Captain was oh so worried [and] sent a boat as near as possible and they all joined voices and screamed for the boat not to venture [into the breakers.]"[41] All safely returned to the *Bear*, and landing operations continued.

In his unofficial letter to Captain Shepard, Healy wrote that while, "I am full to charity to poor Robinson whose body is still on board," he thought that it "must be said that he paid with his life the penalty of carelessness and non compliance to orders reiterated many times before he left the vessel." Healy went on to point out that he questioned the only survivor.

> He replied that no accident would have happened had the steer oar been properly handled or any judgment been displayed. The officer had a coxswain at the steer [oar] to help him. All were cautioned to take off their rubber boots and orders repeatedly given to take no risks whatsoever. Broadbent's boat did not take in a particle of water in the seven or eight trips he made, although he did not land until the next day. [Lieut. George E.] McConnell's boat turned over on the beach caused by carrying away the steering rowlock. All the outfits were landed without loss and with very slight wetting, excepting a few things in Robinson's boat.

The deaths of the officers and sailors created another problem for Captain Healy—what to do with the dead. Healy reported: "The sailors I buried at Icy Bay. [F]irst because I felt that in my own case I would like to be buried where I fell on duty, 2ndly, I knew that Robinson would be given a military funeral here [at Sitka] and the sailors would not. I wished to avoid so marked a distinction in the last rites for the satisfaction of the men." Third Lieut. Leonidas L. Robinson now lies largely forgotten in the National Cemetery at Sitka, Alaska. There are no markers showing the graves of the sailors of the *Bear* who died on the isolated beach at Icy Bay.[42]

The U.S. Coast Guard, beginning in the 1970s, rightfully pointed out that Capt. Michael A. Healy never lost a cutter while sailing in the dangerous and largely uncharted waters of the Bering Sea and Arctic Ocean. The loss of the men from the *Bear*'s small boat at Icy Bay, however, "was one of the few tragedies in the history of American exploration in the Far Northwest."[43]

Captain Healy, with the loss of his crewmen still weighing heavily on his mind, continued his duties as the *Bear* made its way toward the Bering Sea. With him was Sheldon Jackson who had received permission to sail on board the *Bear* in 1891. His official reasons for the trip were to inspect the progress of the schools of the northern regions of the state and to test whether the Chukchi would sell their reindeer. If the Siberian natives could be convinced to sell the animals, then Healy would test whether the reindeer could be transported by sea.

Jackson supplied the barter goods to purchase the reindeer. Captain Healy's contributions lay in his good reputation among the native people of both Alaska and Siberia and in his role as the cutter captain providing transportation of the animals from Siberia to Alaska. As it happened, the natives' good feelings about Healy proved more important than Jackson's influence in Washington, D.C.

Healy and Jackson planned on beginning the project at Indian Point [Mys Chaplina], Siberia. Both men felt that the services of James B. Vincent, the rescued survivor of the *Napoleon* who had lived among the Chukchi, were essential to the plan. They wanted him to act both as an interpreter with the Chukchi and as the first person in charge of the reindeer station. At Port Clarence, they found Vincent, who had risen to the rank of third mate on the whaling ship *Abram Barker*. Even after two long meetings, Healy and Jackson were unable to persuade the captain of the whaling ship to release Vincent from his duties. Charles and Mary Antisarlook, however, both natives of Alaska, joined the *Bear* for the voyage to Siberia. Mary, who was part Russian, could be called upon for interpretation.[44]

On July 8, 1891, the *Bear* arrived off Indian Point, which officially began the experiment. Matters, however, progressed much more slowly than planned. The head of the nearest village refused to give up his animals. He seemed to Jackson to be a wealthy man and uninterested in trading. Noting the role money would inevitably play, Jackson recorded in his journal, "No one expressed a doubt or any intimation of the natives being unwilling to sell from superstitious notions."

An old native man and his son came aboard the *Bear* at Indian Point. Both spoke English, and the young man agreed to accompany the cutter as an interpreter. The father of the boy said that he would never trust white men on ships to take his son, but he did trust Captain Healy.

The natives of this area thought larger herds of reindeer might be found above Cape Serdze Kamen, at least one hundred miles to the north. Ice, however, prevented the cutter from visiting these areas at that time. Instead, Healy shaped a course to Holy Cross Bay [Zaliv Kresta], which lies at the northwestern portion of the Gulf of Anadyr.

Fog, ice, and poorly charted waters made Holy Cross Bay a dangerous location for the cutter. Nevertheless, Jackson managed to make it ashore and two natives agreed to sell five animals. Conditions, however, prevented the cutter's crew from taking them on board. Jackson also contacted the largest herder in the area and arranged for the purchase of twenty-five deer the next year. The *Bear* then departed this dangerous location.

Originally, Jackson and Healy had planned to unload the deer at St. Lawrence Island immediately after purchasing them at Indian Point. They now changed their plan and decided to buy the reindeer later in the summer and transport them to San Francisco, which would undoubtedly provide great publicity for the project. Jackson and Healy released the young interpreter, with a gift of a Winchester repeating rifle and one hundred cartridges. Charles and Mary Antisarlook remained aboard.

Healy set a course for the Alaskan coastline and began working northward on July 24. By August 25, after stopping at Point Hope, Cape Lisbourne, Point Barrow, Point Belcher, and Wainright Inlet, he again turned the *Bear*'s course toward Siberia and set his sights on the purchase of reindeer.[45]

In a region of extreme isolation, weather, ice, and sea conditions, Captain Healy never knew what might happen on a patrol. On Monday, August 17, near Point Belcher—approximately one hundred miles to the southwest of Point Barrow—Healy learned that a strange steamer was heading northward. He decided to investigate. The *Bear* maneuvered cautiously through fog and ice. At 3:30 p.m., Healy finally ordered the cutter anchored to await better visibility. Four hours later, the visibility improved, and the cutter's lookout reported a small Japanese iron steamer nearby. Captain Healy ordered the *Bear* underway to investigate the vessel. What Healy found must have even made this Arctic expert shake his head. A Mr. Carroll of Carrolton, Maryland, accompanied by his bride, "was on a bridal tour around the world, + with a yatching [*sic*] party had come into the Arctic to hunt Walrus + Polar Bear. Ignorant of their danger they had driven their steamer into ice thinking they could force a way to Point Barrow." The cutter lay alongside the steamer for one day, while Michael and Mary Jane visited with the newlyweds. Eventually, the steamer left, this time, presumably on Healy's advice, bound for the south.[46]

On August 27, 1891, the *Bear* anchored off the village of Enchowan, near Cape Serdze. Negotiations with the villagers proved successful. Jackson recorded that the price for four reindeer amounted to "1 Rifle and 200 cartridges." Crewmen on board the *Bear* began making pens on the port side of the deck to hold the animals. The next day—a rainy, overcast Friday—Lieut. David H.

Jarvis supervised the loading of four reindeer into the *Bear's* small boats. Second Lieut. H. M. Broadbent recorded in the logbook that the "four reindeer were taken on board as an experiment. More could have been purchased if desired." Mary Jane watched the animals come on board and recorded in her diary: "They are beautiful creatures and gentle as lambs. I hope we may be able to get them to San Francisco, what a sensation they will create."[47] "This is a great event," Jackson penned in his diary. "It is now to be tested how well they will bear transportation."

Even though Jackson knew they could purchase more animals, without a sure plan for keeping them fed, plus the added uncertainty of how well the animals would travel, Jackson concluded, "we thought it provident to receive only four on board." The *Bear* departed and began to work back to the Alaskan mainland, stopping first at Cape Prince of Wales to allow Charles and Mary Antisarlook to disembark.

En route to the Alaskan coast, the cutter stopped at King Island. There, the cuttermen found the native community in the throes of imminent starvation. Hunting the previous winter had proven poor, and the village's emergency food supply was already used up. Half of the population had left to search for food on the mainland. The remaining people faced a sure death before the return of the November ice, which would bring with it a native food source: seals.

Captain Healy sent a note to his officers. "I know all of you have too deep an interest in the natives of this section to leave them to what seems now a most probable fate," he wrote. "I shall therefore be obliged to test the proverbial generosity of the sailor and the amount of interest each may take in the life or death of these natives." The appeal garnered $150.00, which Healy used to purchase supplies that he felt would be "sufficient to bridge the gap until sealing begins and save [the islanders] from starvation."[48]

The *Bear* continued on into Norton Sound, stopping at St. Michael briefly. Captain Healy then set course once again for Siberia to see if he and Jackson could purchase more reindeer. On September 12, at Glasenapp Harbor, Siberia, the *Bear's* logbook records the apparently indefatigable Lieutenant Jarvis returning aboard with five male and seven female reindeer. With this purchase, Captain Healy then set a course for Unalaska, arriving there on September 18.

Sometime between the purchase of the first reindeer and arriving at Unalaska, the plan for the animals changed once again. On September 21, the *Bear's* logbook recorded that the cuttermen transported nine animals ashore at Amaknak [Amakna] Island—which lies east of Unalaska, near the present-day Cold Bay—and, earlier, seven at Unalaska Island.

Meanwhile, Thornton, uneasy about spending another winter at the village, had returned to the United States with the intention of seeking a wife for himself and another for Lopp, who remained alone at the mission. The remainder of the 1891 patrol seems almost anticlimactic after the incident at Icy Bay and the reindeer experiment. The *Bear* reached San Francisco on December 3, 1891.[49]

Back in the contiguous United States, Jackson once again launched a strong campaign to obtain funding from the federal government. Captain Healy also received orders, on January 19, 1892, to return to Washington for "temporary duty in [the] Interior Department." Healy's long experience in the Arctic, combined with the recent success of the reindeer experiment, made him a natural expert witness for the Interior Department's Department of Education, to which Jackson reported.[50] Once again, however, Congress refused to provide the needed money. Nevertheless, the determined missionary was undeterred. Jackson again joined Healy on board the *Bear* in 1892. The missionary still had money remaining from the 1891 reindeer experiment, and he used this money to buy the barter goods needed to purchase 171 reindeer in eight separate transactions. The crew of the *Bear* landed the first reindeer on the Alaskan mainland at Port Clarence, and Jackson established the first reindeer station at nearby Teller.[51]

Jackson, for the rest of his involvement in the reindeer experiment, carefully pointed out Healy's importance to the project. It was Healy's reputation among the natives alone that made the venture a success. "With a stranger in command," Jackson observed, "I am confident that but little could have been accomplished this season."[52] While Jackson may have been somewhat obsessive about the reindeer project, his awareness of Healy's importance to its success made him careful not to slight, let alone anger, Healy.

Healy, for his part, approved of the project, up to a point. He could see that the reindeer might help the natives and other Alaskans. One of Healy's personality traits, which mirrored that of Jackson, was his obsessive sense of duty to those on the Alaskan maritime frontier. He knew that the *Bear* provided the only governmental services available to anyone in the region and this included law enforcement, medical aid, and search and rescue. Any interference with his duties, such as the reindeer transportation trips, naturally made him uneasy and disagreeable.

Meanwhile, at Wales, during the long winter of 1891–1892, Lopp learned the flip side of using the *Bear*'s cannon as a threat against the Kinugumuts. Some of the Kinugumuts focused their hostility against the revenue cutter upon the mission. Lopp began to regret using the threat, as the most intense hostility came from the beach village, the more aggressive of the two settlements.[53]

Thornton had departed for San Francisco in the fall of 1891. Many years later, Lopp recalled that apparently Healy still held "a grudge" against Thornton because of the bath incident in 1890: "[Healy] refused [Thornton] passage on the *Bear*. He was compelled to travel that long rough voyage on a little schooner."[54] Healy, of course, unless he was ordered by headquarters or compelled by his own judgment to do so, had no obligation to provide transportation to any civilian. Thornton returned to Wales in July 1892 with a bride and another teacher, Ellen Louise Kittredge, from Glyndon, Minnesota. Born in 1868, Ellen was "a very independent, brave, strong-willed, adaptable, intelligent, and highly educated woman for her time."[55] She apparently knew nothing about Lopp's wish to take a wife. Within two months, however, Ellen and Tom were married. The two couples built a new house, this time clearly in the hill village. Although the hill people remained peaceable, they treated the missionaries with very little affection.

Not everything was pleasant between the two couples, either. Unlike the Thorntons, Ellen and Tom were trained and experienced teachers and their intent was more to educate the natives than to convert them to Christianity. Ellen's letters reveal that Thornton's personality was perhaps unsuited to life in an isolated area, especially among a group of volatile people. Even before arriving at Cape Prince of Wales, Ellen noticed that Thornton had a tendency to, as she put it, "tear around," when things did not go as he wished.[56] Ellen also wrote that the feeling among the missionaries of Northwestern Alaska was that while Lopp would persist in the mission, Thornton would not. Another missionary in Alaska, the Rev. Archibald S. McLellan, credited "Mr. Thornton with the large share of the bad and Mr. Lopp a large share of the good traits."[57] In another letter, Ellen wrote that Thornton did not like to take advice.[58] Based on this evidence, it is possible that Thornton may have treated the natives the same way Southerners treated African Americans at that time.

Soon after the new house was built, Thornton asked to meet with Tom and Ellen. Thornton felt that the two couples should divide the house and live separately from each other. Thornton talked at length about how meal preparation would be easier. Ellen wrote: "He talked eloquently, quoted scripture about husband and wife being of the same flesh. I am not sure whether he meant that in connection with their being hungry at the same time or wanting the same things to eat."[59] Nothing escaped Thornton's attention when it came to the division of the house. "Mr. Thornton is a very exact man in some ways," wrote Ellen.[60] To escape Thornton's personality, Ellen and Tom, despite Ellen being pregnant with their first child and against the advice of natives, made a dangerous winter trip to the Point Hope missionary station, fighting numerous blizzards along the way. Upon their safe return, the Lopps confided to their diary the ominous news that Thornton would shoot natives in certain cases. Tom Lopp asked for time to investigate the matter. One native told Lopp that he doubted anyone wanted to harm Thornton. In contrast, Thornton, after a drunken Eskimo tried to stab him, announced in school "that if a Native should come to his door after night and refused to give his name, he would shoot him."[61]

By this time, both Thornton and Lopp were becoming disillusioned with their work at Cape Prince of Wales. Thornton believed the "savage Eskimo" was too difficult to transform "into a comparatively civilized Christian."[62] Lopp, on the other hand, believed that the only thing that would change the Eskimo would be the successful implementation of the reindeer project. Lopp logically then decided to abandon his efforts at Wales, travel some sixty miles southeast to the new reindeer station near Teller, and devote his energies to that task.

Thornton, for whatever reason, decided to remain at Wales. He may have worried about the effect of yet another failure in his life, or he may simply have felt he was superior to his charges, and taken some pleasure in that feeling. As the year progressed, however, he grew more and more worried. He began to feel that his death was inevitable.

After Lopp left Wales in June 1893, matters between Thornton and the natives proceeded relatively peacefully at first. Then three young men, described as "aboriginal juvenile delinquents," began to cause problems.[63] Tensions increased over acts of pilfering and breaking and entering committed by the young natives. Generally, when confronted with evidence of their misdeeds, the guilty youths proved contrite and promised never to do it again, especially when told they would not be allowed to reenter school. In each case, Thornton relented and allowed the boys to resume their studies. But soon thereafter, the boys would again misbehave.

By the summer of 1893, even the Kinugumuts considered these boys outcasts. Thornton grew even more wary. He felt that if he punished the boys, despite their status as outcasts, they might retaliate against him. It seems Thornton was too frightened to deal firmly with the miscreants.

When Healy and the *Bear* arrived at Wales during the patrol of 1893, Thornton asked Healy to arrest a father and son who had allegedly taken a shot at him. Captain Healy replied that if Thornton made an affidavit concerning the charges, he would arrest them and transport them to Sitka. This, however, meant that Thornton and his witnesses would also have to travel to Sitka, which, at the time, meant being gone for one to two years. Thornton decided not to make the affidavit, but still asked Healy to arrest the two Kinugumuts. According to Sheldon Jackson, Healy wanted to know "where he should take them." Sheldon explained: "He could not leave them on the coast to starve. If he did so he would be tried for kidnapping. He could not take them to San Francisco, for there was no one to meet the expenses."[64]

In the end, Healy decided to take the natives on board the *Bear* and demonstrate to them once more the power of the cutter's cannon. As before, the Kinugumuts showed their fear of Healy and his cutter's powerful cannon.

A few days later, Thornton had a native deliver to the *Bear* a letter accusing Healy of not really trying to compel the Kinugumuts to behave. In response, Healy offered to take the missionary and his wife away from Wales. Thornton, however, unable to reach a decision, elected to remain there. Healy promised to stop by again as he returned from the Arctic in August to see whether Thornton had changed his mind.[65]

Once Healy and the *Bear* left the area, the boys again began their breaking and entering. This time Thornton decided that if more whiskey was brought into the beach settlement, he and his wife would leave. On August 19, two barrels of whiskey were brought into the beach village. The missionaries gave up and began closing up their house, expecting the *Bear* to arrive within a week. That night, the missionary couple retired to bed and slept soundly.[66]

Later that night, however, the boys, without telling anyone, stole a whaling gun, loaded it with a steel harpoon, and brought it up the hill. They pressed the barrel of the gun against the door of Thornton's house. One boy knocked and, when the door handle began to turn, another boy fired the whale gun. The harpoon passed through the door and through Thornton. Mrs. Thornton found her husband's body lying in a pool of blood.[67]

The next morning, when the Kinugumuts learned of the murder, they immediately captured two of the boys and killed them. The third boy escaped into the hills behind the village.

The two bodies were shown to Mrs. Thornton, then stripped, and thrown to the dogs. The Kinugumuts, meanwhile, expected the *Bear* to return and destroy their villages. Mrs. Thornton then wrote three messages to Healy. In each, she asked that the lives of the individual Kinugumuts who had helped her be spared. In the last message, she asked that the lives of all the hill villagers be spared. Friendly Kinugumuts then escorted her to the Port Clarence area. There, she expected to hear of the destruction of at least the village on the beach.[68]

One week later, Captain Healy and the *Bear* arrived off the coast of Wales, but Healy saw no sign of life in the villages. He sent two officers ashore to investigate. They found Thornton's body still lying where it fell as well as a message from Mrs. Thornton explaining that she had escaped to Port Clarence. Healy immediately sailed there and brought Mrs. Thornton on board the cutter. He then requested that Lopp come on board so all of them could return to Wales to close up the buildings.[69]

By the time Captain Healy returned to Wales, many of the natives had returned to their villages. When Healy went ashore, he heard rumors that the natives all expected they would be killed and their villages destroyed. This, after all, was what Eskimo justice would demand. Most Eskimos felt that an act was criminal only if it endangered the entire community. Clearly, the natives understood the threat posed to their village should anything happen to the missionaries. By killing the two boys, the natives had fulfilled the Eskimo punishment of those who placed the community in danger.[70]

Healy, hearing the natives' rumors of their impending doom, used their fear to his advantage. He told the natives that the teachers had asked Captain Healy to spare the villagers, because they had already punished Thornton's murderers. According to Mary Jane, who sailed in the *Bear* again that year, had they not already delivered this punishment "he said he would have [destroyed the villages] and would not have a single one of their people alive, and that he would have followed them north and south, over mountains and sea until everyone of them was killed or afraid to say they were of Cape Prince of Wales."[71]

Healy ordered the villagers to capture the one fugitive boy and hold him until the spring when he returned. He would then be transported for trial. Once the *Bear* departed and the ice made it impossible for the cutter to return to Wales, the boy returned to the village. The villagers took the boy up the hill to the site of Thornton's grave. Next to it, they made him dig a shallow grave. They then gave him the choice of his execution: shooting, strangling, or stabbing. The boy chose death by shooting. He was told to lie down in his own grave and then he was shot.[72]

Later, Mrs. Mattie E. McLellan, the wife of Reverend McLellan, responded to the letters from Ellen's family in Minnesota concerning her safety. They had no need to worry about Ellen's safety, Mattie wrote, "for we understand they are much thought of by the Eskimos and Mr. Thornton was not, on account of his peculiar methods."[73] Ellen later wrote that she felt no danger and was "perfectly willing to go back to the cape."[74] The family did return to Wales the following year.[75]

Tom Lopp later interviewed some of the people of Wales. In a letter to Neda Thornton, Harrison Thornton's widow, Lopp claimed the murder was to avenge the Gilley deaths.[76] Ellen was adamant that the natives were not drunk when Thornton was murdered.[77]

The murder of Harrison Thornton, the only churchman to die violently while educating and Christianizing the Eskimo, serves as one of the best examples of the complexities that Captain Healy faced on every one of his patrols in the Far North. Given the racial attitudes of the nineteenth century toward the "lesser breeds," Healy's actions are extraordinary. The naval commander at Angoon, for example, used cannon fire to rake a village and then set fire to it for an act against whites of lesser magnitude. Healy accepted Eskimo justice for a crime against a white man. However, as Ellen Lopp recorded, a man said that "Mr. Lopp and Mr. Thornton must have believed a great deal in God's protecting them from the Natives to have come here and lived, that people around here expected to have heard that they were killed." Ellen further explained: "Here, the people don't think of it as faith in God, but as faith in Captain Healy, his power to kill the people and blow the town up with his big guns, and [white men's] faith in their own firearms."[78]

Healy did not come out of this incident unscathed. Neda Thornton, remembering that her slain husband felt Healy did not want to protect them, began implying that had Healy offered them better protection, her husband would not have died. Ellen Lopp, however, explained in a letter to her parents: "Mrs. Thornton writes me in regard to our returning [to Cape Prince of Wales], 'Doubtless you will be given the protection we were denied.' She is mistaken. She is blaming Captain Healy, but we cannot see that he is to blame. I hope that you have not gotten that idea."[79]

When the time came for the 1894 patrol, it was apparent that the reindeer project was not receiving the Congressional support that Jackson thought it should. Money from the federal government did not materialize. Ice conditions along the Siberian coastline threatened to slow the purchasing and transportation of the animals. At the same time, the Bering Sea Controversy, which will be described below, continued to tax those cutters serving in the Bering Sea.

Healy, who, much like Jackson, was never one to shy away from expressing his opinion, began to show his uneasiness with the project. Before the beginning of the 1894 patrol, and the third year of the reindeer project, Healy wrote to Jackson, "As Congress has in two sessions refused to appropriate money for transporting domesticated reindeer from Siberia to Alaska, it would seem that the project has not the approval of the Government." At the end of the 1894 patrol, in a letter to the Commissioner of Education, Healy wrote, "advantage has been taken of our long absence from our own shores by contraband traders to carry on their illicit traffic, and in my opinion it is not wise for the [Treasury] Department to devote so much time to reindeer to the exclusion of our legitimate Revenue Cutter duties."[80]

Healy continued to express his displeasure with practically everything connected to the reindeer project. As for the person in charge of the Teller Reindeer Station, it "seems to me," Healy wrote to Jackson, "that it would not take much of a man to care for the business at all." Neither did the people hired to teach the natives about herding the animals escape the captain's criticisms.[81]

Some writers have made much of Healy's displeasure with the project. Capt. Charles F. Shoemaker, however, Chief of the U.S. Revenue Cutter Service Division and little known by many who have written on the reindeer project, also expressed his concern. In a March 26, 1895 letter to Healy, Captain Shoemaker wrote that he noted how much time Healy and his crew had spent on acquiring and transporting the animals. He also noted, "this occupation diverts the 'Bear' in too large a measure from her duties and purposes as a revenue cruiser, besides, I conceive that it must be a nuisance to you, as well as a very disagreeable business." Shoemaker wanted Healy's views on the subject so that he might present a plan to the secretary of the treasury. Captain Shoemaker also remarked, "I have thought it possible that vessels could be chartered for this work by the proper Department, and thus relieve our Service as 'common carriers.'"[82]

Healy wrote letters to Jackson, and others, about his disappointment with the reindeer project. Remarkably, his letters apparently did not affect the feelings between the two men. Some surviving letters from Mary Jane to Jackson show that a cordial relationship still existed between the men. In one of Healy's letters to Jackson in which he is critical of the project, he still took the time to say, "Mrs. Healy sends her regards," and then attached a short message from Mary Jane.[83] Healy and Jackson recognized themselves in each other, which led to a wary respect between the two men. There is no written record of Healy ever personally attacking Jackson's character; he focused his criticism on the project and how it hurt his performance of his own duties. Jackson, in turn, recognized Healy's extreme sense of duty and did not take umbrage at his attacks on the reindeer project. There is no way to know just how the profane and hard-drinking captain actually felt about being cooped up in a small cabin for long periods of time with the zealous missionary.

After 1895, Healy had no further official involvement with the reindeer project. It is ironic that the one aspect of Healy's life most commented upon in any history of Alaska is the reindeer importation project, when, in fact, he spent a great deal of energy trying to extricate himself from the project.

The introduction of reindeer into Alaska also sheds light on the only Eskimo woman to gain any recognition in the early years of the Alaskan maritime frontier. One of Healy's duties during the *Bear's* 1890 patrol was to conduct a census of the northern regions. For this he needed an interpreter. He chose two: Mary Antisarlook and her husband, Charlie.

Mary was born to Russian and Eskimo parents sometime between the late 1850s and the 1870s, at St. Michael, Alaska. She had two names: in Russian, she was called Palasha Makikoff, and in Eskimo, Changunak (or Sangruyak), and sometimes went by the nickname "Russian Mary." According to her own account, Mary "came from a poor family." They had "no blankets nor cups or any kind of wares." One day after returning from a caribou hunt in "the hills" the family found "people from the North with skin boats that came to St. Michaels." Charlie Antisarlook, from the Cape Nome area, numbered among the group. "He found Mary + got her for his wife. They went back to North with these people to where Charlie's father lived. . . . They lived on real simple food, like cooked + frozen tom-cods, or dried tom-cods. Whale meat, whale blubber, seal meat, seal oil and other wild animals, like rabbit + ptarmigans."[84] They eventually moved west of Nome to Sinrock. Mary's ability to speak English, Eskimo, and Russian made her an ideal interpreter.

Charlie, a full-blooded Eskimo born around 1863, lived at Cape Nome. He came from a family of traders and thus learned English.[85]

Mary and Charlie Antisarlook were an ideal team of interpreters. Taking both on board a ship kept husband and wife together. According to one source, Mary and Charlie "had served as interpreters and helpers for several years on government vessels along the coast."[86]

Years later, when Mary talked to a group of schoolchildren at Unalakleet about her life and the role she played in the introduction of reindeer to Alaska, a native of Unalakleet wrote down what she said. Later, the unknown transcriber wrote to William T. Lopp: "My brother wrote + I kind of straighten it up + write it. . . . [S]he was suppose to tell of how she first got her deer, but she told more of her trips + life. . . . I never can get a good story [from her]. When I ask her to tell me, she talks of this + that. She never can tell from first start, she tells it mixed."[87] Even if Mary did mix up dates, her account is the only known version from a native perspective of the introduction of reindeer into Alaska.

Mary recalled that during the Nome gold rush "the masts of the ships looked like the forest the boats were so thick" lying off the beach. One day the *Bear* arrived at Nome and four sailors came ashore in a boat and sought her out. After asking her a series of questions, they told her that Captain Healy asked them to bring her on board the cutter. Afraid to go aboard "without her husband," the sailors brought Charlie along. Mary recalled how "bashful" Charlie acted on board the *Bear*. Captain Healy asked her "if her husband fed her well, about his hunting, and if he was good to her." She replied "that he was very nice + a good hunter." Then, Captain Healy "asked her if she'd go along + interpret for them at Point Barrow. So, they talked to Charlie's father before they promised to go." The next morning at 6:30 a.m., a boat arrived to take Mary and Charlie on board the cutter and "they went just as they were, without any-thing."

According to Mary, they set off from Point Barrow in 1890 to purchase reindeer in Siberia. "When they get to Siberia peoples were not polite. They were wild and they never smile." She could not understand their language. As recorded by the unknown transcriber, Jackson told Mary "they wanted to buy reindeer from Siberians."

> They went to the Herder there + she couldn't understand them, so she cried when she couldn't understand or do any interpreting. The Captain [Healy] slapped her on her face when she cried.
>
> This was the biggest herd in Siberia. . . . The herder send a man without a nose to bring the deer. This man without a nose was very poorly dressed. He brought or drove the deer by whistling. . . . They bought four reindeer[,] 2 spotted + 2 blacks from this herder.
>
> When they got back to Cape Prince of Wales they left Mary and Charlie to help Mr. Lopp take care of [a] hundred reindeer. On the first trip they brought four deer + they hauled more after wards.[88]

In 1895, Charlie became the first native to receive reindeer. He moved his herd to the Sinuk River area, some twenty-two miles west of present-day Nome. (Prospectors called the river "Sinrock," from the Eskimo word "singuk," meaning point.)[89] Two years later, Charlie and Mary took part in another famous expedition involving reindeer known as the Overland Relief Expedition, earning themselves a reputation for their work with the reindeer. When, on July 30, 1900, Charlie died of measles and pneumonia, the Nome newspaper reported that the "Reindeer King" had died.[90]

Even though Lieut. John G. Berry, an officer on board the *Bear* in 1898, described Mary as "one of the most intelligent of the natives of Alaska," her fame really began after her husband's death.[91] When Mary took over the herd, she received many offers of marriage from suitors who sought to gain control of the herd. She also fought legal battles to retain the herd of reindeer. In spite of everything, Mary persevered and prospered as the herd steadily increased. Because of the original location of the reindeer herd, she became known as "Sinrock Mary." She eventually relocated the animals to an area near Unalakleet, and then moved them between Unalakeet and St. Michael. She, however, lived at Unalakleet until her death.

In the meantime, while Captain Healy continued with his add-on duties, trouble arose concerning his primary duty of protecting the seals. The controlled harvesting of the fur seals might have continued in its traditional way indefinitely, pumping money into the coffers of the United States, were it not for the increasing demand of the woman's fashion industry for more fur seal pelts. This demand led to pelagic—open sea—hunting of the animal from ships. Traditionally, natives had pursued the seal and harpooned them from their kayaks. The number of seals killed in this manner never interfered with the ecology of the mammal. Moreover, rarely, if ever, did the native lose the animal after harpooning it. This would all change once greed entered the picture. Sealing schooners soon rushed to the Bering Sea and the passes in the Aleutian Islands leading to the sea. Jack London's classic novel, *The Sea Wolf*, takes place on board such a vessel. Hunters from the schooners shot the seals with rifles. Many sank beneath the waves before the ship's crew could arrive and gather the carcasses. Just as bad, hunters killed indiscriminately. Many pregnant and nursing females fell before the bullets. The death of a nursing female also meant the death of a pup, as female seals only nursed their own young. London's novel best describes the scene on board one of these vessels: "It was wanton slaughter, and all for woman's sake. No man ate of the seal meat or the oil. After a good day's killing I have seen our decks covered with hides and bodies, slippery with fat and blood, the scuppers running red; masts, ropes, and rails spattered with the sanguinary color; and the men, like butchers plying their trade, naked and red of arm and hand, hard at work with ripping and flensing knives, removing the skins from the pretty sea creatures they had killed."[92]

By the late 1800s, at least one hundred sealing ships from nations around the world worked in the Bering Sea. On the Pribilof Islands, "the quantity of killable seals decreased to one-fifth the usual number."[93] The Alaska Commercial Company bombarded Washington with requests for help. Treasury officials knew what had happened to another commercially desirable sea mammal, the sea otter, which hunting drove almost to extinction. If the fur seal suffered a similar fate, then the United States would lose a valuable source of income. When the Alaska Commercial Company obtained the lease that allowed them a monopoly on the harvesting of fur seals, the lease contained a provision forbidding the company's hunters to kill fur seals at sea. Citing this provision as the legal basis for stopping the recent uncontrolled slaughter, the Treasury Department turned to its maritime police force to regulate the killing.

In 1886, cutters received orders to seize all U.S. and foreign ships that killed fur seals at sea. Three Canadian ships, operating at least sixty miles off the Alaskan coast, became the first vessels captured under this order. Brought back to Sitka, the ships' officers received a fine and were placed in jail for a month. Not too surprisingly, the British and Canadian press howled at what they considered an outrage against their vessels on the open sea. In response, the United States declared the Bering Sea a *mare clausum*, a closed sea, subject to the enforcement of U.S., not international, law. Predictably, other nations viewed the situation differently. The following year, the U.S. Revenue Cutter Service seized twelve ships, six hailing from the United States and six from Canada.[94] All of this led to the little-known Bering Sea Controversy.[95]

Tensions mounted. In 1891, Washington, D.C., and London established a *modus vivendi* in an attempt to ease the tensions. Both sides renewed the *modus vivendi* in the spring of 1892, with the stipulation that any Canadian ship seized on the high seas would be turned over to Canadian authorities for prosecution.

Nevertheless, in 1892, the United States sent the "largest fleet of American fighting ships ever seen, up to that time, in the North Pacific," under the command of Comdr. Robley D. Evans.[96] "Fighting Bob" Evans, next to Adm. George Dewey, "may have been the most popular naval personality at the turn of the [twentieth] century."[97] President Theodore Roosevelt remarked that the U.S. Navy had perhaps never had an officer "who more thoroughly and joyously welcomed a fight." Known as a man "forthright" and "gruff, who could become nasty," Evans, just prior to his venture in the Far North, had returned from another hot spot. The year before the Bering Sea Controversy took hold, a revolution had taken place in Chile. Despite his knowledge of the Chilean people's dislike for Americans, which stemmed from the United States' support of the recently overthrown government, the commanding officer of the U.S. cruiser *Baltimore* granted liberty to his crew in Coquimbo, north of the capital of Santiago. Riots broke out and two sailors died. Chile claimed the two navy men had started the incident while drunk. The U.S. State Department, not too surprisingly, claimed anti-American feelings had caused the mob to attack the sailors. Diplomatic efforts to investigate and resolve the incident reached an impasse. War loomed. Shortly after the incident, Evans and his gunboat, *York-town*, arrived in the area. Because of his determined stand against the Chileans, he earned the nickname "Fighting Bob" Evans.[98]

Evans' orders in the Bering Sea seemed simple: eliminate the seal poachers, or as some called them, the "seal pirates." Eight ships sailed under his command when Evans began work in the Bering Sea. In addition to the *Yorktown*, the fleet contained the USS *Mohican*, the USS *Adams*, and the USS *Ranger*, a U.S. Fish Commission vessel, the *Albatross*, and the cutters *Rush*, *Corwin*, and, eventually, Healy's *Bear*.[99]

In his autobiography, *A Sailor's Log*, Evans credits Captain Hooper, who commanded the *Corwin*, with making the major capture of seal poachers in 1892. Hooper seized the Canadian ship *Coquitlan*, which was suspected of act-ing as the poachers' supply ship. The *Coquitlan's* hold contained thirty thou-sand sealskins. Evans wrote, "the case against her was so plain that there was no reason for resistance, and she was towed to Sitka as a prize . . . she was bonded for six thousand dollars, which . . . paid most of the expenses of our summer's work."[100]

Although Captain Healy and the *Bear* normally spent more time operat-ing away from the Pribilof Islands, Healy received orders to cooperate with Evans upon his return from the Arctic, beginning on September 28, 1892.[101] This made the *Bear* and the USS *Adams* the last two government ships in the region. The commander of the *Adams*, Comdr. R. M. Nelson, had never ex-perienced weather anything like that which the two vessels faced. His report contained a great deal of information supplied by Healy. This probably did not surprise those within the Treasury Department, who had already read many comments from Healy. Captain Healy let Nelson know which of the two men knew more about operating within the Bering Sea. Nelson reported: "The AD-AMS is unsuited for this duty, and even Captain Healy's strongly built BEAR is of limited usefulness. His [Healy's] long experience in these waters indicates that maintaining patrols so late in the year cannot prevent raids on the Islands by a bold poacher who has no regard for the safety of his vessel." Nelson went on to point out that Captain Healy felt that guarding the islands by vessel was "at most ineffective, expensive and hazardous and severe on a ship's company." Healy felt, and Nelson agreed, that the only way to logically "guard the islands effectively is from the shore."[102]

Prior to departing the Bering Sea, Commander Evans noted that he had "dinner aboard the *Bear* with Captain and Mrs. Healey [sic]." Instead of putting up with the long slow passage aboard the *Bear* from the Bering Sea back to San

Francisco, Mary Jane took what she and Michael felt would be a faster passage aboard the *Yorktown*.[103]

Evans left the Bering Sea on October 1 and arrived in San Francisco on October 10. Mary Jane did not, as it turned out, have a pleasant voyage aboard the larger ship. Commander Evans said they encountered "gales and hurricanes all the way from Unalaska—the worst I have ever known. We were absolutely under water for five days, and I lived in wet clothing. Finally came a hurricane in which we were hove to for twenty hours."[104]

This marked the end of the U.S. Navy's involvement in the Bering Sea Controversy. Evans received recognition for his duties in Chile and the Bering Sea with a promotion to captain in 1893.[105]

That year, an international tribunal took the matter of pelagic sealing into its own hands. Unfortunately for the United States, the tribunal ruled against America and requested payment of $473,151 in damages for the seizure of Canadian ships.[106] The tribunal did lead to regulations concerning the hunting of the fur seal. It helped establish a reservation of sixty miles circling the Pribilofs, stopped the hunting of seals from May 1 to August 1, and established an Anglo-American patrol force for the area. Sixty miles, however, did little to ensure the safety of an animal used to roaming thousands of miles.

Bickering over this issue continued within the U.S. Congress and diplomatic circles. Meanwhile, the fur seal population plummeted. The animal hovered near extinction. By 1911, the seals almost gone, an international agreement finally settled the question and the U.S. Senate ratified the agreement.[107] While many hail this agreement as an example of international diplomacy, the event that more likely saved the fur seals was that the fashion industry no longer dictated the demand of the seals' pelts.

After the U.S. Navy warships departed the Bering Sea, Captain Healy continued his traditional duty of patrolling for seal poachers. One can point out that, while decisive action against poachers began out of concern for a loss of revenue for the federal government, the work of Captain Healy helped prevent the loss of this marine mammal.[108]

The official establishment, in 1895, of a Bering Sea Patrol, with headquarters at Unalaska for the months cutters operated in the Bering Sea, became the spin-off of the Bering Sea Controversy for the U.S. Revenue Cutter Service. The service selected Capt. Calvin L. Hooper as the patrol's first commander. Perhaps, had the cloud of drinking not hung so heavily over Captain Healy, the duty might have been his.

Despondency over the 1890 trial, followed shortly thereafter by the major loss of Lieutenant Robinson and his crewmen at Icy Bay, might have caused lesser men to quit work in the Far North altogether. Healy instead continued to carry out his duties in the Far North, arguably with even greater vigor. The reindeer project should have brought him great fame, but, once again, fate intervened.[109]

The 1894 patrol departed on April 21 and returned on November 14. When preparations for the patrol of 1895 began, Healy had been a seaman for forty years. Fourteen of these years had been spent in command of cutters in one of the world's most unforgiving and uncharted maritime environments. On the wild Alaskan maritime frontier, Healy faced not only death from storms and ice, but also the challenge of dealing with law enforcement issues that often involved people of different cultures. Rarely, if ever, have other sea-going officers faced such complexities, especially during peacetime. Despite these hardships, Healy continued to present what the modern-day military likes to call a command presence.

By 1895, Healy was fifty-four, and the years at sea, with long stretches spent in the cold, windswept crow's nest seeking the best way through the ice, had taken their toll upon the captain. In the only candid photograph of the man, probably taken in 1891 during the days of buying and transporting of reindeer, gray hair protrudes from the edges of his uniform hat, while his mustache is shot with gray. The image captured "Hell Roaring Mike" wearing glasses, making it the only known photograph of him with spectacles. The years at sea caused Healy to look older than Sheldon Jackson, who, in reality, was five years Healy's senior. Strong lines are etched into his face. Among these are the telltale crow's-feet that, at the corners of his blue eyes, show years of squinting through the glare of the sea and ice. During his 1890 hearing, Healy intimated for the first time that the years were taking their toll. He admitted that he now had difficulty making the hard climb up the rigging to the crow's nest. In an unguarded moment, he said that he now preferred to sit in a boatswain's chair (a short narrow board suspended by a bridle made of rope) and be hoisted to the lookout station far above the *Bear*'s main deck.[110]

In 1895, those who did not know Healy, and that included most everyone, with perhaps the exception of Mary Jane, saw a stern, by-the-book officer whose greatest concern was doing his duty to the best of his ability. Capt. Michael A. Healy's work and manner led to the almost natural moniker, the "Czar of the North."[111]

10

"I Steer By No Man's Compass But My Own"

The 1895 Bering Sea Patrol began no differently for Capt. Michael A. Healy than had any other. Capt. Calvin L. Hooper, Healy's former skipper, served as commander of the annual patrol. He already had received reports of sealing vessels congregating near the Shumagin Islands, waiting for the usual bad weather to hit the Aleutian Islands before sneaking into the prohibited area to kill fur seals and harvest a quick, lucrative cargo of illegal pelts. Healy's initial orders of the season called for him to investigate the seas around the Shumagins, a short distance from the Aleutian passes leading to the Bering Sea. Afterwards, Healy and his 198-foot *Bear* were to patrol the Pribilof Islands in search of illegal sealing operations, before moving on to other duties above the Arctic Circle.

June 6 found the *Bear* maneuvering slowly through a thick fog. At 2:30 p.m., Second Lieut. Howard Emery, navigation officer and then officer of the deck, spotted a small island off the port bow through a break in the fog. The lieutenant notified Healy of the sighting and informed him he felt the island resembled Korovin, one of the Shumagins. Captain Healy first ordered slow ahead and then questioned Emery's identification of the island. When the wind freshened about 5:00 p.m., Healy ordered the engines stopped and the mainsail set. He next went below to his cabin, leaving Second Lieut. George M. Daniels, the new officer of the deck, with the responsibility of conning (maneuvering) the cutter without any specific orders. Although this routine practice has taken place millions of time since sailors first went to sea, this seemingly banal act became the harbinger of the fall of Capt. Michael A. Healy.[1]

The various changes in the *Bear*'s speed over the preceding days made an accurate dead reckoning position impossible, Daniels later explained, and placed the ship "in a dangerous position close to the island in conditions of limited visibility."[2] That evening at dinner in the officer's wardroom, Emery expressed his uneasiness about the dangers "of going among the islands in thick fog," while "not knowing the position of the vessel accurately." The other officers in the wardroom echoed his reservations. First Lieut. Albert Buhner, the ship's executive officer, argued, "the ship should have been put into the bay that afternoon."[3] Buhner, an old salt, had served with Healy for many years.

Emery resumed his watch as the officer of the deck at 8:00 p.m., with the cutter's position doubtful, the skipper below in his cabin, and the only orders being "go slow ahead." In a scene that would likely seem strange, if not bizarre, to a modern seagoing officer, Buhner and Daniel joined Emery and began discussing their concern over the present situation. Today, naval officers would not discuss such matters within hearing of an officer of the deck. The fog lifted. Recognizing Korovin Island, First Lieutenant Buhner, as senior officer on deck, took over the officer of the deck's duties for a short time and ordered a course change, one paralleling the island and following a deep channel into Stepovik Bay. He then went below to notify Captain Healy of his actions and receive orders for the night. After knocking at the cabin door and receiving no response, the lieutenant went topside to the pilothouse and wrote the night orders. According to later testimony, Buhner undertook this action on his "own responsibility," something he had never done before: "frequently the Captain had spent 24, 48 or even 72 hours straight on deck, and I thought he needed his sleep." Healy came on deck briefly at 11:00 p.m. and issued orders to reduce sail and continue sailing offshore during the night. He made no other changes to the night orders. Second Lieutenant Emery remembered Healy as being unsteady and "very drunk."[4]

At 4:30 a.m. on June 7, Buhner and Daniels, along with Engineer J. E. Dory, relaxed in the wardroom over coffee before turning in. Suddenly, they heard the captain's service bell ringing for his personal steward. The bell rang several more times before they heard Captain Healy leave his cabin and make his way to the area where the stewards slept. He screamed obscenities and cursed them for not answering the bell before returning to his cabin. Daniels later swore he heard Healy strike one of the Japanese stewards, although he did not actually see Healy strike the man.

The *Bear* spent the next two weeks cruising among the Shumagin Islands. On those rare occasions when Healy appeared on deck, his officers noted that he was "showing the effects of constant drinking." The executive officer finally decided to confiscate his liquor supply "for the Captain's own good," since the ship's doctor had advised that Healy's drinking "was injuring him seriously." In Healy's time, it was legal for naval officers to drink aboard ship, although they were not to drink to excess or, of course, put their ship in danger. Lieutenant

Buhner and the ship's carpenter found an unopened case of whiskey and several additional bottles of liquor, and gave the alcohol to the ship's doctor.[5]

Early August found the *Bear* hove to off Icy Cape, above the Arctic Circle, with the whaling fleet, waiting for the ice conditions to improve before pushing on to Point Barrow. On August 23, Captain Healy decided to wait no longer and ordered the cutter south. Much later, at his trial, some of his officers would try to prove that this decision was the result of Healy's craving for liquor, not his knowledge of Arctic ice navigation. The relations between the officers and the skipper of the *Bear* had degenerated to a dangerous degree, which helps explain what happened next at Unalaska, the patrol headquarters in the Aleutian Islands.

The *Bear* came to in Unalaska on September 11, joining the other vessels participating in the final stages of the 1895 Bering Sea Patrol. As required by regulations and naval custom, Captain Healy immediately called upon the commander of the patrol, Captain Hooper, on board the cutter *Rush*. Later, under oath, Hooper admitted to recognizing the signs that "Captain Healy had been drinking." "[B]ut I would not say he was drunk," Hooper said.[6]

Captain Hooper soon received another visitor from the *Bear*, Second Lieut. (Temporary) Chester M. White, who declared his intentions to file charges of misconduct against Captain Healy. Captain Hooper did not ask for the particulars, but did request that White not pursue his formal charges any further. Hooper subsequently informed Healy of the incident by letter, ordering that the message be delivered only "when Healy was sober."[7]

At the time of the *Bear*'s visit to Unalaska, four other U.S. Revenue Cutter Service cutters—the *Corwin*, the *Grant*, the *Perry*, and the *Rush*—lay at anchor in Unalaska, as well as a British warship, the HMS *Pheasant*. The U.S. Revenue Cutter Service officers spent their time in Unalaska working and socializing. At one social event ashore, Captain Healy, who continued his normal routine of intimidating junior officers, so flustered a young officer that he appealed to both his own commanding officer, Capt. D. F. Tozier of the *Perry*, and patrol commander Captain Hooper to prevail upon Healy to cease his harassment. Later, Capt. Frank A. Garforth of the Royal Navy, who commanded the *Pheasant*, invited all the U.S. Revenue Cutter Service officers anchored at Unalaska to a wardroom party aboard his cruiser. "A lot of whiskey was going around," Captain Hooper much later recalled, "and I would be surprised that anyone got away sober that evening." At one time during the party, Hooper noticed Healy dozing in a chair. As the party began breaking up, Healy's deep commanding voice bellowed across the room: "Ross, be a man." Upon hearing his name, First

Lieut. Worth Ross, of the *Grant*, hurried over to Healy. Ross suggested to Healy that farewells were in order and offered to accompany him back to the *Bear*. When Healy rejected the offer, Ross explained that he meant no disrespect and only made the suggestion "in a friendly spirit."[8]

Healy next turned on Chief Engineer A. L. Broadbent, who had served with him for years. "Broadbent," Healy roared, disoriented either from his nap or drink, "get out of my cabin or I will put you under arrest." Broadbent shot back, "I don't belong to your ship," and walked away.[9] Healy started to rise from his chair, but then sat down again.

Captain Garforth and First Lieut. F. M. Dimmock of the *Rush* next tried to convince Healy to leave. Lieutenant Ross again volunteered his services, eventually coaxing Healy on deck and, with the help of Lieutenant Dimmock, escorted him back to the *Bear*. Later, Lieutenant Daniels claimed the British captain confided to him that, if he "had realized Captain Healy was not a gentleman, he would not have invited him."[10]

Two days later, Captain Healy made his way down the pier to see off the cutter *Perry*. One minute Healy was on the pier and the next, according to amazed observers, he was floundering in the bay. Many blamed drunkenness for his fall. Seaman Benjamin Hutton, however, later testified that Healy had inadvertently tripped on something and, unable to gain his balance, fell into the water. Hauled aboard the *Perry*, the drenched Healy admitted in astonishment to falling overboard. "So, I perceive, sir," replied First Lieut. John G. Barry, while Captain Tozier remarked, "Captain, I regret to see you in this condition." Both Barry and Tozier, according to their later statements, believed Healy was drunk.[11]

Captain Healy spent the next week at the home of Mr. Harvey N. Nice, of the Alaska Commercial Company, recuperating from his plunge into the bay. The *Bear*'s surgeon, Dr. Thomas Bodkin, treated Healy for cuts and bruises.

Meanwhile, Captain Hooper, the senior U.S. Revenue Cutter Service officer on the West Coast, had been presented with a document entitled, "Request for Investigation into the Conduct of Captain Michael A. Healy." It contained the signatures of twenty-five officers. Not too surprisingly, practically all of the junior officers on the four revenue cutters signed their names to the document. Many of the more senior first lieutenants also signed the document. Only First Lieutenants Buhner and Dimmock refused to sign.[12]

The document alleged seven specifications of misconduct. Six dealt with Healy's ungentlemanly conduct and treatment of his junior officers, while the seventh dealt with the event on board the HMS *Pheasant* involving Chief Engineer Broadbent. Surprisingly, none of the misconduct specifications accused Healy of the intemperate use of alcohol. Hooper did not consider this document to level official charges against Healy. He advised the secretary of the treasury to postpone any action until the *Bear* returned to San Francisco in November, stating that a copy of the document had been forwarded to Healy for his reply.[13]

Upon the *Bear*'s return to home port, Lieutenant Daniels, learning of Captain Hooper's refusal to act upon the seven charges, preferred formal charges against his commanding officer. Service regulations required these charges to be routed through the executive officer of the *Bear*, Lieutenant Buhner, passed to Captain Healy for endorsement, and finally sent on to Washington. When Healy delayed his endorsement too long, Buhner went to Healy's home, obtained the documents, and mailed them.[14]

Captain Healy finally returned to the *Bear* on November 29 and, finding Lieutenant Daniels ashore, left orders for him to report to his cabin immediately upon coming aboard the cutter. Fearful that "Hell Roaring Mike" might try in the privacy of his cabin to provoke Daniels into striking him, the lieutenant stationed Emery and Engineer Officer Dory outside the open door. Daniels later swore that upon his entrance Healy called him a liar and spat in his face. Healy, in turn, countered that he had merely expressed his disgust at his subordinate's incorrect ship log entries by spitting upon the deck in front of his feet. The two witnesses carefully placed by Daniels did not actually observe the actions of either Healy or Daniels in the cabin. They reported hearing no mention of the log, but did hear Healy calling Daniels a liar and the lieutenant's immediate exclamation that the captain had spit upon him. Captain Healy left the cutter shortly thereafter.[15] As fate would have it, one of the witnesses to the "confrontation," Lieutenant Emery, remained on board as officer of the deck. This made Emery the senior duty officer on board at the time. What happened next may have modern naval officers again shaking their heads, but given the climate on board the cutter, it is merely a logical escalation of events.

Emery violated every rule of the military chain of command by firing off a telegram to Assistant Secretary of the Treasury Charles Hamlin. Emery signed the message, "1st Lieut. Temporarily in charge," and reported: "Captain Healy is intoxicated on board the *Bear* insulting his officers. Immediate action necessary." Hamlin's reply on November 30 summarily relieved Healy of command pending a Board of Inquiry to consider the charges against him. The assistant secretary also ordered Emery to file new formal charges.[16]

Hamlin's actions are inexplicable today. Surely, anyone familiar with the military would have expected him to reprimand Emery for his violation of the chain of command, since any recommendation for Healy's removal should have come from his immediate superior officer, Captain Hooper. One rationale for the senior Treasury official's decision is that he had grown weary of Healy's behavior, which had, after all, created a major public relations disaster, and felt he needed to be pushed aside. Perhaps Hamlin already knew of the 1890 charges against Healy concerning cruelty and drunkenness and, despite Healy's exoneration, now felt it was time to replace him. Also, just prior to these latest charges against Healy, the service had received bad publicity about the behavior of a number of other senior officers, who had also been accused of excessive drinking. Hamlin may have felt Healy's case could set an example for others.[17]

Captain Healy's friends advised him not to contest the charges. "The cloud is very dark and more threatening than I thought," wrote his brother James A. Healy, Bishop of Portland, Maine.[18] Captain Hooper, Healy's superior officer and longtime colleague, also cautioned against fighting the charges. Nevertheless, Healy's personality coupled with the atmosphere on board the *Bear* makes Healy's decision not all that surprising: he decided to fight. Healy engaged the services of San Francisco attorney Bradley Henley.

As events began to unfold, the newspapers in San Francisco devoted many column inches to anything connected with the trial. Without a doubt, no other single story in the history of the U.S. Revenue Cutter Service on the West Coast ever garnered as much newspaper attention as Captain Healy's tribulations. At times during the proceedings, it was difficult to tell which produced more sensationalism: the trial or the press.

As if scripted for a modern soap opera, an early headline screamed, "Lieutenant White Deserts His Wife: Runs Away With a Chorus Girl." Breathlessly, the first paragraph of the story opened with the information that Lieut. Chester White "not only left his ship and the United States service without leave, but has deserted his young and beautiful wife during a critical illness and gone away with a chorus girl of the 'Passing Show' Company, whither his wife knows not." The loyal and trusting Mrs. White, the story went on to say, would not accept that Chester White had run off, but then "she received a letter from him, dated at Reno, [Nevada], in which he acknowledged that he had run away with [the woman,] and that after a week of anticipated 'real happiness' he would end both his own life and that of the woman who accompanied him."[19]

As in any lurid story of unfaithfulness reported in the press, an engraving of Mabel Howe and Chester White made their way into the newspapers. Mrs. White, after seeing the engraving of Mabel Howe, said she did not think Mabel "was a pretty woman." Mrs. White went on to say, "nor is she attractive. She is, in fact, quite ordinary." Mrs. White did not believe Chester White would carry out his dire threat to kill himself. "Men who boast of such things rarely keep their promises," she said. "I think the probabilities are that he will not."

Attorney Henley immediately sent a letter to Secretary of the Treasury John G. Carlisle, pointing out that the charges against Healy had originally begun with Lieutenant White, who "within the last few days it has been publicly announced . . . resigned from the Service (and incidentally deserted his wife in the process)." Henley continued, "it would seem to indicate that there is an abandonment of the accusation, the existence of which he is mainly responsible for." Secretary Carlisle, however, refused to bow to the implied threat of adverse publicity that might result from a formal trial.[20]

Shortly after the White affair ran in the newspapers, another account described Chester White telegraphing his resignation to headquarters, which refused the resignation, since telegraphic resignations were unacceptable. White then traveled to Washington, D.C., to properly tender his resignation, arriving there on November 27, 1895.

On December 1, White spoke to an unidentified reporter and explained that he had previously "sent a message to Captain Healy from Reno." According to White, he telegraphed his commander that he had resigned from the *Bear* and from the service. White claimed Captain Healy kept this information to himself.

The reporter tried to capture the feelings of the officers aboard the *Bear*. White informed the journalist that he was a protégé of Captain Healy, and that Healy had become extremely distressed by the young man's ingratitude. Further, the reporter claimed that Lieutenant White, while acting as navigating officer, had nearly lost the *Bear* and would have run her aground on Kodiak Island had Captain Healy not come on deck at an opportune moment. Afterward, Captain Healy had placed White under arrest for insubordination. White told the reporter that "he took issue with his commander regarding an order" and was impertinent. Captain Healy kept White detained in his quarters for a day and told White "he would not record his arrest on the log." The reporter, pointing out that Healy, by not placing White's name in the log, had "sought to save him from disgrace," also reported, "White's name has also been mentioned in connection with the unpleasantness of H.M.S. *Pheasant* at Unalaska."

In the meanwhile, Mrs. White told a reporter that she did not think White's abandoning her "'was premeditated.'" She continued: "'I think it was a mad-ness—in fact, I can account for his conduct in no other way. He had been away a good while up there, outside the limit of civilization. It was a sort of crazy streak that came over him and, without realizing what he was doing or considering the consequences, he plunged ahead. But the time will come when he will be sorry for it all. I know that and I feel sorry for him.'" She pointed out that White had known Howe previously, and that she had only learned of the affair when White's letters were forwarded to her once the *Bear* returned to home port.

Readers eagerly followed the continuing story of Chester White. The next revelation came in a story from Boston, dated December 3, 1895. White tried to tell all to another unidentified reporter, stating: "In the first place, I did not prefer charges against Captain Healy, and would not now desire to say anything but in praise of him. I don't think the Captain had a firmer friend in the service than I have been and still am. I left San Francisco on account of him, princi-pally because I did not desire to testify at any hearing that may be held on the charges."

White also pointed out that Lieutenant Daniels had submitted the first written charges against Healy, in which he alleged "drunkenness, tyranny and abusive conduct on the cruise." White further claimed that the current charges against Healy originated from Lieutenant Emery and therefore insisted that he did not "have anything to do with the charges." White said that Emery and Daniels had served in the *Bear* for only a year, while he "had been on the cutter on the Pacific station four years": "I was the navigating officer, and I was not transferred at the end of my three years' service, but assigned again to the *Bear* on special duty as navigating officer, because Healy wrote to have me retained. I left San Francisco November 9th, within twenty-four hours after the *Bear* got into port. As I said, I do not care to testify against the Captain, and I supposed that my evidence would be very important to the men who had made the charges against the Captain, because I had been under him so long and knew more about him than they did."

Chester White then continued: "The only way I saw out of it was to resign from the service. I had received an offer from a large Chicago house to enter commercial life, to do business for them in Alaska. I thought it a very good opportunity, and coming at this time, my decision to resign on account of the charges against Captain Healy was more easily arrived at."

White also told a reporter that just "before leaving San Francisco" he had made the following arrangements:

I telegraphed to the department at Washington, resigning from the service and asking them to forward the acceptance to Chicago. Ordinarily, resignations from the Revenue Service are accepted, and I waited four days in Chicago to hear concerning my request to be relieved. Then I went to Washington and saw Assistant Secretary Hamlin and Captain Shoemaker, chief of the Revenue Marine Division. I talked with them about my resignation, and they both told me that on account of the charges which had been preferred against Captain Healy, inasmuch as I was the Navigating Officer of the *Bear*, the Department did not wish to accept my resignation.

White then received orders to report to the cutter *Dallas* in Boston. Returning to his comments on the charges against Healy, White said, "I feel that an injustice has been done me in the statement that I preferred the charges against Captain Healy, and the whole affair looks to me like an attempt to force me out of the service."

About the Mabel Howe revelations, White said: "It has been stated that I was seen in Oakland November 16th, with Miss Howe, but I was not in Oakland with her, as I left San Francisco the day before. Mrs. White knew of my departure, and also of the circumstances for I wrote to her from Reno, Nevada. She did not expect to come East, as she was sick at the time. I wrote her again from Chicago, telling her of the situation and of my plans."

Yet another article, datelined December 3, 1895, from Washington, D.C., informed readers that an investigation into Lieutenant White's alleged elopement was now underway by the service. Four days later, newspapers reported that Chester White had once again offered his resignation, and that this time it was accepted. With this act, Chester White ended his journey along the twisted path that culminated in the pivotal moment of Healy's life.

The many newspaper accounts of Chester White's strange tale point to either the service or the Treasury Department's desire to rid itself of Capt. Michael A. Healy. If the accounts are to be believed, it appears that once the decision-makers learned of White's refusal to testify against Healy, they quickly disposed of their problem by letting White resign.

While the Chester White story played out largely in Boston and Washington, D.C., residents in the San Francisco Bay area on November 29, 1895, read that Captain Healy had received orders detaching him from the *Bear*. One reporter said that at nine o'clock in the morning of November 28, Healy called the crew of the *Bear* to quarters and "made a brief speech to the officers and crew, telling them he was no longer in command." After this announcement, Healy said that Lieutenant Buhner, the executive officer, was now in temporary command. The reporter wrote that the news came as "a great surprise to the crew of the *Bear*, though the officers expected it." Not surprisingly, the account mentioned that Healy appeared "greatly agitated" as he turned over the command of the *Bear* to Buhner.

A rival reporter viewed the proceedings differently: "At muster yesterday morning Captain Healy appeared a bit nervous. He held the telegram in his hand. As soon as the men were lined up he stepped forward and announced that he was no longer in command, and that he had received instructions from the Secretary of the Navy [*sic*] to turn the vessel over to Lieutenant Buhner. Then, thanking the crew for their faithfulness, he made way for the temporary commander."

The journalist went on to state: "No one on the vessel appeared to be the least bit sorry over the change. All are now anxiously looking forward to the instructions that will probably be received from headquarters regarding the trial of Captain Healy."

Before the service headquarters announced its decision to hold a trial, Healy's son, Frederick, wrote to the head of the Healy clan, Bishop James A. Healy, in Portland, Maine. Frederick Healy asked the bishop about using his influence to help his younger brother, Michael A. Healy. Bishop Healy's response proved disillusioning to Frederick and Mary Jane Healy. "From present indications I think his best plan is to ask to be placed on the retired list and as to the trial to plead *nolo conterere* [*sic*]."[21] Bishop Healy either did not know, or chose to ignore the fact, that unlike the U.S. Navy, the U.S. Revenue Cutter Service did not have a retirement system.

Although the San Francisco newspapers favored their colorful captain, Healy did not escape their damaging pretrial publicity. Shortly after accounts ran that Healy was awaiting orders for a trial, a story appeared that began by slyly noting that Healy now resided on "a hard cot in the Home for Inebriates at North Beach." The account detailed that Healy had "always risen superior to his difficulties, but now that his difficulties are now in the ascendancy he goes weakly to the wall."

The story went on to relate how Healy, after learning of the forthcoming trial, felt dejected. A group of his cronies found it extremely easy to start Healy drinking so much in the Occidental Hotel that the "old sea dog" fell out of his chair. Healy, the article said, picked himself up and "declared that he would drink everyone under the table." Soon after that, he became "unmanageable" and "began abusing people, and the junior officers of the *Bear* came in for a share of his stentorian wrath." After Healy's conduct became "dangerously violent," his friends placed something in his drink that put Healy to sleep. His cronies then rushed him "to the Home for Inebriates, where he is now under medical care."

After relating all the unsavory details, the article's mood shifted to a pious tone, explaining that such behavior did not bode well for Healy. The reporter, however, tried to close with the best possible explanation. "His friends," the newspaper said, "plead the sudden turn in his fortunes as provocation for his latest escapades."

Another reporter, whose article serves as the antithesis of the Occidental Hotel piece, pointed out that Healy had walked into the Home for Inebriates "accompanied by his son [Frederick]" and "of his own accord and asked for treatment of his lungs, a severe congestion having set in rather suddenly." The father and son had planned to visit Captain Smith of the cutter *Commodore Perry*, when the congestion began. "The doctor said he saw at a glance that Healy was a sick man and put him to bed immediately." The reporter noted that, at one point, Healy had "several hemorrhages of the lungs" that continued for two days. At another point, Healy's condition became so bad that the physician sent for "Mrs. Healy and a priest, as he feared that death was at hand." Fortunately, Healy rallied and regained his strength. Friends and the doctor were "empathic" in pointing out that Healy may have had something to drink "to dull his humiliation in having his command taken away from him," but never during his thirty-six-hour stay at the home did a doctor treat him for alcoholism or "delerlum [*sic*] tremens."

The article also responded to the newspaper report of Healy's actions at the Occidental Hotel. One of the permanent residents of the residential hotel said that Healy "was not in the saloon at the time he was alleged to have been tossing glasses about and making himself a nuisance." Lastly, the article reported that, despite Healy's "feeble condition," the attending physician decided the captain could "leave the institution . . . and go to his home in Sausalito, where he could be assured of quiet and rest." The article concluded, "His wife and son accompanied him across the bay."

These sensational press stories about Healy's alleged actions at the Occidental Hotel proved to foreshadow what lay in store for readers in the Bay area over the next few months. Charge and countercharge filled the papers.

On December 7, newspapers jump-started the story again: "The troubles on the revenue *Bear* seem to be without end. Lieutenants Daniels, Dory and

White have been held up as the principal accusers of Captain Healy, but the fact is that Lieutenants Ross and McConnell and Chief Engineer Swartze [of the cutter *Grant*] were the prime instigators of the movement." At the same time, the two officers most quoted about the charges, Daniels and Dory, found themselves facing charges. Later, newspapers reported: "[the] officers are cleared of the charges brought against them, which are said to have been merely newspaper gossip. There were some members of the *Bear*'s crew who had grievances against the officers in question, but the charges they brought were not specific; therefore the court found that there were not any grounds for suspension. This disposes of the rumors that Daniels and Dory were guilty of all manner of breach of discipline."

Even before the trial began, news accounts revealed a rift between the commissioned officers' feelings about their captain and those of the warrant officers and enlisted men. One story related: "no matter what may be the feeling between Captain Healy and his officers, the men say with one accord that a better master never issued an order. . . . [S]everal days ago the following communication was circulated through the forecastle and signed by all the men: 'To the Editors of the San Francisco Daily Papers—Gentlemen: We the undersigned members of the crew of the United States Steamer *Bear*, having read in the columns of your papers an article reflecting on the ability and courtesy of the Captain, M.A. Healy, deem it necessary to refute such statements as misleading and containing not a particle of truth that can be substantiated.'" Twenty-eight members of the crew signed the document, including the boatswain, the master at arms, the gunner, and the carpenter, Richard Cain.

The Treasury Department announced the members of the trial board: Capt. D. B. Hodgedon, of the cutter *Fessenden* at Detroit, who served as president of the board; Capt. Louis N. Stoddard, Captain of the Port of New York; Capt. W. C. Coulson, on duty with the U.S. Life-Saving Service and a friend of Healy's; First Lieut. H. H. Rogers, of the cutter *Hartwell* in the Bay area, who served as recorder; and First Lieut. William E. Reynolds, of the *Grant*, who served as the prosecuting officer.

"It is the general opinion among the Treasury officials that Captain Healy will be found guilty," read an article datelined January 4, 1896, in Washington, D.C. "His splendid record as an officer, however, is well known, and it is believed that the punishment inflicted will be as light as the law will allow." The unknown reporter quoted Treasury officials as saying: "'Captain Healy is one of the ablest seamen in the Navy [*sic*]. In fact, he has no superior in that respect. He is also a man of splendid intellect, and has spent a great deal of time in studying every question peculiar to the revenue-cutter service. His one failing is drink, and that alone has been the cause of all his troubles, both past and present." The reporter went on to inform readers that Healy could be suspended, "during which time Captain Healy will be on waiting orders, and will draw but two-thirds pay."

Six days later, a small article about the service, which most readers probably skimmed over in their desire to read the more exciting news of the upcoming trial of Captain Healy, appeared in the newspapers. The few lines of print related that hearings were again being held in Washington, D.C., on whether the U.S. Revenue Cutter Service should, like the U.S. Navy, have a retirement system.

Healy realized his alleged misconduct aboard the British ship could prove extremely damaging. In hopes of limiting the damage, he wrote to the Royal Navy captain, who replied, "as far as I and my officers are concerned, you did not give any cause whatever for offense." In one of the trial's many strange events, Captain Garforth later wrote to Secretary Carlisle about Healy's letter. "Captain Healy who I fancy was hardly sober when he came aboard," the British officer informed the secretary, "after a time went to sleep in an armchair, and when some officers tried to wake him up, he had an idea he was aboard his own ship, as he ordered one of the officers of the U.S. Revenue Service belonging to another ship to go out of his cabin."[22]

Captain Hodgedon's first official act as president of the trial board moved the trial from the cutter *Rush* to the more spacious Room 83 of the Appraisers Building in San Francisco. The preliminaries began on Saturday, January 18, 1896, with the introduction of documentary exhibits.

Newspapers informed their readers that the court would "sit during the investigation with closed doors": "if any of the inquiry are divulged for publication the publicity will be given without the official knowledge or consent of the court. . . . [C]ourts of this character are not conducted in this star-chamber fashion, but the rule has been adopted in the revenue cutter service to allow the accused to elect whether the court shall sit with open or closed doors. In this investigation Captain Healy, through his counsel, Bradley Henley, signified a desire for an inquiry with closed doors."

Those who wished to test the closed-door policy arrived on the top floor of the Appraisers Building to find "an officer of the *Bear*, in full dress uniform, with a scabbard containing an ugly-looking cutless [*sic*] hanging by his side [who] walked up and down in front of the door to keep out intruders," as well as many other officers "in resplendent uniforms." Reporters, while excluded from the proceedings, wrote that besides the court officials "there were present thirty first and second lieutenants belonging to the Coast Revenue Marine Service" and concluded, "It is doubtful if a United States Army or Navy trial ever surpassed the one now going on in the Appraisers building for splendor of the attire of the officers participating in it." Representative officers from all of the cutters in San Francisco sat in the room and "several Japanese sailors off the *Bear* were also present in their pretty blue and white uniforms."

At one o'clock in the afternoon, the proceedings began. "Captain Healy, looking a trifle nervous and anxious, was on hand quite early." Healy sat at a long table in front of the room.

The coming trial would be worthy of the pen of Herman Wouk. The prosecuting officer read the six charges: Healy had engaged in conduct unbecoming an officer and, on specified occasions, he had been intoxicated while on duty in command of the *Bear*, thereby hazarding its safety and the accomplishment of its mission. The most serious charge against Healy, of course, was that he had hazarded the safety of his vessel, which, even today, would result in at least immediate loss of command, if not dismissal from the service. Healy's attorney entered his plea of "not guilty" on all accounts. Attorney Henley would later tell the trial board that this was a "melancholy case, as melancholy as any recorded in the naval or military annals of our country."[23] He also feared that a conviction would erase the name of Captain Healy from history.

The prosecution called the first witness. First Assistant Engineer Levin T. Jones described and provided details about the events aboard the HMS *Pheasant*, the altercation with Chief Engineer Broadbent, and the captain's fall from the dock. Henley's cross-examination revealed that Jones had made several critical and disparaging comments concerning his captain to the officers of the cutter and within hearing of the enlisted men. Engineer Jones denied conspiring against his commanding officer, but did admit to forming "a common interest early in the cruise" with other officers and their agreement "to observe incidents that might form a basis on which to initiate some form of official action" against Healy.[24] Interestingly enough, Harvey Nice, in whose home Healy had recuperated after his fall, swore that his guest had not been drunk during his stay. The *Bear*'s surgeon, Dr. Thomas Bodkin, despite pointed cross-examination, steadfastly maintained the only liquor he knew of Healy consuming during the 1895 cruise was the medicinal brandy mixed with quinine prescribed by himself for a severe cold. Later, however, Dr. Bodkin noted, "one drink of any high liquid shows very perceptively on Captain Healy."[25]

Lieutenant Daniels covered the same ground as Jones, but refused to admit to making derogatory remarks about Healy or conspiring against him. Daniels also denied that "his testimony was motivated by any personal malice" toward his captain. Nine officers testified on Healy's alleged behavior aboard the British warship. When Chief Engineer Broadbent took the stand, however, he testified to having "no recollection whatever of the incident." Later, even a direct order from Assistant Secretary Hamlin that Broadbent tell all he knew of Healy's drinking failed to shake Broadbent's testimony.[26]

A mere five days after the trial began, the press described the members of the trial board as "perturbed," because someone was routinely leaking the proceedings of the trial to the newspapers, which promptly printed them. The truth of their suspicions can easily be confirmed. A researcher in the twenty-first century only has to compare the newspaper articles to the official transcripts in the National Archives to learn that the press had reported most of the trial verbatim.

Captain Hooper testified several times during the trial, always attempting to cast Healy in the best light. His careful responses demonstrate that a nicely worded evasion is not a modern invention. When questioned about the Arctic legend's sobriety, he answered: "That I hardly know, some claim he drinks a good deal, and others claim he does not. I do not know exactly what would constitute a reputation. In the manner of his reputation as a sailor, that is universal." Healy, Hooper continued, "was always considered a strict if not severe commanding officer," who treated his junior officers "always good until this year," when "complaints" began surfacing.

In response to the question of Captain Hooper's opinion of Healy's qualifications as an officer, as well as of his diligence, good judgment, courage, and sobriety, Hooper responded: "Healy did not lack in any of them, except possibly in sobriety. . . . Captain Healy has occasionally taken a drink—perhaps too much—in days past, ever since I have known him, and at times which he ought not to have done it. Otherwise he is an exceptionally good officer, an able, intelligent, bright, skillful officer." When asked if he had advised Healy to plead guilty to the charges, Captain Hooper said, "As I have stated before, and it is no secret, my advice to him was to acknowledge the fact that he was under the influence those three days in Unalaska."[27]

Capt. D. F. Tozier, of the cutter *Grant*, also, interestingly enough, considering his observations of Healy when he fell into the harbor, shuffled around the question. Was Healy an efficient officer, a strict disciplinarian, abusive to subordinates, and so forth? The *Grant*'s captain explained that Captain Healy was "strict, and perhaps annoying": "I cannot explain myself any better than that. He is a hard man to sail with. They [the junior officers] dread to go near him. . . . I have heard a great many complaints of his abusive treatment of officers, and that he would frequently send them to the crow's nest to punish them." Captain Tozier told of Healy working on deck continuously for seventy-two hours or more at a time. "He works his officers hard," Tozier testified, "but works hard himself."[28]

As the trial progressed, the schism between the young commissioned officers of the *Bear* and the grizzled warrant officers and enlisted men concerning Healy became pronounced. To a man, the warrant officers and enlisted men denied ever seeing their captain in an intoxicated condition or doing anything wrong, for that matter. The following, for example, took place when the prosecutor attempted to examine the incident with the Japanese wardroom attendants. Unfortunately for Reynolds, the prosecuting officer, F. Sumii is listed as a "witness for the prosecution."

> "Did Captain Healy strike, kick, or ill-treat you, early in the morning of the 7th of June last?" asked Reynolds.
>
> "I have no rememberance of that."
>
> "Did Captain Healy use any profane language to you?"
>
> "I have no rememberance of it."
>
> "Did not Captain Healy say to you, 'You damned son-of-a-bitch, get up!' or words to that effect?"
>
> "He did not say that."

Then Attorney Henley asked Sumii: "Did Captain Healy treat you kindly always?"

> "Captain Healy was very kind to me. And besides, he asked Mr. Hamilton to teach English to me. For that reason, I think the Captain was very kind to me."

The transcript shows that Reynolds gave "notice that I desire at a future time to impeach the testimony of this witness as being directly contrary to what he told me on preliminary examination."

The other cabin attendant, T. Ohno, also denied being "struck or ill-treated by any officer" of the *Bear*.[29]

William F. Quintall, a quartermaster, when asked if Healy had "been habitually kind and good to his men and officers," replied, "Yes, sir, he has been pretty good, sir." He also denied that Healy had placed the ship in danger. Frederick

Arnold, an ordinary seaman, said, "I have always seen [Captain Healy] sober since I have been in the ship."[30]

Newspapers enjoyed the friction between the two groups. One account claimed that part of the *Bear*'s crew mutinied after returning to port because of their loyalty to Captain Healy. Lieutenant Daniels once again took center stage in the drama. The article claimed: "Lieut. Daniels yesterday ordered Joseph Byrnes, one of the crew of the cutter in irons. Byrnes is a witness for Capt. Healy. He resisted and a row ensued. Lieut. Daniels ordered the crew to overpower Byrnes. Instead of obeying, the men shouted to their comrade to stand his ground. . . . In the excitement Byrnes escaped, and searching parties failed to find him. The mutineers sullenly returned to their posts. Arrests will be made."

One of the U.S. Revenue Cutter Service commissioned officers, realizing how the young officer corps appeared in the press, said to a reporter:

Look there at that group of a dozen officers [waiting to testify]. Do they look like men who would conspire against an old officer to bring him into trouble? No; they are honorable, upright men, who have at heart the good of the service, and in this affair many of them have been misrepresented and maligned. One officer, against whom charges were preferred by the crew, was the subject of inquiry and acquited [*sic*]. It was alleged and so published that he was drunk for three days, but when the inquiry established the fact that he was sober and on duty and he was acquitted and vindicated, only a line or two announced the results.

As the trial continued, however, more newspaper articles commented on actions taken against the enlisted men for testifying in favor of Healy than commented on actions taken against the commissioned officers.

Meanwhile, back in the closed court, Lieutenant Buhner, after relentless prodding by Reynolds, reluctantly admitted to changing course off the Shumagin Islands without authority, because Healy "had been drinking." He also admitted to confiscating the alcohol in Healy's cabin. The executive officer steadfastly maintained that at no time was Captain Healy so drunk that he could not understand what he was doing. When questioned about Healy's treatment of his officers, Buhner replied that the "Captain is strict, but he is just." Although, as would be the case on any ship, he heard "a lot of wardroom carping and complaining," he had "just learned to ignore it."[31] Reynolds became so frustrated with Buhner's loyalty to his captain that he resorted to an unprecedented action. The prosecutor sent off a telegram to Assistant Secretary

Hamlin requesting that Hamlin order Buhner to tell the truth about Healy's drinking. Hamlin replied the next day directly to Buhner with the order: "[g]ive your testimony without reservation or concealment."[32]

In his next appearance before the trial board, the executive officer responded to the telegram with indignation. "This is an insult," he stated, for "it touches upon my integrity." Furthermore, the executive officer stated, "I demand to know of this honorable body, if it has been in correspondence with the Treasury Department concerning my testimony."[33] Reynolds readily admitted to sending a message to Washington, after becoming convinced that Buhner had not been forthcoming in his answers.

The San Francisco newspapers jumped on this latest revelation as another example of the department's hostile attitude toward Healy. Hamlin "will probably pass finally upon Captain Healy's case," blasted the San Francisco *Chronicle*, and the "chances for the Captain's reinstatement in the service are considered to be very poor." The *Chronicle*'s Washington, D.C., correspondent also reported an unnamed official source at the Treasury Department as saying Buhner "and one or two others are so anxious to shield Captain Healy that they are endangering their own reputations . . . and that is the reason Asst. Secty. Hamlin wired him as he did." Ominously, the department officially designated Capt. Francis Tuttle the new commanding officer of the *Bear*.

When the court reached the infamous spitting charge, newspapers reported, "At this stage in his [Daniels'] testimony the witness appeared to be overcome by the recollection of events described, and burst out into a prolonged giggle."

> "Funny wasn't it?" queried one of the captain's attorneys, imitating the Daniels giggle the best he could.
>
> "Well, yes, it was rather funny," replied the lieutenant, and he giggled again.
>
> "By the way, Mr. Daniels, when the captain spat in your face what did you do?" asked the attorney.
>
> "I wiped off my face," was the witness' answer, whereat a smile circulated about the judicial chamber.
>
> "Did you say anything? Any bad words, for instance?"
>
> "I asked the captain what he meant," answered Daniels, "and he said that if I accused him of such an insult I was a liar."
>
> "That was all there was to the little affair, was it?" inquired the captain's representative.

"Yes," answered Daniels, "that was all."

"And the captain was really drunk?"

"Oh, yes," was the lieutenant's answer, "very drunk."

As became clear during the trial, the friction between Lieutenant Daniels and Captain Healy had continued throughout the entire patrol of 1895. Daniels claimed that at one point, in private, Healy had wanted him to remove his uniform coat so that he could fight him. When Daniels refused to do so, Healy allegedly made an ominous statement about the two of them going hunting together sometime: "one of us would not come back; there would be an accident." To counter this claim, Healy said that what actually took place at Dutch Harbor, Alaska, happened while he was shooting at birds from the bridge of the *Bear* and Lieutenant Daniels was serving duty on the quarterdeck as the officer of the deck. Healy called to Daniels to come to the bridge to see how well he could shoot. The Lieutenant arrived on the bridge and took the rifle, asking Healy to name the target. Healy replied: "You go on the quarter deck and I will stay up here. If you hit me, well and good. If I hit you, well and good." Daniels dropped the rifle and walked quickly away. Healy claimed: "I was only speaking in jest. I was not going to shoot a man on the deck of a ship." Given this rancor between the two men, it seems inevitable that tempers did finally get out of hand at the trial. The boiling point came while Daniels testified to Healy staggering about the *Bear*'s decks, making "himself obnoxious to his officers": "Suddenly Daniels bounded from [the witness] chair, burning with anger and tembling [*sic*] with excitement, and accused Healy of hissing through his closed teeth and muttering 'liar' under his breath."

Healy also leaped to his feet and "indignantly denied the charge." News accounts related that it "was a trying moment": "every one expected that the lie would be passed. The accused and the accuser stood facing each other in a menacing attitude, but only for a few seconds. The members of the court and the counsel rose and started forward as if to prevent the expected clash, and for a few minutes the room was all confusion."

Both men retreated to their respective seats. Healy's attorneys "assured the court that the witness must have been mistaken, for they were both seated so close to their client that they must have heard any sounds that came from the lips" of Healy. After this tense moment subsided, the hearing continued.

Not all of the drama took place within the courtroom. One reporter wrote: "As the afternoon session opened, a man attempted to enter the room in which the investigation was going on. His entry was, however, barred by an individual in uniform, who after flourishing a bayonet in midair drew with it an imaginary line on the floor in front of the door, remarking grimly as he did so: 'That's the dead line.'"

News accounts related that when Lieutenant Emery took the stand, his testimony took longer than most: "[he] spent from two to five minutes 'in rumination deep and long.' Being asked his reasons for that, he said he wanted to be sure of what he was saying. When his answers told against the captain, however, they came without delay, a circumstance which caused the old man [Healy] to glare more than once in indignation."

One evening, a reporter interviewed Healy. Captain Healy said his attorneys would not allow it: "but, hang it! a man must speak sometimes or he'll burst! This whole thing is a job put up by a few young fellows who don't want to work and hate to obey. And then I suppose the boys think the old men ought to get out of the way and give them a chance. Perhaps they're right, but even though I am an old man I don't relish being run out by men whom I have made. After all I'm not quite a fossil, even if I'm not so young as I might be."

Assistant Secretary Hamlin delayed the trial so Dr. Benjamin Sharp, a Philadelphia scientist who accompanied the *Bear* for part of the 1895 cruise, could come to San Francisco to testify. Some at the time felt this might indicate Hamlin's desire to obtain a guilty sentence. The thirty-six-year-old Doctor Sharp, however, carried impressive credentials. Born in Philadelphia in 1858, he studied at Swarthmore College and at the Coffin School, on Nantucket Island, Massachusetts. He went on to receive a medical degree from the University of Pennsylvania and studied in Europe, where he received a Ph.D. in zoology. He chose not to practice medicine. Sharp once said, "I have not killed anyone yet, but then, I never really practiced medicine; I have helped to take a man's leg off at the knee joint; the leg was saved, but not the man."

Sharp began as a professor of zoology at the University of Pennsylvania and conducted research at a number of locations. "He soon acquired considerable fame as a scientist and published extensively." The noted Arctic explorer, Robert Perry, selected him as the zoologist in charge of Perry's first trip to Greenland in 1891. In 1894, he received the nomination and induction into the Academy of Natural Sciences, "which seemed to propel him increasingly into international research and lecturing."[34]

With Sharp's credentials, how could a politician such as Hamlin not accept Sharp's offer to testify at the hearing? To give Hamlin his due, he might have thought that the testimony of such a noted person outside of the U.S. Revenue Cutter Service would add more objectivity to the hearing. If Hamlin felt this way, he did not know how Doctor Sharp felt about Captain Healy. To say that Sharp did not care for Healy is to understate on a grand scale. The newspapers greedily sought out information on the "Sharp versus Healy" relationship, hoping to find even more material with which to tantalize their readership. They would not be disappointed.

Doctor Sharp related that he held no malice toward Captain Healy, but "thought it his duty, inasmuch as he was a guest of the Government on the cruise to report the flagrant misconduct of the commanding officer." Sharp, the newspapers reported, would "testify that Captain Healy was gloriously drunk during the cruise" and "cite several of his strange acts in support of the assertion." The article elaborated: "[One of these was] that one night during the mess Captain Healy took a plate of mashed potatoes, poured gravy over it and after stirring it up with his hands proceeded to eat it with his fingers. This is a sample of Captain Healy's actions which made him a boor in the eyes of Professor Sharp and the other officers of the *Bear*."[35]

Sharp later explained that his dislike of the captain stemmed from a single action of Healy's. The captain had cited a departmental regulation and used it to forbid Doctor Sharp from trading with the Eskimos for artifacts or specimens that he hoped to find for the Philadelphia Museum. Sharp did admit, however, that Healy had treated him courteously, once even taking the *Bear* out of its way so that the scientist could collect specimens.[36]

Newspapers called Henley's cross-examination of Sharp "scorching": "He accused [Sharp] of keeping a memorandum book during his voyage on the *Bear*, wherein he scrupulously noted from day to day every thing which could be construed to Captain Healy's discredit, even by fantastically forced interpretations."

The article continued: "'With that book hugged close to his breast with one hand,' pursued Mr. Henley, 'Dr. Sharp scrupled not to extend the other to receive the gifts which the captain generously gave him—rare curios and quaint mementoes of the Arctic which were valuable in more ways than one. This monster of ingratitude is the one who seems to have exerted himself more than all the smaller fry of his kind to bring disgrace and ruin down upon the gray head of his host. No convict in the gloomy precincts of San Quentin would even dream of descending to such depths of baseness.'"

Once Reynolds announced that the prosecution rested, attorney Henley began presenting the defense's case, by calling crewmen, whalers, and so forth. All spoke favorably of Captain Healy. Captain Hooper returned to the stand again to praise Healy's skills. During cross-examination, Reynolds repeatedly asked about Healy's sobriety while on the patrol. In his hands, the prosecuting officer had copies of the letters Hooper had written from Unalaska to Captain-Commandant Shoemaker, which gave details about Healy's drinking and his being drunk on duty. Once alerted by an unidentified member of the trial board to the existence of these letters, Hamlin not only ordered Captain Shoemaker to send copies to Reynolds, but also forbade him from warning Captain Hooper. The Captain, however, ignored his superior and wrote to Hooper. Thus, forewarned, attorney Henley rose to object when Hooper's testimony was in danger of being impeached. "We do not contest the issue of Captain Healy's having been intoxicated during that period," he said, before claiming this line of questioning was "improper." In answer to Reynolds' question, "You are conceding this issue then?" Henley simply stated, "Yes." Captain Hooper then stepped down without answering.[37]

Captain Healy now took the stand to defend his actions and professional career. With his intoxication at Unalaska already conceded, he needed to challenge only the allegations of mistreating his officers and the more serious charge of hazarding his vessel.

"I play no favorites," Healy testified.

I go up there to do my duty and to do right as far as I can, and I expect every officer to do the same. I seldom speak to an officer roughly, unless it is the third time I have to speak. I want to say, though, that when I am in charge of a vessel, I think I always command. I think that I am put there to command, and I do command, and I take all the responsibility and all the risks, and the hardships that my officers would call upon me to take. I do not steer by any man's compass but my own. I do not phrase my words with an 'if you please.' I say 'set the mainsail' or whatever the order may be.

During cross-examination, Reynolds asked Healy only two questions:

"Do you always treat your officers justly?"
    "Yes."
    "Then why are there so many complaints of unjust treatment?"
    "I cannot account for it all, I think that I have been too good to them."[38]

Prior to the summation of the case, a short newspaper article, datelined Port Townsend, Washington, declared "there may be another side" to the trial besides the one being reported by the newspapers. One "official" reported that his testimony had "been utterly distorted by whoever gave it out to the newspapers" and further declared that "Captain Healy's friends are attempting to try the case in the newspapers and that the prosecution will be found very strong when the findings are made public."

In his summation, Henley pleaded with the trial board to give the greatest credence to the testimony of the enlisted men, for most had sailed with Healy for more than ten years. The testimony against him, on the other hand, came from junior officers who were personally antagonistic toward Healy because he subjected them to the tough discipline demanded by the dangerous conditions of the Arctic frontier. In closing, attorney Henley elaborated upon Healy's professional qualifications, strongly suggesting "that no other officer would be capable of replacing him as captain of the BEAR."[39]

Lieutenant Reynolds in his summation to the board brushed off the statements made by the warrant officers and enlisted men by remarking that the "testimony of these men is avowedly and unmistakably hostile towards the officers who have complained of Captain Healy's conduct." Reynolds had spent a great deal of time during the hearing showing how the enlisted men owed their employment to Healy. That is, Healy controlled which enlisted men were signed on board the *Bear*. He went on to say, "The officers who have testified have no motive to deceive, each may have jeopardized his own future career by coming forward as witnesses against their commanding officer." Reynolds did not mention Surgeon Bodkin's testimony, which echoed the remarks of the enlisted men. He also did not repeat the testimony of Capt. Horatio D. Smith, who commanded the cutter *Perry*. Not only did Captain Smith describe Healy as "one of the best navigators in the service and most competent commander in the Bering Sea patrol," but he also denied ever seeing the Arctic pilot drunk on duty and reported that he had merely observed Healy having an occasional social drink.[40]

The prosecuting officer met with the formidable task of dealing head on with Captain Healy's reputation as a great Arctic navigator. Healy possessed excellent professional abilities when sober and "a record of which all are proud," Reynolds admitted, but also wondered "might not others have done as well?" The lieutenant, however, did admit to accepting Healy as the only officer with high qualifications for Arctic duty. Nevertheless, Reynolds hammered at the following point. "Quick judgment should be possessed by those who follow the sea," he reminded the board members. "A brain clouded by alcohol cannot work rapidly, and is incapable of grasping a situation of peril."[41]

Whether or not Healy's "friends" attempted to try the case in the newspapers cannot be proved at this late date. The newspapers, of course, eagerly sought out any information they could obtain. There appears no doubt, however, that most, if not all, of the newspapers in the San Francisco Bay area were on Healy's side. When the time came for reporting the summations, one newspaper account devoted twenty-three column inches to Henley's comments, while Reynolds received almost a reprimand from the paper. A reporter commented that there "was nothing sensational, oratorical or even ingenuous in Lieutenant Reynolds' presentation of his case," concluding, "He is not a lawyer nor a public speaker, and he made not an attempt at argument." Although the newspaper mentioned that Reynolds spoke for two hours, he received a mere two column inches of comment.

The trial board adjourned to begin their deliberations on February 27, 1896, after more than a month of hearing evidence and the testimony of fifty-eight witnesses that produced a transcript totaling 992 typewritten pages. On March 5, the board sent to the Treasury Department their finding and recommendations. The board found Capt. Michael A. Healy, at one time the most popular man in the Far North, guilty of all charges. The board recommended that Healy be dismissed from the service.[42]

Little known to most people, however, is the fact that the board made a highly unusual recommendation to Secretary of the Treasury John G. Carlisle, the final authority in the trial. The board wrote that although they found no "mitigating circumstances in the case, . . . we do think that we should not fail to call your attention to the valuable services performed by this officer during his connection with the Revenue Cutter Service, covering a period of nearly thirty years, and to respectfully recommend that such clemency as may be consistent with the gravity of the case and welfare of the Revenue Cutter Service may be extended to him."[43]

Secretary Carlisle's staff must have pointed out the inconsistencies in the trial and, most importantly, the political pressures involved in the case. Assistant Secretary Hamlin, for example, confided to his diary that "[s]trenuous efforts were made by friends" of Captain Healy. "Congressmen, Senators, and hundreds of others, among whom was Bishop Healy of Portland, Maine, a brother of Captain Healy, all joined in begging such a reversal."[44] *The Call,* using its sources in Washington, D.C., confirmed that Hamlin had recommended Healy's dismissal. "There was so much perjury on both sides," confided a board member after the trial, "that much of the testimony had to be disregarded in its entirety."[45]

On June 20, 1896, the Treasury Department issued U.S. Revenue Cutter Service Special Order Number 20 containing the final verdict. Because of the "rec-ommendation for clemency, and giving to the accused the benefit of the slight conflict in the testimony as to the most serious charge" Carlisle ordered the fol-lowing: "[that] Captain Michael A. Healy be dropped to the foot of the list of Captains of the Revenue Cutter Service, and that he retain that place hereafter, that he be suspended from rank and command for a term of four years, and that he be publicly reprimanded by reading this order on board all vessels of the Revenue Cutter Service, by the commanding officer of each, at a muster of the commissioned officers, and admonished that if again found guilty of excessive use of intoxicants during the term of his sentence or hereafter, whether afloat or on shore, he will be summarily dismissed from the service."[46]

With the announcement of the trial, some of the younger officers of the U.S. Revenue Cutter Service may have felt they had made the first step in replacing an old school officer. They, however, did not know Captain Healy. On the other hand, Michael A., Mary Jane, and Frederick Healy may have felt their lives could not get worse. They, too, did not understand the true tragedy of Michael A. Healy's life.

11

"A Desperate and Dangerous Man"

After Capt. Michael A. Healy received Secretary of the Treasury John G. Carlisle's final decision in the trial, Michael and Mary Jane retreated to the St. Nicholas Hotel in San Francisco. For the first time since he ran away to sea at the age of fifteen, Captain Healy found himself forbidden to go to sea for an extended time. True, he received at least one half of his regular pay, but for an overachiever like Healy and someone who had known only the sea, such a sentence seemed catastrophic. A year after his sentence, however, fate seemed ready to snatch Healy from the jaws of defeat. But, like Sisyphus, he would rise only to plunge back down into the depths of despair. These strange vagaries of fate came about because of a situation near far-off Point Barrow, Alaska.

In the early autumn of 1897, Charlie Brower, calling upon his years of experience at Point Barrow, sensed that potential problems lay in wait for the Arctic whaling fleet. He began storing extra game in his ice cellars. His premonition proved correct. Eventually, eight ships lay either crushed or trapped in the ice near Point Barrow. Thus began the Whaling Disaster of 1897.[1]

By 1897, at least ninety-four whalers routinely made their way to Point Barrow. Brower had fixed up an old whaling station building to shelter the men. The crews from the ships straggled into Point Barrow via dog sled.[2]

Brower, and others at Point Barrow, felt that they had everything under control. They decided, however, to send out two messengers to the south to report the problems even as they felt "there was no cause for undue worry." George Fred Tilton, third mate of the *Belvedere*, received the toughest route. He "cut a new and difficult trail down the west coast of Alaska to the Pacific Ocean." The other man, Charles Walker, took the relatively "easy" route via Herschel Island, to the east of Point Barrow, proceeding to the Mackenzie River in the Canadian Arctic, and then southward. Both men traveled more than 1,700 miles on foot and, amazingly enough, both arrived in the United States just a few days apart.[3]

Meanwhile, another ship, the *Alexander*, reached San Francisco on November 3, bringing the first word of the trapped ships. John D. Spreckels, the wealthy publisher of the San Francisco newspaper, *The Morning Call*, known simply by the city's readers as *The Call*, must have looked upon this news as a gift from heaven. Three days later, U.S. Navy Lieut. George M. Stoney, the naval officer who had twice explored the Kobuk River, offered his solution. Stoney, now on duty at the San Francisco Naval Rendezvous, informed the newspaper, "there is a chance to succor the icebound whalers, although it is a slim chance and desperate one." The exploring naval officer felt, with a properly equipped and provisioned ship, he could reach the northern part of Norton Sound. He would then gather reindeer at Port Clarence and drive them northward as food for the starving whalers.[4]

Four days later, *The Call*'s Sunday front page screamed, "Arousing the Government to Send Immediate Aid to the Ice-Bound Whalers." The first article related how the newspaper had been "swift to urge upon the Government the need of immediate relief for the [whaling] fleet," but pointed out that Congress needed to appropriate the money for such an expedition.[5]

The editor warned that to wait for a decision from Congress was "to abandon the enterprise and leave the sailors to the fate that threaten[ed] them." In the manner of New York City newspapers, *The Call* offered to "furnish supplies required" for any relief ship as "soon as the Government gets it ready."

A sidebar pointed out that a meeting of the President's Cabinet, scheduled for November 9, planned on taking up the matter: "The voice of humanity demands that earnest efforts be made to save these sailors imprisoned in the frozen ocean, and THE CALL will promptly co-operate with the Government in sending the help that will bring them safe to their homes and their loved ones." Clearly, the publisher and reporters of *The Call* now looked upon the fate of the whalers as *their* cause.

The Call's correspondent in the nation's capital, C. C. Carlton, interviewed Secretary of the Navy John D. Long on the navy's plans to help the whalers. Secretary Long mentioned that the provisions at the federal refuge station at Point Barrow made it unnecessary to send naval ships northward. Carlton quickly responded that the station had been "abandoned and the supplies sold to private parties." Understanding he had Long at a disadvantage, Carlton said, "There is nothing but starvation and death in store for these men unless the government takes prompt action." In response, the secretary finally admitted that the navy had no vessel capable of helping. Long asked Carlton to provide a letter from *The Call* on the plight of the trapped ships at Point Barrow, which he would present to the cabinet meeting. The journalist sent Long a letter, along with clippings from *The Call*, on the situation.

The letter elaborated the newspaper's understanding that the navy could not supply the ships needed to bring aid. Carlton pointed out that if the people of San Francisco "make a determined effort the Treasury Department might be induced to send the revenue cutter *Bear*, notwithstanding the objection of [Captain] Shoemaker, who says that she cannot possibly go until next spring. Of all vessels the *Bear* is believed to be most admirably adapted for such an expedition."

Another headline in the Sunday edition of *The Call* proclaimed "San Francisco People Thoroughly Aroused." Readers learned that the Chamber of Commerce planned to petition "President McKinley to dispatch an expedition without delay." The newspaper reported that Capt. William L. Merry, secretary of the Chamber, emphatically recommended "Captain Healy of the revenue service": "He is by all odds the best-posted man on Arctic navigation and climatic conditions in the country, and he, of all men, would be best fitted to command such an expedition."

Following up on this lead, the journalist reported: "Every whaling master in port named Captain Healy as the one man above all others who should be given command of the relief ship. They assert that with his knowledge of the Alaskan coast and waters he could take the ship farther north at this season than anybody else and safely land her cargo where almost anybody else would fail to get near the shore."

The reporter informed readers that Captain Healy had "expressed the opinion that there was every chance of rescuing" the whalers, "if the necessary steps were taken without delay." Furthermore, Healy believed that only the government could successfully carry out such an expedition. The ship selected, Healy continued, would have to be capable of "battling with the ice" and have a picked crew. "There is no reason I can see," said Healy, "why such a ship cannot reach the north shore of Norton Sound, or even Cape Prince of Wales, where the first reindeer station is located."

When the reporter asked Healy whom he might recommend to lead such an expedition, he replied, interestingly enough, "Lieutenant Stoney of the navy." Healy failed to mention Lieut. John C. Cantwell, who was the first to find the headwaters of the Kobuk and who led an expedition at the same time Stoney did. As Doctor White's diary revealed, Healy, and the other officers of the *Bear*, felt Cantwell faked sickness to escape duty during the 1889 patrol. One of Healy's strongest values focused on doing one's duty. He apparently had never forgiven Cantwell for this neglect of duty. Or, perhaps Healy felt that Stoney, who was already in San Francisco, was the logical choice.

The reporter also asked Healy if he would undertake the expedition. Healy replied: "Most willingly[,] if I should be called upon. At least I would undertake the sea expedition and I believe I could reach the north coast of Norton Sound or even Cape Prince of Wales."

Next, the reporter asked would Healy "be willing to lead the land party?" Healy replied, "Yes, if I were asked to do so, but it would be an unusual proceeding for a captain to leave his ship for such a long period." Healy went on to say that, in his opinion, the *Bear* remained the best choice for the mission. Second choice fell to any steam whaler now in San Francisco. Healy suddenly seemed on track to redeem himself by leading a headline-grabbing relief expedition.

One of the leading steam whaling captains in San Francisco made an astute observation. "Let THE CALL agitate the manner and the Government will speedily act," said Capt. Lew Wallace.

On November 9, *The Call* printed the San Francisco Chamber of Commerce's telegram to President McKinley: "In the name of humanity and patriotism the Chamber of Commerce . . . respectively urges upon you the prompt dispatch of the revenue steamer *Bear* to the Arctic under command of Captain Healy with discretionary orders, fully fueled and provisioned, to rescue over 200 American seamen imprisoned by ice near Point Barrow, and with authority to use, if necessary, reindeer at Government stations to facilitate land transportation."

The wire went on to explain the reasoning behind the Chamber's recommendation of both the ship and the captain to command it: "Captain M. A. Healy's previous services to our whaling fleet in the Arctic while commanding the *Bear* are well known to the [Treasury] department. His years of experience in Arctic navigation and his indomitable courage and energy specially qualify him for his service and promise a successful result if attainable by human effort."

Captain Merry, apparently under the mistaken assumption that Healy's sentence only entailed one year ashore, wrote, "It may seem a little presumptuous on our part to recommend an officer whose term of suspension for one year has not yet expired, but as it will soon expire and as Captain Healy has had vast and successful experience in ice navigation, we deem it best to suggest him."

Merry went on to inform readers that an ordinary seagoing navigator might "become alarmed at the prospect of contending with the obstacles" of Arctic ice. Merry claimed that Captain Healy, on the other hand, knew "the dangers and how best to avoid them": "We talked with Senator Perkins and many captains who have seen service in the Arctic, and their judgment agreed with ours that Captain Healy was the best man available. He is resolute, courageous and able. He would succeed where others might fail." Captain Merry also had no illusions about what Healy stood to personally gain if placed in command of the expedition. Healy, Captain Merry felt, "would be particularly anxious to achieve success in order to reinstate himself in the service."

The recommendations reached President McKinley. Not too surprisingly, the U.S. Revenue Cutter Service received the mission and selected the *Bear* to transport the expedition.[6] The president's selection of a commander proved surprising, however. Capt. Francis Tuttle, the officer who had taken over the *Bear* when Healy received his sentence, found himself in charge of a cutter manned by volunteers.

While the recommendation of the San Francisco Chamber of Commerce carried some influence, there appears to be no question as to the fact that the U.S. Revenue Cutter Service never considered Healy as the leader of any rescue attempt. Once again, Stoney stood a very good chance of taking the spotlight away from the service. Interservice rivalry, therefore, might have played a larger role than Arctic experience. This, perhaps, explains why Tuttle, who had only one year and eight months of experience as a commanding officer in the Arctic, received the nod. The Overland Relief Expedition, as it became known, consisted of First Lieut. David Jarvis, in charge, with three years and seven months of experience in Alaska; Second Lieut. Ellsworth Bertholf, with no experience; and Dr. Samuel Call, who "had first seen the country more than a dozen years earlier" and who entered the service in 1891.[7]

The Overland Relief Expedition departed Seattle on November 27, 1897, and closely followed Healy's recommendations. When ice prevented Captain Tuttle from reaching the northern portion of Norton Sound, he landed the expedition at Cape Vancouver, near Nunivak Island, on December 16. Jarvis, Call, and Bertholf made their way to Teller.

Little noted is the fact that Sinrock Mary and her husband, Charlie, played an important role in the Overland Relief Expedition. Jarvis's official report tells of his uneasiness with what he was given to accomplish once he reached Teller. He looked upon the Antisarlooks as "old friends." Now he had to "convince them to give up their deer and convince them that the Government would return an equal number at some future time. . . . These deer were their absolute property." Charlie and Mary "held a long and solemn consultation."

They agreed to the request, even though, as Jarvis pointed out, they "were poor except for the deer herd, which was all they had to depend upon."[8]

William T. Lopp and native herders, including Charlie Antisarlook, volunteered to help drive the animals northward. The expedition traveled over 1,500 miles in the dead of an Alaskan Arctic winter, a tremendous achievement.[9]

Remaining at Cape Vancouver for the winter, Captain Tuttle pushed the *Bear* northward in 1898. Heavy ice slowed the progress, and not until July 28 did Jarvis finally welcome the *Bear* to Point Barrow. On September 13, the cutter returned to Seattle to a tumultuous welcome.[10]

Jarvis, Bertholf, and Call each received a special gold medal from the U.S. Congress. The government printed a 144-page publication, complete with maps, containing all the reports from the service officers. The report proved larger than either of the publications authored by Healy. In a rare bit of honesty, the government report admitted that President McKinley learned of the whalers "by the Chamber of Commerce and people of San Francisco." The fact that the wealthy John Spreckels owned the newspaper that advocated the expedition did not, however, receive notice.[11]

Lieut. John G. Berry, of the *Bear*, after returning to home port, told the San Francisco *Call* that Sinrock Mary came out to greet Charlie when the cutter arrived back at Teller. "She was 'tickled to death' to get Charley back, even if he did not have any reindeer with him. When Jarvis asked for the deer last winter, Mary predicted that Charley would return without any deer and that the people would laugh at him." Eventually, Charlie and Sinrock Mary received both reindeer and payment in supplies and goods for the use of their herd.[12]

The Overland Relief Expedition became a very high profile newspaper item for a short period of time, and then quickly faded from memory. For years, it received a great deal of publicity within the U.S. Coast Guard. By the twenty-first century, however, it had also largely dimmed in the service's institutional memory.[13]

Already suffering from the shame of suspension, Healy endured additional torment during the events of the Whaling Disaster of 1897. For a three-week period, it appeared to Healy that he might have the chance to resume the long months in the ice that had honed his talents as an ice master and thereby redeem his tarnished record. He then watched as this chance quickly faded away.

In Healy's mind, ambitious officers had wronged him, seeking advancement at his expense. Had it not been for these self-serving younger men, he could have laid claim to being the person largely responsible for both introducing reindeer to Alaska and leading a great humanitarian expedition using these same animals. Surely, the Overland Relief Expedition would have been the capstone of his career, ensuring his enduring fame. Instead, Healy faced ignominy. Capt. Michael A. Healy had two more years to finish out his sentence—two years to continually mull over these thoughts in his mind.

The four-year banishment from command put a strain on Michael and Mary Jane's finances. Mary Jane revealed to Sheldon Jackson that in 1897 the couple had moved to the St. Nicholas Hotel. She hated to move from Room 8 in the Occidental Hotel because, she said, "it was our home for so many years and I know so many of the people there." The Occidental Hotel also provided a location convenient to the San Francisco docks and the center of the city. Mary Jane revealed that the "Doctor recommended it because the Captain was in poor health, but we have lovely rooms and the food is better." Still, she continued to visit their former lodgings.[14]

Two years into his sentence, a June 10, 1898, entry in Healy's service record reads: "Request to go to Alaska granted. Remain as long as you desire."[15] Before the Treasury clerk recorded the blunt reply to Healy's request, the new Assistant secretary of the treasury, W. B. Howell, had already moved on the matter. Eight days before the entry in Healy's service record, on June 2, 1898, Howell had taken a course of action that might have pleased the future J. Edgar Hoover of the Federal Bureau of Investigation. Howell gave the Treasury's special agent in San Francisco the following orders: "institute an investigation and exercise surveillance over his [Healy's] movements and habits." While Special Agent H. A. Moore's inquiry was to be "wholly confidential," the assistant secretary especially expressed his desire to be informed regularly of Healy's conduct and habits "in the matter of excessive use of intoxicating liquors."[16] No record of Moore's report has been found. Special Agent Moore, an old friend of Healy's, probably took umbrage at his new orders and simply neglected to carry them out. His actions remind the authors of the old Chinese saying, loosely translated, "The Emperor is far away and many high mountains lie in between."

Mary Jane, in a chatty letter to Sheldon Jackson, dated October 28, 1898, revealed her husband's reasons for taking the trip to Alaska. Michael, she informed Jackson, had just returned from exploring several potential commercial ventures in far-off Alaska. Besides visiting Unalaska, he had traveled to Cape Nome and Bristol Bay. While at Cape Nome, Mary Jane reported, "The Captain had been offered a claim at Nome by a friend but hadn't taken it, and he is sorry now because some of the officers and men in the service who had taken advantage of the opportunities which came their way, were well off now." The command of a paddle-wheeled steamer on the Yukon River, carrying passengers and freight to the gold strikes in the Klondike, had been offered, but Healy had declined it.[17]

Michael and Mary Jane not only had to contend with the problems of Michael's sentence, but their son Frederick was also causing them concern. Mary Jane's diaries and letters show that both parents doted on Fred, not too surprisingly, since they had lost two previous children. Fred, however, seemed to have inherited some of Michael's rebellious traits and, along with them, his reputation. According to family tradition, Fred, enrolled at the Jesuit Santa Clara College to the south of San Francisco, climbed the church's bell tower and decorated "the cross with some feminine underclothes."[18] He quickly found himself expelled and back living with his parents in San Francisco in 1896, just before his father's trial began. True to form, Michael blamed everything on the Jesuits. He also demanded that Fred leave San Francisco, but Mary Jane wanted Fred nearby. Michael then stormed against the Jesuits for expelling his son for a young man's prank. In the midst of his anger he focused on the "foibles of his own teachers through life and Fred's at present." Michael then simmered down, and Fred apparently later resumed his studies. San Francisco newspaper editors, perhaps with increased readership in mind owing to Captain Healy's trial, must have smiled at the thought of the readers they would attract with the next installment of Frederick A. Healy's life.

On April 2, 1896, in a headline that might prove the envy of modern supermarket tabloids, the San Francisco *Chronicle* reported: "Frederick Healy's Rash Marriage: Love, Cocktails and Sudden Separation."[19] Interestingly enough, at the time, Fred was reading the law at the office where Henley, the attorney who defended his father, worked.

The *Chronicle*, which described Fred as a "popular young man about town," went on to say that a witness told a reporter that Fred "had been on a bat for about a week." The witness explained: "the more he drank the more he wanted to marry Viola, and when they both got good and mellow he made her believe he was a reformer, and that if he married her she would soon grow wings and be an angel in his mansion . . . [They married on a Friday.] By Saturday [Fred] Healy was in such a condition that he needed medical attention." The *Chronicle*, using the method that at the time alerted readers to certain salacious facts, reported that Viola "was formerly Miss Lucretia M. Carpenter, late of Denver and the Far East, who had, however, been widely known in certain circles in San Francisco as 'Miss Viola' during her four months sojourn" in that city.

Finally sobering up, Fred took Viola to Henley's office and had the marriage annulled. A few weeks later, on Wednesday, April 28, Michael and Mary Jane put Fred on the 137-foot barkentine *Tropic Bird* bound for Tahiti. Fred enlisted in the U.S. Army shortly thereafter and served during the Philippine Insurrection. He wrote a series of letters about his experiences that the San Francisco *Call* published. By 1898, as revealed in one of her letters to Jackson, Mary Jane had come to feel pride in what her son had accomplished. She wrote that Fred "stood high with the officers and men of his regiment and never drinks."[20]

In 1899, a year before the expiration of his sentence, Healy's reputation remained high enough in San Francisco that a reporter sought out the colorful captain. Michael, like Mary Jane, still cared to visit the Occidental Hotel. While visiting the hotel, the aging Healy, who was always willing and ready to tell a good sea story, demonstrated that he remained an expert in the art (see chapter 2 for the story Healy told).

Healy knew nothing but the sea and the U.S. Revenue Cutter Service. He had nothing to fall back on once ashore. With little to occupy his days, he had too much time to think and his thoughts turned to those who were against him.

Meanwhile, Mary Jane continued to work to restore her husband to command. In January 1900, the year Healy's sentence expired, she wrote to Jackson asking for help in her efforts. "You yourself know well that during the years you were with him," she wrote, "he never drank on his vessel or while on duty . . . the whole thing is only a matter of influence."[21] As it turned out, new events in Alaska and an unexpected sickness restored Capt. Michael A. Healy to command.

During Healy's absence from the Far North, gold had drastically changed the region. The new problems emerging as a result of gold fever forced the U.S. Revenue Cutter Service to employ new tactics in order to maintain at least a semblance of law. The 1897–1898 gold rush attracted thousands of prospectors, both veterans and amateurs, into the Yukon River area. They, and the inevitable camp followers, transformed the region into a wild, lawless land, best described by the novels of Jack London and the poems of Robert Service. The U.S. Revenue Cutter Service sought to establish a year-round federal law enforcement presence by stationing on the Yukon River a unique cutter that would winter over there. First Lieut. John C. Cantwell, Healy's former chief explorer on the Kobuk River, commanded the 207-foot sternwheeler *Nunivak*, which plied the river from 1898 to 1902.[22]

In 1899, word reached the outside world that Nome's creeks, and even its sandy beach, contained gold that was simply there for the taking. Gold fever immediately launched a flood of ships, loaded with those who knew they would soon be millionaires, from San Francisco and Seattle to Unalaska. There, the ships, many of them unseaworthy, had to wait for the ice near Nome to break up before they could continue on to the latest gold strike. It soon became apparent that a revenue cutter needed to be rushed north for special duty to inspect the merchant vessels congregated at Unalaska, check out the situation at Nome, and transport supplies to the *Nunivak* on the Yukon River.

Capt. W. C. Coulson, with thirty-three years of service, received the assignment. Captain Coulson commanded the newest major cutter in the service's fleet. At 219 feet and displacing 1,280 tons, the *McCulloch* held the distinction of being the service's largest cutter to date.[23] On May 25, 1900, however, Coulson wired Washington, D.C.: "Wife very ill. Dr. says I should not leave her. Will Department assign temporary commander until return last [of] June and grant me temporary leave?"[24] Headquarters quickly approved the emergency leave. Captain Coulson suggested as his replacement, Captain Healy. Captain Charles F. Shoemaker, knowing Healy's four-year sentence was about to end, agreed with the suggestion and ordered Healy to the *McCulloch*.[25] Ironically, the officer that Captain Healy temporarily relieved had sat on the board of officers that placed Healy on the beach for four years.

Interestingly, Shoemaker, on May 3, while inspecting West Coast units, wrote to his wife that, according to service etiquette, he must call upon Mary Jane Healy. He looked upon the visit as a task because he knew he would have "to listen . . . to a tearful appeal [on] behalf of *gentle* Mike." (Shoemaker's emphasis.) Furthermore, if he did not visit Mary Jane, she might, Shoemaker confided, "think I have a personal grudge against Mike."[26]

Later, once Mary Jane had learned of her husband's selection to command the cutter, she dashed off a letter to a friend declaring that the orders indicated her husband had been unjustly convicted.[27] Equally for Captain Healy, the order to command the service's newest cutter in the Far North reinforced his own belief that a cabal of younger officers had stopped his career and now the service had finally recognized this fact.

Before departing San Francisco for the Far North, Healy arranged for an allotment of $150.00 from his pay sent to Mary Jane. With the assurance that Mary Jane had enough money to tide her over in his absence, Captain Healy ordered his cutter's course toward the Bering Sea on May 28, 1900. After an uneventful transit, Healy brought the *McCulloch* to anchor in the familiar harbor on Unalaska Island.[28]

After eight days of checking safety conditions and cargoes of ships at Unalaska, the *McCulloch* weighed anchor on June 22. Captain Healy's navigation officer shaped a course to Nome. Three days later, the cutter arrived at the roadstead of the town hard by the Bering Sea.[29]

Staring in toward the shore from the *McCulloch*, Healy, who knew only the small town of Nome, witnessed an unbelievable sight. Tents stretched along the beach for almost thirty miles. The new gold rush had attracted an estimated 20,000 people, who sheltered in the canvas city. The official United States census of 1900, however, recorded only 12,488 people in Nome. Nevertheless, one-third of all whites recorded as residing in Alaska lived in Nome, which was now a far cry from the town Healy recalled from before his four-year exile.[30]

Underway the next morning, Captain Healy brought the *McCulloch* to anchor off St. Michael, the settlement near the mouth of the Yukon River. There, crewmen of the *McCulloch* and the *Nunivak* began the hard work of transferring supplies. Four crewmen and the *McCulloch*'s doctor also transferred to the sternwheeler. Captain Healy knew the doctor; it was James Taylor White, the diary-writing physician who served in the *Bear* in 1889. Before departing St. Michael, Captain Healy took a passenger on board, Mrs. Ada P. French, "for passage to Seattle." Working quickly, the crews of the two cutters completed their work in only one day, after which the *McCulloch* departed. Healy again briefly touched at Nome, before setting a course southward toward Unalaska.[31]

As usual, official and personal mail awaited the *McCulloch* at Unalaska. Upon opening one letter from service headquarters, Healy read orders detaching him from the *McCulloch* to "assume command of the 'Seminole' at Baltimore, Md." After over twenty years and nine months on the Pacific Station, with nine years and one month of duty spent in Alaska, his service decided to return the aging captain to the East Coast. The orders shook Healy. Even Mary Jane Healy wished to remain on the West Coast, mainly to be near their only son, Frederick. The chain of events that subsequently followed is a perfect example of the fact that sometimes misperceptions can lead to mistaken conclusions.[32]

Rightly or wrongly, Captain Healy believed the orders were meant to punish him. He believed the junior officers on the West Coast had worked against him to produce the new orders. As early as April 17, 1893, Healy had written to Captain Shepard that these officers wanted to drive him out of the service. Their strategy, Healy wrote then, seemed simple. The juniors said to the captains, "Hooper and Healy want to run the whole Pacific Coast." The captains, Healy felt, believed the juniors.[33] It is not surprising, given Healy's longstanding feelings, that Healy looked upon the orders to the *Seminole* as punishment. Shoemaker, on the other hand, might well have intended the orders to break up Hooper and Healy's perceived power in the region, but he nevertheless sought to sweeten a pill that he likely knew would be bitter for Healy to swallow. The records of the U.S. Coast Guard show that the 188-foot, steel-hulled, steam-propelled *Seminole*, commissioned on September 3, 1900, and home ported at Boston, was the most modern and prestigious for an officer to command.[34] Throughout his career, Healy's record shows that, even though he was born in Georgia, he considered Massachusetts his home. Shoemaker no doubt thought Healy, coming off four years on the beach, might look upon a new cutter in his home state as a favor. Given Healy's personality, it is not surprising that the cutter captain took the opposite meaning.

Here, race again enters the story. Healy felt betrayed. After serving in the U.S. Revenue Cutter Service for over thirty-five years, he felt his service had turned against him. Captain Healy knew that, by 1900, some within the American Catholic Church, as well as some of their parishioners, had begun openly discussing their suspicion that brothers James and Patrick had an African American heritage.[35] At this time, those who practiced Catholicism were still not embraced by mainstream American society; therefore, the rumors did not reach the isolated north, the West Coast, or the service's headquarters. But, if Healy were to return to Massachusetts, would people not begin to make the connection? How soon would it be before the rumor reached U.S. Revenue Cutter Service headquarters? Then what?

Many people feel that a sea cruise is a delightful way to shake loose from the cares of the world. Unbeknownst to these part-time seafarers, sea duty for some can mark a period of intense introspection, especially when one is working long hours in isolated locations with very little time for relaxation. No one has ever accused Captain Healy of not working long, hard hours, bearing major responsibilities, and taking very little time out to relax. Even today, those in command of ships have few people to talk to on off duty hours while underway. In the gritty atmosphere of a small cutter, little things can begin to magnify, taking on gigantic proportions. An unintentional slight becomes a major insult. Given the psychological baggage Michael A. Healy carried, the only surprise is that what happened next did not happen sooner.

The *McCulloch* reached Unalaska near the end of June. Michael probably read the letter containing his orders no later than July 1. Four days after that, the cutter departed for Seattle. A friend of Healy's wife wrote to Fr. Patrick F. Healy that Mary Jane Healy "was so delighted at [Michael's] reinstatement."[36] She made plans to meet the *McCulloch* when it arrived at Seattle.

Two days out of Unalaska, while the cutter cruised in the Gulf of Alaska, Mrs. French sent for the executive officer, First Lieut. P. W. Thompson. Upon reaching her cabin, Lieutenant Thompson found something not covered in the U.S. Revenue Cutter Service's manual. On the deck outside Mrs. French's locked door sat Capt. Michael A. Healy. When Mrs. French realized Thompson stood outside the door, she shouted out that "the captain had just threatened to take his life and that he was constantly calling her and she feared for her life."[37]

Unlike the officers on board the *Bear* in 1895, the officers of the cutter *McCulloch* approached this highly unusual situation in an orderly manner. Lieutenant Thompson had the boatswain pass the word for all officers to "lay to" (report to) the wardroom. Once assembled, Thompson reported his discovery of the captain on the deck outside of Mrs. French's cabin. The understandably highly excited and nervous Mrs. French had demanded protection. After discussing the situation, the shocked officers quickly transferred Mrs. French from her room to the wardroom. Thompson next entered Mrs. French's testimony into the *McCulloch*'s logbook:

> At 5:00 this morning the Captain called repeatedly to me and asked me, "For Christ's sake come out for my sake," and kept calling me at intervals until 10:00 at which hour he asked me "if I would be friends with him," I said that was impossible. At about 10:30 he called me repeatedly until I was obliged to answer, "What is it?" [H]e replied, "I am going to kill myself and right now." I was dreadfully frightened and rang the bell repeatedly for the boy and knocked on the floor for help, but for some minutes could get none, at last the boy came and I sent for Mr. Thompson and appealed to him for protection, saying that I preferred to sleep on the deck to remaining in the cabin.

After Lieutenant Thompson completed his log entry, the executive officer next learned that Captain Healy seemed in "a state of intoxication." Thompson summoned another officer's call in the wardroom. This time the discussion turned on whether to relieve Captain Healy of command. Relieving a captain of a naval ship while underway is something that is not undertaken lightly. Thompson understood that, at any inquiry held once back in port, if the charges against Healy proved false, at best, he and his brother officers stood a chance of receiving a record of misconduct, which would ruin their careers. At worst, they stood a very good chance of facing the serious charge of mutiny. These thoughts, plus Captain Healy's well-known reputation for being a drunk, ran through the mind of Lieutenant Thompson. Protecting himself from any future charges, Thompson wrote in the logbook, "It was finally decided that as long as [Captain Healy] did nothing to jeopardize the safety of the vessel or her personnel, no drastic measures should be resorted to."

Unfortunately for Lieutenant Thompson, the "drastic measures" presented themselves the next evening. At 6:14 p.m., Captain Healy came out on deck. Mrs. French stood nearby. Glancing over at her, Healy said, "Good-bye Madam," and promptly threw both legs over the stern rail in preparation for leaping into the cold North Pacific Ocean. Luckily, Second Assistant Engineer J. J. Bryan stood nearby. Engineer Bryan managed to grab Healy and, in a fierce struggle, wrestled him to the deck. Then, Bryan and other cuttermen took the captain to his cabin.

The executive officer now had the boatswain pass the third officer's call in two days. Lieutenant Thompson ordered Captain Healy brought to the wardroom to face his officers. The executive officer then informed Healy that, as of this moment, he no longer commanded the *McCulloch*. Thompson next entered into the cutter's log: "That Capt. Healy's mental condition, brought on by intemperance, was such as to render him a desperate and dangerous man, that he was manifestly determined to take his own life, and that his further remaining in command would imperil the lives of those on board as well as jeopardize the safety of the vessel, for the best interests of all concerned, do hereby declare it necessary to relieve Capt. M. A. Healy RCS of the command of the Revenue Steamer *McCulloch* and to restrict him in confinement to his cabin, under Guard, until the Department is communicated with." All officers present signed the log to record their agreement in the removal of Healy from command. Later, the officers held a muster of the crew and informed them that Lieutenant Thompson now commanded the cutter. Over forty years before the novelist Herman Wouk wrote his classic novel of World War II, *The Caine Mutiny*, life presaged art in the North Pacific Ocean.

Lieutenant Thompson and his brother officers on board the *McCulloch* pursued the only course of action available to them. Faced with an unusual situation, far out at sea, and without any way of reaching an officer of higher rank, they proceeded in a manner to protect themselves. Thompson's logbook, a legal document recognized by any inquiry or court, clearly spelled out the problem and his actions. Furthermore, Thompson also had a civilian witness, Mrs. French, to the whole episode. The executive officer no doubt felt relieved, but anxious to return to Seattle. Thompson's problems, however, had just begun.

Having been ordered to guard the captain in his cabin, Seaman C. W. Stidham remained awake early in the morning of July 10. Without any warning, Healy suddenly leaped out of bed, raced past the seaman, gained the deck, and tried to throw himself into the sea. Despite his captain's unexpected burst of speed, Stidham proved even faster. He caught hold of Healy just in time to prevent him from leaping to his death. To prevent any further attempts at jumping overboard, Lieutenant Thompson ordered Healy's cabin door locked, with his guard keeping the key.

Half an hour later, Seaman Stidham called for an officer. "Captain Healy," recorded Thompson in his by now ever-present logbook, "had gotten something from his pantry and hidden it in his bunk, Lieutenant Joynes searched same and found a glass concealed at the foot of his bed." Thompson then ordered a "lattice to be nailed across [the pantry's] door."

Healy attempted suicide two more times that day. At 5:15 p.m., he tried to hang himself with a curtain cord. Seaman Stidham once again frustrated Healy's suicide attempt. Four hours later, Healy tried again. He managed to "cut his wrist slightly with a small, jagged piece of glass," but another seaman, who had relieved the alert Stidham, prevented him from doing himself any further injury. As a precaution, the officer of the deck removed "two pairs of binoculars and two pairs of spectacles" from Healy's cabin.

Adding to Lieutenant Thompson's problems, the passenger steamer *Nome City* requested assistance in the Strait of Juan de Fuca. The cutter officer had no choice but to take the ship under tow and make for Port Townsend, Washington.[38]

By now, Thompson feared that Healy might succeed in his suicide attempts. To avoid this danger, he planned to transfer Healy as soon as possible to the U.S. Marine Hospital in Port Townsend, approximately one hundred miles northwest of Seattle. Nevertheless, the lieutenant worried about the outcome and ramifications of this terrible voyage.

Thompson had good reason to fret. At midnight, on July 12, one day out from Port Townsend, Captain Healy almost succeeded in killing himself. Second Lieut. Henry Ulke, Jr., the officer of the deck, wrote in the logbook that the guard in the captain's cabin rushed up to him and reported that Healy, "while lying in his bunk with hands hidden from view had cut his left forearm badly with a watch crystal and was bleeding profusely." I entered the cabin and found him lying in his bunk in a pool of blood. Noticed that he had severed an artery and at once bound upper arm tightly with a handkerchief, holding my hand tightly over the wound, which was a wide, triangular gash, to staunch the flow of blood. Sent for First Lieutenant Thompson, who provided medical supplies and more aid from the watch. Meanwhile Captain Healy struggled vigorously, it requiring the combined efforts of four men to keep him in his bunk. . . . Chief Engineer Chalker assisted by the other officers and seamen . . . tied up the arteries and sewed up the wound. All the officers agreed that, as a last resort, in order to prevent Capt. Healy from finally taking his life, his well arm must be confined, did so by putting it in a splint from arm-pit to his hand. Put wounded arm in a splint and gave watch strict instructions to keep his hands in sight and not allow him out of the bed.

As soon as the *McCulloch* anchored in the harbor of Port Townsend, Lieut. Thompson hurried ashore to the Marine Service Hospital. Surgeon C. H. Gardner, in charge of the hospital, refused to admit Captain Healy unless two escorts accompanied and watched over him. Thompson quickly detailed two seamen, who brought Healy to the hospital.

The *McCulloch* arrived in Seattle the same afternoon. Thompson quickly telegraphed headquarters about Captain Healy. The executive officer requested orders "to Washington at once, [to] properly explain extraordinary case."[39]

Seattle newspapers quickly learned of the events on board the *McCulloch*. One headline screamed, "Captain Healy Insane: Revenue Cutter Commander a Raving Maniac." Unlike the officers involved in the events of 1895–1896, the *Seattle Post-Intelligencer* reported that the "officers of the *McCulloch* . . . refused point blank to be interviewed concerning the insanity of Capt. Healy."[40]

Meanwhile, Surgeon Gardner, of the Marine Service Hospital in Port Townsend, formally charged Healy with insanity. A special session of the Superior Court of Jefferson County, Washington, the county in which Port Townsend is located, convened at the hospital on July 14 to examine the charge. The doctors found that Captain Healy had "had many attacks of insomnia, lasting a week or more" due to "mental worry" during the years he chaffed under his court martial sentence. The physicians then concluded that Healy's "intemperate use of liquors, within the last two weeks" caused his suicidal "mania."[41] After the hearing, Capt. Michael A. Healy, once the most famous man in the Far North, found himself confined within the Western Washington Hospital for the Insane at Fort Steilacoom. Interestingly, the *Post-Intelligencer* reported that, according to his wife, Healy's drinking had nothing to do with what happened. The newspaper also reported that while the doctors "do not think there is any chance of the unfortunate man recovering his mind, his many friends here are hopeful that his derangement is only temporary, and that under the scientific treatment at the state hospital he will be well again."[42] Despite Mary Jane's statements to the newspapers, she admitted in a letter to a friend her suspicion that "the 4th of July celebrations at Unalaska unsettled his mind."[43]

In 1976, Fr. Albert S. Foley authored another view of the events, which further complicates one's understanding of what happened on board the cutter. According to Father Foley: "Michael had become distraught after a wild Fourth of July in Unalaska. He had been so drunk that he had to be carried aboard his ship by his men." The ship then got underway for Seattle under the command of Lieutenant Thompson. When Captain Healy sobered up, he realized "he had become liable to another court-martial for dereliction of duty and drunkenness while in command of a naval vessel." This realization led to Healy's suicide attempts. Father Foley also writes that Healy's "loyal junior officers shielded him from a further court-martial by reporting simply that he had lost his mind."[44] The material in the National Archives, however, clearly states that the officers felt Healy's problems stemmed from his being drunk while on board the *McCulloch*.

A more shocking revelation, according to Father Foley, comes from a letter written by Mary Jane to Father Patrick. In her letter to Michael's older brother, Mary Jane writes:

> I am truly broken-hearted and cannot understand why I have to go through so much. Mine has been a chain of crosses for the past five years. It seems I must succumb under the weight. This last blow has been such a shock it will take some time for me to recover from it. I was so in hopes we were to be on our feet again, and I felt sure that Michael would again achieve a greater name than he had before, but it seems that our dear Lord wills it otherwise. . . . It is hard to say, but if it was God's will and Michael well prepared, it would be better that He take him, for then we would not dread the future for him. Don't think me unkind in speaking this way, but I dread what any day may bring him, for he looks very badly, but is improving.[45]

Meanwhile, an interesting drama unfolded on board the *McCulloch*. Lieutenant Thompson, with every reason to expect an inquiry concerning Healy's latest behavior, gathered the testimony of the officers and crew of the cutter. He expressed willingness to travel to Washington, D.C., and state his case. And yet, no investigation followed, and neither did Thompson receive orders to headquarters. Instead, Captain Coulson returned to take over his command. On July 26, Captain Coulson forwarded the reports of Thompson and the crew of the *McCulloch* to headquarters. A silence settled over what became known as the "Healy case." On December 24, 1900, Coulson wrote his official report on the 1900 cruise. His laconic comment—"Captain Healy being indisposed was sent to the Marine Service Hospital"—became the official explanation of the case.[46]

Even more remarkable, records in the Jefferson County Courthouse show that the hospital discharged Healy on September 12, 1900, roughly just two months after Healy was confined to the state mental hospital. An entry in his service record has Captain Healy arriving home on September 2, 1900, and being placed again on awaiting orders status.[47]

Surprisingly, Captain Healy received orders on July 16, 1901, placing him in command of the harbor cutter *Golden Gate* in San Francisco.[48] What happened?

Capt. Michael A. Healy's tribulations on board the *McCulloch* in 1900, and the immediate aftermath of the incident, are little known. Eighty-five years after the Healy case, in 1985, historian Gary C. Stein, Ph.D., seeking to shed light on the incident, published an article in *The Alaska Journal*. In the course of his research for the article, Stein found that all of the statements of the officers of the *McCulloch*, along with all other correspondence related to the event, were missing from the files of the service, which are now shelved in the National Archives. Stein managed to piece together what took place by locating the abstracts of relevant letters and using as his primary source of information the logbook of the *McCulloch*. By 2005, the logbook was missing too; a search request for the logbook, placed in the National Archives by one of the authors of this biography, returned only the news that the National Archives personnel could not locate the journal. Researchers are now forced to follow what took place using only the brief abstracts of the letters and Stein's article.

Doctor Stein, using the only evidence available to him, based his narrative upon the comments of the officers of the *McCulloch*, who stated that Capt. Michael A. Healy's difficulties stemmed from the excessive use of liquor. In turn, the doctors who examined Healy based much of their diagnosis on the officers' observations. The doctors reported that Healy's "intemperate use of liquors within the last two weeks" had caused his suicidal "mania." The officers of the *McCulloch* knew of Healy's reputation and, not surprisingly, based their conclusions upon it. Moreover, the medical doctors based their diagnosis upon the *McCulloch*'s officers' observations. Everyone reporting on the case, both then and years later, knew of Captain Healy's reputation. Recent research suggests, however, that there are two other possible ways of viewing what happened on board the cutter *McCulloch* in the summer of 1900.

No one has yet provided written evidence that Michael A. Healy drank during the 1900 cruise of the *McCulloch*. As noted, only the officers of the cutter stated that Healy staggered because of drunkenness. Based on the evidence available, the officers on the cutter seem to have harbored no animosity toward their temporary captain; thus, a desire to rid themselves of him can be ruled out. However, because Doctor White transferred to the *Nunivak* at St. Michael, the *McCulloch* had no doctor on board who could give his medical opinion of Healy's condition.

Beginning around the middle of the twentieth century, Father Foley, a Jesuit, spent many years studying the lives of James A., Patrick F., and Michael A. Healy. Father Foley was the first to publish, in a major New York publishing house, the racial heritage of the Healy family. Although he never wrote a book on Michael, Foley's papers reveal his strong interest in Captain Healy. Buried within Foley's papers is the remarkable statement that he believed Captain Healy's staggering did not result from strong drink, but from epilepsy. Unfortunately, Father Foley never documented either how he reached this conclusion or wherefrom he obtained this amazing revelation. If, and only if, Healy drank prior to departing Unalaska in 1900, then this consumption of alcohol, combined with epilepsy, might have triggered the incident.[49]

Two surviving pieces of evidence point to what most likely happened on board the *McCulloch*. Captain Healy's service record for July 18, 1900, records that Surgeon Gardner admitted the captain to the hospital with a diagnosis of "suicidal tendency." A brief of a letter from the Marine Hospital Service, dated July 25, 1900, diagnoses Captain Healy as suffering from "acute melancholia."[50]

In the twenty-first century, Healy might be diagnosed with either severe depression or bipolar disorder, which is also known as manic depression. Healy had just returned to duty after four very frustrating years away from the service. Healy and his wife strongly felt that he had been wronged. Then, once again, out of need for an officer experienced in the Far North, the service recalled him to take temporary command of a cutter. When Healy returned to Unalaska, he received the letter informing him of a transfer that he looked upon as a punishment.

The key to understanding what took place on the *McCulloch* is this order to the East Coast. Healy had too much time to brood on the meaning of the letter. *If* he drank at Unalaska, then it is likely that his depression intensified. Alcohol abuse is "very common among people with bipolar disorder." Furthermore: "[m]anic-depression distorts moods and thoughts, incites dreadful behaviors, destroys the basis of rational thought, and too often erodes the desire and will to live. . . . [It is a disorder] that brings in its wake almost unendurable suffering, and not infrequently, suicide." Moreover, the following feelings and behaviors are often given as signs that those with the disorder are at risk for suicide: "feeling hopeless, that nothing will ever change or get better; feeling helpless, that nothing one does makes any difference; [and] abusing alcohol or drugs . . ."[51] Clearly, *if* Captain Healy suffered from the disorder, then the upcoming transfer to the East Coast alone could have proved the catalyst for his actions, with alcohol never entering into the picture. In other words, through no fault of their own, the officers of the *McCulloch* misread Captain Healy's actions as evidence of alcohol abuse, a misreading that engendered a flawed interpretation of his life that has lasted into the twenty-first century.

Mary Jane Healy's comment to the *Post-Intelligencer* that drinking did not cause the incident on the cutter can be brushed off as being simply a devoted wife's attempt to defend her husband. The reporter who wrote the piece on Captain Healy in the Seattle newspaper apparently took this attitude, as he did not follow up on her comments. Perhaps Mary Jane Healy knew of her husband's mental affliction and recognized that he had suffered a serious attack of what is now called bipolar disorder. Even in the twenty-first century, people are often reluctant to discuss such matters outside of their immediate family. Likewise, Mary Jane Healy would be unlikely to mention why she believed drinking had not caused Captain Healy's tribulations aboard the *McCulloch*. She knew as well as her husband that if such information were to reach the ears of those in the U.S. Revenue Cutter Service headquarters, his career would be over.

It is also possible, of course, that Captain Healy did drink to excess while in Unalaska. Surely, he would have wanted to renew ties with old acquaintances now that he once again commanded a cutter in the Far North. In Healy's life, such gatherings of old friends often led to heavy drinking. Neda Thornton, the widow of murdered missionary Thornton, wrote to Mrs. William T. Lopp that she had heard that Mrs. Healy felt "the 4th of July celebration at Unalaska unsettled [Healy's] mind."[52] Again, Captain Healy, having just returned from four years on the beach and already suffering from "mental worry" over what he viewed as an injustice, then received the letter to move back to the East Coast. This might have caused Healy to drink heavily, both ashore and on board the *McCulloch*. If so, Captain Healy may well have suffered from delirium tremens.

Whatever interpretation one cares to defend concerning the incident on the *McCulloch*, one more significant question still looms about Captain Healy's life. After he was placed on waiting orders following his stay in the mental hospital, Healy received orders transferring him to the harbor cutter *Golden Gate* on July 16, 1901. Shortly thereafter, he received orders to also command the harbor cutter *Hartley*.[53] Both the *Golden Gate* and the *Hartley* were small cutters for such a senior officer as Healy. Perhaps, the service wanted to prepare Healy for the position of superintendent of construction on the West Coast.[54] Indeed, much of Healy's correspondence while aboard the cutters focused on making needed repairs. Captain Healy's long experience made him an expert on the service's craft and cutters and a logical choice for such a position.

During this period, Captain Healy received an amazing telegram. On November 28, 1901, just over a year after he returned from the mental hospital, Healy read the following message from Captain Shoemaker: "Reported hundred fifteen destitute men from Nome stranded at Unalaska. Do you credit report? Want you to take *McCulloch*, go there bring away destitute. Think better send *McCulloch* as she is in fine condition. Can have as many officers and men as desire along. Can I implicitly depend on you? Very important answer."[55] Though wary of Healy's reputation and recent mental instability, the head of the service still depended upon Captain Healy's expertise in the Far North.

Healy began to make preparations for another possible command. As a caring husband and father, he requested that an allotment from his pay be made out to his son, Frederick. Apparently, Captain Healy planned on taking Mary Jane with him and wanted Fred to handle his financial affairs, or else he felt that Fred was old enough to handle the family's financial affairs no matter whether Mary Jane accompanied Healy on the cruise. On December 2, however, headquarters sent Healy another telegram, advising him that there was "no vessel to go north." Headquarters, true to their usual worry over money, then sent another letter, dated December 11, informing Healy that his request for an allotment was "not favorably considered . . . as [the Department did] not intend to send him North at present."[56]

One month later, Captain Healy received yet another puzzling, albeit extremely welcome, communication. The letter of January 11, 1902, noted for its brevity and lack of explanation, reads: "Hereby restored to his original position on the list of Captains in the R.C.S., next after Capt. Loring N. Stodder, or *No. 7 on the list* and his name will so appear on the next Register."[57] (Emphasis in the letter.) According to all the traditions of the naval services, this letter meant that headquarters now judged Capt. Michael A. Healy's 1896 sentence unjust. Perhaps the inconsistencies of the trial seemed to someone in the Treasury Department cause for reasonable doubt. In any case, no one has yet discovered the reasoning behind this ruling.

Captain Healy may have felt that nothing could improve upon the letter that restored him to his original position on the captain's list, but, given his apparent lot in life, he received equally good news on April 4. Orders arrived for Healy to leave the *Golden Gate* and the *Hartley* in San Francisco and report as captain "without delay" to the cutter *Thetis*.[58]

Once again, near the end of May, Healy sailed from San Francisco to the Far North. Mary Jane accompanied him on this patrol, as she would during the following 1903 patrol. This time, Healy requested that an allotment of $75.00 a month be made to his son. All in all, the 1902 patrol proved uneventful. The *Thetis* returned to San Francisco on September 23.[59]

Prior to the 1902 patrol, an event at Washington, D.C., directly affected Healy's future. On April 2, 1902, after decades of indecision, the Congress finally authorized the U.S. Revenue Cutter Service to place officers who had reached the age of sixty-five on a retired list with a pension.

On January 7, 1903, during the winter layover in San Francisco, Captain Healy received orders to Washington, D.C. Although no written record exists of the reasons for this summons, it most likely dealt with his forthcoming retirement. By February 21, Captain Healy had reported back on board the *Thetis*. A month later, on March 20, Healy received a letter from the U.S. Revenue Cutter Service stating that "upon reaching the age of sixty-five next September" he should consider himself eligible for retirement. The letter, however, contained a surprising clause. Healy was to remain in command of the *Thetis*, "unless otherwise ordered."[60]

On May 26, the *Thetis* departed Seattle and Captain Healy ordered a course northward. A sign of the changing times came in a letter from the Treasury Department prior to his departure. From the time outsiders had first entered the Bering Sea and areas above the Bering Strait, they had routinely bartered with the Alaskan and Siberian natives. The Department now forbade "bartering or trading with natives in Alaska for furs, curios, etc."[61] Without the benefit of diaries from either Michael or Mary Jane, the thoughts of "Hell Roaring Mike" about his last patrol north have to be left to the field of speculation.

Apparently, at least one major change had occurred in the captain's behavior. During the 1903 patrol, a master of a merchant ship requested help from the cutter captain. The master felt that some of his crew were mutinous and might desert. He insisted that the troublemakers be shackled and confined. "I refused to do so," Healy wrote to the Treasury Department, "referring him to the U.S. attorney on shore, and informing him that I would uphold the legal decision of whatever nature it might be."[62] The refusal revealed a captain entirely different from the "Hell Roaring Mike" of two decades previous. If anyone foolishly thought that Captain Healy had become kinder and gentler, they would quickly change their minds after looking at his service record. His file recorded that on October 17, 1903, he received a reprimand "for using uncalled for, unofficer like, and indecent language in presence of his officers and crew."[63]

On October 30, Captain Shoemaker wrote to his wife that "it was very nice of old Healy to remember you" and their daughter Dorothy by sending a polar bear skin to them even in the face of Healy making "a blackguard of himself, and F[rancis] an ass of himself."

The next week, on November 6, Captain Shoemaker, in one of his long letters to his wife, explained what led up to the entry in Healy's record. Captain Healy, on the bridge, had yelled to the forecastle, where Third Lieut. Francis R. Shoemaker stood, "Lower that boom, and be damned to you." Shoemaker "took umbrage, and demanded an apology from Healy, which he refused to make, other than to say 'the order was impersonal, and not addressed to you.'" Not caring for Healy's explanation, Third Lieutenant Shoemaker "preferred charges of 'unofficerlike and ungentlemanly conduct' against the old man."

Despite being related to the young officer, Captain Shoemaker appreciated Captain Healy's rebuttal to Third Lieutenant Shoemaker. "Of course that disclaimer of Healy's left F[rancis] not an inch of ground to stand on—and he was severely reprimanded by the Dept. for preferring frivolous charges. Healy was also reprimanded for the use of the language—that's all."

Captain Shoemaker reminded his wife that all this brouhaha happened during his absence from Washington, and that he "had no hand in it," except to advise his assistant what to write Healy and Shoemaker. "I have no doubt, whatever, knowing Healy as I do," admitted the captain to his wife, "that he nagged Frank to desperation and that the fellow was driven practically to do what he did."[64]

Captain Healy's service record shows him detached from the *Thetis* on October 26, 1903, and placed on waiting orders. The last few entries in his official record only raise additional questions about his life and career.[65]

In late October 1903, officially retired but still in command of the *Thetis*, Healy received a letter from the Treasury Department asking him to supply the reason for his absence from the cutter from October 13 to 16. Healy received another letter in November, stating that his explanation for the absence was "not satisfactory." The Treasury Department demanded that he "apply for leave" or else be considered "absent without leave" and have his "pay deducted" for that period. Furthermore, the Department wanted an explanation as to "why Mrs. Healy remained aboard 'Thetis' after arrival at Sausalito to the end of October." Left with no choice, Healy applied for, and received, permission to take leave during the period of October 13–16.[66] He also may have explained Mary Jane's presence on board the *Thetis*, but records documenting his explanation either have not survived or have been misfiled.

That a very senior retired officer in the U.S. Revenue Cutter Service should receive such a spate of petty bureaucratic letters seems strange, to say the least. But the strangeness continued. On March 24, 1904, headquarters required Captain Healy to resubmit his voucher for his retired pay of $2,625 per year because he failed to add the word "retired" to his title "Capt. Michael A. Healy, U.S. Revenue Cutter Service."[67]

Healy now faced days with little to do. His age prevented him from gaining employment. He had no grandchildren. While there is an old tradition that senior retired naval officers retreat to gardens to tend roses, one has a difficult time imagining "Hell Roaring Mike" pruning roses. Instead, Michael and Mary Jane moved back into Room 8 of the Occidental Hotel, where Healy became "a daily habitué of the lobby."[68] There, he hoped to see old cronies and learn any news of the north. On July 15, 1904, Captain Shoemaker, himself nearing retirement, received a letter from a nephew who practiced medicine in the Marine Hospital in San Francisco. "I see Captain Healy often + he always asks after each of you, neither he nor Mrs. H have been very well of late; age mostly + on his part a 'strenuous life.'"[69]

On August 31, 1904, *The Call* headlined the current events in the now little-remembered Russo-Japanese War. After reading about these international events, readers who eventually worked their way to page 12 read a much smaller headline, "Death Calls Captain Healy, Noted Mariner."

The short article reported: "Captain Michael A. Healy, one of the best known navigators of the Pacific, ended his long and eventful career shortly after

10 o'clock last evening, when he passed quietly away at the Waldeck Hospital. Captain Healy had been sick for some time, but his condition did not take a serious turn until a few days ago, when he was advised to go to the hospital. A failing heart and a general breaking down of what was once a robust constitution hastened his end."[70]

Within eight years of Michael A. Healy's death, everyone in his immediate family died. Mary Jane, Healy's devoted wife who made many trips to the Far North to help her husband, passed away in 1907. His only son, Frederick, returned to San Francisco and became a newspaperman, a flour merchant, a broker, an insurance agent, and a partner in a grain, flour, and insurance company. He married, legally this time, had three sons, and in 1911 moved to Santa Barbara, California, where he died on January 7, 1912, at the age of forty-two.[71] The graves of Michael A. Healy and his immediate family are located in the Holy Cross Cemetery, near Coma, California, south of San Francisco.

Sixteen years after his death, most of Healy's friends and enemies within the U.S. Revenue Cutter Service had also died. His most influential friends, Captains Leonard G. Shepard and Calvin L. Hooper, preceded him in death. Shepard died on active duty in Washington, D.C., on March 14, 1895, and Hooper, also while still on active duty, died on April 29, 1900, at Oakland, California.[72]

John A. Henriques, who commanded the *Reliance* and the *Rush* when Healy and Henriques sailed around the Horn, retired as a captain on April 12, 1902, at Providence, Rhode Island, and died in the same city on March 29, 1906. Albert Buhner, who served alongside Healy on the *Moccasin* and as Healy's very loyal executive officer on the *Bear*, eventually gained the rank of captain on February 20, 1901, and retired on June 2, 1902. He passed away on September 15, 1911.

David H. Jarvis, the ambitious officer who helped with the purchase of the first reindeer, continued to advance in the U.S. Revenue Cutter Service. Described as "one of the brainiest men in the Revenue Cutter Service," Jarvis accepted, at the "urgent personal request of President Theodore Roosevelt," the post of customs collector of Alaska. Jarvis, however, did not give up his position on the captain's list of the service. He received permission to take the position for four years beginning in 1902. Jarvis resigned from the collector position on March 1, 1905, made temporary captain on March 29, and resigned from the service on May 1. Jarvis became part of the Morgan-Guggenheim Syndicate in Alaska and "became embroiled in the controversy that erupted over access to the rich copper mines and coal fields in Southern Alaska. . . . Tired and worn out, he became unable to withstand the abuse and accusations leveled at him." David H. Jarvis committed suicide in 1911.[73]

The two officers most influential in bringing Healy to trial in 1896, Lieutenants Emery and Daniels, remained in the service. George M. Daniels reached the rank of captain on July 14, 1913, and died that year on August 31, at Burlington, Vermont. Howard Emery reached the rank of senior captain on July 6, 1911, and retired that year on August 31. Emery lived a long life, outliving every U.S. Revenue Cutter Service officer that played a part in Healy's story. Howard Emery passed away on December 30, 1941, at Laconia, New Hampshire.[74]

John C. Cantwell, who explored the Kobuk River, also lived a long life. Cantwell, after continued service in Alaska, received orders to the East Coast and eventually, on March 25, 1898, to the cutter *Morrill*. While serving in the cutter, Cantwell, along with the other officers and men of the cutter, received a bronze medal for his action near Havana during the Spanish American War. Cantwell's next assignment had him commanding the stern wheel cutter *Nunivak* on the Yukon. He wrote an excellent government publication on his duties along the Yukon and received his commission as captain on October 11, 1904. He received a letter of reprimand for grounding the cutter *Manning* on November 11, 1907, in Prince William Sound, Alaska. On October 3, 1917, Cantwell received a commission as a senior captain, just two days after he took command of the Naval Reserve Training Camp in San Diego, California. Cantwell retired on April 6, 1920, died at Sausalito, California, on October 8, 1940, and received a burial at sea on October 10, 1940.[75]

Of the U.S. Navy officers who crossed Healy's bow, Lieut. George M. Stoney attained the rank of commander and died on April 20, 1905, at Annapolis, Maryland. Robley D. "Fighting Bob" Evans, who commanded the navy's force during the Bering Sea Controversy in 1892, went on to further fame. He is noted for his actions at Santiago Bay, Cuba, during the Spanish War of 1898, along with other accomplishments such as leading the "Great White Fleet" around the world. He retired from the U.S. Navy on February 22, 1909, and died of a heart attack on January 3, 1912, in Washington, D.C.[76]

Of the civilians who played a part in Healy's story, Sheldon Jackson continued to cause controversy and eventually, in 1908, ended his affiliation with the Bureau of Education and Alaska. Seriously ill, he moved from Washington, D.C., to Asheville, North Carolina. He died on Sunday, May 2, 1909, and is buried in Minaville, New York. As one writer noted, "Sheldon Jackson himself surely believed that he had fought the good fight, to the best of his ability, on all of the several battlefields where he had encountered conditions dangerously detrimental to the fulfillment of America's enlightened destiny."[77]

William T. "Tom" Lopp and Ellen L. (Kittredge) Lopp left Alaska in 1902 and settled in Seattle, Washington. Tom continued working for the Native People of Alaska through the reindeer project and education. He died in Seattle on April 10, 1939. Ellen continued to manage a household of eight children and handle the family's finances. She died in Seattle on October 19, 1947.[78]

Mary Antisarlook—"Sinrock Mary"—outlived them all. Mary became the "reining [sic] [granddame of reindeer herders], sought out by journalists and artists visiting Unalakleet." Despite becoming a legend in own lifetime, Sinrock Mary "remained in outlook an Eskimo woman" who fished, prepared seal meat and fish for the winter, and carried out the other tasks traditionally needed to survive in the Far North. "She was one of the first Eskimo women to play a role successfully in two cultures, for she combined a commercial success, highly regarded by the white man, with qualities greatly esteemed by the Eskimo." Sinrock Mary died at Unalakleet in 1948.[79]

The U.S. Revenue Cutter Service's 1903 register records that Capt. Michael A. Healy served for a total of thirty-eight years in the U.S. Revenue Cutter Service. He spent twenty-two years and eight months on the Pacific Station, and served an amazing nine years and six months in Alaska. In all the time he spent in the foggy, storm-driven, and poorly charted Arctic waters Healy never lost a ship. The officer with the closest amount of experience in Alaska, Capt. Francis Tuttle, served just four years and eight months in the Far North. The service began publishing information about the amount of time officers served in Alaska in 1895. From 1895 until Healy's retirement in 1903, no other captain in the U.S. Revenue Cutter Service served as long in Alaska.[80] It is doubtful that any officer in the history of the U.S. Revenue Cutter Service served as long in the Arctic. Yet, very few members of the U.S. Coast Guard know the location of Capt. Michael A. Healy's grave and rarely, if ever, does anyone from the service visit and honor the final resting place of the ice master and Arctic lifesaver of their service.

EPILOGUE

The story of Michael Augustine Healy has enough adventure to fill a Hollywood sea epic. Beyond the dramatic exploits, his is the story of a complex individual and the questions associated with such a person. Like Russian matryoshka dolls, opening one question for examination only reveals another. After the passage of over a century, and the burning of Healy's diaries, some of the answers to these questions can only be surmised. Today, five important questions remain that continue to add to the mystery of Michael A. Healy.

Race

The question of race has loomed so large as to dominate every discussion of Michael A. Healy. Some claim that his ability to pass as white and his acceptance by his colleagues and the general public as being white *makes* him *white*. Some African Americans do not believe Healy should be regarded as a true African American, since he deliberately passed as white. Others, without giving any reasons for their comment, state that he simply could not have been an African American. A few even maintain that his fellow service officers must have known about his racial heritage.

Even though some people question both Eliza Clark Healy's ethnic origins and name, the evidence is clear concerning her racial heritage. Michael A. Healy learned very early in life that his mother's race led to unpleasant consequences. He knew that his father threatened to turn his dogs loose upon the man who called his children by the racially derogatory term "yard children."[1] Until Michael A. Healy reached the age of twenty-six, the law considered him a slave. Even after the Civil War, racial segregation in the United States prevented Healy from ever obtaining fame in mainstream American society. With light skin and blue eyes, Michael A. Healy had two choices in life. He could declare his racial heritage and enter society as a slave, or he could pass.

After Michael A. Healy's racial heritage became widely known in the early 1970s, a new question arose. Did anyone know that Captain Healy was an African American?

Maritime and naval historians in the United States have spent a great deal of time researching and writing about African Americans and the sea. Granted, African Americans could find a freedom at sea that was not available to them on shore. They shared the same quarters and responsibilities as their white shipmates, *except* for the chance to rise to the position of officer. This arrangement included sailors serving in the merchant marine, on board whalers, and in the U.S. Navy. The "equality" continued until, roughly, 1898. After that, African Americans found themselves relegated to the role of an officer's seagoing servant.[2] In other words, present research confirms that no known African American held the command of a federal ship until World War II.[3]

Prof. James M. O'Toole, in an article on Michael A. Healy, offers the most telling explanation for why no one in the U.S. Revenue Cutter Service knew about Healy's racial heritage. An unfortunate human trait, Professor O'Toole points out, is the tendency when we are angry with someone to call them the worst name we can think of. Given the bitter nature of the 1896 trial in San Francisco, during which one officer called Captain Healy "an Irish Catholic son of a bitch," had there been any suspicion of Healy's racial heritage, would a more racial expletive not have been used?[4] The newspapers of San Francisco, moreover, eagerly snapped up any scrap of information leaked during the trial. Certainly, Healy's opposition, had they known, would have shared his racial heritage with anyone who would listen. Furthermore, had anyone in the Treasury Department learned of Healy's background, there is no doubt that they would have immediately removed him from the officer corps.

Despite what James Michener's novel, *Alaska*, has to say on the matter, the authors have failed to locate a single record to suggest that anyone knew of Michael A. Healy's secret during his lifetime.[5] Thirty-five years of examining books, articles, diaries, archival records in many locations, and other material concerning Captain Healy have uncovered no evidence that anyone knew of Healy's secret.

A more difficult question still remains. Did Mary Jane and her son, Frederick A., know the Healy secret? Mary Jane probably knew, and likely before their marriage. Healy and Mary Jane guarded their secret very carefully. Frederick, in 1883, when he was thirteen years old and accompanying his father on an Alaskan cruise, recorded in his diary that he "was the first white boy" on an island.[6] This indicates that either he did not know about his grandmother or that his father and mother had so coached him into passing for white that he automatically recorded his whiteness. By the early 1950s, however, most of the Healy family knew about their racial heritage.

An editorial in an online publication, the *Interracial Voice*, shows yet another side of how race dominates the story of Michael A. Healy. A. D. Powell believes that the Healy family is a shining example of "racial kidnapping." The family, according to Powell, should be considered Irish-American. She hammers at the point that the "Healy family's achievements do not show what 'blacks' could do in the 19th century because they were NOT BLACK." Furthermore, she believes "that various degrees of 'negro blood' were accepted into the 'white race,' even in the Deep South."[7]

Powell correctly points out that the Healy family stressed their Irish Catholic heritage and faith. She does not seem to understand, however, the consequences the Healy family would have faced had they declared that they had an African American racial heritage. The idea that a person's blood could determine their social status in American society may seem outrageous—and, indeed, is outrageous—but Powell, and others, must understand that prior to the 1960s in the United States this was the prevailing thought concerning race.

Powell contends that since "Captain Healy and his siblings succeeded in establishing themselves as second-generation Irish Americans," they should be so considered because they had "embraced the identity that they believed best defined them." The Healy family made this choice, she points out, despite the fact that "both Irish and Catholics faced massive discrimination" at the time. "If the Healy's wanted to social climb," she added, "they could have become Protestants." Powell even labels the U.S. Coast Guard's decision in 1997 to christen its biggest and most modern icebreaker the "*Michael A. Healy*," "a racial insult" that "tarnished" the captain's "memory" because, in doing so, the U.S. Coast Guard stressed Healy's African American, rather than Irish Catholic, heritage.[8]

Liquor

Another pressing question concerning Capt. Michael A. Healy centers on whether he drank to excess and, if he did, whether this affected his ability to command. The evidence is too strong to deny that Healy drank, sometimes to excess. He came from the merchant marine, whose members have a long tradition of drinking, which earned them reputations as ne'er-do-wells. As late as the

1920s, public opinion of all sailors had sunk so low that seven states disqualified them from voting.[9]

Both the nature of the times and of Healy's profession almost made it mandatory for officers to drink. Capt. Calvin L. Hooper once recalled that he would have been surprised had anyone come away sober from that infamous officer's party on board the HMS *Pheasant* in 1895. Healy took the pledge in 1880 not to drink, strong evidence that his heavy drinking had to be reined in. Recognizing his dependence upon alcohol, Healy asked Mary Jane to accompany him on many of his voyages. On those patrols, Healy did not encounter any problems. The 1900 incident on the *McCulloch* may, or may not, have had its root cause in drinking, but his wife, had she been present, might have prevented his bizarre behavior and attempted suicides.

After his recovery, Mary Jane sailed with Michael on his last two northern patrols, during which no drinking occurred. In 1892, a number of Healy's friends wrote to Sumner I. Kimball, general superintendent of the U.S. Life-Saving Service, recommending Captain Healy for duty therewith. Healy professed that he knew nothing of this move. The authors believe that Healy knew he needed help and that a position ashore with Mary Jane to help him stay sober seemed the best option. According to Healy, however, Kimball felt that no Catholic should hold any responsible position in the U.S. government. Healy expended a great deal of ink and paper over the next few years explaining how he could never accept a position working for Kimball and, in fact, how he planned on making Kimball sorry for the comment. There is no evidence that any implied action against Kimball ever materialized. The alleged comments by Kimball, of course, also worked on Healy's psyche.[10]

Guilty or Not Guilty

The story of Michael A. Healy is one in which things are never as they seem on the surface. The trials of 1890 and 1896 prove this statement. In the 1890 trial, for example, the two charges—cruelty and drunkenness—actually have other meanings that serve as subtexts.

By the 1880s, there grew in the United States a movement that focused on injustices in the social and political fabric of the country. This current, or movement, became a reform political force known as the Progressive movement. Progressives, drawn from both political parties, sought to address the excesses of runaway growth. Two of the Progressives' social goals directly impacted Healy. The first of these began in towns in Ohio and New York in 1873 when women, concerned about the destructive power of liquor, met in churches to pray and then marched to saloons to ask the owners to close down. Realizing that success could only come by organizing nationally, in 1874 the women organized the Woman's Christian Temperance Union (WCTU) and, that year, began a crusade against liquor.[11]

Many reformers wished to improve the lives of working people. Some believed that unions offered the only solution. This concern led to the second current that impacted Healy in 1890. Improving the lot of those who followed the sea proved difficult. A worker ashore could refuse work and just walk away. A sailor, on the other hand, if he wished to work on a ship, had to sign Articles of Agreement, which amounted to a contract. A mariner who refused work faced the charge of mutiny and draconian measures, such as tricing up, to make him return to his duties. If the sailor left his ship before the end of a voyage, he faced the charge of desertion. In 1790, the federal government passed legislation that provided for arresting, imprisoning, and returning sailors that deserted. Those who served before the mast found themselves "wards of the admiralty, under the care of their guardian, the state." In reality, they found themselves treated, as the sailor advocate Andrew Furuseth liked to point out, little better than slaves.[12]

Andrew Furuseth, a Norwegian who came to this country as a sailor, became one of the early advocates for the rights of seamen. He joined the Coast Seaman's Union in San Francisco in 1885. Two years later, he held the position of secretary of the union, "the highest office in the union."[13] At one time, he resigned his position and returned to sea. Eventually, members persuaded him to resume his former position, and he worked tirelessly to support legislation that helped sailors. When threatened with jail, Furuseth, according to the classic story, responded: "You can put me in jail. But you cannot give me narrower quarters than as a seaman I have always had. You cannot give me coarser food than I have always eaten. You cannot make me lonelier that I have always been." Given such rhetoric it is easy to see why, among those who followed the sea, Furuseth has earned the title, the "Abraham Lincoln of the seas."[14]

Some have wondered why the WCTU and a sailor's union joined forces in 1890 against Capt. Michael A. Healy. Rightly or wrongly, "Hell Roaring Mike's" reputation offered reformers a perfect target for using publicity to advance their cause, a tactic not unknown in the twenty-first century. In 1890, some saw the advocates not as reformers, but as agitators, which may also help explain why the trial board found Healy not guilty. It is interesting to speculate whether the women of the WCTU and the Coast Seaman's Union actually targeted Healy *before* the 1889 patrol. It may explain why Mrs. M. B. Eden, of the WCTU, had known seaman Henry Spicer for a period of time before the trial. Further, Captain White, head of the board, accused seaman Spicer of keeping a written record of Healy's activities during the patrol for the union.

Yet another obvious question about the 1890 trial has not been answered. Did Captain White's son, Doctor White, ever discuss the patrol with his father or share his diary with him?

The 1896 trial was host to even more subterranean activities and continues to prompt even more questions. One of the largest debates about the 1896 trial centers on whether Assistant Secretary of the Treasury Charles Hamlin set out to rid the service of the troublemaker he saw in Captain Healy. At present, the historical evidence does not completely support the idea that Hamlin deliberately wished to destroy Healy. Hamlin's diaries and papers, now archived in the Library of Congress, show that he tried to approach the matter in a judicial manner. Hamlin accepted the testimony of the officers at the trial. In other words, he felt that those who testified were officers and gentlemen who told the truth. Why he chose to do so is clear; he had only to look at Healy's record, which already contained three previous charges of drunkenness. Even though Healy was found innocent of one of those charges, it nevertheless sowed the seed of doubt in the minds of many.

There were two groups within the service itself who seem to have been intent upon finding Healy guilty. The young officers on board the *Bear* and other cutters, who wished to rid themselves of older officers so they could advance in their own careers, are among the most suspect. The second group comprises the unnamed senior U.S. Revenue Cutter Service officers who were jealous of Healy's reputation and influence. Historian Gerald O. Williams felt that once Captain Shepard died, Healy had no one left in the service to defend him. The result of the 1896 trial vindicates Williams' observation.[15]

Another source of debate about the 1896 trial is Healy's punishment: did he receive too severe a sentence? Capt. Fredrick M. Munger faced charges of drunkenness while commanding the cutter *Corwin* in the Bering Sea. Much like Healy, a lieutenant sent charges to Captain Hooper. Even worse than Healy's charges, the lieutenant stated that Munger's drunkenness led to the death of a sailor. Captain Hooper not only dismissed the charges, but also recommended Munger for the special duty of overseeing the construction of a new cutter in Seattle. This so angered the lieutenant that, much like Lieutenant Emery, he by-passed Hooper and sent his charges to Washington. Munger again escaped the charges. On the other hand, on October 16, 1896, Capt. Jefferson A. Slamm, convicted of drunkenness, found himself lowered from number fourteen to number thirty-four on the captain's list. Slamm received this large demotion for a first time offense. Captain Healy's sentence was further complicated by two previous reprimands for drinking and one suspected charge of drunkenness.[16] Three things are clearly illustrated by these examples. First, those in leadership positions within the service meant to show that, in the presence of strong evidence, drinking to excess by senior officers would not be tolerated. Second, in Munger's case, in which the charges seemed weak, those in leadership indicated that charges must be substantiated and that weak charges stood a chance of being dismissed. Captain Healy's sentence, therefore, seems justifiable. This line of reasoning, of course, presumes him guilty of the charges. The investigation following the 1896 trial shows that some doubt lingered as to whether Healy had in fact placed the *Bear* in danger.[17]

Finally, why did the service, in 1903, reverse its decision and restore Captain Healy to his original position on the captain's list? Perhaps, as mentioned in chapter 11, the questions raised by the conflicting testimonies left sufficient cause for reasonable doubt. At present, however, there is no surviving evidence that can be used to conclusively identify the reasons for this decision.

While one should never judge events of the past by modern standards, it is interesting to note how military lawyers in the twenty-first century see the 1896 trial. The U.S. Coast Guard now treats charges of excessive drinking by both the officer corps and the enlisted force as very serious. It is highly probable that in the twenty-first century U.S. Coast Guard, Captain Healy would have been cashiered from the service, along with Captains Munger and Slamm.

Running below the charges and countercharges of drunkenness is a subtle current that began in 1870 when someone tried to right a poor practice. As mentioned earlier, prior to 1870, the U.S. Revenue Cutter Service recruited its officers from the merchant service, where the new revenue officers had put in many years at sea learning their trade. The collector of customs made these appointments and, since the collectors changed each time the political power in Washington changed, the revenue office's posts depended on politics. Moreover, collectors of customs in some cases held great power. The collector at the Port of New York, for example, had "power and responsibility . . . greater than those of most Cabinet officers; and the pay, as things were constituted, could exceed even that of the President. Politically, it was the ultimate plum."[18] The collectors, therefore, felt strongly about keeping control of their "navy." Then,

Sumner Increase Kimball, a lawyer and former politician from Maine and a longtime Treasury Department employee, took over the reins of the service. Kimball felt politics had no place in the service, and he changed the methods of appointing new officers. He created a "School of Instruction" with a cadet system that eventually evolved into today's U.S. Coast Guard Academy. From then on, younger officers learned the ways of the sea at school instead of through a long apprenticeship at sea and practical on-the-job training. The school also provided a means for the service's future commanders to keep pace with the rapid changes in technology at sea. The movement away from political appointees, especially by the collectors of customs, and the fielding of well-educated officers familiar with the current technology reflected greatly the beneficial effects of the School of Instruction.[19]

There was, however, yet another subtle effect of this embryonic service academy. The young officers graduating from the School of Instruction, like those from the U.S. Navy Academy at Annapolis, considered themselves officers and gentlemen and superior to the old-time officers, especially to those who began as ordinary seamen and came up through the ranks. The service academies have "long been accused of being . . . aristocratic institution[s], which churned out an elitist and privileged class of officers for a nation dedicated to equality, democracy and the common man."[20]

Complicating the situation even further, the service did not have a retirement system. The school-trained and highly ambitious young officers viewed Healy and other senior officers as the old guard, backward men lacking the social graces of a gentleman. These uncouth elderly officers, more importantly, clung tenaciously to their positions and ranks, thereby blocking the young officers from promotions they felt they richly deserved owing to their academic training. Many officers, as a result, developed an "us against them" mentality. In retrospect, it is not at all surprising that the school-trained officers aboard the *Bear* in 1895, especially Lieutenants Daniels and Emery, signed charges against Captain Healy. As the tenth most senior captain in the service, the *Bear*'s skipper delayed the promotion of those below him and therefore personified what these new officers so hated about the old guard. Paul H. Johnson, former librarian at the U.S. Coast Guard Academy, feels had there been a retirement system in effect, there would never have been a trial in San Francisco.[21] Had such a system existed, the older officers would have left the service sooner, secure in the knowledge they would be financially taken care of, thereby opening their billets to the younger men. Healy's life after 1896 confirms Johnson's observation.

Trouble Maker?

Many old salts who have heard of Captain Healy's two trials, each marked by a charge of drunkenness, question the wisdom of the U.S. Revenue Cutter Service's decision to keep such a man within its ranks. There are, however, two simple explanations for this decision.

When Captain Healy's troubles first began, he was likely allowed to continue to serve both because of his seagoing abilities and the influence of his inheritance and his high-ranking brothers in the Catholic Church. As the years passed, his continued abilities as a master mariner and Arctic navigator came to the attention of senior officers. These officers, namely Capt. John W. White, Capt. Calvin L. Hooper, and most especially Capt. Leonard G. Shepard, watched over Healy's career and protected him as much as possible. For instance, it appears that Captain White, the head of the 1890 trial, did not really want to prosecute Healy, but was forced to obey orders.

In the end, it was solely his skill as a sailor in the dangerous waters of the Bering Sea, the Arctic Ocean, and the maritime frontier of Alaska that saved him. His abilities as an Arctic navigator far exceeded those of any other commanding officer in this important region.

Even Capt. Charles F. Shoemaker, who labored valiantly to weed out troublemakers and ineffective older officers from the service's rolls, recognized Healy's strong reputation in the Far North. Later, when most of the service's leadership seemed to turn against Healy, Captain Shoemaker again turned to Captain Healy as an expert on Alaska. Quite simply, the service could not afford not to employ Capt. Michael A. Healy.

Also, unrecognized by many is the fact that a small woman from Boston largely ensured Healy's continued employment in the service. When he finally recognized his dependency upon strong drink and signed the pledge to abstain from alcohol in 1880, Healy turned to the one person he could always depend upon, his wife, Mary Jane (Roach) Healy. In her diaries and letters, Mary Jane admitted her dislike, and even fear, of the Far North. There was good reason for her dread. Many sailors, even those with decades of sea duty under their belts, hesitated to challenge the dangers of the northern latitudes. She also recorded in her journal an incident in which a wardroom steward went "a little insane," but was quickly placed under guard. Mary Jane recorded that while she now felt secure, she had previously worried about the man "paying them a call."[22] As a woman, she encountered few people, either on the vessel or ashore, to pass a pleasant conversation with. Her diaries contain many entries that describe her sitting alone for hours in her cabin and only occasionally record her joy at a rare visit with another woman at an isolated mission.

Despite the danger, isolation, and separation from friends in San Francisco, Mary Jane sailed north year after year, because "her husband needed her." Captain Healy made eighteen patrols to the Far North from 1881 to 1903, and Mary Jane accompanied him at least five times. Without her presence on board to steady Healy, his fall from grace may have been permanent. Had Mary Jane accompanied him in 1889, 1895, and 1900, might not Captain Healy's place in history have been far greater?

Hero or Colorful Failure?

Should Capt. Michael A. Healy be considered a hero? Or, as some hint, should he be considered an ordinary government official, a sailor by trade, who helped introduce reindeer into the Far North and had an interest in the welfare of the people living there, but nevertheless ended his days as a colorful failure?

Many Americans want their heroes to be without normal human faults and foibles. Anyone labeled a "hero," according to them, must not have feet of clay. Unfortunately, Captain Healy does not fit this mold. Instead, he demanded strict obedience to his orders, used punishments that today seem inhumane to enforce his edicts, swore like a sailor, and sometimes drank to excess. At times, he could exhibit all the required manners of polite nineteenth and early twentieth century society. At other times, he exhibited all the manners of a drunken sailor.

As was the case with his brothers and sisters, Healy's intelligence and ambition soon brought him recognition. He succeeded first in the merchant marine and then in the U.S. Revenue Cutter Service. Those who went down to the sea in ships in the nineteenth century found themselves in a brutal and dangerous world. Strangely enough, in some ways, the life of a sailor, especially one who sailed before the mast, proved to be not all that different from the lives of those in bondage in the South. Most of American society looked down upon those who plied the seas, whether they were an officer or a common sailor. Since many believed that a life at sea required little intelligence, they shunned sailors.

Happy to be free of the discipline of Catholic schools, Michael A. Healy willingly entered this world. To succeed, one needed not only to meet toughness with either a stronger brute force or superior aggressiveness, but also intelligence. The young Healy exhibited the superior aggressiveness, toughness, and intelligence to move up the ranks. The financial inheritances from his parents and Mary Jane's family, plus the influences of his older brothers, surely helped, but ultimately his own abilities played the greatest role in propelling him forward. His love of the sea, and its influence on him, stayed with him throughout his life, as did his sense of duty. Healy never looked upon himself as an African American, an Irish American, a devout Catholic, or a white person. Until the day he died, Healy thought of himself as a sailor. In some ways, he remains the archetypal sailor.

For his own reasons, Healy wished to succeed in his profession. Like his siblings, while he did not reach the pinnacle of his profession, he nevertheless obtained a station far above most. No matter the depths to which his life plunged, he persevered, and rose once again.

By 1865, Michael A. Healy had met and married Mary Jane Roach of Boston. Eager for a family life, he promptly left the merchant marine and entered the U.S. Revenue Cutter Service because he could not bear to sever all connections with his beloved sea. His desire for a family highlights another strong factor in Healy's psyche. As his later career clearly demonstrated, Healy succeeded with the help of Mary Jane; without her help, he might have failed.

With the United States' purchase of Alaska in 1867, the U.S. Revenue Cutter Service struggled to man the new missions needed to police the northern possession, and Healy's entire life and career at sea changed. Previously, Healy's duties had centered mainly on customs enforcement in local areas. After the purchase of Alaska, these duties grew and became those of a deepwater maritime officer with the responsibilities of enforcing federal law, carrying out search and rescue missions, providing medical care, advancing science and exploration, protecting wildlife, and caring for native peoples, all in an international setting. Healy's work on the maritime frontier of Alaska makes him eligible for inclusion among the greats of U.S. and international maritime history.

Unfortunately, most people in the United States recognize only a few names of their maritime heroes. Only the names of a handful of U.S. Navy heroes, such as John Paul Jones, Oliver Hazard Perry, George Dewey, and Ernest J. King, even sound familiar to the general public. Not everyone who goes to sea faces dangerous military situations. In other words, not everyone can become a Fleet Adm. Ernest J. King. As a result, only a few recognize the names of outstanding captains who sailed in the merchant marine or the U.S. Revenue Cutter Service.

Every year that Capt. Michael A. Healy sailed north, he entered a brutal, dangerous, and isolated environment. While heroism did not come to Healy amid blood-soaked decks and the deafening roar of naval cannon, it did come to him in lonely, gale-swept seas, and in a numbing cold that seemed to sear the soul.

The region Healy operated in had a long and wicked reputation for lawlessness without any form of government, let alone law enforcement. To compound his problems, the federal government in Washington provided him with no clear-cut guidelines. Healy characteristically enforced federal law as he saw fit and in a manner not generally noted for its gentility. When it came to the Eskimos, however, he dispensed justice with a grain of charity. In most cases of law-breaking within the Eskimo community, Healy let their leaders decide the fate of the guilty party, even going so far as to allow them to sentence and carry out executions. Yet, in the event the natives attacked whites, Healy's response proved quick and effective.

In an age when Americans gave very little thought to the welfare of native people, Captain Healy witnessed the mass starvation of natives on St. Lawrence Island and began fearing the extinction of the Eskimo. After a great deal of thought, Healy took action to head off such a catastrophe by helping to spearhead the introduction of Siberian reindeer into Alaska, thereby transforming the native hunters of Alaska into herders.

Literally hundreds of sailors owed their lives to Healy's willingness to exhaustively search for anyone lost or otherwise in danger in the Bering Sea and the Arctic. He may have cursed the whaling masters for risking their ships and crews for increased profits, but, when a whaler turned up missing, Healy and his cutter searched the long shores of Siberia and Alaska to rescue them. Congress officially commended Captain Healy for his Arctic lifesaving work in 1885. He received a published testimonial in the San Francisco *Chronicle* in 1888 by the masters and crews of four whalers for his work to rescue them after they were wrecked off Point Barrow. Fifty owners and masters of whalers gathered in San Francisco that year to present yet another testimonial to his rescue work. In truth, he could be called a Master Lifesaver of the Arctic. Healy's accomplishments should have gained him great fame. Yet, even within the maritime world, he is little known. The cause of this virtual anonymity can be attributed to his personality. Some might say he had a "prickly" disposition, an overbearing personality. There are many observations recorded from Healy's fellow officers that describe him as constantly hounding his junior officers. In 1903, for example, Capt. Charles F. Shoemaker observed that Healy "nagged an officer" to such desperation that he struck back and received a reprimand.[23] To this day, there are captains whose leadership style focuses on seeing how well their junior officers and enlisted men hold up under stress. Such captains may be great seamen, but officers and enlisted men usually approach serving on their ships with something closely approaching fear. Most Americans do not like their heroes to have this type of personality; heroes must be saintly and without blemish. In no way can Capt. Michael A. Healy ever be considered a saint. To his death, he remained a tough, profane sailor. He also drank.

Not all heroes are saintly. Most, being human beings, possess all the weaknesses and strengths of the human animal. All of the special people who have entered into the American pantheon of heroes have demonstrated the ability to overcome or rise above complex social and psychological forces. Despite what life throws at them, they persevere and accomplish great things. Michael Augustine Healy belongs to this class of hero. He deserves a better place in the history of the United States.

APPENDIX 1

Important Dates in the Life of Capt. Michael A. Healy

1839	September 22, born in Jones County, Georgia, near Macon.
1850	May 19, death of mother, Eliza Clark Healy.
1850	June 22, entered the College of the Holy Cross at Worcester, Massachusetts. Fire in 1851 canceled classes.
1850	August 27, death of father, Michael Morris Healy.
1853	By September, Healy had returned to Holy Cross.
1855	Sent by oldest brother to the English College at Douai, France.
1855[?]	Ran away to sea and sailed in the merchant marine.
1865	January 31, married Mary Jane Roach, of Boston, Massachusetts.
1865	March 7, entered U.S. Revenue Cutter Service as a third lieutenant.
1865	April 27, assigned to cutter *Stevens* at New York City.
1865	November 5, birth of son John James, who died the same day.
1866	January, serving on board cutter *Chase*, at Ogdensburg, New York.
1866	June 6, commissioned as a second lieutenant.
1866	November 1, birth of son, Eugene.
1866	December 15, reported on board cutter *Pawtuxet*, at Boston.
1867	June 5, reported on board cutter *Active*, at Philadelphia, Pennsylvania.
1867	August 1, reported on board cutter *Reliance* at Baltimore, Maryland. Made journey around Cape Horn to cutter's home port in San Francisco, California.
1868	November 23, *Reliance* took station at Sitka, Alaska. This was Healy's first service in Alaskan waters.
1869	April[?], transferred temporarily to cutter *Lincoln* for patrol to the Far North. This duty was not entered in his official record.
1869	May 16, first duty in the Bering Sea.

1869   November or December, transferred from the *Lincoln* to the East Coast.

1870   January 5, death of son, Eugene. Cause of death given as "croup."

1870   July 20, commissioned as a first lieutenant.

1870   August 5, reported on board cutter *Seward* at Wilmington, North Carolina.

1870   October 5, birth of son, Frederick Aloysius Healy.

1870   December 3, reported to cutter *Vigilant* at Boston.

1871   September 21, ordered to cutter *Moccasin* at Newport, Rhode Island.

1871   December 2, reprimanded for drunkenness.

1872   January, ordered to cutter *Active* at New Bedford, Massachusetts.

1874   July 13, ordered to new cutter *Rush* at Boston and then sailed around Cape Horn to cutter's home port of San Francisco. First duty as acting commanding officer for a lengthy period while cruising along the West Coast.

1877   November 29, detached from *Rush* and ordered to East Coast.

1877   December 3, began examination for captain in Washington, D.C.

1877   December 17, received orders for cutter *Chandler* at New York City. First cutter commanded by Healy.

1878   January 14, successfully completed examination for captain.

1880   May 20, reported for duty on board cutter *Corwin* at San Francisco, for search to find the naval exploring ship *Jeannette* above Arctic Circle.

1880   November 1, reported for temporary command of cutter *Rush* at San Francisco, for duty in Alaska.

1882   February 24, reported for duty as the commanding officer of the cutter *Corwin* at San Francisco.

1883   March 3, promoted and commissioned as a captain.

1886   April 9, ordered to command the cutter *Bear* at San Francisco.

1890   March 3, charged with inhuman treatment of merchant seamen and drunkenness. Exonerated of all charges.

1891   August 28, first purchase of reindeer in Siberia.

1895   November 7, received thanks from the Treasury Department for duties in the Bering Sea and Arctic.

1896   January 10, faced board of investigation on charges of drunkenness.

1896   June 9, found guilty of charges, dropped to bottom of list of captains, and placed on waiting orders for four years.

1900	May 26, ordered to temporarily command the cutter *McCulloch* on voyage to Alaska.
1900	June 22, received orders to command the cutter *Seminole* at Baltimore, Maryland.
1900	July, attempted suicide on voyage from Alaska to Seattle, Washington.
1900	July 18, confined to Washington State Institution for the Insane.
1900	September 2, released from Washington State Institution for the Insane. Arrived in San Francisco. Placed on waiting orders.
1901	July 16, ordered to temporarily command the cutter *Golden Gate* at San Francisco.
1901	October 25, directed to command cutter *Hartley* at San Francisco.
1902	January 11, returned to original position on list of captains (number 7).
1902	April 11, reported as commanding officer of cutter *Thetis* at San Francisco.
1903	September 22, officially retired from the U.S. Revenue Cutter Service, but kept in command of *Thetis* until November. At time of retirement, ranked third among all captains in the U.S. Revenue Cutter Service.
1903	October 17, reprimanded for using uncalled-for and indecent language unbecoming an officer in presence of his officers and crew.
1904	August 30, died of a heart attack at San Francisco, California.
1907	February 27, death of wife, Mary Jane (Roach) Healy, at San Francisco, California.
1912	January 7, death of son, Frederick, at Santa Barbara, California.

APPENDIX 2

The Family of Michael Augustine Healy[1]

Mary Jane Roach. (Wife) Born July 27, 1836, in Boston, of Irish immigrant parents and married Michael Augustine Healy on January 31, 1865, in Boston. Mary Jane (Roach) Healy died February 27, 1907, in San Francisco, California.[2]

John James Healy. (Son) Born November 5, 1865, in Boston, and died the same day.

Eugene Healy. (Son) Born November 1, 1866, in Boston, and died January 5, 1870.

Frederick Aloysius Healy. (Son) Born October 5, 1870, in Boston, and died January 7, 1912, in Santa Barbara, California. He is buried with his mother and father in San Francisco.

Michael Morris Healy. (Father) Born September 20, 1796, in Athlone [?], Ireland, and immigrated to the United States. By 1818, had moved to Georgia and became a successful plantation owner near Macon. Began living with Eliza Clark, an African American slave, as man and wife sometime before 1829. Died near Macon, Georgia, on August 27, 1850.

Eliza Clark. (Mother) Date and place of her birth are unknown. Began living with Michael Morris Healy as a married couple sometime before 1829 and died near Macon, Georgia, on May 19, 1850.

James Augustine Healy. (Brother) Born April 6, 1830, near Macon, Georgia, and brought to the North in 1837. He graduated from the College of the Holy Cross, Worcester, Massachusetts, in 1849. Entered the Catholic Church and studied at Sulpician seminary in Montreal, Canada, and Paris, France. He was ordained in Notre Dame Cathedral, Paris, in 1854. James began his duties in Boston and eventually served at a home for homeless boys, as secretary to the Bishop, and as chancellor. He then served as pastor in one of Boston's largest parishes. In 1875, James became the Bishop of Portland, Maine. Died in Portland on August 5, 1900.

Hugh Clark Healy. (Brother) Born April 16, 1832, near Macon, Georgia, and brought to the North in 1838. Graduated from the College of the Holy Cross, Worcester, Massachusetts, in 1849. Hugh entered business in New York City with John Manning. Died as a result of an accident on September 17, 1853, in New York City.

Patrick Francis Healy. (Brother) Born February 27, 1834, near Macon, Georgia, and brought to the North in 1838 [?]. Entered the College of the Holy Cross, Worcester, Massachusetts, in 1844, and graduated in 1850. Entered the Jesuit order the same year. Taught at a school in Philadelphia and returned to teach at the College of the Holy Cross. In 1858, entered Georgetown College to begin concentrated theological studies. In 1860, began studies at Louvain in Belgium, and earned an advanced degree in theology. Ordained at Liege, Belgium, in 1864, he became "prefect of studies" at Georgetown University, Washington, D.C., in 1869, and on May 24, 1873, became president of the university. Left that post in 1882 and died January 10, 1910. Patrick F. Healy is buried in the priests' graveyard on the campus of Georgetown University, Washington, D.C.

Alexander Sherwood Healy. (Brother) Born January 24, 1836, near Macon, Georgia, and brought to the North in 1844. Entered the College of the Holy Cross, Worcester, Massachusetts, the same year, but did not graduate from the school. He withdrew from school in 1850 because of health and, two years later, attended the Sulpician seminary in Montreal, Canada. Entered the Sulpician seminary in Paris in 1853, was ordained in the Cathedral of Notre Dame in 1858, and was assigned to work in an orphanage in Boston's North End in 1860. Began to rise to prominence in the church in Boston. In 1864, joined the faculty of Saint Joseph's Seminary in Troy, New York. After becoming the confidant of and aide to the Bishop of Boston, he accompanied the Bishop to the First Vatican Council of 1869–1870, where he suffered a physical collapse. Alexander Sherwood never returned to important duties in Boston because he never completely recovered his health. Died in Boston on October 21, 1875.

Martha Ann Healy. (Sister) Born March 9, 1838, near Macon, Georgia, and brought to Boston in 1844 [?]. Entered an academy run by the Congregation de Notre Dame in Montreal, Canada, and in August 1850, decided to enter the Church. Made her first profession of vows as a member of the Congregation de Notre Dame, in September 1855, becoming known as Sister Saint Lucie. Martha left the church in 1863 and married Jeremiah Cashman, of Boston, on July 25, 1865, with whom she had one son and three daughters. Martha A. (Healy) Cashman died on May 18, 1920, in Watertown, Massachusetts.

Eugene Healy. (Brother) Born June 30, 1842, and lived only five weeks.

Michael Augustine Healy. Born September 22, 1839, near Macon, Georgia, and died August 30, 1904, in San Francisco, California.

Amanda Josephine Healy. (Sister) Born January 9, 1845, near Macon, Georgia, and brought to New York City in June 1851. Two years later, entered elementary school and the academy of the Congregation de Notre Dame in Montreal, Canada, and graduated in 1861. Traveled on a Mediterranean cruise with older brother James in 1868 and in 1873 joined the Sisters of the Good Shepard, but left after three months. On November 21, 1873, she entered the Religious Hospitallers of Saint Joseph in Montreal, Canada. In December 1875, she took her final vows. Suffering from poor health, Sister Amanda J. Healy died July 23, 1879, in Montreal, Canada.

Eliza Dunamore Healy. (Sister) Born December 23, 1846, near Macon, Georgia, and brought to New York City in June 1851. Entered elementary school and the academy of the Congregation de Notre Dame in Montreal, Canada, and graduated in 1861. Traveled on a Mediterranean cruise with older brother James in 1868 and in the early 1870s decided to enter the Congregation de Notre Dame. She took her final vows in July 1876 and received the name "Sister Saint Mary Magdalen." She became noted as a teacher and Mother Superior in Canada. Sister Mary Magdalen also saw service in Chicago and, by 1903, had taken a position as Mother Superior of an academy in St. Albans, Vermont. Left in 1918 for a Notre Dame Convent and school on Staten Island, New York. Failing health caused her to retire to Montreal, where she died on September 13, 1919. Sister Mary Magdalen (Eliza D. Healy) was eventually placed in the sisters' vault in the cemetery located on Mont Royal, in the heart of Montreal.

Eugene Healy. (Brother) Born January 23, 1849, near Macon, Georgia, and brought to New York City in June 1851. His brother James placed him in the English College at Douai, France, in 1863, but Eugene left after one year. He traveled from job to job in various locations, including Utah. In 1876, Eugene served jail time in Boston. He remained in low-paying sales positions in the Boston area. Eugene apparently married, but his wife and children, if he had any, are not known. Eugene Healy died in March 1914.

APPENDIX 3

Original Charges Brought Against
Capt. Michael A. Healy in 1896 Trial[1]

Second Lieut. George M. Daniels placed two sets of charges.
First Lieut. Howard Emery placed charges.
First Asst. Eng. Levin T. Johns placed charges.

Charge 1.
   Conduct to the prejudice of good order and discipline. Seven specifications.
Charge 2.
   Conduct unbecoming an officer and gentleman. One specification.
Charge 3.
   Tyrannous and abusive conduct to inferiors. Four specifications.
Charge 4.
   Conduct detrimental to discipline. One specification.
Charge 5.
   Placing a vessel of the Government in a perilous position while in an intoxicated condition. One specification.

By Lieutenant Daniels (second set) and Lieutenant Emery (charges and specifications identical).

Charge 1.
   Insulting and abusive treatment of officers. Three specifications.

By Engineer Jones.

Charge 1.
   Drunkenness to the scandal of the Service. Two specifications.

Findings

First set of charges and specifications by Lieut. George M. Daniels:

Charge 1. Guilty.

Charge 2. Guilty.

Charge 3. Guilty.

Charge 4. Guilty.

Charge 5. Guilty.

Of the charge preferred by First Asst. Eng. Levin T. Jones.

Charge 1. Guilty.

Of the charges by First Lieut. Howard Emery and Second Lieut. George M. Daniels (second set).

Charge 1. Guilty.

Recommendation

And the Board therefore recommends that the accused officer, Capt. Michael A. Healy, United States Revenue Cutter Service, be dismissed from the service.

Board of Investigation

The Board of Investigation upheld the recommendation of the trial board and an addition requesting clemency. The board sent the following to the Secretary of the Treasury:

> Sir:
>
> Although the Board do not find any mitigating circumstances in the case of Capt. M. A. Healy, R.C.S., recently under investigation, we do not think that we should fail to call your attention to the valuable services performed by this officer during his connection with the Revenue Cutter Service, covering a period of nearly thirty years, and to respectfully recommend that such clemency as may be consistent with the gravity of the case and the welfare of the Revenue Cutter Service may be extended to him.

NOTES

Abbreviations

ADB   Archives, Diocese of Boston, Massachusetts.
ADP   Archives, Diocese of Portland, Maine.
AGU   Archives, Georgetown University, Washington, D.C.
AHC   Archives, College of the Holy Cross, Worcester, Massachusetts.
AJB   Archives, Josephite Brothers, Baltimore, Maryland.
AMJP   Archives, Maryland Jesuit Province, in AGU.
FAH   Frederick Aloysius Healy.
GDAH   Georgia Department of Archives and History, Atlanta, Georgia.
JAH   James Augustine Healy.
MAH   Michael Augustine Healy.
MJH   Mary Jane (Roach) Healy.
NARA   National Archives and Records Administration, Washington, D.C.
PFH   Patrick Francis Healy.
RG26   Record Group 26, Records of the U.S. Coast Guard, in NARA.

Introduction

1. An unidentified and undated newspaper clipping in a scrapbook located in the Papers of Elliot Snow, Container 24, Manuscript Division, Library of Congress, Washington, D.C., hereinafter cited as Snow, Scrapbook.

2. Ibid.

3. Quoted in Evans, *Coast Guard*, 121.

4. *The Morning Call* (San Francisco), August 31, 1904, 5, hereinafter this newspaper will be cited as *The Call*.

5. Snow, Scrapbook.

6. Charges Against RCS Officers, Seamen and Vessels. Legal Cases, ca. 1808–1896. General Court, Capt. M. A. Healy, 1896. Box 10, RG26, NARA, hereinafter cited as "General Court, Healy, 1896."

7. Ibid.

8. O'Toole, *Passing for White*, 14–20.

9. Ibid., 12–14.

10. Ibid., 20.

11. PFH to Fr. George Fenwick, December 11, 1854, AMJP.

12. JAH to Fenwick, December 21, 1854, AHC.

13. Healy, *Corwin, 1885,* 9; Van Dorn, *Oceanography,* 187.

14. Ray, *Eskimos of Bering Strait,* 200.

15. Diary, MJH, June 20, 1894, Michael A. Healy Papers, Huntington Library, San Marino, California, hereinafter MJH Diary, with appropriate date(s).

16. "General Court, Healy, 1896."

17. MJH Diary, September 22, 1894.

18. Elizabeth Cunningham to Albert S. Foley, March 1, 1951, Papers of Albert S. Foley, AJB, hereinafter cited as Foley Papers.

19. Foley to "Carol and Bo," July 1951, ibid.

20. Peter Guilday to Thomas O'Donnell, June 20, 1942, Box 3; Coleman Knot to O'Donnell, April 21, 1942, ibid.

21. Foley to Paul H. Johnson, July 10, 1974, "Michael Healy," ibid.

22. Foley, *Bishop Healy*; Foley, *Dream of an Outcaste.*

23. See "Michael A. Healy," Foley Papers.

24. Williams, "Healy," 430.

25. "Healy, Court, 1896."

26. Richard McKenna gives the best-written nonfiction description of an outrageous sailor act. His essay described Coxswain Duke Lee, "who wore chin whiskers, went barefoot, scarcely even talked, kept an ancient and equally silent parrot in number four hold and smoked opium in the cordage locker." In a bar in Shanghai's Blood Alley, he "vomited the contents of his stomach over a table, then used a pair of chopsticks to pick up the solid pieces and swallow them again." McKenna, "USS *Goldstar*," in Shenk, ed., *The Left-Handed Monkey Wrench,* 130.

27. Hensley, "Jack London's Use of Maritime History in *The Sea Wolf*," 1–8, completely dispels this myth.

28. Dennis L. Noble heard the latest telling of this story at a holiday gathering on December 18, 2004, in Sequim, Washington.

29. Stein, "Desperate and Dangerous Man," 39–45.

Chapter 1. The Georgia Plantation

1. "Years later, one of his sons [Patrick], became fascinated in old age by genealogy, sketched in more detail. The son traced the family to the town of Athlone." O'Toole, *Passing for White,* 6. See also Patrick F. Healy's genealogical notes of May 23 and September 18, 1884, in PFH Diaries, AHC.

2. The first researcher to publish books on the Healy family, Fr. Albert S. Foley, SJ (Foley, *Bishop Healy* and *Dream of an Outcaste*), also caused frustration for historians following him. Although he held a Ph.D. and spent many years researching the Healys, Father Foley, for some unaccountable reason, did not document his sources. Foley also did not place bibliographies in his two biographies concerning the older brothers of Michael A. Healy. Some of Father Foley's statements can be proved with a great deal of research, but others cannot. It is our opinion that much of what cannot be verified in Foley's two books came from Healy family members, who are

now deceased. Therefore, material attributed to Father Foley that the authors of this book could not personally locate will be prefaced in the narrative by "according to tradition," or "according to family tradition," with proper citation to Foley's works in the notes.

3. Father Foley has Michael Morris Healy enlisted in the British Army and ordered to Canada during the War of 1812. From there, he deserted and eventually made his way to Georgia. Foley, *Dream of an Outcast*, 1. Prof. James M. O'Toole, however, believes that this is just a family legend "that got better with each retelling." O'Toole, *Passing for White*, 6. For information on the cousin, see Carolyn White Williams, *Jones County*, 72. Edward W. Phillips, a professional genealogist, "searched several books on the origins of Irish Immigrants, looked for records on roster lists of War of 1812 participants from Canada (with no success), and searched a computerized list of Irish immigrants with only one finding[:] A Michael Healy arrived on the Brig *Foundling* from Sligo, [Ireland], at New York 30 June 1816." This seems a reasonable supposition, as Sligo is seventy-three miles north of Athlone. Phillips used the following sources—Passenger and Immigration Lists: Irish Immigrants to North America, 1803–1871; Family Tree Maker's Family Archives, CD #257 (Broderbund), at the Federal Records Center, NARA, Waltham, Massachusetts, e-mail, Phillips to Dennis L. Noble, June 13, 2005, page 1. Healy's sisters eventually returned to Ireland. O'Toole, *Passing for White*, 6.

4. The naturalization oath, dated April 3, 1818, is in Deed Book K (1818–1819): 144, Jones County, Microfilm copy in GDAH.

5. O'Toole, *Passing for White*, 6.

6. Ibid., 6–7, 12.

7. Ibid., 6.

8. Average temperature data comes from www.cityrating.com/cityweather.asp?city=Macon and www.worldtravels.com/travelguide/countries/Ireland/Climate/, both sites accessed October 13, 2004; Olmsted, *Seaboard Slave States*, 538; Sherwood, *Gazetteer of Georgia*, 50, 183–184; Hall, *Travels in North America*; quoted in Lane, ed., *Rambler in Georgia*, 79; O'Toole, *Passing for White*, 7.

9. For cotton production in Georgia, see Bonner, *Georgia Agriculture*, 51–63; Reidy, *From Slavery to Agrarian Capitalism*; Stone, "Economic Conditions in Macon, Georgia," 217–18.

10. O'Toole, *Passing for White*, 7–8.

11. Brown, *Slave Life in Georgia*, 171–79.

12. Coulter, *Georgia*, 57–58; Jordan, *White Over Black*, 262–64; slave populations are found in Appendix 1, Table A of Berlin, *Slaves Without Masters*, 396–97; Chapell, *Miscellanies of Georgia*, Part 2, 2; Flanders, "Two Plantations," 4.

13. Foley, *Dream of an Outcast*, 3.

14. Jones County Inferior Court Minutes (1824–1827): 251–54 and Jones County Superior Court Minutes, microfilm in the GDAH. The value of $200 is found in Economic History Service, "What Is the Relative Value?" www.eh.net, accessed October 14, 2004, hereinafter cited as "Relative value."

15. Foley, *Bishop Healy*, 7; Foley, *Dream of an Outcast*, 4.

16. Foley, *Bishop Healy*, 7–8; Foley, *Dream of an Outcast*, 3–5; O'Toole, *Passing for White*, 14; Williams, *Jones County*, 72–74; photocopy of an article by Natalie Ganley, "Patrick Healy—Georgetown's Second Founder," *Irish Echo* (July 1, 1984), AHC.

17. Foley, *Bishop Healy*, 8.

18. O'Toole, *Passing for White*, 14.

19. Ibid., 14–15.

20. Ibid., 17.

21. For Healy's slave holdings, see the federal slave census of 1830 and 1850, GDAH. Healy hired William Hornaday as his overseer; see 1850 census of free inhabitants of Jones County, microfilm, GDAH.

22. O'Toole, *Passing for White*, 20.

23. U.S. Census, Agriculture (Jones County), 1850. Microfilm in GDAH.

24. Morris, *Southern Slavery*. On the law of slavery in Georgia, see Jordan, *White Over Black*, 124–26, 169–70; Berlin, *Slaves Without Masters*, 139–40; Rogers, "Free Negro Legislation," 27–37; Flanders, "The Free Negro in Georgia," 250–72; O'Toole, *Passing for White*, 10.

25. Williams, *History of Jones County*, 72–74; O'Toole, *Passing for White*, 19.

26. O'Toole, *Passing for White*, 13–14.

27. Sale of the Healy estate in December is recorded in Jones County Superior Court, Book R, 390–91. Microfilm in GDAH.

28. Books in Healy's estate are listed in his estate on December 3 and 16, 1850, Jones County Court of Ordinary, Inventories, etc., N: 16–26, microfilm in GDAH.

29. Ibid., 23.

30. Ibid., 24.

31. Ibid., 25; Foley Papers.

32. Foley, *Bishop Healy*, 18–19; Foley, *Dream of an Outcaste*, 12–14.

33. O'Toole, *Passing for White*, 26.

34. Ibid., 26.

35. See Schultz, *Fire & Roses*.

36. O'Toole, *Passing for White*, 27.

37. Ibid., 28.

38. Material on the contents and inventories pertaining to Healy's will is found in the Jones County Court of Ordinary, Inventories, etc., M: 392–94; N: 16–26; P: 5–6; Q: 268–69; hereinafter cited as "Healy's will." The relative value of Eliza Clark Healy's trust fund is found in "Relative value."

39. Baptismal record, November 18, 1844, Thomas Mulledy Papers, 1: 2, AHC; confirmation record, June 21, 1845, Episcopal Register, Archives of the Archdiocese of Boston. The person recording the baptism erred in the boy's home county.

40. Quoted in Sharrow, "John Hughes and a Catholic Response," 255–56. Material on Catholic attitudes toward slavery can be found in Miller, "Slaves and Southern Catholicism," in John B. Boles, ed., *Masters and Slaves in the House of the Lord: Race and Religion in the American South, 1740–1870*, 127–52; "Abolition and Negro Equality," *Brownson's Quarterly Review*, 186–209. Ironically, Brownson's son attended Holy Cross with the Healys.

41. O'Toole, *Passing for White*, 34.

42. Ibid., 36–37.

43. JAH Diary, July 25, 1849, JAH Papers, ACHC.

44. Foley, *Dream of an Outcaste*, 26.

45. HCH to Fenwick, July 6, 1850, 71:13, AMJP.

46. O'Toole, *Passing for White*, 44, 49. In June 1975, Father Foley had a stone marker and plaque erected at the gravesite of Michael and Eliza. See photocopies of newspaper clippings in Foley Papers.

Chapter 2. Down to the Sea

1. The story of the missing diaries is yet another of the many twisted paths in the life of Michael A. Healy. The burning of the diaries by a later member of the family is detailed in the introduction, with the source given as the papers of Fr. Albert S. Foley. Yet, Foley, in his biography of Patrick F. Healy (*Dream of an Outcaste*, 293), states that the destruction of the volumes was "probably [the result] of the San Francisco fire in 1906." Although Foley is currently the only known source about the diaries, the authors are convinced that at one time Healy kept a diary. The circumstantial evidence pointing to this is simply that his brothers, James, Patrick, and Sherwood, all kept diaries. Mary Jane Healy also kept diaries while sailing on some patrols with Michael. In addition, Captain Healy told his son, Frederick, that if he kept a diary while on board the *Corwin* in 1882, he would buy him a shotgun. In other words, Michael A. Healy came from a family that practiced the keeping of diaries and passed this practice on to his wife and son. It is highly probable, therefore, that he kept a record of his exploits. Another reason to record his exploits would have been his desire to show his older brothers that he too succeeded in life. Mary Jane and Frederick Healy's diaries are housed in the Huntington Library, San Marino, California.

2. O'Toole, *Passing for White*, 45–50.

3. Ibid., 27, 45–46. The earnings of a laborer are found in U. S. Department of Commerce, *Historical Statistics*, 165.

4. Woodson, *Free Negro Slaves*, 3–4.

5. O'Toole, *Passing for White*, 46–47; Jones County Court of the Ordinary, Inventories, Appraisements, Sales, Returns, Book O, 1853–1854, 254. Microfilm copy in GDAH.

6. O'Toole, *Passing for White*, 49.

7. *The Matricula of The College of the Holy Cross*, 12. The 1851 fire at Holy Cross destroyed the records of classes offered. We used material found in Gleason, "Curriculum of the Catholic College," 102, and the published listing of a catalogue of classes in the 1856 *Catalogue of Holy Cross, 1856–1857*, located in AHC. Gleason's article used James A. Healy's diary of December 8, 1848, through August 24, 1849, as one of its main primary sources. The diary is found in AHC.

8. PFH to George Fenwick, November 1853, AMJP, located in AGU.

9. O'Toole, *Passing for White*, 80.

10. PFH to Fenwick, December 11, 1854, AMJP, AGU.

11. Quoted in Foley, *Dream of an Outcaste*, 51.

12. JAH to Fenwick, December 22, 1854, AMJP, AGU. James also sent the youngest sibling, Eugene, to Douai from 1863 to 1864 and also stated that it was not to train Eugene for the priesthood, but to provide a religious education. O'Toole, *Passing for White*, 99–102.

13. The Bible is sometimes referred to as the Douai Bible. *Catholic Encyclopedia*, 879–80.

14. One source also states that Eliza Clark Healy may have come from Central America and Michael may have wished to explore the land of his mother. Photocopy of an article by Natalie Ganley, "Patrick Healy—Georgetown's Second Founder," *Irish Echo* (July 1, 1984), AHC.

15. Quoted in Harlow, *The Making of a Sailor*, 4.

16. Raban, *Passage to Juneau*, 7.

17. See, Bolster, *Black Jacks*, and Nalty, *Strength for the Fight*, especially for the changing status of African Americans in the U.S. Navy.

18. The actual hawse pipe aboard a ship is "the iron castings in the bow through which the anchor chains run." Bradford, *Mariner's Dictionary*, 122.

19. Villiers, *Way of a Ship*, 171, 251.

20. Valle, *Rocks and Shoals*, endpapers.

21. Quoted in Villiers, *Way of a Ship*, 275.

22. Ibid., 171, 173.

23. Cordingly, *Women Sailors & Sailor's Women*, 109–15; Druett, *Hen Frigates*, 184–85. For a fictional account of one woman who took command of a ship, see the young adult book, Merlith, *Mary Patten's Voyage*, and another fictional work, Lasker, *Voyage of Neptune's Car*. The hospital at the U.S. Merchant Marine Academy is named after Mary Anne Patten. Druett, *Hen Frigates*, 185.

24. Foley, *Dream of an Outcaste*, 293.

25. MAH to Sheldon Jackson, March 1893, Alaska File of the Revenue Cutter Service, 1867–1914, National Archives Microfilm Publication, Microcopy Number 641, Roll 3, hereinafter cited as Alaska File, with letter date and roll number.

26. "How a Dead Man Made a Will," 17. See Raban, ed., *Oxford Book of the Sea*, 327–30, for an example of sea stories.

27. When Sherwood departed New York City to study in Paris, Hugh, then living in the city, rented a boat to follow the steamer out of the harbor. His dory, struck by another ship, threw him into the water. Although he managed to swim ashore, the exposure to the bad harbor water and September temperatures brought on a fever from which he did not recover. O'Toole, *Passing for White*, 59–60. For the lives of James, Patrick, Sherwood, and Martha to this period, see ibid., 42–64, 62–82.

28. O'Toole, *Passing for White*, 62–82.

29. Ibid., 46–47; U.S. Department of Commerce, *Historical Statistics*, 163.

30. O'Toole, *Passing for White*, 47–48.

31. Ibid., 48. The statement that Nancy was the sister of Eliza Clark Healy is attributed to Foley. Foley did not explain how he learned the genealogy of Eliza. Foley, *Dream of an Outcaste*, 26.

32. U.S. Department of Commerce, *Historical Statistics*, 165; McCusker, "How Much Is That?" 297–373; Derks, ed., *The Value of a Dollar*.

Within the Georgia Archives is the inventory of the Healy plantation. As mentioned in the narrative, someone in the Healy house had a musical instrument. One wonders today what Michael Morris and Eliza Clark would make of the fact that a musical was written about their lives. Hood and Hardy, Jr., *River of Redemption*.

33. O'Toole, *Passing for White*, 72.

34. Quoted in Villiers, *Way of a Ship*, 176.

Chapter 3. Love and the Sailor

1. Unless otherwise noted, all material on Mary Jane Roach and her immediate family is located in Phillips, "The Life of Mary Jane Roach."

2. Evans, *U.S. Coast Guard*, 5.

3. The naming of the U.S. Revenue Cutter Service and its command and control structure is complicated. As mentioned in the narrative, the service first became known as a system of cutters. "In April 1843, the secretary of the treasury established a Revenue-Marine Bureau, which centralized control but by 1854 the service was once again merely a 'system of cutters,' essentially under sectional (Collectors of the Ports), rather than national, control. Congress first referred to the service as a named organization in a law passed in 1863, in which the term 'Revenue-Cutter Service' received official sanction. Then, in 1871, the secretary of the treasury reestablished the Revenue-Marine Bureau and assigned it the duty of administering both the cutters and the lifesaving stations. On 3 March 1875, Congress formally established the Revenue-Marine Division, giving a permanence to a centralized, or headquarters, organization. By an act of 31 July 1894, Congress required the head of the division be a captain of the Revenue Cutter Service." Strobridge, "The Coast Guard, 1790–1983," 265–66, in Higham and Mrozek, eds., *A Guide to Military History: Supplement II*, 266. The machinations of the merging of the two services are in Noble, *That Others Might Live*, 149–55. In 1939, the U.S. Light-House Service was brought into the U.S. Coast Guard and, finally, in 1949, the Bureau of Marine Inspection became the last small federal maritime organization to make up the modern day U.S. Coast Guard. Noble, *Lighthouses & Keepers*, 37–41; Johnson, *Guardians of the Sea*, 261–61.

4. Chapelle, *American Sailing Ships*, 178–81, 182; Kern, *John Foster Williams*, 3–4, 11–12, 21–24.

5. Chapelle, *American Sailing Ships*, 11–13, 180. All vessels in the modern U.S. Coast Guard over sixty-five feet in length are called cutters.

6. Ibid., 176–78.

7. Noble, *Gulf Coast and Western Rivers*, 5; Canney, *Cutters, 1790–1935*, 11.

8. Ibid.

9. Strobridge and Noble, *Alaska and the USRCS*, 5.

10. Ibid., 5–11.

11. Ibid., 24–26.

12. Unless otherwise noted, all quoted material on Healy's application is in Revenue Cutter Service Personnel and Payroll, Applications for Positions in the Revenue Cutter Service, 1844–1880, Har to Hil, Box 12, RG26, NARA.

13. An obituary in a San Francisco newspaper, *The Call*, stated when "fifteen years old he ran away to sea and traveled the entire world in the merchant service, where he rapidly rose from a cabin boy to the position of captain." *The Call*, August 31, 1904, 5. Mr. Len Barnett, a professional maritime researcher who specializes in merchant marine records in London, England, exhaustively searched the records of Lloyds of London and the Public Records Office and could find no trace of Healy, or of the *Jumna*. (He also searched under the name *Juma*.) Barnett also found no record of the *Boomerang*, mentioned in Healy's story the authors relate in chapter 2.

The *Jumna* was built in 1855 in Portsmouth, New Hampshire, and boasted: two decks; three masts; a length of 166 feet, five inches; a breadth of thirty-one feet, seven inches; a depth of fifteen feet, eight inches; and a weight that measured seven hundred and eight tons. Custom House Declaration, RG 41 Bureau of Marine Inspection and Navigation, NARA.

Healy's recollection of his first ship was off by one year. However, it is still not possible to know the years Healy served on the *Jumna*, or apparently on any other ships sailing out of Boston. Normally, ships entering Boston would file their crew listing with the Custom House, but, according to Nathaniel Wiltzen, Archives Specialist/Volunteer Coordinator, NARA Northeast Region (Boston), "Unfortunately, a fire in 1894 at the Customs House warehouse destroyed most of customs records for Boston prior to 1890. There are virtually no crew lists that did survive for the time you are looking for (1855–1865). I did browse through the 7 crew lists that did survive for that period and I found no Jumna." E-mail, Edward Phillips to Dennis L. Noble, March 28, 2006.

14. "Governors of Massachusetts. John Albion Andrew 1818–1867," <www.mass.gov/state-house/massgovs/jandrew.htm>, accessed October 20, 2004.

15. Photocopy of marriage certificate, Michael Healy and Mary J. Roach, Cathedral of the Holy Cross, Boston, Massachusetts, January 31, 1865, located in Folder, "Mike Healy. Chapter IV. First Command," Foley Papers; Diary of Hillary Tucker, January 31, 1865, ADB. Mary Jane Roach's birth certificate gives her birth date as July 27, 1836, while her death certificate and her gravestone give it as 1837. We have used the date given on her birth certificate. See Phillips, "The Life of Mary Jane Roach." Martha Ann Healy, Michael's oldest sister, made her first profession of vows as a member of the Congregation de Notre Dame in September 1855 and was to be known as Sister Saint Lucie. She left the order in 1863 and married Jeremiah Cashman, of Boston, on July 25, 1865. Martha had one son and three daughters. Martha Ann (Healy) Cashman died on May 18, 1920, at Watertown, Massachusetts. O'Toole, *Passing for White*, 52–55, 172–76, 220–21.

16. *USRCS Registers, 1853–1875*, 69.

17. Service Record of Calvin Hooper, Records of Officer Personnel, 1797–1913, Entry 265 (NC-31), RG26, NARA, hereinafter cited as "Service Record, Hooper." The service records of the U.S. Revenue Cutter Service contain very little personal data, being mostly the hand-written records of transfers and promotions in large journals. There are, however, comments on disciplinary actions.

18. Service Record of Leonard G. Shepard, Records of Officer Personnel, 1797–1913, Entry 265 (NC-31), RG26, NARA, hereinafter cited as "Service Record, Shepard"; Leonard G. Shepard Collection, MVF-252, located in the files of the Historian of the U.S. Coast Guard, U.S. Coast Guard Headquarters, Washington, D.C., hereinafter cited as "Shepard," Historian, USCG.

19. Canney, *Cutters, 1790–1935*, 35; Strobridge and Noble, *Alaska and the USRCS*, 9–11; Service Record of Michael A. Healy, Records of Officer Personnel, 1797–1913, Entry 265 (NC-31), RG26, NARA, hereinafter cited as "Service Record, Healy."

20. "Service Record, Healy"; Phillips, "The Life of Mary Jane Roach"; The *Chase* was decommissioned in 1875, Canney, *Cutters, 1790–1935*, 34.

21. *USRCS Register, 1867*, 140.

22. The *Pawtuxet* was decommissioned March 31, 1867, Canney, *Cutters, 1790–1935*, 32; "Life of Mary Jane Roach"; "Service Record, Healy."

23. See Raymond Fisher, *Bering's Voyages*; Frost, ed., *Bering and Chirikov*.

24. Bailey, *Diplomatic History*, 363–71.

25. Strobridge and Noble, *Alaska and the USRCS*, 1.

26. Phillips, "The Life of Mary Jane Roach"; "Service Record, Healy"; The *Active* was disposed of later in 1867, Canney, *Cutters, 1790–1935*, 38.

27. "Service Record, Healy"; USCG, *Record of Movement*, 345.

28. Unless otherwise noted, all material on Healy's time on board the *Reliance* is located in

Transcript of log book of *Reliance*, Entry 157A, RG26, NARA; Bradford, *Mariner's Dictionary*, 127.

29. *USRCS Register, 1867*, 139–40.

30. Strobridge and Noble, *Alaska and the USRCS*, 35, 38–39.

31. Quoted in Murphy, *Rounding the Horn*, 253.

32. Ibid., 255–57.

33. "Michael A. Healy," Foley Papers.

34. Quoted in Landauer, *Scammon*, 16.

35. "Michael A. Healy," Foley Papers.

36. O'Toole is uncertain who kept the diary of this voyage, but believes it was "most probably Mary Jane Healy." O'Toole, *Passing for White*, 177–78, 255n11.

37. Quoted in MacPhail, "Early Days in San Diego," 31.

Chapter 4. Eastern Interlude

1. Unless otherwise noted, all material on the *Reliance*'s activities in Alaska are found in Abstracts of log book of the *Reliance*, 1867–1869, Entry 157A, RG26, NARA.

2. The members of the Chilcal tribe that visited the cutter on the afternoon of December 1, 1868, normally came from around Klukwan, near Haines and possibly near Skagway. The tribal members near the cutter on the afternoon of January 2, 1869, usually came from around Chilkoot Lake or possibly from a village around Skagway. The reasons why members of both of these tribes were at Sitka can include "any or all of the following: trading, potlaching, visiting relatives, warfare, or hiding from the naval authorities." E-mails, Rosemary Carlton, Curator, Sheldon Jackson Museum, Sitka, Alaska, to Dennis L. Noble, May 18–19, 2005.

3. MAH to the Secretary of the Treasury, January 10, 1868, Box 46, Letters from Officers, 1833–1869, RG26, NARA.

4. Unless otherwise noted, all material on Healy's voyage on the cutter *Lincoln*, and on the cutter itself, is found in USCG, *Record of Movements*, 403; Abstracts of log book of the *Lincoln*, May–November 1869, RG26, NARA (April is missing from the records); Muster Rolls for cutter *Lincoln*, May–November 1869, RG26, NARA (April is missing from the records).

5. "Service Record, Healy"; Phillips, "The Life of Mary Jane Roach."

6. *USRCS Officers, Register, 1865–1876*, 152.

7. "Service Record, Healy." For information on the *Seward*, see www.uscg.mil/hq/g-cp/history/WEBCUTTERS/Seward_1864.html, accessed November 2, 2004.

8. Phillips, "The Life of Mary Jane Roach."

9. Another older brother, Eugene, died in infancy and Hugh, the second son born to Michael Morris and Eliza, died of complications from an accident in 1853. O'Toole, *Passing for White*, 20, 59, 105–6, 113–18, 124–25.

10. "Service Record, Healy"; Canney, *Cutters, 1790–1935*, 38.

11. "Service Record, Healy"; Canney, *Cutters, 1790–1935*, 36.

12. Records of Officer Personnel, 1797–1913, Entry 265 (NC-31), RG26, NARA, hereinafter cited as "Service Record, Buhner."

13. Unless otherwise noted, all entries concerning the *Moccasin* are found in Abstracts of log book of the *Moccasin*, 1871–1872, Entry 157A, RG26, NARA.

14. "Service Record, Healy."

15. George S. Boutwell to S. W. Macy, December 2, 1871, Letters Sent, 1790–1871, Entry 143A (NC-31), 1871, Vol. 44, RG26, NARA, hereinafter cited as Letters Sent; O'Toole, *Passing for White*, 209.

16. "Service Record, Healy."

17. Boutwell to MAH, November 2, 1871, Letters Sent.

18. *Register USRCS Officers, 1865–1876*, 152.

19. Ibid.

20. "Service Record, Healy."

21. Canney, *Cutters, 1790–1935*, 44–45.

22. Abstracts of log book of the *Richard Rush*, 1874–1877, Entry 157A, RG26, NARA. Unless otherwise noted, all material on Healy while on board the *Rush* is from this source.

23. "Service Record, Healy"; Phillips, "The Life of Mary Jane Roach."

24. Phillips, "The Life of Mary Jane Roach"; *Historical Statistics*, 165.

25. "Service Record, Healy."

26. Captain Henriques was transferred to the cutter *Dobbin* at Baltimore, Maryland. "Service Record, Henriques."

27. Capt. George W. Bailey entered the USRCS as a third lieutenant on March 7, 1865, was promoted to second lieutenant on June 6, 1866, thence to first lieutenant on November 11, 1867, and obtained his captaincy on June 30, 1874, Noble, comp., *Historical Register*, 2.

28. Quoted in e-mail, Freya Anderson, Reference Librarian, Alaska State Library, to Dennis L. Noble, July 5, 2005.

29. Strobridge and Noble, *Alaska and the USRCS*, 1, 15.

30. Williams, *Bering Sea Dispute*, 7.

31. Strobridge and Noble, *Alaska and the USRCS*, 15. See also "Islands of the Seals," 1–125. For a monograph that strongly condemns the treatment of the Aleuts who worked to harvest the seals, see Jones, *Century of Servitude*.

32. Martin, *The Golden Fleece*, 30.

33. Van Nostrand, "The Seals Are About Gone," 12–14.

34. Strobridge and Noble, *Alaska and the USRCS*, 16.

35. Van Nostrand, "The Seals Are About Gone," 14, 16.

36. A handwritten and undated history of the U.S. Revenue Cutter Service on the stationery of the Treasury Department, 6, in Alaska File, Roll 19. The history seems to be from the U.S. Revenue Cutter Service to the Department of State.

37. Capt. George W. Bailey to John Sherman, Secretary of the Treasury, August 8, 1877, "Alaska File," Roll 1. Unless otherwise noted, all letters from Captain Bailey concerning the 1877 Alaska patrol are from the "Alaska File," Roll 1, and only the dates will be cited.

38. Ibid.

39. A few of the log books from Mount Ballyhoo are stored at the Historian of the U.S. Coast Guard's office, U.S. Coast Guard Headquarters, Washington, D.C., hereinafter cited as Historian.

40. Bailey to Sherman, August 8, 1877.

41. Ibid., November 8, 1877.

42. Ibid.

43. Ibid.

44. "Service Record, Healy"; Canney, *Cutters, 1790–1935*, 38.

45. Unless otherwise noted, all entries concerning the cutter *Chandler* are found in Abstracts of log book of the *Chandler*, 1878–1880, Entry 157A, RG26, NARA. Healy's service record states that he reported to his next cutter on May 20, 1877, but the abstract of the log of the *Chandler* shows otherwise.

46. MAH to unknown politician, October 20, 1890, "Alaska File," Roll 2.

47. "Service Record, Hooper."

Chapter 5. Healy's Polar Passion

1. John, *Libby*, 14.

2. Mary Jane and Fredrick lived in the household of Harriet K. Floyd in Portland, Maine. Phillips, "The Life of Mary Jane Roach," n. 25.

3. Bockstoce, *Whales, Ice, & Men*, 21, 25.

4. Quoted in ibid., 23.

5. Ibid., 21.

6. Ibid., 21, 25.

7. Quoted in ibid., 23.

8. Bockstoce, *Steam Whaling*, 17.

9. Ibid.

10. Ibid.

11. Ibid.

12. Ibid.

13. Bockstoce, *Whales, Ice, & Men*, 100, 346–47.

14. Bockstoce, *Steam Whaling*, 20.

15. Ibid., 20–21.

16. For a discussion of Franklin's expedition and other expeditions to the Canadian Arctic regions, see Delgado, *Across the Top of the World*.

17. Lloyd, *Mr. Barrow*, 144.

18. Mowat, *The Polar Passion*, 11.

19. Quoted in Guttridge, *Icebound*, 17.

20. Ibid., 36–41.

21. Ibid., 68–69. Young mounted two private expeditions in the attempt both to search for the lost Franklin Expedition and to sail through the Northwest Passage in a single season. The first began in 1875, but impenetrable ice in Peel Sound forced his ship to retreat. He started again the following year, only to be diverted by the Admiralty to check on the government's expedition at Smith Sound. Young never tried again. Delgado, *Across the Top of the World*, 175; Savours, *Search for the Northwest Passage*, 304.

22. Quoted in Guttridge, *Icebound*, 162.

23. Williams, "Healy," 52–53; Evans, *Coast Guard*, 102–3.

24. E. W. Clark to Calvin L. Hooper, May 15, 1880, Revenue Marine Semi-Official Correspondence, RG26, NARA.

25. Ibid.

26. USCG, *Record of Movements*, 191–93; Canney, *Cutters, 1790–1935*, 44–45.

27. Unless otherwise noted, all material on the 1880 cruise of the *Corwin* is from Hooper, *Corwin, 1880*.

28. Baker, *Geographic Dictionary of Alaska*, 553.

29. Bailey, *Report Upon Alaska*, 26–27.

30. Article from unknown publication, with a handwritten "1888" on it, page 81, Scrapbook of MJH, located in the Michael A. Healy Papers, Huntington Library, San Marino, California, hereinafter cited as MJH Scrapbook, with appropriate date(s) and page(s), when provided in the scrapbook.

31. For a brief history of the *Reliance/Leo*, see Hinckley, "Cutter, Smuggler, Colporteur" in *The Sea in Alaska's Past*, 182–205.

32. Quoted in Bockstoce, *Whales, Ice, & Men*, 176–79. Gerald O. Williams has Captain Bauldry's name as "Baudry" and his ship as the "*Helen Marr*." We have used Bockstoce's spelling for both names, as it is consistent in both of his works on whaling in the Arctic.

33. According to Williams, Healy was in charge of the surveying. Williams, "Healy," 60–61.

34. Bockstoce, *Whales, Ice, & Men*, 179.

35. Ibid.

36. Guttridge, *Icebound*, 176–79, 184–85, 203, 235, 251, 258.

37. Williams, "Healy," 69; MJH Scrapbook, 81.

38. Hooper to Clark, October 23, 1880, RG26, NARA.

39. Bailey, *Report Upon Alaska*, 3.

40. Clark to Healy, November 15, 1880, Revenue Marine Semi-Official Correspondence, RG26, NARA. There is no notation of a reprimand in Healy's service record.

41. Ibid.

42. Ibid.

43. Clark to Healy, December 9, 1880, Revenue Marine Semi-Official Correspondence, RG26, NARA.

44. "Service Record, Healy"; Healy's cruise reports are located in Alaska File, Roll 1.

Chapter 6. Cannons, Expeditions, Shipwrecks, and Reindeer

1. Quoted in Hinckley, "Punitive," Part 1, 8.

2. In 1864, Col. John M. Chivington, of the Colorado militia, led an attack of volunteers on the Cheyenne village of Chief Black Kettle at Sand Creek, Colorado. Most historians of the American Indian War period agree that Chief Black Kettle was a peace-seeking Native American and that what took place at Sand Creek can rightfully be called a massacre. Four years later, the ill-fated Black Kettle was attacked again, this time on the Washita River in Oklahoma Territory by Col. George A. Custer and the Seventh Cavalry. Although this second attack was not on the same scale as the attack at Sand Creek, many historians also agree that there was nothing to be proud of about this engagement, and it received much criticism in the press. For information on both incidents, see Utley, *Frontier Regulars*, 97, 111, 113, 114, 150, 152, 408. For the Washita, see Greene, *Washita*.

3. USCG, *Record of Movements*, 193.

4. Ibid., 193–94; Bockstoce, *Steam Whaling*, 80. There was another *Mary and Helen* built by the same shipbuilders in 1882. Bockstoce, *Steam Whaling*, 82.

5. De Laguna, *A Tlingit Community*, 25.

6. Ibid.

7. Ibid., 158.

8. Hinckley, "Punitive Action," 6.

9. Ibid., 9.

10. Quoted in ibid., 8.

11. Hinckley, "Punitive Action," 9.

12. De Laguna, *A Tlingit Community*, 159.

13. Ibid.

14. Hinckley, "Punitive Action," 43.

15. Morris, *1879 Report*, 126.

16. Quoted in Hinckley, "Punitive Action," 44.

17. Beardslee, *1882 Report*, 13.

18. De Laguna, *A Tlingit Community*, 162.

19. Beardslee, *1882 Report*, 13.

20. De Laguna, *A Tlingit Community*, 162.

21. Morris, *1882 Report*, 2.

22. Ibid.

23. Ibid.

24. Ibid.

25. Ibid.

26. Healy, *1882 Report*, 2.

27. De Laguna, *A Tlingit Community*, 165.

28. Morris, *1882 Report*, 2.

29. Ibid.

30. Merriman's letter is within Merriman, *Report*, 4.

31. Ibid.

32. De Laguna, *A Tlingit Community*, 166.

33. Merriman, 2.

34. De Laguna, *A Tlingit Community*, 169.

35. Ibid., 159. On October 21, 1973, the residents of Angoon approved the offer of $90,000 from the federal government as reparations for the bombardment by the *Corwin*. *Southeastern Alaska Empire* (Juneau), October 24, 1973, 1.

36. USCG, *Record of Movements*, 194.

37. Caswell, *Arctic Frontiers*, 198.

38. Strobridge and Noble, *Alaska and the USRCS*, 82–83.

39. Murphy, "Cutter Captain," 1, 6–7.

40. Healy, *Corwin, 1884*, 29.

41. Ibid., 57, 74.

42. Healy, *Corwin, 1885*, 6, 83.

43. Murphy, "Cutter Captain," 13.

44. Bockstoce, *Whales, Ice, & Men*, 304.

45. Unless otherwise noted, all material on Healy's rescue work on August 10, 1885, is in Healy, *Corwin, 1885*, 9–10.

46. Van Dorn, *Oceanography*, 187.

47. Cantwell's description of his expedition is in Healy, *Corwin, 1884*, 23–52; Caswell, *Arctic Frontiers*, 199–200. Neither Healy nor McLenegan recorded Seaman Nelson's first name.

48. Ibid.

49. Healy, *Corwin, 1884*, 17.

50. Healy, *Corwin, 1885*, 88.

51. Cantwell, "Healy's Reindeer," 27.

52. In 2005, the highest price offered by a rare book dealer for the 1884 report was $566.87, while the 1885 report price tag was $297.15. See American Book Exchange, www.abe.com, accessed January 5, 2005.

53. Healy, *Corwin, 1884*, 20.

54. Ibid.

55. Ibid.

56. U.S. Revenue Cutter Service, *Overland Expedition*; Cantwell, *Report of the Nunivak*.

Chapter 7. The Captain and the Immortal *Bear*

1. Wead, *Gales, Ice, and Men*, 4.

2. For a very good account of the Greely Expedition, see Guttridge, *Ghosts of Cape Sabine*.

3. Noble and Strobridge, "Arctic Adventures of the *Thetis*," 3.

4. Ibid.

5. Wead, *Gales, Ice, and Men*, 8–9.

6. Quoted in Caswell, *Arctic Frontiers*, 111–12.

7. Ibid., 113.

8. Noble and Strobridge, "Arctic Adventures of the *Thetis*," 4.

9. Wead, *Gales, Ice, and Men*, 61–63.

10. Healy, *Corwin, 1885*, 20.

11. Ibid.

12. USCG, *Record of Movements*, 164.

13. Officers, *Below Zero*, 11.

14. Wead, *Gales, Ice, and Men*, 104; Healy, *Corwin, 1884*, 17.

15. Wead, *Gales, Ice, and Men*, 107.

16. "Service Record, Healy"; Wead, *Gales, Ice, and Men*, 110–11.

17. Healy, *Corwin, 1885*, 19.

18. Allen, "Saved by the *Bear*," in Heckman, ed., *Yankees Under Sail*, 119; MJH, Scrapbook.

19. Allen, "Saved by the *Bear*," 120.

20. Ibid.

21. The original block of wood carved by Vincent is in the collection the New Bedford Whaling Museum.

22. MJH, Scrapbook.

23. Quoted in Allen, "Saved by the *Bear*," 125; MJH, Scrapbook.

24. Unless otherwise noted, all material on the Point Barrow Refuge is found in Bockstoce, "Point Barrow," 5–10, 20–21.

25. Why did Healy change his mind? Even Bockstoce, a recognized expert on Arctic Alaska, writes, "It is less easy to understand Healy's apostasy," especially after his long experience in Arctic waters and his strong support of the station. Bockstoce, "Point Barrow," 20.

26. "Today the station remains under [the ownership of the Cape Smythe Whaling and Trading Company] and stands, slightly altered, as Brower's Restaurant—Arctic Alaska's oldest frame building—near where it was built in 1889." Bockstoce, "Point Barrow," 21.

27. "Service Record, Healy"; Alaska File, Reel 3. Healy, *Corwin, 1884*, 22.

28. MAH to Shepard, April 28, 1893, Alaska File, Reel 3.

29. PFH Diary, June 18 and December 7–11, PFH Papers. Diary and papers located in AHC.

30. Unless otherwise noted, all quotes from newspaper article are found in MJH, Scrapbook, 83.

Chapter 8. "Monster Healy"

1. R. W. Bartleman to Secretary of the Treasury, March 8, 1889, copy located in Box 8, "Michael Healy," Foley Papers; Letter, I. H. Maynard to Bartleman, March 16, 1889, ibid. See Howe, *The Humane Society*, for information on the society.

2. I. H. Maynard to Bartleman, March 16, 1889, and Maynard to Bartleman, March 16, 1889, "Michael Healy," Foley Papers.

3. The civilian head of the Revenue Marine Bureau in the Treasury Department, Sumner I. Kimball, reorganized the lifesaving stations within the Treasury in 1871. This eventually became U.S. Life-Saving Service (USLSS) in 1878. Kimball had two chains of command reporting to him. One was administrative and made up of personnel from the USLSS. The other consisted of U.S. Revenue Cutter Service (USRCS) officers. Their duties centered on inspecting the stations of the USLSS in each lifesaving district. Furthermore, they were required to investigate any shipwrecks within their area of operations. Lieutenants carried out the actual inspections and investigations. The lieutenants in each district reported to a Captain of the USRCS, who reported to Kimball. The East and West coasts had one captain. See Noble, *That Others Might Live*; E-mail, Dr. Robert M. Browning, Jr., Chief Historian of the U.S. Coast Guard, to Dennis L. Noble, January 24, 2005.

4. Unless otherwise noted, all quotations concerning the 1889 patrol are found in the diary of Dr. James Taylor White, Accession number 4966, Special Collections, University of Washington Libraries, Seattle, Washington, hereinafter cited as "White diary, 1889."

5. Record of Letters of the U.S. Revenue Marine Service, April 11, 1888 to October 20, 1890, in U.S. Revenue Cutter Service, Manuscript Division, Library of Congress, Washington, D.C., hereinafter cited as Record of Letters of the USRMS.

6. Williams, "Healy," 263–64.

7. Unless otherwise noted, all newspaper accounts concerning the 1890 hearing are found in Snow, Scrapbook. One of the handbills is preserved in Snow, Scrapbook.

8. Murphy, "Two Standards," 374.

9. Ibid. The "Major" was for his former Civil War service.

10. Unless otherwise noted, all material dealing with the 1890 hearing is located in "Charges Against RCS Officers, Seamen and Vessels, Legal Cases, ca. 1830–1896," folder "Capt. M. A. Healy," Box 11, RG26, NARA, hereinafter cited as "Healy, Court, 1890." Some of the records for the 1890 hearing have been inadvertently placed in Box 10, Healy's 1896 hearing. Researchers should consult both boxes.

Chapter 9. The Czar of the North

1. MJH to PFH, July 23, 1884, Folder 2, Box 2, Patrick F. Healy Papers, AGU.

2. MJH Diary, June 20, 1894.

3. Stewart, *Sheldon Jackson*, 18–23, 31, 35–38.

4. Tower, *Reading, Religion, Reindeer*, 2.

5. Montgomery, "Murder of Thornton," 167.

6. Jackson, "Education in Alaska, 1890–1891," 957–58.

7. Montgomery, "Murder of Thornton," 168.

8. Ibid.; Smith and Smith, *Ice Window*, 7.

9. Montgomery, "Murder of Thornton," 168.

10. Ibid.

11. Ibid.

12. Quoted in Bockstoce, *Whales, Ice, & Men*, 189.

13. Hooper, *Corwin, 1880*, 20.

14. Bailey, *Letter to Secretary of the Treasury, 1880*, 15.

15. Nelson, "The Eskimo in Bering Strait," 299.

16. Bockstoce, *Whales, Ice, & Men*, 189.

17. Quoted in Bockstoce, *Whales, Ice, & Men*, 189–91.

18. Ibid., 191.

19. Montgomery, "Murder of Thornton," 168.

20. "Notes for Neda S. Thornton," March 21, 1933, William Thomas Lopp Papers, Ax58, Special Collections & University Archives, University of Oregon Libraries, Eugene, Oregon, hereinafter "Notes," Lopp Papers.

21. Montgomery, "Murder of Thornton," 168.

22. Ibid., 169.

23. Johnshoy, *Apaurak in Alaska*, 105.

24. Ray, *Eskimos of Bering Strait*, 246.

25. Ibid., 247.

26. Ibid.

27. MJH Diary, July 16, 1890.

28. Record of Letters of the USRMS.

29. Ray, *Eskimos of Bering Strait*, 246.

30. Ibid., 247.

31. Unless otherwise noted, all material and quotations on the shooting of the native is from Brower's autobiography, Brower and Anson, *Fifty Years Below Zero*, 145–48.

32. Ray, *Eskimos of Bering Strait*, 246.

33. Hooper, *Corwin, 1880*, 7–12; Cantwell, "Healy's Reindeer," 27.

34. Cantwell, "Healy's Reindeer," 27.

35. Ray, *Eskimos of Bering Strait*, 228.

36. MAH to W. D. Harris, December 6, 1890, "Alaska File," Roll 1.

37. Ibid.

38. Ray, *Eskimos of Bering Strait*, 228.

39. Imlay, "Seal Patrol," 28–32. Unless otherwise noted, all quotes about the deaths are located in MAH to Capt. Leonard G. Shepard, June 9, 1891, "Alaska File," Roll 2. The official letter to the Secretary of the Treasury is at the same location.

40. MJH to "My Dearest Brother," June 10, 1891, located in the Papers of PFH, AHC. Even though the letter is in the papers of Patrick Healy, within the letter are references to the fact that the "Dearest Brother" had not seen Alaska, which indicate that the letter is not addressed to Patrick Healy, who had made a journey to Alaska on board the *Bear*. Near the end of Bishop James A. Healy's life, brother Patrick put his older brother's papers in order. It is believed that the letter then made its way into Patrick's papers.

41. MJH Diary, June 6–7, 1891.

42. The enlisted sailors could not be buried with military honors, as only the commissioned officers of the USRCS possessed a military status. See Imlay, "Seal Patrol," 31–32.

"The present feature called Icy Bay was filled with ice in 1891. The feature then called Icy Bay was just to the east, at the mouth of the Yahtse River. I'd guess that the victims were probably buried on the first beach ridge above the high tide mark. To the best of my knowledge, there is no monument [to the sailors.]" E-mail, Dr. Geoffrey T. Bleakley, Historian, Wrangell–St. Elias National Park and Preserve, Copper River, Alaska, to Dennis L. Noble, February 7, 2005.

43. Sherwood, *Exploration of Alaska*, 80.

44. Unless otherwise noted, all quotes concerning the purchase of the first reindeer are located in Log Book of U.S. Revenue Steamer *Bear*, July 11, 1891, through September 21, 1891, Entry 159, RG26, NARA, hereinafter cited as *Log, Bear*, with appropriate date(s); Diary of Sheldon Jackson, July 11, 1891, through September 21, 1891, Sheldon Jackson Papers, Presbyterian Historical Society, Philadelphia, Pennsylvania, hereinafter cited as SJ, PHS. Charles A. Anderson edited this diary and it is located in the following: Jackson, "Exploring for Reindeer in Siberia," Part 1, 1–24; Jackson, "Exploring for Reindeer in Siberia," Part 2, 87–114; Imlay, "Seal Patrol."

John C. Cantwell wrote a long, detailed article on the purchase of the first reindeer in 1935. Cantwell's biographer, John F. Murphy, however, points out Cantwell was not present at the time, having been transferred to the School of Instruction in April 1887. Although there is some evidence that Healy did not hold Cantwell in high esteem, Cantwell appears to have respected Healy's abilities as a seaman. Murphy believes the account "contains details known only to the participants and is probably the account given to Cantwell by Healy." Murphy, "Cutter Captain," 49n17. See Cantwell, "Captain Healy's Reindeer," 26–29, 58–60 for another view of what took place in Siberia.

45. *Log, Bear*, August 27, 1891; Bockstoce and Batchelder, "Gazetteer of Whaler's Place Names," 261, 263.

46. MJH Diary, August 21, 1891.

47. MJH Diary, August 28, 1891.

48. Healy to wardroom officers, September 1, 1891, Andrews Papers, Sheldon Jackson College, Sitka, Alaska.

49. USCG, *Record of Movements*, 165.

50. "Service Record, Healy"; Secretary of the Treasury to Secretary of the Interior, December 15, 1891, Letters Sent, Vol. 90, Entry 144C, RG26, NARA.

51. The first reindeer were "placed on Amaknak and Unalaska islands without herders, merely, as Jackson said, 'to answer the question whether the reindeer could be purchased and transported alive.' At the end of two years, all had died." Ray, *Eskimos of Bering Strait*, 229.

52. Jackson, "Report on Education in Alaska," 946.

53. Montgomery, "Murder of Thornton," 169.

54. "Notes," Lopp Papers.

55. Smith and Smith, *Ice Window*, 4.

56. Ibid., 23.

57. Ibid.

58. Ibid., 24.

59. Ibid., 45.

60. Ibid., 50.

61. Ibid., 52–53.

62. Thornton, "Incidents in Alaska Life," 363.

63. Montgomery, "Murder of Thornton," 171.

64. Ray, *Eskimos of Bering Strait*, 247.

65. Montgomery, "Murder of Thornton," 171.

66. Ibid., 171–72.

67. Ibid., 172.

68. Ibid.

69. Ibid.

70. Ibid.

71. Quoted in Ray, *Eskimos of Bering Strait*, 248.

72. Montgomery, "Murder of Thornton," 172.

73. Smith and Smith, *Ice Window*, 75.

74. Ibid., 73.

75. Ibid., 91.

76. Montgomery, "Murder of Thornton," 172.

77. Smith and Smith, *Ice Window*, 93.

78. Ibid., 66.

79. Ibid., 93.

80. MAH to Sheldon Jackson, March 5, 1893, "Alaska File," Roll 3; Letter, Healy to Commissioner of Education, December 17, 1894, Ibid.

81. MAH to Jackson, April 4, 1892, Correspondence, 1891–1894, SJ, PHS; MAH to Jackson, "Alaska File," Roll 3.

82. Charles F. Shoemaker to MAH, March 26, 1895, Semi-Official Correspondence, March 20, 1895 through January 4, 1897, RG26, NARA.

83. MAH to Jackson, "Alaska File," Roll 3.

84. "Story of Sinrock Mary," n.d., n.p., a handwritten, undated manuscript in Lopp Papers, hereinafter cited as "Story of Sinrock Mary." We have left the original syntax of the manuscript

as recorded, so readers may "hear" Mary's voice, which may have been very close to that of the unknown recorder.

85. Ray, "Sinrock Mary," 98–99.

86. Ray, *Eskimos of Bering Strait*, 218.

87. "Story of Sinrock Mary."

88. Ibid.

89. Ray, "Sinrock Mary," 101.

90. Quoted in ibid., 103.

91. *The Call*, September 13, 1898, 2.

92. London, *The Sea Wolf*, 128. Mineola, N.Y.: Dover Publications, 2000.

93. Hinckley, "Rustlers of the North Pacific," 27.

94. Ibid.

95. The Library of Congress' catalog lists many official reports concerning seals and published papers of the arbitration, but only two books on the history of the Bering Sea Controversy: Williams, *The Bering Sea Fur Dispute*, and Gay, *American Fur Seal Diplomacy*.

96. Hinckley, "Rustlers of the North Pacific," 28.

97. Cooling, "Introduction," in Evans, *A Sailor's Log*, xxii.

98. Quoted in ibid., xxviii; Turk, "Robley D. Evans: Master of Pugnacity," in Bradford, *Admirals of the New Steel Navy*, 80–82.

99. Evans, *A Sailor's Log*, 324–25.

100. Ibid., 342–43.

101. "Alaska File," Roll 3.

102. MAH to Nelson, November 28, 1892, Area 9, RG45, Naval Records Collection of the Office of Naval Records and Library, Area Files, NAB; Nelson to the Secretary of the Navy, December 17, 1892, Area 9, RG45.

103. Evans, *A Sailor's Log*, 371.

104. Ibid., 373–74.

105. Cooling, "Introduction," xxiii.

106. Hinckley, "Rustlers of the North Pacific," 29.

107. Ibid., 29–30. For the diplomatic and political machinations concerning the controversy, see Bailey, "The North Pacific Sealing Convention of 1911," 1–14.

108. Most accounts of the fur seals state that, once the pressure of indiscriminate hunting passed and the change in fashion occurred, the mammals made a large comeback. By 2005, however, scientists and those who live on the Pribilofs had noticed a marked decline in the seal population. The reason for the decline is not yet known. See O'Harra, "A Puzzle in the Pribilofs," 14–20.

109. The greatest of all ironies concerning the reindeer project—a circumstance that may indeed shed a different light on everything that has ever been written about the project—is reported by anthropologist Dorothy Jean Ray in her classic book *The Eskimos of Bering Strait, 1650–1898* (Seattle: University of Washington Press, 1975). "Even so," she reported, "Lopp, who later became an important figure in the reindeer industry, said that Jackson's plan to import reindeer may have rested on merely a quip because 'Healy was a critical kidder and told Jackson [that the Eskimos] needed reindeer more than schools.'" Ray gives as evidence for this startling quote a

"handwritten note from Lopp inserted in C. L. Andrews' bound reindeer reports, Andrews Collection, Sheldon Jackson College, Sitka, Alaska" (page 227 and 227n4). In October 2004, Dennis L. Noble attempted to locate in the college's library the note in the Andrews' bound reindeer reports, with no success. In a letter to Noble, Ray states she did not make a copy of the note. She feels, and Noble agrees, that, unfortunately, the note, in the more than thirty years since her book came out, has been lost or misplaced. Letter, Ray to Noble, November 18, 2004.

110. Bradford, *Mariner's Dictionary*, 26.

111. Foley, "Michael Healy," AJB.

Chapter 10. "I Steer By No Man's Compass But My Own"

1. Williams, "Healy," 4–6.

2. "General Court, Healy, 1896."

3. Williams, "Healy," 4–6.

4. "General Court, Healy, 1896."

5. Williams, "Healy," 6–7; "General Court, Healy, 1896."

6. "General Court, Healy, 1896."

7. Williams, "Healy," 6–7.

8. "General Court, Healy, 1896."

9. Ibid.

10. Williams, "Healy," 20–21.

11. "General Court, Healy, 1896."

12. Ibid.

13. Williams, "Healy," 20–21.

14. Ibid., 419–20.

15. "General Court, Healy, 1896."

16. Williams, "Healy," 419–20; "General Court, Healy, 1896."

17. Williams, "Healy," 418; William R. Wells II, who has spent many years researching the records of the U.S. Revenue Cutter Service, states that a number of senior officers near the time of Healy's trial were accused officially of excessive drinking, e-mail, Wells to Noble, June 6, 2003.

18. Quoted in Foley, *Dream of an Outcaste*, 24.

19. Unless otherwise noted, all quotations concerning the events leading up to the trial, the trial itself, and the aftermath of the trial, are found in Snow, Scrapbook. In most cases, the dates and sources of the newspaper clippings are not identified.

20. Williams, "Healy," 421–27.

21. JAH to Fred Healy, December 3, 1895, ADP.

22. Lieut. Comdr. Frank A. Garforth, RN, to MAH, November 25, 1896; MAH to the Secretary of the Treasury, December 2, 1896, enclosing letter of Garforth; Garforth to Carlisle, December 12, 1896, RG26, NARA.

23. "General Court, Healy, 1896."

24. Ibid.

25. Ibid.

26. Ibid.

27. Ibid.

28. Ibid.

29. Ibid.

30. Ibid.

31. Ibid.

32. Lieut. Reynolds to Secretary of the Treasury, January 26, 1896; Hamlin to Buhner, January 30, 1896, RG26, NARA.

33. "General Court, Healy, 1896."

34. Unless otherwise noted, for all material on Sharp, see Frank Milligan, "The Best Nantucketer of Us All," Nantucket Historical Association, www.nha.org/history/hn/HNBenSharp.htm, accessed February 2, 2005. Sharp died in 1915. The American artist Thomas Eakins (1844–1916) painted an oil-on-canvas portrait of Doctor Sharp entitled "The Oboe Player (Portrait of Dr. Benjamin Sharp)" in 1903. His widow donated the painting to the Philadelphia Museum of Art in 1944; see www.davidrumsey.com/amico/amico1344080110118.html, accessed February 2, 2005.

35. Most of the potato incident is also recorded in "General Court, Healy, 1896."

36. Williams, "Healy," 443.

37. "General Court, Healy, 1896."

38. Ibid.

39. Ibid.

40. Ibid.

41. Ibid.

42. U.S. Revenue Cutter Service Special Order Number 20, June 8, 1896, 2, "Alaska File," Roll 5, hereinafter cited as "Special Order 20," with appropriate page(s).

43. "Special Order 20," 2–3.

44. Diary, 245–46, Charles S. Hamlin Papers, Manuscript Division, Library of Congress, Washington, D.C.

45. Quoted in Williams, "Healy," 430.

46. "Special Order 20," 3.

Chapter 11. "A Desperate and Dangerous Man"

1. For a detailed examination of the disaster, see Bockstoce, "Arctic Whaling Disaster," 27–42; Bockstoce, *Whales, Ice, & Men*, 316.

2. Bockstoce, *Whales, Ice, & Men*, 318–19.

3. "It was thought that Walker, had he pressed on, should have beaten Tilton by a month. Later the men learned that Walker had spent valuable weeks drinking at Herschel Island." Ibid., 319.

4. For a brief biography of Spreckels, see "San Diego Biographies, John D. Spreckels (1853–1926)," <sandiegohistory.org/bio/spreckels/spreckels.htm>, accessed February 11, 2005; *The Call*, November 9, 1897, 1–2.

5. Unless otherwise noted, all quotes concerning *The Call*'s efforts to move the government to undertake an expedition are found in *The Call*, November 7 and 9, 1897, pages 1, 2.

6. *The Call*, November 9, 1897, 1.

7. E-mail, Dr. Robert M. Browning, Historian of the U.S. Coast Guard, to Noble, November

21, 2005. Samuel J. Call was born in Missouri in 1858. He received a medical degree from Cooper Medical College in San Francisco. He died in Hollister, California, on February 16, 1909. Cocke, "Dr. Samuel J. Call," 181–88.

8. *Overland Relief Expedition*, 50–51.

9. For a short, concise account of the expedition, see Foundation, *Overland Relief Expedition*.

10. Ibid.

11. *Overland Relief Expedition*, preface, n.p.

12. *The Call*, September 13, 1898, 2.

13. For years, the only published work, other than the official report, solely devoted to the Overland Relief Expedition, remained Foundation, *Overland Relief Expedition*, along with a few scattered articles. Beginning in 2005, however, interest in the expedition began to revive. Works representative of this renewed interest in the Overland Relief Expedition include Shallow, *Rescue at the Top of the World*, which is not, however, an entirely historical work as it contains imaginary dialogue, and Taliaferro, *In a Far Country*.

Since 1897–1898, the Overland Relief Expedition has been held as one of the outstanding examples of the USRCS's humanitarian efforts in Alaska. Buried in a few early memoirs of those who either explored or lived in the Far North, however, are comments that question the need for the reindeer drive. The noted Arctic explorer, Vilhjalmur Stefansson, for example, wrote that it "was as heroic an undertaking then as the carrying of mail is to-day to Point Barrow, and is done three times a winter for the munificent pay of the American postal department." Stefannson, *The Friendly Arctic*: 580. Ray, in *The Eskimos of Bering Strait*, 239–40, also feels the expedition needless. Bockstoce, "Arctic Whaling Disaster," 41, sums up the comments. While it now appears that the whalers were not in danger of starvation, this does not mean that the USRCS knew this at the time. The reindeer drive still remains an excellent true-life adventure story.

14. Quoted in Williams, "Healy," 464.

15. "Service Record, Healy."

16. Quoted in Williams, "Healy," 467.

17. Ibid., 464.

18. Foley is the only person who has written of Fred's expulsion from Santa Clara College. He implies that the expulsion took place shortly after Patrick Healy sailed with Michael in 1883, and that the annulled marriage took place shortly after the patrol ended. Foley, however, is somewhat off in his chronology. Carol Lamoreaux, the Registrar of Santa Clara University, places Fred A. Healy at the school during the years 1885, 1886, 1887, and 1889. It therefore appears that the expulsion happened in 1889. The archives of the university show Fred in attendance at the then college every year from August to June 1885 through August to June 1889, but his "name does not appear in the register of graduates in 1889." Sheila Conway, Assistant Archivist, notes that it "is hard to verify" transgressions by students. "However, the rules for behavior at Santa Clara were very strict, and if Mr. Healy did commit the alleged prank . . . , he probably would have been expelled. However, I don't know if he would have been readmitted." Santa Clara College at the time, much like Holy Cross, "served as a grammar and high school for boys." As will be shown in note 19, below, the annulled marriage took place in 1896. We believe that Foley repeated Healy family history, which did not have the events in proper chronological order. Foley, *Dream of an Outcaste*, 223–24; e-mail: Carol Lamoreaux, Registrar of Santa Clara University, to Dennis L.

Noble, January 9, 2006; E-mail, Sheila Conway, Assistant Archivist, Santa Clara University, to Dennis L. Noble, January 12, 2006.

19. All material on Frederick's annulled marriage is found in (San Francisco) *Chronicle*, April 2, 1896, 16.

20. Quoted in Williams, "Healy," 464.

21. Ibid., 466.

22. Murphy, "Cutter Captain," 73–80. Cantwell authored the largest of all publications that the service produced on their work in Alaska: Cantwell, *Report on the Nunivak*, which totals 325 pages.

23. *USRCS Register, 1900*, 6–7; Strobridge and Dennis L. Noble, "North in the Spring," 60–69; Noble, "The *McCulloch*," 12–17.

24. Telegram, Coulson to Secretary of the Treasury, May 25, 1900, Letters Received, U.S. Revenue Cutter Service, RG26, NARA.

25. "Service Record, Healy."

26. Charles F. Shoemaker to wife, May 3, 1900, Papers of Charles F. Shoemaker, Manuscript Division, Library of Congress, Washington, D.C., hereinafter cited as CFS Papers.

27. MJH to PFH, August 2, 1900.

28. Briefs of Letters Sent, Vol. 22, September 24, 1900, page 179, RG26, NARA, hereinafter cited as Briefs, with volume(s), date(s), and page number(s); Stein, "A Desperate and Dangerous Man," 40.

29. Stein, "A Desperate and Dangerous Man," 40.

30. "Nome, Alaska," 2, www.fairbanks-alaska.com/nome-alaska.htm, accessed February 28, 2005.

31. As explained in the narrative, all correspondence dealing with the cutter *McCulloch*'s events during the 1900 voyage north has been pulled from the records of the U.S. Revenue Cutter Service. In 1985, Dr. Gary C. Stein published an article in *The Alaska Journal* dealing with the events that took place on board the cutter. He based his narrative upon the log book of the cutter and abstracts—now called briefs—of the correspondence in the service's registers. In 2005, the National Archives personnel in the Maritime Records, where the records of the U.S. Coast Guard and its predecessors are located, could not locate the log book of the *McCulloch* for the 1900 incident. Prof. James M. O'Toole, who devoted a chapter to Captain Healy in his book on the Healy family, *Passing for White*, graciously copied his detailed notes concerning the *McCulloch*'s log entries of 1900 and sent them to the authors. O'Toole to Noble, June 7, 2005. Until the log book can be located, unless otherwise noted, all material on the incident on board the *McCulloch* is taken from O'Toole's notes; Stein, "A Desperate and Dangerous Man," 39–45; and Briefs, Letters Sent, Vol. 86, July 14, 24, 26, 1900, pages 240, 276, 290.

32. Letter detaching Healy from the *McCulloch* to command the *Seminole*, located in Briefs, Letters Sent, Vol. 21, June 20, 1900, page 220.

33. MAH to Shepard, April 17, 1893, "Alaska File," Roll 3.

34. Canney, *Cutters, 1790–1935*, 58–59, 61.

35. On some comments about James A. Healy, the oldest brother, see O'Toole, *Passing for White*, 129–31; on Patrick F. Healy, see ibid., 155–60.

36. Eliza Harris Carrigan to "My Dear Father Healy," August 2, 1900, PFH.

37. Briefs, Letters Received, Vol. 86, July 14, 1900, page 240.

38. Ibid., July 13, 1900, page 240.

39. Ibid.

40. *Seattle Post-Intelligencer*, July 15, 1900, 11.

41. Physicians Certificate, Healy Case, Jefferson County Probate No. 241. Jefferson County Courthouse, Port Townsend, Washington.

42. *Seattle Post-Intelligencer*, July 15, 1900, 11.

43. Letter, Neda Thornton to Mrs. Lopp, August 4, 1900, "Correspondence: Neda Thornton, 1900–1903; 1927–1937," Lopp Papers.

44. Foley, *Dream of an Outcaste*, 274, does not record the evidence used in coming to this conclusion.

45. Quoted in ibid. Foley does not record where he obtained this letter. A search of the archives at the College of the Holy Cross and the archives at Georgetown University, both locations holding records of Patrick Healy, failed to uncover the letter. In a communication with the author, Professor O'Toole also reports failing to locate the letter in his research. E-mail, O'Toole to Noble, September 2, 2005. This, of course, does not mean the letter did not exist, only that Foley did not record the location of the letter.

46. Letter, Coulson to Secretary of the Treasury, December 24, 1900, "Alaska File," Roll 8.

47. Jefferson County Probate No. 241. Jefferson County Courthouse, Port Townsend, Washington; "Service record, Healy."

48. "Service record, Healy."

49. "Michael Healy," Foley Papers, AJB.

50. "Service Record, Healy"; Briefs, Letters Sent, Vol. 86, July 25, 1900, page 295.

51. Kay Redfield Jamison, *An Unquiet Mind* (New York: Random House, 1995), 6; "Bipolar Disorder," National Institute of Mental Health, National Institutes of Health, April 9, 2004, 2–4, www.nimh.nih.gov/publicat/bipolar.cfm, accessed March 9, 2005. See comments on a form of bipolar disorder called "cyclothymic disorder" that "may contribute to a person's success in business, leadership, achievement, and artistic creativity. However, it may also cause uneven work and school records, frequent change of residence, repeated romantic breakups or marital failure, and alcohol and drug abuse." Further, bipolar disorder may be triggered by seasonal changes. "The depressive and manic episodes often recur according to the season; for example, depression occurs in the fall and winter, and mania occurs in the spring or summer." "Manic-Depressive Illness," *Merck Manual of Medical Information*, 620–21.

52. Letter, Neda Thornton to Mrs. Lopp, August 4, 1900, "Correspondence: Neda Thornton, 1900–1903; 1927–1937," Lopp Papers.

53. "Service record, Healy."

54. Williams, "Healy," 482–83.

55. Briefs, Letters Sent, Entry 144C(2) Vol. 24, November 28, 1901, page 170, hereinafter cited as Letters Sent, with Volume number(s), date(s), and page number(s).

56. Ibid., December 2, December 11, 1901, pages 170, 172.

57. Ibid., January 11, 1902, page 175.

58. "Service Record, Healy."

59. Ibid.; Letters Sent, Vol. 24, April 18, 1902, page 191.

60. "Service Record, Healy"; Letters Sent, Vol. 24, March 20, 1903, 189.

61. Letters Sent, Vol. 26, May 9, 1903, page 171.

62. MAH to Secretary of the Treasury, June 11, 1903, "Alaska File," Roll 9.

63. "Service Record, Healy."

64. Shoemaker to wife, November 6, 1903, CFS Papers.

65. "Service record, Healy."

66. Ibid.; Letters Sent, Vol. 27, November 16, 1903, page 165.

67. Letters Sent, Vol. 27, March 24, 1903, page 185. Ironically, in November of the same year that Healy received his bureaucratic complaints, Capt. Charles F. Shoemaker, senior officer of the service, sent a letter to the civilian head of the service complaining about a similar bureaucratic criticism. While on an inspection trip, he stopped in Portland, Oregon: "I had occasion to assume a prerogative similar to which I had before exercised when away from the Department at other times, though under the Assistant Secretaries. I simply did this: granted leave to two officers, and wired the Department *requesting confirmation* of my action, as is customary. In response I received . . . a most unusual and humiliating [telegram.] You will readily appreciate the mortifying position in which the young snob (A.) has placed me."

The telegram, from R. B. Armstrong, Assistant Secretary, stated, "Department denied applications . . . for leaves. Hereafter do not grant officers leave without first consulting Department."

Trying to control his anger, Captain Shoemaker went on to say that Armstrong "is entirely out of place where he is. In the meantime let loose your dogs and cut this fellow's wind!" Warming to the subject, Shoemaker hit his stride: "It may as well be borne in mind that I am nearing the completion of forty years of honorable service 'under the flag,' and a record without a blemish should at least give immunity from snubs by a swelled head on the shoulders of an inexperienced boy. I hope he may find other channels, and that soon, in which to exhibit his *chestiness*." One wonders if the "inexperienced boy" sent the letters to Healy. Shoemaker to [no name given in copy of the letter], November 3, 1904. A copy of the telegram, dated November 2, 1904, is attached to the letter, CFS.

68. *The Call*, August 31, 1904, 5.

69. Alanson Weeks, MD to CFS, July 15, 1904, CFS Papers.

70. *The Call*, August 31, 1904, 5.

71. Mary J. Healy's date of death is recorded as February 27, 1906, but the death certificate is dated 1907. Cause of death is listed as heart failure. She was buried in the same grave as her husband in Holy Cross Cemetery on February 28, 1907. State of California Certification of Vital Records, Original Certificate of Death, number 7-004903. Frederick A. Healy's date of death is recorded as January 7, 1912, with cause listed as "cerebral hemorrhage." In the block for color or race he is listed as "white." Certified copy of vital records, I00001778. Comments on Frederick A. Healy are located in e-mail, Frederick Sherman, Researcher California Genealogical Society, Oakland, California, to Dennis L. Noble, January 17, 2002.

72. "Service Record, Shepard"; "Service Record, Hooper."

73. "Service Record, Henriques"; "Service Record, Jarvis"; Tower, "Captain David Henry Jarvis," 1–21.

74. "Service Record, Daniels"; Information on Emery is located in U.S. Coast Guard Academy Alumni *Bulletin*, III, No. 12 (February 1942): 184.

75. "Service Record, Cantwell"; Murphy, "Cutter Captain," 160–98.

76. *Register of Alumni*, 25; Turk, "Robley D. Evans," 83–92.

77. Bender, *Winning the West for Christ*, 190–92, 205.

78. Smith and Smith, *Ice Window*, 14, 357–58.

79. Ray, "Sinrock Mary," 107.

80. *USRCS Register, 1903*, 6–9.

Epilogue

1. Foley, *Bishop Healy*, 13.

2. Nalty, *Strength for the Fight*, 26–28, 32–34, 58, 64–64, 78–87.

3. In "World War II . . . the U.S. Coast Guard assigned Lieut. Clarence Samuels as Commanding Officer of Lightship No. 115, operating in the Panama Sea Frontier. Thus, he became the first admitted Black to command a cutter, as well as the first one to be a commanding officer of a Coast Guard vessel during wartime." Greco and Strobridge, "Black Trailblazer," 12.

4. O'Toole, "Racial Identity," 199.

5. Michener's novel incorrectly describes Healy and helps further the myth of the man. According to Michener, Healy had "a foul vocabulary, an insatiable craving for strong drink and an inherited willingness to use his fists." He further described him as a "hulking six feet two with a temper he could not control. . . ." Furthermore, Captain Healy "was an American Negro . . . [who] had learned to wear a hat that covered his dark forehead and a large mustache that obscured the blackness around his mouth, so that many people knew him for some time before they realized he was a black man." Michener, *Alaska*, 404, 410.

6. FAH, Diary, September 8, 1883, Huntington Library.

7. A. D. Powell, "'Racial Kidnapping,' and the Case of the Healy Family," *Interracial Voice*, 2, <http://webcom./~intvoice/powell118.html>, accessed March 17, 2005.

8. Ibid., 1–4.

9. Fisher, Jr., *Guardians of the Republic*, 210.

10. See "Alaska File," Roll 3, for the many letters written by MAH to Captain Shepard concerning Kimball.

11. See Hogan, ed., *Rhetoric and Reform*. For a history of the WCTU see Bordin, *Woman and Temperance*.

12. Berwick, *The Abraham Lincoln of the Sea*, 7.

13. "Andrew Furuseth, 150th Anniversary," 2.

14. Ibid., 2, 9.

15. Williams, "Healy," 514.

16. *USRCS Register, 1896*, 6–9; Munger also remained in the service, see *USRCS, 1904*, 6–7.

17. "Special Order 20," 1–3. The material on Munger is found in Snow, Scrapbook.

18. McCullough, *Mornings on Horseback*, 171.

19. Strobridge and Noble, *Alaska and the USRCS*, 175–76.

20. Strobridge, "West Point, Thayer & Partridge," 85.

21. Paul H. Johnson, "Healy, Part III," 29.

22. MJH, Diary, September 8, 1890.

23. CFS to wife, November 6, 1903, CFS Papers.

Appendix 2. The Family of Michael Augustine Healy

1. All material on Michael Augustine Healy's father, mother, and siblings is extracted from O'Toole, *Passing for White*.

2. Material on Mary Jane (Roach) Healy and Frederick A. Healy is contained in Edward Wallace Phillips, "The Life of Mary Jane Roach," New England Ancestry Revealed, Upton, Massachusetts, May 2005, in the files of the authors.

Appendix 3. Charges Brought Against Capt. Michael A. Healy in 1896 Trial

1. All material comes from Special Order, Revenue Cutter Service, Number 20, Washington, D.C., June 8, 1896, located in Alaska File, M-641, Microfilm Roll 5, Records of the U.S. Coast Guard, RG26, National Archives and Records Administration, Washington, D.C.

SELECTED BIBLIOGRAPHY

Primary Material Depositories

Alaska State Museum, Juneau, Alaska.

Archives, Archdiocese of Boston, Boston, Massachusetts.

Archives, College of the Holy Cross, Worcester, Massachusetts.

Archives, Diocese of Portland, Portland, Maine.

Archives, Georgetown University, Washington, D.C.

Archives, Josephite Fathers, Baltimore, Maryland.

Columbia River Maritime Museum, Astoria, Oregon.

Georgia Department of Archives and History, Atlanta, Georgia.

Historian of the U.S. Coast Guard, U.S. Coast Guard Headquarters, Washington, D.C.

Historical Society, San Francisco, California.

Huntington Library, San Marino, California.

Mystic Seaport Museum Library, Mystic, Connecticut.

New Bedford Whaling Museum Library, New Bedford, Massachusetts.

Manuscript Division, Library of Congress, Washington, D.C.

Merseyside Maritime Museum, Liverpool, England.

Museum of the Aleutians, Unalaska, Alaska.

Music Division, Library of Congress, Washington, D.C.

National Archives and Records Administration, Washington, D.C.

Peary-MacMillan Arctic Museum, Bowdoin College, Brunswick, Maine.

Presbyterian Historical Society, Philadelphia, Pennsylvania.

Sausalito Historical Society, Sausalito, California.

Sheldon Jackson College Library, Sitka, Alaska.

Sheldon Jackson Museum, Sitka, Alaska.

Special Collections and University Archives, University of Oregon Libraries, Eugene, Oregon.

Special Collections, University of Washington Libraries, Seattle, Washington.

U.S. Navy Library, Washington Navy Yard, Washington, D.C.

Newspapers

New York Times
(San Francisco) *The Morning Call*
San Francisco Chronicle
(Seattle) *Seattle Post-Intelligencer*
(Juneau) *Southeastern Alaska Empire*

Articles, Books, Theses

"Abolition and Negro Equality." *Brownson's Quarterly Review*, National Series 1 (April 1864): 186–209.

Alleged Shelling of Alaskan Villages, Letter from the Secretary of the Treasury, In Resolution of the House of Representatives Relative to the Alleged Shelling of Two Villages in Alaska by the Revenue Cutter Corwin. 47th Cong., 2d sess., House Exec. Doc. No. 9.

Allen, Everett S. "Saved by the *Bear*." In *Yankees Under Sail*. Ed. Richard Heckman. 38–45. Dublin, N.H.: Yankee, Inc., 1968.

"Andrew Furuseth, 150th Anniversary." *West Coast Sailor*, March 12, 2004, 1–2.

Bailey, George W. *Report upon Alaska and Its People*. Washington, D.C.: Government Printing Office, 1880.

Bailey, Thomas A. "Why the United States Purchased Alaska." *The Pacific Historical Review* 3, no. 1 (1934): 39–49.

———. *A Diplomatic History of the American People*. Englewood Cliffs, N.J.: Prentice-Hall, 1974.

Baker, Marcus. *Geographic Dictionary of Alaska*. Washington, D.C.: Government Printing Office, 1902.

Bancroft, Hubert H. *History of Alaska, 1730–1885*. San Francisco, Calif.: A. L. Bancroft Company, 1886.

Bender, Norman J. *Winning the West for Christ: Sheldon Jackson and Presbyterianism on the Rocky Mountain Frontier, 1869–1880*. Albuquerque: University of New Mexico Press, 1996.

Berleth, Richard. *Mary Patten's Voyage*. Morton Grove, Ill.: Albert Whitman & Company, 1994.

Berlin, Ira. *Slaves Without Masters: The Free Negro in the Antebellum South*. New York: Pantheon, 1974.

Berwick, Arnold. *The Abraham Lincoln of the Sea: The Life of Andrew Furuseth*. Santa Cruz, Calif.: Odin Press, 1993.

Bockstoce, John R. *Steam Whaling in the Western Arctic*. New Bedford, Mass.: Old Dartmouth Historical Society, 1977.

———. "The Arctic Whaling Disaster of 1897." *Prologue* 9, no. 1 (Spring 1977): 27–42.

———. "Arctic Castaway: The Stormy History of the Point Barrow Refuge Station." *Prologue* 11, no. 3 (Fall 1979): 152–69.

———. *Whales, Ice, & Men: The History of Whaling in the Western Arctic*. New Bedford, Mass.: New Bedford Whaling Museum, 1986. Reprint, Seattle: University of Washington Press, 1995.

Bockstoce, John R., and Charles F. Batchelder. "A Gazetteer of Whaler's Place Names for the Bering Strait Region and Western Arctic." *Names* 26, no. 3 (1978): 258–70.

Bolster, W. Jeffrey. "An Inner Diaspora: Black Sailors Making Selves." In *Through a Glass Darkly:*

Reflections on Personal Identity in Early America. Ed. Ronald Hoffman, Mechal Sobel, and Fredrika J. Teute. 419–48. Chapel Hill: University of North Carolina Press, 1997.

———. *Black Jacks: African American Seamen in the Age of Sail*. Cambridge, Mass.: Harvard University Press, 1997.

Bonner, James C. *A History of Georgia Agriculture, 1732–1819*. Athens: University of Georgia Press, 1964.

Bordin, Ruth Birgitta Anderson. *Woman and Temperance: The Quest for Power and Liberty, 1873–1900*. New Brunswick, N.J.: Rutgers University Press, 1990.

Brevig, J. *Apaurak in Alaska: Social Pioneering Among the Eskimos*. Philadelphia, Pa.: Dorrance & Company, 1944.

Brooks, Maria. *The Odyssey of Captain Healy*. Oakland, Calif.: Waterfront Soundings Productions, 1999.

Brower, Charles D., and Lyman Anson. *Fifty Years Below Zero: A Lifetime of Adventure in the Far North*. New York: Dodd, Mead and Company, 1947.

Brown, John. *Slave Life in Georgia: A Narrative of the Life, Sufferings, and Escape of John Brown, A Fugitive Slave, Now in England*. London: W. M. Watts, 1855.

Buell, Thomas B. *Master of Sea Power: A Biography of Fleet Admiral Ernest J. King*. Boston: Little, Brown, 1980.

Canney, Donald. *U.S. Coast Guard and Revenue Cutters, 1790–1935*. Annapolis, Md.: Naval Institute Press, 1995.

Cantwell, John C. *Report of the Operations of the U.S. Steamer* Nunivak *on the Yukon River Station, Alaska, 1899–1901*. Washington, D.C.: Government Printing Office, 1902.

———. "Captain Healy's Reindeer." *Marine Corps Gazette* 19, no. 2 (May 1935): 26–29, 58–60.

Carlton, Rosemary. *Sheldon Jackson, The Collector*. Juneau, Alaska: Alaska State Museums, 1999.

Caswell, John Edwards. *Arctic Frontiers: United States Explorations in the Far North*. Norman: University of Oklahoma Press, 1956.

Catalogue of the Students of Holy Cross, Worcester, Massachusetts, for the Academic Year, 1856–1857. Worcester, Mass.: Henry J. Howland, 1857.

Chance, Norman A. *The Eskimo of North Alaska*. New York: Holt, Rinehart and Winston, 1966.

Chapell, Absalom. *Miscellanies of Georgia, Historical, Biographical, Descriptive*. Atlanta, Ga.: J. F. Meegan, 1874.

Chapelle, Howard I. *The History of American Sailing Ships*. New York: Bonanza Books, 1935.

Cocke, Albert K. "Dr. Samuel J. Call." *Alaska Journal* (Summer 1974): 181–88.

Cocke, Albert K. "The Deer Men." An unpublished manuscript dated March 1, 1979, in the files of the Historian of the U.S. Coast Guard, U.S. Coast Guard Headquarters, Washington.

Cocke, Mary, and Albert Cocke. "Hell Roaring Mike: A Fall from Grace in the Frozen North." *Smithsonian* 13, no. 11 (February 1983): 119–20, 122, 125–26, 128, 130, 132, 134–37.

Cordingly, David. *Women Sailors & Sailors' Women: An Untold Maritime History*. New York: Random House, 2001.

Coulter, E. Merton. *Georgia: A Short History*. Chapel Hill: University of North Carolina Press, 1960.

De Laguna, Frederica. *The Story of a Tlingit Community: A Problem in the Relationship Between Archeological, Ethnological, and Historical Methods*. Washington, D.C.: Government Printing Office, 1960.

Delgado, James P. *Across the Top of the World: The Quest for the Northwest Passage*. New York: Checkmark Books, 1999.

Derks, Scott, ed. *The Value of a Dollar: Prices and Incomes in the United States, 1860–1989*. Detroit, Mich.: Gale, 1994.

Druett, Joan. *Hen Frigates: Wives of Merchant Captains Under Sail*. New York: Simon & Schuster, 1998.

———. *Petticoat Whalers: Whaling Wives at Sea, 1820–1920*. New Zealand: Collins Publishers, 1991. Reprint, Hanover, N.H.: University Press of New England, 2001.

Eames, Aled, Lewis Lloyd, and Bryn Parry, eds. *Letters from America: Captain David Evans of Talsarnau, 1817–1895*. Denbigh, Wales: Gwynedd Archives Service, 1975.

Evans, Robley D. *A Sailor's Log: Recollections of a Sailor's Life*. New York: Appleton, 1901.

Evans, Stephen H. *The United States Coast Guard, 1790–1915: A Definitive History: With a Postscript, 1915–1950*. Annapolis, Md.: Naval Institute Press, 1949.

Farr, James. "A Slow Boat to Nowhere: The Multi-Racial Crews of the American Whaling Industry." *The Journal of Negro History* LXVIII, no. 2 (Spring 1983): 159–70.

Fisher, Ernest, Jr. *Guardians of the Republic: A History of the Noncommissioned Officer Corps of the U.S. Army*. New York: Ballantine Books, 1994.

Fisher, Raymond H. *Bering's Voyages: Whither and Why*. Seattle: University of Washington Press, 1977.

Flanders, Ralph B. "Two Plantations and a County of Antebellum Georgia." *Georgia Historical Quarterly* 12 (March 1928): 1–24.

———. "The Free Negro in Ante-Bellum Georgia." *North Carolina Historical Review* 9 (July 1932): 250–72.

Foley, Albert S. *Bishop Healy, Beloved Outcaste: The Story of a Great Man Whose Life Has Become a Legend*. New York: Farrar, Straus and Young, 1954.

———. *Dream of an Outcaste: Patrick F. Healy: The Story of the Slave-Born Georgian Who Became the Second Founder of America's Great Catholic University, Georgetown*. Tuscaloosa, Ala.: Portals Press, 1989.

Frost, O. W., ed. *Bering and Chirikov: The American Voyages and Their Impact*. Anchorage: Alaska Historical Society, 1992.

Gay, James Thomas. *American Fur Seal Diplomacy: The Alaskan Fur Seal Controversy*. New York: Peter Lang, 1987.

Gleason, Philip. "The Curriculum of the Old-Time Catholic College: A Student's View." *Records of the American Catholic Historical Society of Philadelphia* 88 (1977): 20–35.

Greco, Joseph, Jr., and Truman R. Strobridge. "Black Trailblazer Has Colorful Past." *U.S. Coast Guard Commandant's Bulletin*, Issue Number 7-75 (February 14, 1975): 11–12.

Greene, Jerome A. *Washita: The U.S. Army and the Southern Cheyennes, 1867–1869*. Norman: University of Oklahoma Press, 2004.

Gruening, Ernest. *The State of Alaska*. New York: Random House, 1954.

Guttridge, Leonard F. *Icebound: The Jeannette Expedition's Quest for the North Pole*. Annapolis, Md.: Naval Institute Press, 1986.

———. *Ghosts of Cape Sabine: The Harrowing Story of the Greeley Expedition*. New York: G. P. Putnam's Sons, 2000.

Hall, Basil. *Travels in North America*. Edinburgh: N.p., 1829.

Harlow, Frederick Pease. *The Making of a Sailor: Or Sea Life Aboard a Yankee Square-Rigger*. Salem, Mass.: Marine Research Society, 1928. Reprint, New York: Dover Publications, 1988.

Healy, M. A. *Report of the Cruise of the Revenue Marine Steamer* Corwin *in the Arctic Ocean in the Year 1884*. Washington, D.C.: Government Printing Office, 1889.

———. *Report of the Cruise of the Revenue Marine Steamer* Corwin *in the Arctic Ocean in the Year 1885*. Washington, D.C.: Government Printing Office, 1887.

Hensley, Dennis E. "Jack London's Use of Maritime History in *The Sea Wolf*." *The Pacific Historian* 28 (1979): 1–8.

Hinckley, Ted [Theodore] C. "Punitive Action at Angoon," Part 1, *Alaska Sportsman* 39 (January 1963): 8–9, 43–45.

———. "Rustlers of the North Pacific." *Journal of the West* II, no. 1 (January 1963): 22–30.

———. "Punitive Action at Angoon." Part 2, *Alaska Sportsman* 39 (January 1963): 8–9, 43–45.

———. "Cutter, Smuggler, Colporteur and Trader—The *Leo* (Formerly USRM *Reliance*)." In *The Sea in Alaska's Past: First Conference Proceedings*, 182–205. Anchorage: Alaska Division of Parks, 1979.

Hogan, J. Michael, ed. *Rhetoric and Reform in the Progressive Era*. East Lansing: Michigan State University Press, 2003.

Hood, John B., and Benjamin A. Hardy, Jr. *River of Redemption: A Musical*. Mentone, Ala.: N.p., 1998.

Hooper, Calvin L. *Report of the Cruise of the Revenue Steamer* Corwin *in the Arctic Ocean, 1880*. Washington, D.C.: Government Printing Office, 1881.

———. *Report of the Cruise of the Revenue Steamer* Corwin *in the Arctic Ocean, 1881*. Washington, D.C.: Government Printing Office, 1882.

"How A Dead Man Made A Will: As Told By Captain Healy, Late of the Rev. Cutter 'Bear.'" San Francisco *Bulletin* LXXXVII (August 13, 1899), 17.

Howe, M. A. *The Humane Society of the Commonwealth of Massachusetts: An Historical Review, 1785–1916*. Boston: Riverside Press, 1918.

Hunt, William R. *Arctic Passage: The Turbulent History of the Land and People of the Bering Sea*. New York: Charles Scribner's Sons, 1975.

Imlay, Miles. "A Seal Patrol Resurrects the Leonidas Robinson Tragedy." U.S. Coast Guard Academy Alumni *Bulletin* XXVIII, no. 1 (January/February 1966): 28–32.

"Islands of the Seals: The Pribilofs." *Alaska Geographic* 9, no. 3 (1987): 1–125.

Jackson, Sheldon. *Preliminary Report to W. T. Harris, Commissioner of Education, Department of the Interior, on the Introduction of Reindeer into Alaska, November 12, 1890*. Washington, D.C.: Government Printing Office, 1892.

———. "Report on Education in Alaska." In *Report of the Commissioner of Education for the Year 1890–91*, vol. 2, 923–60. Washington, D.C.: Government Printing Office, 1894.

———, with an introduction by Charles A. Anderson. "Exploring for Reindeer in Siberia: Being the Journal of the Cruise of the U.S. Revenue Steamer *Bear*." *Journal of the Presbyterian Historical Society* 31, no. 1 (March 1953): 1–24.

———. "Exploring for Reindeer in Siberia: Being the Journal of the Cruise of the U.S. Revenue Steamer *Bear*." *Journal of the Presbyterian Historical Society* 31, no. 2 (June 1953): 87–112.

Jamison, Kay Redfield. *An Unquiet Mind.* New York: Random House, 1995.

John, Betty. *Libby: The Alaskan Diaries & Letters of Libby Beaman, 1879–1880.* Boston: Houghton Mifflin Company, 1989.

Johnshoy, J. Walter. *Apaurak in Alaska: Social Pioneering Among the Eskimos.* Philadelphia: Dorrance, 1944.

Johnson, Paul H. "Portrait of Captain Michael A. Healy, Part II." *The Bulletin: U.S. Coast Guard Academy Alumni Association* 41, no. 2 (March/April 1979): 22–27.

Johnson, Robert Erwin. *Guardians of the Sea: History of the United States Coast Guard, 1915 to the Present.* Annapolis, Md.: Naval Institute Press, 1987.

Jones, Dorothy Knee. *A Century of Servitude: Pribilof Aleuts Under U.S. Rule.* Washington, D.C.: University Press of America, 1980.

Jordan, Winthrop D. *White Over Black: American Attitudes Toward the Negro, 1550–1812.* Chapel Hill: University of North Carolina Press, 1968.

Kaplan, H. R., and James F. Hunt. *This Is the Coast Guard.* Cambridge, Md.: Cornell Maritime Press, 1972.

Karsten, Peter. *The Naval Aristocracy: The Golden Age of Annapolis and the Emergence of Modern Navalism.* New York: The Free Press, 1972.

Kennedy, Randall. *Interracial Intimacies: Sex, Marriage, Identity, Adoption.* New York: Pantheon Books, 2003.

Kern, Francis. *John Foster Williams' U.S. Revenue Cutter* Massachusetts, *1791–1792.* Washington, D.C.: Alised Enterprises, 1976.

———. *Patrick Dennis' U.S. Revenue Cutter* Vigilant, *1791–1798.* Washington, D.C.: Alised Enterprises, 1976.

King, Irving H. *The Coast Guard Expands, 1865–1915: New Roles, New Frontiers.* Annapolis, Md.: Naval Institute Press, 1996.

Kroeger, Brooke. *Passing: When People Can't Be Who They Are.* New York: Public Affairs, 2003.

Kuzniewski, Anthony J. *Thy Honored Name: A History of The College of the Holy Cross, 1843–1994.* Washington, D.C.: The Catholic University of America Press, 1999.

Landauer, Lyndall Baker. *Scammon: Beyond the Lagoon: A Biography of Charles Melville Scammon.* San Francisco, Calif.: Associates of the J. Porter Library, 1986.

Lane, Mills. *The Rambler in Georgia.* Savannah, Ga.: Beehive Press, 1990.

Langley, Harold D. *Social Reform in the United States Navy, 1798–1862.* Urbana: University of Illinois Press, 1967.

Lasker, Joe. *The Strange Voyage of Neptune's Car.* New York: Viking Press, 1977.

Lloyd, Christopher. *Mr. Barrow of the Admiralty.* London: Collins, 1970.

Luchetti, Cathy. *I Do! Courtship, Love and Marriage on the American Frontier.* New York: Crown, 1996.

MacDonald, R. St. J., ed. *The Arctic Frontier.* Toronto: University of Toronto Press, 1966.

MacPhail, Elizabeth C. "Early Days in San Diego, The Memoirs of Augusta Barrett Sherman." *The Journal of the San Diego Historical Society* 18, no. 4 (Fall 1972): 31.

Malcomson, Scott L. *One Drop of Blood: The American Misadventure of Race.* New York: Farrar, Straus, Giroux, 2000.

Marszalek, John F. *Assault at West Point: The Court-Martial of Johnson Whittaker.* New York: Macmillan Publishing Company, 1972.

Martin, Fredericka. *The Hunting of the Golden Fleece*. New York: Greenberg, 1946.

McCullough, David. *Mornings on Horseback*. New York: Simon and Schuster, 1981.

McCuster, John J. "How Much Is That Worth in Real Money? A Historical Price Index for Use as a Deflator of Money Values in the Economy of the United States." *Proceedings of the American Antiquarian Society* 101 (1994): 297–373.

McKenna, Richard. "Life Aboard the USS *Goldstar*." In *The Left-Handed Monkey Wrench: Stories and Essays by Richard McKenna*, ed. Richard Shenk. Annapolis, Md.: Naval Institute Press, 1986.

Meagher, Walter J., and William J. Grattan. *The Spires of Fenwick: The History of the College of the Holy Cross, 1843–1963*. New York: Vantage Press, 1966.

Merick Manual of Medical Information. Second Home Edition. Whitehouse Station, N.J.: Merick Research Laboratories, 2003.

Merlith, Richard. *Mary Patten's Voyage*. Morton Grove, Ill.: Albert Whitman & Company, 1994.

Michener, James A. *Alaska: A Novel*. New York: Ballantine Books, 1988.

Miller, Randall M. "Slaves and Southern Catholicism." In *Masters and Slaves in the House of the Lord: Race and Religion in the American South, 1740–1870*. Ed. John B. Boles. 127–52. Lexington: University of Kentucky Press, 1988.

Montgomery, Maurice. "The Murder of Missionary Thornton." *Pacific Northwest Quarterly* 54, no. 4 (October 1968): 10–25.

Morris, Thomas D. *Southern Slavery and the Law, 1619–1860*. Chapel Hill: University of North Carolina Press, 1996.

Morris, William Gouverneur. *Report Upon the Customs District, Public Service, and Resources of Alaska Territory*. 45th Cong., 3d sess. Sen. Exec. Doc. No. 59.

Mowat, Farley. *The Polar Passion*. Boston: Little, Brown, 1967.

Muir, John. *The Cruise of the Corwin*. Boston: Houghton Mifflin, 1917. Reprint, San Francisco, Calif.: Sierra Club Books, 1993.

Murphy, Dallas. *Rounding the Horn: Being the Story of Williwaws and Windjammers, Drake, Darwin, Murdered Missionaries and Naked Natives—A Deck's-Eye View of Cape Horn*. New York: Basic Books, 2004.

Murphy, John F. "Two Standards of Judgment." U.S. Coast Guard Academy Alumni *Bulletin* XXVII, no. 5 (September/October 1965): 5–13.

———. Cutter Captain: The Life and Times of John C. Cantwell. Ph.D. diss., the University of Connecticut, 1968.

———. "Portrait of Captain Michael A. Healy." *The Bulletin: U.S. Coast Guard Academy Alumni Association* 41, no. 1 (January/February 1979): 14–18.

Nalty, Bernard C. *Strength for the Fight: A History of Black Americans in the Military*. New York: The Free Press, 1986.

Naval Historical Foundation. *The Incredible Overland Expedition*. Washington: Naval Historical Foundation, 1968.

Nelson, Edward William. "The Eskimo in Bering Strait." In *Eighteenth Annual Report of American Ethnology*. Washington, D.C.: Government Printing Office, 1899.

New Catholic Encyclopedia. Sd. ed., vol. 4. Detroit: Gale, 2003.

Noble, Dennis L. *Recollections of Vice Admiral J. E. Stika, U.S. Coast Guard, on the U.S. Revenue Cutter Service and Bering Sea Patrol*. Washington, D.C.: U.S. Coast Guard, 1975.

———. "The Little War of the *McCulloch*." *Sea Classics* 9, no. 3 (May 1976): 12–17.

———. *Gulf Coast and Western Rivers: A Brief History of Coast Guard Operations.* Washington, D.C.: U.S. Coast Guard Historian's Office, 1989.

———. *Historical Register U.S. Revenue Cutter Service, 1790–1914.* Washington, D.C.: U.S. Coast Guard Headquarters, Historian's Office, 1990.

———. *That Others Might Live: The U.S. Life-Saving Service, 1878–1915.* Annapolis, Md.: Naval Institute Press, 1994.

———. *Lighthouses & Keepers: The U.S. Lighthouse Service and Its Legacy.* Annapolis, Md.: Naval Institute Press, 1997.

Noble, Dennis L., and Truman R. Strobridge. "The Revenue Cutter *Tahoma*." *The Alaska Journal* 6, no. 2 (Spring 1976): 118–22, 128.

———. "The Arctic Adventures of the *Thetis*." *Arctic, Journal of the Arctic Institute of North America* 30, no. 1 (March 1977): 2–12.

———. "The Polar Exploits of the *Thetis*." *Sea Classics* 11, no. 4 (July 1978): 6–13, 82.

———. "Early Cuttermen in Alaskan Waters." *Pacific Northwest Quarterly* 78, no. 3 (July 1987): 74–82.

———. "'Hell Roaring Mike' on Trial." *Naval History* 15, no. 2 (April 2001): 34–39.

Officers of the U.S. Revenue Cutter Service and Some of Their Friends. *Below Zero: Songs and Verses from Bering Sea and the Arctic.* Astoria, Ore.: J. S. Dellinger Company, 1903.

O'Harra, Doug. "A Puzzle in the Pribilofs." *Smithsonian* 35, no. 12 (March 2005): 14–20.

Olmsted, Frederick Law. *A Journey in the Seaboard Slave States.* New York: Dix and Edwards, 1856.

Oswalt, Wendell H. *Eskimos and Explorers.* Novato, Calif.: Chandler & Sharp Publishers, 1979.

O'Toole, James M. "Passing: Race, Religion, and the Healy Family, 1820–1920." *Proceedings of the Massachusetts Historical Society* 108 (1996): 1–34.

———. "Racial Identity and the Case of Captain Michael Healy, USRCS." *Prologue* 29, no. 3 (Fall 1997): 190–201.

———. *Passing for White: Race, Religion, and the Healy Family, 1820–1920.* Amherst: University of Massachusetts Press, 2002.

Phillips, Edward Wallace. "The Life of Mary Jane Roach." An unpublished genealogical report. Upton, Mass.: New England Ancestry Revealed, June 5, 2005.

Postell, Alice. *Where Did the Reindeer Come From? Alaska Experience, The First Fifty Years.* Portland, Ore.: Amaknak Press, 1990.

Raban, Jonathan, ed. *Oxford Book of the Sea.* New York: Oxford University Press, 1993.

———. *Passage to Juneau: A Sea and Its Meanings.* New York: Pantheon Books, 1999.

Rankin, Robert H., and H. R. Kaplan. *Immortal* Bear: *The Stoutest Polar Ship.* New York: G. P. Putnam's Sons, 1970.

Ray, Dorothy Jean. *The Eskimos of Bering Strait, 1650–1898.* Seattle: University of Washington Press, 1975.

———. "Sinrock Mary: From Eskimo Wife to Reindeer Queen." *Pacific Northwest Quarterly* 75, no. 3 (July 1984): 20–28.

Rediker, Marcus. *Between the Devil and the Deep Blue Sea: Merchant Seamen, Pirates, and the Anglo-American Maritime World, 1700–1750.* New York: Cambridge University Press, 1989.

Reidy, Joseph P. *From Slavery to Agrarian Capitalism in the Cotton Plantation South: Central Georgia, 1800–1880*. Chapel Hill: University of North Carolina Press, 1992.

Reports of L. A. Beardslee, Relative to Affairs in Alaska, and the Operations of the U.S.S. Jamestown Under His Command, While in the Waters of the Territory, 1882, Forwarded by William H. Hunt, Secretary of the Navy. 47th Cong., 1st sess. Sen. Ex. Doc. No. 71, in Vol. 4.

Rogers, W. McDowell. "Free Negro Legislation in Georgia Before 1865." *Georgia Historical Quarterly* 16 (January 1932): 27–37.

Savours, Ann. *The Search for the Northwest Passage*. New York: St. Martin's Press, 1999.

Schultz, Charles. *Forty-Niners 'Round the Horn*. Columbia: University of South Carolina Press, 1999.

Schultz, Nancy Lusignan. *Fire & Roses: The Burning of the Charlestown Convent, 1834*. New York: The Free Press, 2000.

Shallow, Shawn. *Rescue at the Top of the World*. Arcata, Calif.: Paradise Cay, 2005.

Sharrow, Walter G. "John Hughes and a Catholic Response to Slavery in Antebellum America." *Journal of Negro History* 57 (July 1972): 254–69.

Shelling of an Indian Village in Alaska, Letter by William Gouverneur Morris, Nov. 9, 1882. 47th Cong., 2d sess., House Exec. Doc. No. 9, Pt. 2.

Shepard, Isabel S. *The Cruise of the United States Steamer "Rush" in Behring Sea*. San Francisco, Calif.: Bancroft Company, 1889.

Sherwood, Alfred. *A Gazetteer of Georgia*. Macon, Ga.: S. Boykin, 1860.

Sherwood, Morgan B. *Exploration of Alaska*. New Haven: Yale University Press, 1965.

Simon, Lizzie. *Detour: My Bipolar Road Trip in 4-D*. New York: Atria Books, 2002.

Skates, John Ray. *The Invasion of Japan: Alternative to the Bomb*. Columbia: University of South Carolina Press, 1994.

Smith, Kathleen Lopp, and Verbeck Smith, eds. *Ice Window: Letters from a Bering Sea Village, 1892–1902*. Fairbanks: University of Alaska Press, 2001.

Standard, William L. *Merchant Seamen: A Short History of Their Struggles*. New York: International Publishers, 1947.

Stefansson, Vilhjalmur. *The Friendly Arctic: The Story of Five Years in Polar Regions*. New York: Macmillan Company, 1921.

Stein, Gary C. "A Desperate and Dangerous Man: Captain Michael A. Healy's Arctic Cruise of 1900." *Alaska Journal* 15, no. 2 (Spring 1985): 39–45.

Stewart, Robert Laird. *Sheldon Jackson: Pathfinder and Prospector of the Missionary Vanguard in the Rocky Mountains and Alaska*. New York: Fleming H. Revell Company, 1908.

Stone, James H. "Economic Conditions in Macon, Georgia, in the 1830s." *Georgia Historical Quarterly* 54 (Summer 1970): 209–25.

Strobridge, Truman R. "Blacks and Lights." *Shipmates* III, no. 4 (Summer 1975): 14–17, 31.

———. "The Coast Guard, 1790–1983." In *A Guide to the Sources of United States Military History, Supplement II*. Ed. Robin Higham and Donald J. Mrozek, 260–96. Hamden, Conn.: Archon Books, 1986.

———. "West Point, Thayer & Partridge." *Military Review* 49, no. 10 (October 1989): 78–86.

Strobridge, Truman R., and Dennis L. Noble. "Polar Icebreakers of the United States Coast Guard." *Polar Record: Journal of the Scott Polar Institute* 18, no. 115 (January 1977): 351–60.

———. "North in the Spring, South in the Fall." *Alaska Journal* 8, no. 1 (Winter 1978): 60–69.

———. *Alaska and the U.S. Revenue Cutter Service, 1867–1915*. Annapolis, Md.: Naval Institute Press, 1999.

Strobridge, Truman R., and T. Michael O'Brien. "Blacks and Cutters." *The Chief* 2, no. 5 (June/ July 1976): 13–16.

Taliaferro, John. *In a Far Country: The True Story of a Mission, a Marriage, a Murder, and the Remarkable Reindeer Rescue of 1898*. New York: PublicAffairs, 2006.

Thornton, Harrison R. "Incidents in Alaska Life." *American Missionary* XLVII (1893): 362–75.

Tower, Elizabeth A. *Reading, Religion, Reindeer: Sheldon Jackson's Legacy to Alaska*. Anchorage, Alaska: Elizabeth T. Tower, 1988.

———. "Captain David Henry Jarvis: Alaska's Tragic Hero—Wickersham's Victim." *Alaska History* 5, no. 1 (Spring 1990): 1–21.

Turk, Richard W. "Robley D. Evans: Master of Pugnacity." In *Admirals of the Steel Navy: Makers of the American Naval Tradition, 1880–1930*. Ed. James C. Bradford. 73–96. Annapolis, Md.: Naval Institute Press, 1990.

U.S. Coast Guard. *Record of Movements: Vessels of the United States Coast Guard, 1790–December 31, 1933*. Washington, D.C.: U.S. Coast Guard, [N.d.].

———. *Bering Sea Patrol*. Washington, D.C.: U.S. Coast Guard, 1942.

U.S. Department of Commerce. *Historical Statistics of the United States, Colonial Times To 1970* (Part 1). Washington, D.C.: Government Printing Office, 1975.

U.S. Revenue Cutter Service. *Cruise of the Revenue Steamer* Corwin *in Alaska and the N. W. Arctic Ocean: Notes and Memoranda: Medical and Anthropological; Botanical; Ornithological* Washington, D.C.: Government Printing Office, 1883.

———. *Register of Officers*. Washington, D.C.: Government Printing Office, various years.

———. *Report of the Cruise of the U.S. Revenue Cutter* Bear *and the Overland Expedition for the Relief of the Whalers in the Arctic Ocean from November 27, 1897, to September 13, 1898*. Washington, D.C.: Government Printing Office, 1899.

Utley, Robert M. *Frontier Regulars: The United States Army and the Indian, 1866–1890*. New York: Macmillan, 1973.

Valle, James E. *Rocks and Shoals: Order and Discipline in the Old Navy, 1800–1861*. Annapolis, Md.: Naval Institute Press, 1980.

Van Dorn, William G. *Oceanography and Seamanship*. New York: Dodd, Mead and Company, 1974.

Van Nostrand, Jeanne. "The Seals Are About Gone." *American Heritage* (June 1963): 10–17, 78–80.

Villiers, Alan. *The Way of a Ship: Being Some Account of the Ultimate Development of the Ocean-Going Square-Rigged Sailing Vessel, and the Manner of Her Handling, Her Voyage-Making, Her Personnel, Her Economics, Her Performance, And Her End*. New York: Charles Scribner's Sons, 1953. Reprint, New York: Charles Scribner's Sons, 1970.

———. *The War with Cape Horn*. New York: Charles Scribner's Sons, 1971.

Wead, Frank. *Gales, Ice, and Men: A Biography of the Steam Barkentine* Bear. New York: Dodd, Mead and Company, 1937.

Williams, Carolyn White. *History of Jones County, Georgia, For One Hundred Years, Specifically 1807–1907*. Macon, Ga.: J. K. Burke Company, 1957.

Williams, Gerald O. *The Bering Sea Dispute*: *A Monograph on the Maritime History Dispute*. Eugene, Ore.: Alaska Maritime Publications, 1984.

———. Michael J. [*sic*] Healy and the Alaskan Maritime Frontier, 1880–1902. Master's thesis, University of Oregon, 1987.

Woodson, Carter G. *Free Negro Slaves in the United States in 1830*. 1924. Reprint, New York: Negro Universities Press, 1968.

INDEX

Page numbers in italic type indicate illustrations.

Abolitionist movement, 27; Healy, Alexander S., and, 27

Abram Barker (ship), 132, 184

Active (ship), 55, 71, 131

African Americans: as sailors, 34, 254, 282, 302n3; as slave owners, 30; U.S. Navy and, 282n17

Age of Sail, 5–6; Cape Horn reputation during, 61; class structure during, 34

Alabama (ship), 48

Alaska, *118*; Civil War's influence on purchase of, 55; *Corwin* voyage to, 120–36; Eskimo law in, 177, 191; gold rush in, 177, 234–37; Mary Jane Healy in, 9, 180, 232–33; Michael Augustine Healy and, 7, 66–67, 84–101, 172–200, 232–33; Inside Passage to, 147; Kinugumuts in, 174, 176, 187–88; lack of government in, 122–23; lawlessness in, 176–77; missionaries in, 172–76, 188–89; Native American population in, 121–28; *Reliance* in, 66–68; sale of, from Russia, 54–55; sealing industry in, 77–79; Seward and, 55; umealit in, 176; U.S. purchase of, 15, 54–55; vigilante groups in, 178–79; white settlers v. Native Americans in, 122–23. *See also* Arctic region; Sitka, Alaska

Alaska (Michener), 12, 254; Michael Augustine Healy, as character in, 302n5

Alaska Commercial Company, 76–77, 81, 153; fur seal industry and, 77, 196–97

The Alaska Journal, 243, 299n31

Alaska Maritime Frontier, 172

Alaskan fur seals, 77–79; bachelor bulls, 78; government studies of, 78–79; Michael Augustine Healy and, 196–97; mating habits of, 78; resurgence of, after overhunting, 295n108. *See also* Fur seal industry

Albatross (ship), 198

Alcoholism, of Michael Augustine Healy, 3, 8, 148, 152, 202, 255–56; bipolar disorder influenced by, 245, 300n51; causes of, 12–13; suicide attempts as result of, 243–44

Alcohol use: by Native Americans, 122–23; sailing as profession and, 255–56, 296n19

Aldrich, Herbert L., 144

Alert (ship), 138

Alexander (ship), 227

Allen, William, 32

American Indian Wars, 120, 288n2

American Revolution, U.S. Revenue Cutter Service during, 46

Amethyst (ship), 141–42

Andrew, John Albion, 51

Angoon, Alaska, 121; attacks on Native Americans in, 126–28

Antisarlook, Charles, 184–86, 194–96, 230–31

Antisarlook, Mary, 184–86, 194–96, 230–31, 252, 294n84; Eskimo name for, 194

An Unquiet Mind (Jamison), 300n51

Arctic region, *119*; *Corwin* in, 89–101; early exploration of, 87–89; lost ships in, 89–90, 97–98; native starvation in, 94; polar icebreakers in, 90–91; *Polaris* Expedition to, 88; U.S. Army camp in, 137–38. *See also* Alaska

Arnold, Frederick, 216–17

Avery, E. O., 158

"Awaiting orders," 71–72

Bailey, George W., 76, 79–82, 94, 101, 174; death of, 101; promotion history for, 286n27; on *Richard Rush*, 94, 101

Bailhache, T. H., 158

Baleen, 85–86

Balls, John G., 90

Baltimore (ship), 197

Barnes, Winslow B., 79

Barnett, Len, 283n13

Barrow, John, 87–88

Barry, John G., 204

Bartleman, R. W., 150

Bartlett, C. W., 126

Basker, Roland, 61

Bass, D. F., 164

Bauldry, George, 95

Beaman, Libby, 84

Bear (ship), 1–2, 9, *107*, 137–49, 198; on Bering Sea
    Patrol, 147, 201–5; burial of dead and, 183; en-
    listed crewmen of, *115*; Greeley Relief Expedition
    and, 139; Michael Augustine Healy on, 137–49;
    mutiny on, 14; obtained by U.S. Revenue Cutter
    Service, 140; patrol area for, 141; rescue opera-
    tions by, 150; Sharp on, 13–14; tensions between
    officers on, 203; testimony about treatment of
    crew on, 159–66; tricing up on, 162; Tuttle as
    commander of, 230–31; whalers and, 142

Beardslee, Leslie A., 124

Belvedere (ship), 226

Bennett, James Gordon, 88

Bent, Silas, 88

Bering, Vitus, 53

Bering Sea, 76–77, *119*; Bailey in, 79; declared as
    closed by U.S., 197; separate theaters of operation
    in, 137; U.S. response to poaching in, of fur seals,
    197–98

Bering Sea Controversy, 197–200

Bering Sea Patrol, 101; Michael Augustine Healy on,
    147, 201–5

Berry, John G., 196, 231

Berry, M. P., 123

Bertha (ship), 167–68

Bertholf, Ellsworth, 230

Bipolar disorder, 245, 300n51

Black Defenders of America (Greene), 11

Black Kettle (Chief), 288n2

Blossom (ship), 96

Bodkin, Thomas, 204, 214

Boomerang (ship), 283n13

Borden, Gilbert B., 146

Boston Nautical College, 52

Boutwell, George S., 70–71

Bowhead whales, 86–87

Boyle, Edward, 80

Bravo (ship), 48

Brewery Workers Union, 155

Broadbent, A. L., 90, 204

Broadbent, Howard M., 182, 186

Brooks, Maria, 12

Brooks, Richard, 63

Brower, Charles D., 178, 226

Brown, Charles, 63

Brownson, Orestes, 26

Bryan, J. J., 239

"Bucko mate," 44

Budd, James H., 120

Buhner, Albert, 70, *114*, 151, 165, 202, 250

Burantt, Andrew, 51

Burke, Edmund, 90

Burke, R., 49

Bynes, Joseph, 217

Cain, Richard, 212

The Caine Mutiny (Wouk), 239

Calico Jim, 142

Call, Samuel J., 153, 230, 297n7

Cantwell, John Cassin, 130, 134, 150, 179, 228, 234,
    251; on reindeer purchases, 293n44

Cape Horn, 57–58, *117*; Age of Sail and reputation
    of, 61; sailing difficulties near, 57–58

Cape of Good Hope, 87

Carlisle, John G., 207, 224, 226

Carlton, C. C., 227

Carpenter, Lucretia M., 233

Carter, John C., 58, 63

Catholic Church: James A. Healy in, 41–42, 45–46,
    63; on slavery, 26–27

Catholicism, 24–25; antagonism toward, 25; in
    Georgia, 24; of Michael Morris Healy, 24; slavery
    and, 26–27

"Cat of nine tails," 35

Chanties (sailor's songs), 37

Chase (ship), 53

Chick, George, 60

Chick, James, 58, 60

Chilcal tribe, 285n2

Chivington, John, 288n2

Chukchi (Siberian natives), 8, *111*, *113*; program for
    buying from, 8, 175–77, 180–81, 192–93; reindeer
    herding by, 8, 134, 179–80

Civil War (U.S.), 55; purchase of Alaska influenced
    by, 55

Clark, Ezra W., 89–90

Clark Healy, Eliza, 4, 10, 12, 14, 18–28, 271; background of, 19, 253, 281n14; family members of, 27, 31, 42–43, 282n31; interracial marriage of, 11, 18–28; settling children up north by, 23–28; slave owners of, 19, 43; social ostracism of, 21; sudden death of, 4, 27

Class structure in sailing, 34; during Age of Sail, 34

Cleveland, Grover, 146

College of the Holy Cross: establishment of, 25; Michael Augustine Healy at, 5, 29, 31–32; Healy family at, 4–5, 25–27; Jesuits' role in, 25; *The Matricula of the College of Holy Cross*, 281n7

Commodore Perry (ship), 203, 211

Conning the ship, 148. *See also* Polar icebreakers

Conrad, Joseph, 15

Conway, Sheila, 298n18

Cooper, George, 58, 60, 63; service record of, 284n17

Coquitlan (ship), 198

Cornell, Stephen, 49–50

Corwin (ship), 6–7, 83–85, 89–101, 149, 198, 203; attacks on Native Americans by, 126–28; Michael Augustine Healy on, as commanding officer, 120–36; as polar icebreaker, 91, 99; as rescue ship, 97–98; voyage to Alaska, 120–36

Cotton industry: cotton gin and, 17; in Georgia, 17–18; slave labor for, 18

Coulson, W. C., 212, 235

Cowan, Lemuel C., 56

Crimean War, 54

"Crimps," 37

Cruzan, J. A., 156

Cunningham, Bessie, 9–10

Custer, George Armstrong, 123, 288n2

Cyclothymic disorder, 300n51

Daeweritz, Otto, 156, 158, 161, 167–69; mutinous behavior of, 169

Dallas (ship), 209

Daniels, George M., 201, 215, 251, 275

Darcout, Richard, 156

Deepwater sailing, 57–58; strict rationing during, 58

De Long, Emma, 88

De Long, George Washington, 88

Denbigh Castle (ship), 57

Denneark, Robert, 63

Desertion, 36

de Stoeckl, Edouard, 55

Dewey, George, 197, 263

Dexter class, of cutters, 73

Dimmock, F. M., 204

Dolliver, James, 51

Dory, George H., 130

Dory, J. E., 202

Douay-Rheims Bible, 32

Drake Passage, 57; *Reliance* in, 61–62

E. A. Stevens (ship), 53

Eakins, Thomas, 297n34

Eden, M. B., 157, 164, 258

1890 trial, of Michael Augustine Healy, 158–71; testimony about treatment of crew in, 159–69; WCTU and, 157, 257–58; West Coast Seaman's Union and, 155, 158, 257–58

1896 trial, of Michael Augustine Healy, 1–3, 205–25, 275–76; Carlisle role in, 207, 224, 226; charges of personal threats in, 219; as closed, 213–14; crewmen v. officers in, 212, 216; defense case in, 221–22; deliberation portion of, 224; Michael Augustine Healy, testimony of, 222; misconduct charges in, 203–6, 214; news reports on, 206–8, 216–18; officers' testimony in, 2; pretrial predictions of guilt in, 212; pretrial publicity for, 210–11; prosecution's case in, 205–21; reversal of verdict of, 247, 259; sentencing after, 3, 225; summation of, 222–25; verdict of, 224; Chester White, and, 206–9

Eliza (ship), 146

Elliott, Henry Wood, 78–79

Emery, Howard, 201–2, 251, 276

English College (in Douai), 5; Eugene Healy at, 281n12; Michael Augustine Healy at, 32–33

Epilepsy, Michael Augustine Healy and, 13, 244

Eskimo law, in Alaska, 177, 191

Eskimos: banning of firearm sales to, 99; Chukchi, 8, *111, 113*, 179–80; Michael Augustine Healy and concern for, 7–8; lawlessness among, 189–91; missionaries and, 173, 189; racism toward, 99. *See also* Chukchi

Eskimos of the Bering Strait (Ray), 180, 295n109

Estella (ship), 158–59, 161–69; mutinous behavior of crew on, 166, 169; testimony about treatment of crew on, 161–69

Evans, Robley D. "Fighting Bob," 197–98, 251

Evans, Stephen H., 9

Fairlong, Edward B., 63

Favorite (ship), 125–27

Fenwick, Benedict, 25, 31

Fernda, Andre, 130

Ferral, Robert, 156

Fessenden (ship), 212

Finnety, Thomas, 156

Fitzpatrick, John Bernard, 24

Flogging, 35

Foley, Albert S., 9–10, 16, 242, 278n2, 279n9

Foundling (ship), 279n3

Framsden, Roy, 156, 158, 160–61; mutinous behavior of, 170

Franklin, John, 87–88

Franklin Expedition, 88, 145, 287n21

French, Ada P., 236

Fugitive Slave Law, 30–31; Healy children and, 30–31

Fuhrman, Alfred, 156–57

"Furious fifties," 57

Fur seal industry, 77–79; Alaska Commercial Company and, 77, 196–97; poaching within, 79, 198; Pribilof Islands and, 77–78

Furuseth, Andrew, 156, 257

Gallatin (ship), 70

Gardner, C. H., 241

Garforth, Frank A., 203

General Harmony (ship), 66

George and Susan (ship), 132

Georgia: Catholicism in, 24; cotton industry in, 17–18; division of land in, 16–17; Michael Morris Healy in, 16–28; interracial marriage in, 19–20; Native American treatment in, 16–17; slave codes in, 21–22

Gibbons, Edward, 22

Golden Gate (ship), 243, 247

Gold rush, in Alaska, 177, 234–37; U.S. Revenue Cutter Service during, 234

Grant (ship), 203, 212

Gray, M. F., 170

Greeley, Adolphus W., 137–41

Greeley Expedition, 138

Greeley Relief Expedition, 138–40; *Bear* as part of, 139

Greene, Robert E., 11

Grieve, Walter, 138

Griswold, Samuel, 17, 19, 42–43

Guttstadt, Herman, 156

Hamilton, Alexander, 46

Hamlin, Charles, 205, 258

Hand, W. H., 95

Hardeman, Robert, 29

Harlow, Frederic Pease, 32

Harris, W. D., 180

Hartley (ship), 246

Hartwell (ship), 212

Hassell, Horace, 151; drinking problems of, 151

Hawse pipe, 282n18

Healy, Alexander S., 4–5, 20, 69, 282; abolitionism and, 27; at College of the Holy Cross, 4–5, 25–27

Healy, Amanda J., 4, 20, 63, 273

Healy, Eliza D., 4, 20, 63–64, 273

Healy, Eugene (son of Michael A. Healy), 69, 271

Healy, Eugene (son of Michael M. Healy), 4, 20, 273; at English College, 281n12

Healy, Frederick A., 69, 84, *105*, 210, 225, 233–34, 250, 271; annulled marriage of, 298n18; army enlistment of, 234; death of, 301n71; expulsion from college, 298n18; newspaper coverage of, 233–34; rebellious behavior of, 233

Healy, Hugh C., 4, 20, 272; at College of the Holy Cross, 4–5, 25–27; death of, 41, 282n27; return to Georgia, 31

Healy, James A., 4–5, 9, 11, 20, 84, *102*, 182, 206, 210, 271; in Catholic Church, 41–42, 45–46, 63; at College of the Holy Cross, 4–5, 25–27; political influence of, 45–46, 51; slave purchase by, 43

Healy, John James, 53, 271

Healy, Martha A., 4, 9, 20, 272–73; religious history of, 284n15

Healy, Mary Jane, 64, *104*, *108–9*, 225, 261–62, 271; in Alaska, 9, 180, 232–33; death of, 250, 301n71; diaries of, 281n11; inheritance of, 74–75; return to San Francisco, 199. *See also* Roach, Mary Jane

Healy, Michael Augustine, *106*, *108–10*; in Alaska, 7, 66–67, 84–101, 172–200, 232–33; in *Alaska*, as character, 302n5; alcoholism of, 3, 8, 148, 152, 202, 255–56; on *Bear*, 137–49; on Bering Sea Patrol, 147, 201–5; bipolar disorder in, 245, 300n51; as biracial, 11–12, 253–55; burial of dead crewmen and, 183, 293n42; at College of Holy Cross, 5, 29, 31–32; on *Corwin*, 89–101, 120–36; as "Czar of the North," 200; death of, 249–50; diaries of, 281n11; dismissal from service of, 224–26; early sailing history of, 5; 1890 trial of, 158–71; 1896 trial of, 1–3; at English College, 5, 32–33; epilepsy and, 13, 244; erratic behavior of, in Unalaska, 152–53, 203–4; as heroic figure, 262–65; hiding of racial background by, 11–12, 14–15, 44; on HMS *Pheasant*, 203–4, 207; hospitalization of, 242–43; humane treatment of crew by, 163–64; humanitarian efforts of, 9; Indian Point project under, 184–85; insanity charges against, 241–42; as inspiration for *The Sea Wolf*, 14; Irish heritage of, 4; Kobuk River expedition of, 130–33; law enforcement under, 176–77; letters to family by, 152–53, 203–4, 293n40; lifetime safety record of, 252; marriage of, to Mary Jane Roach, 51; as master storyteller, 38–41; on *McCulloch*, 235–43, 299n31; in merchant fleet, 41; misconduct charges against, 203–6, 214; Native Americans and, 7; news reports on, 158, 160–61, 163, 206–8, 216–18, 241–42, 283n13; nicknames for, 6; promotion to captain for, 128; protection of seals as duty of, 196–97; public drunkenness of, 71–72; public protests against, 155–58; public support for, 156; race as factor for, 253–55; rank history of, 6, 43, 53–54; rebellious adolescence of, 32–33; reinstatement of service for, 235–37, 245–46; on *Reliance*, 55–56, 58–65; relieved of command, 205; retirement of, 249–50; on *Richard Rush*, 72–77; *Seminole* and, reinstatement on, 236–37; sentencing of, 3; as sole Alaska maritime representative, 7; suicide attempts by, 14, 238–41; surveillance of, 232; testimony against, 159–69; on *Thetis*, 247–49; transfer requests by, 67–68; tricing up on orders of, 162; on use of tricing up of sailors, 168–69; in U.S. Revenue Cutter Service, 46, 52–53; Whaling Disaster of 1897 and, calls for reinstatement after, 228–30; James Taylor White, and, reports on drunkenness of, 153–55; on *William E. Chandler*, as first permanent command, 82–83; written reports of, 135–36. *See also* 1890 trial, of Michael Augustine Healy; 1896 trial, of Michael Augustine Healy

Healy, Michael Morris, 3–4, 12, 14, 16–28; Catholicism of, 24; death of, 4, 28; educational beliefs of, 22–23; emigration to U.S., 16; estate of, 29–30, 43; in Georgia, 16–28; interracial marriage of, 11, 18–28; Manning and, 23, 25–26; military service of, 279n3; settling children up north by, 23–28; as slave owner, 20–21, 30, 42–43, 280n21; social ostracism of, 21

Healy, Patrick F., 4–5, 11, 20, 31, *103*, 272; at College of the Holy Cross, 4–5, 25–27; family genealogy by, 278n1

Helen Mar (ship), 95, 98

"Hell Roaring Mike," 6. *See also* Healy, Michael Augustine

Henderson, Robert, 79

Henley, Bradley, 2, 206, 213

Henriques, John A., 56, 250; on *Reliance*, 59–60, 68; on *Richard Rush*, 73

Herald (ship), 88

The History of the Decline and Fall of the Roman Empire (Gibbons), 22

HMS *Osprey* (ship), 124

HMS *Pheasant* (ship), 203–4, 207, 256

Hodgedon, D. B., 212

Holben, Alfred, 156, 158, 167; mutinous behavior of, 169

Hooper, Calvin L., 52, 54, 83, 90, 92, 101, *116*, 174, 199, 201, 215, 250, 256, 261

Hoover, J. Edgar, 232

Hornaday, William, 280n21

Howard, James, 59

Howard, William H., 59–60

Howe, Mabel, *113*, 206–9; Chester White and, 206–9

Howell, W. B., 232

Hughes, James, 157, 159–63; testimony of, 159–63

Hunter (ship), 144

Hutton, Benjamin, 204

Hutton, H. W., 158, 164, 171

In a Far Country (Taliaferro), 298n13

Indian Point project, 184–85

Inside Passage, to Alaska, 147

Interracial marriage, 11; in Georgia, 19–20; laws against, 19–20; social ostracism as result of, 21

Interracial Voice, 255

Jackson, Sheldon, 8, 172–77, 190, 200, 232, 251–52; federal reindeer herding programs and, 8, 175–77, 187, 192–93; as missionary, 172–73

James Crawford (ship), 68

Jane Grey (ship), 155

Jarvis, David H., 146, 152, 182, 185–86, 230, 250–51; suicide of, 251

Jeanette (ship), 6, 89, 94, 97–98, 100, 120, 130, 149

Jeanette Expedition, 6, 89

Jefferson, Thomas, 49

Jesuits, College of the Holy Cross and, 25

John Barleycorn, 3

Johnson, Andrew, 55

Johnson, Rosamond, 157

"Jonahs," 37–38

Jones, John Paul, 263

Jones, Levin T., 214, 275

Jumna (ship), 50, 283n13

Kelly, William H., 155
Kenrick, Francis, 26
Key, Francis Scott, 58
Kialy, John, 60
Kimball, Sumner I., 145, 256, 260; U.S. Revenue
     Cutter Service under, 291n3
King, Ernest J., 263
Kinugumuts, 174, 176, 187–88; murders by, 190
Kipling, Rudyard, 37
Kittredge, Ellen Louise. *See* Lopp, Ellen L.
Kjellman, William, 176
Knowles, Josiah N., 146
Kobuk River expedition, 130–33

LaFitte, Jean, 48
Lamoreaux, Carol, 298n18
Law. *See* Eskimo law, in Alaska
Lee, Margaret, 45
Leo (ship), 95
Lewis, Frank, 130, 131
Limuel (ship), 51
Lincoln (ship), 55, 68–69, 83
Littlefield, A. D., 70
Livingston, David, 88
Loch Garry (ship), 138
Loleta (ship), 96
London, Jack, 7, 14, 196, 234
Long, John D., 227
Long, Robert, 63
Loomis, Jarvis, 48
Lopp, Ellen L., 188, 192, 252
Lopp, William Thomas, 174–75, 192, 194–95, 231,
     252; missionary activities of, 189–90
Louisiana (ship), 48

Mabel (ship), 7, 132–33
Mackay, W.J.D., 156
Macy, S. W., 70
Makikoff, Pasha. *See* Antisarlook, Mary
Manning (ship), 251
Manning, John, 23; as Healy family guardian, 25–26,
     29, 31
Marriage. *See* Interracial marriage
Marsh, William G., 131
Mary and Helen (ship), 120
Mary W. Thomas (ship), 177
Massachusetts (ship), 47
Massachusetts Humane Society, 150
Mating habits, of Alaskan fur seals, 78

The Matricula of the College of Holy Cross, 281n7
Maynard, I. A., 150
McCarthy, Charles, 29
McCulloch (ship), 235–43; Michael Augustine Healy
     removed as commander of, 239, 299n31
McCulloch, James, 60, 63
McKenna, Richard, 278n26
McLellan, Archibald S., 188
McLellan, Mattie E., 191
McLenegan, Samuel B., 130
Melville, George, 98
Merrimack (ship), 53
Merriman, E. C., 124
Merry, William L., 228–29
Michael A. Healy (ship), 12
Michener, James, 12
Miller, James, 130
Misconduct charges, against Michael Augustine
     Healy, 203–6, 214; news reports of, 206–8; for
     spitting at officers, 218–19
Missionaries in Alaska, 172–76, 188–89; attacks on,
     175–76; Eskimos and, 173, 189; murder of, 190
Moccasin (ship), 70–72, 100
Moore, H. A., 232
Moreland, William, 29
The Morning Call, 1, 156, 224, 227–29, 249; Whaling
     Disaster of 1897 and, 227–29
Morrill (ship), 251
Morris, William Gouverneur, 125
Mount Wollaston (ship), 89, 97–98, 149
Mowat, Farley, 88
Mulledy, Thomas, 26
Mullett, Thomas B., 56
Munger, Frederick M., 258
Myrick, C. D., 90

Napoleon (ship), 131, 143–44, 184
Native Americans: in Alaska, 121–28 (*see also* Eski-
     mos); introduction to alcohol, 122–23; Chilcal
     tribe, 285n2; clashes with white settlers, 122–23;
     Corwin attacks on, 126–28; demands for com-
     pensation by, 127–28; Michael Augustine Healy,
     and, 7–8; mass starvation of, 134; misperceptions
     about, 124; new diseases' effects upon, 122; as
     nomadic, 121–22; Northwest Trading Company
     and, 124–25; population of, 122; in Sitka, 123;
     Tlingit people, 121; U.S. government policy
     toward, 125–26; U.S. government treatment of, in
     Georgia, 16–17

Naugatuck (ship), 53

Naval Historical Foundation, 298n13

Nelson, Edward William, 174

Nelson, R. M., 198

Newspaper articles: 1896 trial of Michael Augustine
    Healy, 206–8, 216–18, 223–24; Frederick A.
    Healy, 233–34; Michael Augustine Healy, 158,
    160–61, 163, 206–8, 216–18, 241–42, 283n13;
    manipulation of, accusations of, 223–24; miscon-
    duct charges, against Michael Augustine Healy,
    206–8; Whaling Disaster of 1897 and, 227–29

New York Herald, 160–61

New York Times, 158, 163

Nice, Harvey N., 204, 214

Nicholas Riggio (ship), 51

Noble, Dennis L., 278n28, 295n109

Nome City (ship), 240

North America, Russian occupation of, 54. *See also*
    Alaska

North Star, 145

Northwest Passage, 87

Northwest Trading Company, 121; Native Ameri-
    cans and, 124–25

Nunivak (ship), 234, 251

Nye, Ebenezer, 89, 98

O'Connor, William, 164–65

Odyssey (ship), 6

"The Odyssey of Captain Healy," 12

Ohno, T., 216

"One-drop rule," 19

O'Toole, James M., 12, 254, 279n3, 299n31

Otter (ship), 66

Overland Relief Expedition, 195, 230–31, 298n13;
    success of, 231; U.S. Revenue Cutter Service and,
    298n13

Overland Relief Expedition (Naval Historical Foun-
    dation), 298n13

Owen, F. E., 90

Pacific Steam Whaling Company, 145–47

Pandora (ship), 89

Passing, as white, 11–12, 253–55

Passing for White (O'Toole), 299n31

Pawtuxet (ship), 53, 55

Pelagic seals. *See* Alaskan fur seals

Perry, Oliver Hazard, 263

Perry, Robert, 220

Petermann, August Heinrich, 88

Peter the Great, 53

Phelps, T. G., 158

Phillips, Edward W., 279n3

Piracy, U.S. Revenue Cutter Service and, 48

Plover (ship), 96

Poaching: in Bering Sea, U.S. response to, 197–98;
    within fur seal industry, 79, 198

Point Barrow, Alaska, 226–30. *See also* Whaling
    Disaster of 1897

Polar icebreakers, 90–91; *Corwin*, 91, 99

Polaris Expedition, 88

The Polar Passion (Mowat), 88

Powell, A. D., 255

Pribilof Islands, 77–79

Progressive Movement, 256–57

Pulitzer, Joseph, 148

Quintall, William F., 216

"Racial kidnapping," 255

Ray, Dorothy Jean, 180, 295n109

Reindeer herding: by Chukchi (Siberian natives),
    8, 134, 179–80; federal programs for, 8, 175–77,
    180–81, 192–93, 295n109; Overland Relief Expe-
    dition and, 195; for purchase, 293n44

Reliance (ship), 55–56, 58–65, 95, 125; in Alaska,
    66–68; in Chile, 62; crew problems on, 59–60;
    in Drake Passage, 61–62; Henricus on, 59–60,
    68; mutiny on, 59; officers on, 56; personnel
    discharges from, 60, 63

Rescue at the Top of the World (Shallow), 298n13

Rescue operations, 7; by *Bear*, 150; Franklin Expedi-
    tion, 88, 145, 287n21; in *Jeanette* Expedition, 6,
    89; for Whaling Disaster of 1897, 226–30

Retirement system, for U.S. Revenue Cutter Service,
    213, 247, 260

Reynolds, William E., 212, 217–18

Richard Rush (ship), 72–77, 79–80, 94, 198, 203;
    Bailey on, 94, 101; new technology of, 73–74

Right whales, 87

Riley, John, 63

Roach, John, 45–46, 51; estate of, 74–75

Roach, Margaret, 51

Roach, Mary Jane, 3, 9; family history of, 45–46;
    marriage of, to Michael Augustine Healy, 51. *See
    also* Healy, Mary Jane

"Roaring forties," 57

Robinson, Leonidas L., 182

Rogers, H. H., 212

Rogers, N. B., 73

Roosevelt, Theodore, 197

Ross, Worth, 204

Roys, Thomas, 84–85, 145

Russell, Israel C., 181

Russia: after Crimean War, 54; North American occupation by, 54; Pribilof Islands, 77–79; sale of Alaska by, 54–55

Russians: North American occupation by, 54; in Sitka, Alaska, 124

Sailing, as profession: African Americans and, 34, 254, 282, 302n3; alcohol use and, 255–56, 296n19; "bucko mate," 44; captains' authority in, 35; chanties for, 37; class structure in, 34; "crimps," 37; death and, 5; deepwater, 57–58; desertion, 36; flogging, 35; harsh living conditions of, 5, 33–35; "Jonahs," 37–38; officers v. sailors within, 34; oral history of, 38; spouses and, 36–37; tricing up and, 35

Sailors, drinking habits of, 100

A Sailor's Log (Evans), 198

Salamatov, Matrona, 108

Samborska, Ania, 116

Samuels, Clarence, 302n3

San Francisco Chronicle, 218, 233

Santa Clara College, Frederick Healy and, 298n18

Scammon, Charles, 92

Schley, Winfield S., 138

"Screaming sixties," 57

Sea captains: authority of, 35; onboard spouses of, 36–37; shipowners and, 36

Search and rescue operations, 7

Searle, William, 47

Seattle Post-Intelligencer, 241–42

The Sea Wolf (London), 14, 196

Seminole (ship), 236–37

Service, Robert, 234

Seward, William, 55

Shallow, Shawn, 298n13

Sharp, Benjamin, 13–14, 220–21

Shepard, Leonard G., 52–54, 72, 166, 181, 250, 261; service record of, 284n18

Sherman, Augusta Barrett, 64–65

Sherman, John, 82

Ships. See Steel ships; specific ships

Shoemaker, Charles F., 193, 235, 261, 264, 301n67

Shoemaker, Francis R., 248

"Sinrock Mary." See Antisarlook, Mary

Sitka, Alaska, 76; Native Americans in, 123; Russians in, 124

Slamm, Jefferson, 259

Slave auctions, 42–43

Slave codes, 21–22

Slave owners: African Americans as, 30; of Eliza Clark Healy, 19, 43; James A. Healy as, 43; Michael Morris Healy as, 20–21, 30, 42–43, 280n21

Slavery, 18; African-American slave owners, 30; Catholicism and, 26–27; cotton industry and, 18; Fugitive Slave Law, 30–31; "one-drop rule" and, 19; private freeing of, 22; slave codes and, 21–22; U.S. Revenue Cutter Service and, 48

Smith, E. E., 95

Smith, Horatio D., 223

Smith, James, 19

Smith, S. P., 143, 177

Spanish War of 1898, 251

Spicer, Henry, 157, 164–66, 258; mutinous behavior of, 169

Spoils system, 49

Spreckels, John D., 227, 231

Stanley, Henry M., 88

"The Star-Spangled Banner," 58

Steam engines, U.S. Revenue Cutter Service use of, 74

Steel ships, in U.S. Revenue Cutter Service, 139–40

Stefansson, Vilhjalmur, 298n13

Stein, Gary C., 243, 299n31

Stephen, Alexander, 138

Stidham, C. W., 240

Stoddard, Louis N., 212

Stodder, Loring N., 247

Stonehill, E. B., 158

Stoney, George M., 128–30, 227, 241

St. Paul (ship), 80

Straits of Magellan, 74

Suicide, attempts by Michael Augustine Healy, 14, 238–41; alcoholism and, 243–44

Sumii, F., 216

Sumner, Charles, 156

Sun, 1

Superior (ship), 85

Taliaferro, John, 298n13

Temperance movements, 157; within Progressive Movement, 256–57

Thetis (ship), 138–39, 146, 166, 247; construction of, 138–39; Michael Augustine Healy on, 247–49

Thomas Corwin (ship), 75

Thompson, P. W., 238

Thornton, Harrison Robinson, 173; missionary activities of, 189; murder of, 190

Thornton, Neda, 192, 245

Tilton, Fred, 226

Tlingit people, 121

Townsend, Charles H., 131; botanical reports by, 134–35

Tozier, D. F., 203, 215–16

Transcontinental railroad, 87

Tricing up, of sailors, 35; on *Bear*, 162; as common practice, 168–69; on *Estella*, 158–59, 164; on *Wanderer*, 165

Tropic Bird (ship), 234

Tuck, John, *109*

Tuck, Mary, *109*

Tucker, William, 35

Turner, Nat, 21

Tuttle, Francis, 230–31

Umealit (leaders), 176

United States (U.S.): American Indian Wars and, 120; Bering Sea Controversy and, 197–200; Civil War in, 55; "closing" of Bering Sea by, 197; Progressive Movement in, 256–57; purchase of Alaska by, 15, 54–55; War of 1812 and, 58

The United States Coast Guard, 1790–1914 (Evans), 9

U.S. *See* United States

U.S. Army, in Arctic region, 137–38

U.S. Coast Guard: formation of, 5–6, 47, 283n3; on safety record of Michael Augustine Healy, 183

U.S. Life-Saving Service (USLSS), 5, 47, 145, 291n3

USLSS. *See* U.S. Life-Saving Service

U.S. Merchant Marines, Michael Augustine Healy in, 41

U.S. Navy, 80; African Americans and, 282n17

U.S. Revenue Cutter Service, 5–6, 46–50; administration issues of, 49; during Alaska gold rush, 234; during American Revolution, 46; application process for, 50; "awaiting orders" in, 71–72; *Bear* obtained by, 140; coal transport by, 80; command structure of, 283n3; commissions of, political influence of, 49; crew size of, 47; *Dexter* class of cutters, 73; dismissal of Michael Augustine Healy from, 224–26; enforcement of federal laws by, 79, 97–99, 123; establishment of, 46–47, 283n3; freeing of slaves by, 48; Michael Augustine Healy in, 46, 52–53; *Jeannette* Expedi-

tion and, 6; under Sumner Kimball, 291n3; native peoples and, interactions with, 98–99; Overland Relief Expedition and, 298n13; personnel recruitment for, 49; piracy and, 48; polar icebreakers in, 90–91; primary duties of, 47–48; recreational activities in, 80; retirement system for, 213, 247, 260; revenue officers of, 47–48; seniority system in, 52; ship size, during early years of, 47; during slave trade, 48; spoils system of, 49; steam engine use by, 74; transition to steel ships, 139–40; during wartime, 49. *See also* Search and rescue operations

USS *Adams*, 125–26, 198

USS *Columbus*, 35

USS *Jamestown*, 124

USS *Mohican*, 198

USS *Ranger*, 198

USS *Rogers*, 120, 128

USS *Saginaw*, 67

USS *Wolcott*, 124

U.S. Treasury department: 1896 trial, of Healy, Michael Augustine, and, 205–25; maritime operations under control of, 6, 46. *See also* U.S. Revenue Cutter Service

Vanderbilt, J. M., 125

Vigilant (ship), 56, 69–70, 89, 97–98, 149

Vigilante groups, in Alaska, 178–79

Vincent, James B., 143–45, 150, 184

Walker, Charles, 226

Wanderer (ship), 157, 162, 168; tricing up on, 165

War of 1812, 58

Wars: American Indian Wars, 120, 288n2; Crimean War, 54; Spanish War of 1898, 251; U.S. Civil War, 55; War of 1812, 58

Wayanda (ship), 79

Wayson, James, 90

WCTU. *See* Woman's Christian Temperance Union

Wead, Frank, 9

Webster, Daniel, 24

West Coast Seaman's Union, 7, 155, 158, 257–58. *See also* Temperance movements

Westmoreland, William, 30

Whaling Disaster of 1897, 226–30; Michael Augustine Healy and reinstatement requests after, 228–30; *The Morning Call* and, 227–29; Overland Relief Expedition and, 230–31

Whaling industry, 85–87; baleen in, 85–86;

bowhead whales and, 86–87; development of, 85–87; fatalities in, 87; government assistance for, 146; harsh conditions within, 86; oil and, 85; right whales and, 87; shipwrecks as risks in, 145; support for Michael Augustine Healy, 155; technology for, 86

"Wharf rats," 36

White, Chester M., *113*, 203, 206–9; extramarital affair of, 206–9; Howe and, 206–9; resignation of, 207–8

White, James Taylor, 150–55, 158; reports on drunkenness of Michael Augustine Healy, 153–55

White, John W., 75, 123, 150, 158, 261

White, passing as, 11–12, 253–55

Whitman, H., 156

Whitney, Eli, 17

Wilbur, Horace, 130

William E. Chandler (ship), 82–83, 148

William H. Allen (ship), 174–75

William H. Seward (ship), 69

Williams, Gerald O., 12, 258

Williams, John Foster, 47

Wiltzen, Nathaniel, 283–84n13

Windom, William, 157–58

Woman's Christian Temperance Union (WCTU), 7, 157, 257–58. *See also* Temperance movements

Woodson, Carter, 30

The World, 148

Wouk, Herman, 1, 214, 239

Wyckoff, John, 90, 96

Yorktown (ship), 198–99

Young, Allen, 89, 287n21

Young, Clay, *116*

Young, Nina, *116*

Yukon (ship), 155

Dennis L. Noble entered the U.S. Coast Guard in 1957 and retired in 1978 as a Senior Chief Petty Officer. Sea duty took Noble six times to the Arctic and twice to the Antarctic. After retiring from the U.S. Coast Guard, he earned a Ph.D. in U.S. history from Purdue University.

Noble is the author of twelve books and now writes full-time. He lives in Sequim, Washington, with his wife, Loren.

Truman R. Strobridge, a native of Sault Ste. Marie, Michigan, served in the U.S. Army Air Forces as a sergeant in World War II. After his discharge, he gained an intimate knowledge of Alaska as Historian of the U.S. Army, Alaska, and the Joint Alaska Command from 1963 to 1967.

His thirty years of employment with the U.S. Federal Civil Service as an historian included work with the U.S. Army, Coast Guard, Marine Corps, National Archives, Joint Chiefs of Staff and three (Alaskan, European, and Pacific) of its unified combatant commands. His best-known work is his coauthored official campaign history, *Western Pacific Operations: The History of the U.S. Marine Corps in World War II*, Vol. 4 (1971).

New Perspectives on Maritime History and Nautical Archaeology

Edited by James C. Bradford and Gene Allen Smith

Maritime Heritage of the Cayman Islands, by Roger C. Smith (1999; first paperback edition, 2000)

The Three German Navies: Dissolution, Transition, and New Beginnings, 1945–1960, by Douglas C. Peifer (2002)

The Rescue of the Gale Runner: *Death, Heroism, and the U.S. Coast Guard*, by Dennis L. Noble (2002; first paperback edition, 2008)

Brown Water Warfare: The U.S. Navy in Riverine Warfare and the Emergence of a Tactical Doctrine, 1775–1970, by R. Blake Dunnavent (2003)

Sea Power in the Medieval Mediterranean: The Catalan-Aragonese Fleet in the War of the Sicilian Vespers, by Lawrence V. Mott (2003)

An Admiral for America: Sir Peter Warren, Vice-Admiral of the Red, 1703–1752, by Julian Gwyn (2004)

Maritime History as World History, edited by Daniel Finamore (2004)

Counterpoint to Trafalgar: The Anglo-Russian Invasion of Naples, 1805–1806, by William Henry Flayhart III (paperback edition, 2004)

Life and Death on the Greenland Patrol, 1942, by Thaddeus D. Novak, edited by P. J. Capelotti (2005; first paperback edition, 2014)

X Marks the Spot: The Archaeology of Piracy, edited by Russell K. Skowronek and Charles R. Ewen (2006; first paperback edition 2007)

Industrializing American Shipbuilding: The Transformation of Ship Design and Construction, 1820–1920, by William H. Thiesen (2006)

Admiral Lord Keith and the Naval War Against Napoleon, by Kevin D. McCranie (2006)

Commodore John Rodgers: Paragon of the Early American Navy, by John H. Schroeder (2006)

Borderland Smuggling: Patriots, Loyalists, and Illicit Trade in the Northeast, 1783–1820, by Joshua M. Smith (2006)

Brutality on Trial: "Hellfire" Pedersen, "Fighting" Hansen, and the Seamen's Act of 1915, by E. Kay Gibson (2006)

Uriah Levy: Reformer of the Antebellum Navy, by Ira Dye (2006)

Crisis at Sea: The United States Navy in European Waters in World War I, by William N. Still Jr. (2006)

Chinese Junks on the Pacific: Views from a Different Deck, by Hans K. Van Tilburg (2007; first paperback edition, 2013)

Eight Thousand Years of Maltese Maritime History: Trade, Piracy, and Naval Warfare in the Central Mediterranean, by Ayse Devrim Atauz (2007)

Merchant Mariners at War: An Oral History of World War II, by George J. Billy and Christine M. Billy (2008)

The Steamboat Montana *and the Opening of the West: History, Excavation, and Architecture*, by Annalies Corbin and Bradley A. Rodgers (2008)

Attack Transport: USS Charles Carroll *in World War II*, by Kenneth H. Goldman (2008)

Diplomats in Blue: U.S. Naval Officers in China, 1922–1933, by William Reynolds Braisted (2009)

Sir Samuel Hood and the Battle of the Chesapeake, by Colin Pengelly (2009)

Voyages, The Age of Sail: Documents in Maritime History, Volume I, 1492–1865, edited by Joshua M. Smith and the National Maritime Historical Society (2009)

Voyages, The Age of Engines: Documents in Maritime History, Volume II, 1865–Present, edited by Joshua M. Smith and the National Maritime Historical Society (2009)

H.M.S. Fowey Lost . . . and Found!, by Russell K. Skowronek and George R. Fischer (2009)

American Coastal Rescue Craft: A Design History of Coastal Rescue Craft Used by the United States Life-Saving Service and the United States Coast Guard, by William D. Wilkinson and Commander Timothy R. Dring, USNR (Retired) (2009)

The Spanish Convoy of 1750: Heaven's Hammer and International Diplomacy, by James A. Lewis (2009)

The Development of Mobile Logistic Support in Anglo-American Naval Policy, 1900–1953, by Peter V. Nash (2009)

Captain "Hell Roaring" Mike Healy: From American Slave to Arctic Hero, by Dennis L. Noble and Truman R. Strobridge (2009; first paperback edition, 2017)

Sovereignty at Sea: U.S. Merchant Ships and American Entry into World War I, by Rodney Carlisle (2009; first paperback edition, 2011)

Commodore Abraham Whipple of the Continental Navy: Privateer, Patriot, Pioneer, by Sheldon S. Cohen (2010; first paperback edition, 2011)

Lucky 73: USS Pampanito*'s Unlikely Rescue of Allied POWs in WW II*, by Aldona Sendzikas (2010)

Cruise of the Dashing Wave*: Rounding Cape Horn in 1860*, by Philip Hichborn, edited by William H. Thiesen (2010)

Seated by the Sea: The Maritime History of Portland, Maine, and Its Irish Longshoremen, by Michael C. Connolly (2010; first paperback edition, 2011)

The Whaling Expedition of the Ulysses, *1937–1938*, by LT (j.g.) Quentin R. Walsh, U.S. Coast Guard, edited and with an Introduction by P.J. Capelotti (2010)

Stalking the U-Boat: U. S. Naval Aviation in Europe During World War I, by Geoffrey L. Rossano (2010)

In Katrina's Wake: The U.S. Coast Guard and the Gulf Coast Hurricanes of 2005, by Donald L. Canney (2010)

A Civil War Gunboat in Pacific Waters: Life on Board USS Saginaw, by Hans K. Van Tilburg (2010)

The U.S. Coast Guard's War on Human Smuggling, by Dennis L. Noble (2011)

The Sea Their Graves: An Archaeology of Death and Remembrance in Maritime Culture, by David J. Stewart (2011)

CPSIA information can be obtained
at www.ICGtesting.com
Printed in the USA
BVHW04s2312220518
517074BV00002B/92/P

9 780813 054858